D0385403

Chicago Public Library
C
P
L
REFERENCE
Form 178 rev. 11-00

Facts On File
BIOGRAPHICAL ENCYCLOPEDIA OF ARTISTS

SIR LAWRENCE GOWING
GENERAL EDITOR

VOLUME 4

JUSEPE DE RIBERA – FRANCISCO DE ZURBARÁN

Facts On File, Inc.

Published in North America by:
Facts On File, Inc.
132 West 31st Street
New York, NY10001

The Brown Reference Group plc
(incorporating Andromeda Oxford Ltd)
8 Chapel Place
Rivington Street
London EC2A 3DQ

Library of Congress Cataloging-in-Publication Data

LC Control Number: 2005040500
Type of Material: Text
Main Title: Biographical encyclopedia of artists / edited by Lawrence Gowing.
Published/Created: New York: Facts On File, c2005.
Projected Pub. Date: 0504
Related Names: Gowing, Lawrence.
Description: p. cm.
ISBN: 0816058032
Contents: v. 1. Alvar Aalto–Paul Durand-Ruel -- v. 2. Albrecht Dürer–Jan Lievensz -- v. 3. Limburg Brothers–Francisco Ribalta -- v. 4. Jusepe de Ribera–Francisco de Zurbarán.
Subjects: Artists--Biography. Artists--Encyclopedias.
LC Classification: N40 .B535 2005
Dewey Class No.: 709/.2/2 B 22

Volume 4 ISBN 0-8160-5807-5
Set ISBN 0-8160-5803-2

Facts On File books are available at special discounts when purchased in bulk quantities for businesses, associations, institutions, or sales promotions. Please call our Special Sales Department in New York at (212) 967-8800 or (800) 322-8755.

You can find Facts On File on the World Wide Web at http://www.factsonfile.com

Cover design by Cathy Rincon

Printed in China

10 9 8 7 6 5 4 3 2 1

The publisher wishes to thank the following individuals and institutions for their help in the preparation of this work:

INDIVIDUALS: Margaret Amosu, Professor Manolis Andronikos, Janet Backhouse, Claudia Bismarck, John Boardman, His Grace the Duke of Buccleugh, Richard Calvocoressi, Lord Clark, Curt and Maria Clay, James Collins, Bryan Cranstone, Mrs E.A. Cubitt, Mary Doherty, Judith Dronkhurst, Rosemary Eakins, Mark Evans, Claude Fessaguet, Joel Fisher, Jean-Jacques Gabas, Dr Oscar Ghez, Paul Goldman, G. St G.M. Gompertz, Zoë Goodwin, Toni Greatrex, A.V. Griffiths, Victor Harris, Barbara Harvey, Maurice Howard, A.D. Hyder, Jane Jakeman, Peg Katritzky, Moira Klingman, Andrew Lawson, Betty Yao Lin, Christopher Lloyd, Jean Lodge, Richard Long, Lorna McEchern, Eunice Martin, Shameem Melluish, Jennifer Montagu, Sir Henry Moore, Richard Morphet, Elspeth O'Neill, Alan Peebles, Professor Dr Chr. Pescheck, Pam Porter, Professor P.H. Pott, Alison Renney, Steve Richard, Andrew Sherratt, Richard Shone, Lawrence Smith, Don Sparling, Graham and Jennifer Speake, Annamaria Petrioli Tofani, Mary Tregear, Jim Tudge, Betty Tyers, Ivan Vomáčka, Tom Wesselmann.

INSTITUTIONS: Ashmolean Museum, Oxford; Bibliothèque Nationale, Paris; Bodleian Library, Oxford; British Library, London; British Museum, London; Courtauld Institute of Art, London; Gulbenkian Foundation, Lisbon; Louvre, Paris; Merseyside County Museums, Liverpool; Metropolitan Museum, New York; Museum of Modern Art, New York; Museum of Modern Art, Oxford; Oriental Institute, Oxford; Oxford City Library; Petit Palais, Geneva; Phaidon Press, Oxford; Pitt Rivers Museum, Oxford; Sainsbury Centre for the Visual Arts, Norwich; Sotheby Parke Bernet & Co., London; Tate Gallery, London; Victoria and Albert Museum, London; Warburg Institute, London.

The publisher wishes to thank the numerous individuals, agencies, museums, galleries, and other institutions who kindly supplied the illustrations for this book.

The publisher also wishes to acknowledge the important contributions of Judith Brundin, Ann Currah, Bernard Dod, Herman and Polly Friedhoff, Juliet Grindle, Jonathan Lamède, Giles Lewis, Andrew McNeillie, Penelope Marcus, and Louise Pengelley.

Ribera Jusepe de 1591–1652

The Spanish painter Jusepe de Ribera was born in Játiva (Valencia). He is believed to have been a pupil of Francisco Ribalta in Valencia, but nothing more is known of his working life in Spain. He went to Italy at an early age. After visiting Emilia and Rome, where he became a member of the Accademia di San Luca, he had settled by 1616 in Naples, where he lived for the rest of his life and was one of the leading artists.

His early style was close to that of Caravaggio in its realism and tenebrism, but it was also typically Spanish in its depth of religious feeling. He was soon patronized by the Duke of Osuna, the Spanish Viceroy in Naples, who commissioned a group of religious works for the collegiate church of Osuna in Andalusia. These include his early masterpiece, the large *Crucifixion* (1616–20), in which the composition recalls Reni, though the style is strongly Caravaggesque. In addition to many Neapolitan patrons, Ribera frequently worked for the King of Spain and for Spanish religious orders, who channeled commissions to him through successive Viceroys. He proudly emphasized his Spanish origin in the wording of the signatures on his paintings, while his style retained a Spanish flavor throughout his career.

Jusepe de Ribera: The Club-footed Boy; oil on canvas; 164×92cm (65×36in); 1642. Louvre, Paris

In the middle 1630s Ribera's palette became more colorful, as in the large *Immaculate Conception* (1635; center of the main altarpiece, Augustinian monastery, Salamanca). This work was commissioned by the Count of Monterrey, then Viceroy in Naples, for his newly founded convent of Augustinian nuns in Salamanca. It influenced painters of the School of Madrid from Juan Carreño de Miranda to Claudio Coello. After a few years during which Venetian color-schemes predominated, as in the *Isaac and Jacob* (1637; Prado, Madrid), Ribera returned *c*1640 to the darker tones of his early period. The increasing vigor and movement in his works were typical of the High Baroque, but his main figures were usually concentrated into a shallow area of foreground, with landscape relegated to an unobtrusive background role.

Ribera was best known for his rugged half-length philosophers, his usually bearded apostles and aged saints (particularly St Jerome), his scenes of *The Martyrdom of St Sebastian* (numerous versions) and *St Bartholomew* (1630; Prado, Madrid), and his sometimes gruesome mythological subjects like *Apollo and Marsyas* (1637; S. Martino, Naples). But he was not impervious to physical beauty, as in *The Penitent Magdalen* (*c*1640; Prado, Madrid) and *The Holy Family with St Catherine* (1648; Metropolitan Museum, New York). Outstanding among his rare portraits were the *Jesuit Missionary* (1638; Museo Poldi-Pezzoli, Milan) and the bearded woman *Magdalena Ventura* (1631; Duke of Lerma Foundation Museum, Toledo). He also executed a number of fine etchings.

Ribera's thick fleshy handling of paint was imitated briefly by his outstanding pupil, Luca Giordano. His influence had earlier affected most of the contemporary Neapolitan painters, from Massimo Stanzione onwards, of whom he remained to the end a keen and successful rival.

Further reading. Felton, C.M. *Jusepe de Ribera: a Catalogue Raisonné*, Pittsburgh (1971). Pérez Sánchez, A.E. and Spinosa, N. *L'Opera Completa del Ribera*, Milan (1978). Trapier, E. du G. *Ribera*, New York (1952).

Sebastiano Ricci: St Peter Released from Prison; fresco; 165×138cm (65×54in); 1722–3. S. Stae, Venice

Ricci family
17th and 18th centuries

The Ricci were painters born in Belluno, active mainly in Venice. The historical importance of Sebastiano Ricci (1659–1734) lies in his successful revival of the great tradition of Venetian history painting after a century of decadence, preparing the way for the achievements of G.A. Pellegrini, Piazetta, and Tiepolo. After an early career that included visits to Bologna, Parma, and Rome, he established himself in Venice *c*1700, setting the pattern for his successors by making several further extended journeys abroad, visiting Vienna (1701–3), Florence (1706–7), London (1712–16), and Paris (1716). The breadth of his artistic experience is reflected in the eclecticism of his style, which variously reveals the influence of Antonio Correggio, the Carracci, Pietro da Cortona, and especially Paolo Veronese. At times, indeed, Ricci's paintings come dangerously close to becoming more pastiches of Veronese's, and he has been accused of lacking original inspiration; but quite apart from the novel gaiety and lightness of his palette, and the sheer brilliance of his painterly technique, his very choice of sources was to be of crucial importance for the next generation of Venetian painters.

Marco Ricci (1676–1730), Sebastiano's nephew and occasional collaborator, was by contrast a specialist in landscape painting. Within this genre, his historical position roughly parallels that of his uncle, and his early assimilation of a wide range of foreign influences, including Salvator Rosa, Claude Lorrain, and perhaps also the Dutch, was to help lay the foundations for the development of Venetian landscape and townscape painting in the 18th century.

Richard of Verdun *fl.* 1288–1318

Richard of Verdun was a French illuminator who lived in Paris. He was the son-in-law of Master Honoré, and as no work by his own hand has been identified his career is interwoven with that of the older master. He is first recorded in 1288, when he was witness to the sale of a manuscript by Honoré. Like him, he lived in the main residential quarter for lay illuminators in Paris (now Rue Boutebrie), and in 1292 the tax paid by him was substantial. He continued to enjoy the royal patronage accorded to Honoré, and is last recorded in 1318. This was in conjunction with an associate, Jean de la Mare, who had collaborated with him on the illumination of three Antiphonaries for the Sainte Chapelle. The attribution to him of various manuscripts, including *La Légende de Saint Denis* which was presented to Philip V in 1317, is purely hypothetical.

Richards Ceri 1903–71

The Welsh artist Ceri Giraldus Richards was born of Welsh-speaking parents near Swansea. He attended Swansea School of Art (1920–4) and the Royal College of Art, London (1924–7). Receptive to new visual ideas, he quickly assimilated the decorative economy of Matisse's portraits and the metamorphism of Picasso, Max Ernst, and other Surrealists. Such influences are discernible in his early reliefs (for example *Bird and Beast*, 1936; Scottish National Gallery of Modern Art, Edinburgh), but the whimsy and invention displayed in them are his own. They are among his finest achievements.

Throughout the 1930s and 1940s Richards often used the Surrealist techniques of free association and metamorphism to illustrate his favorite theme, the cycle of life. After the war he developed this further in many semi-abstract compositions, most notably perhaps in the series *Homage to Dylan Thomas* (1953–5; examples in the Tate Gallery, London; Cecil Higgins Art Gallery, Bedford; Glyn Vivian Art Gallery, Swansea). Here the richness of the forms themselves express the continual triumph of the life force over death.

Ceri Richards: Blossoms; oil on canvas; 51×61cm (20×24in); 1940. Tate Gallery, London

Richier Germaine 1904–59

Germaine Richier was a French sculptor. During the 1930s she was influenced by the classicism of Charles Despiau and Aristide Maillol. *The Toad* of 1942, on one level a conventional nude, also refers obliquely to the title in its pose and is the first of her sculptures to use the human body as an analogy for animal life. While this penchant for visual metaphor relates her to Surrealism, her sinister zoomorphic images find parallels in the works of other postwar sculptors, notably César. So does her concern for richness of texture in her handling of bronze, sometimes emphasized by gilding or polychrome.

Richter Gerhard 1932–

The German painter Gerhard Richter was born in Dresden. He studied at the Kunstakademie in Dresden (1951–6) and the Kunstakademie in Düsseldorf (1961–3). In 1962 he began to create paintings based on photographs, in gray, black, and white. His work was about the act of painting itself, not the subject—emphasized by the mundane photographs he chose. By the 1970s Richter began creating purely abstract works, sometimes exploring one color or gestural brushstroke. He continued to create figurative works inspired by photographs, in particular his controversial series of paintings *Oct. 18, 1977* (1988) based on forensic photographs of a group of German radicals who died in prison.

Riemenschneider Tilman c1460–1531

First mentioned in Würzburg in 1478/9, the German sculptor Tilman Riemenschneider settled there in 1483 and became a citizen and master two years later. During his journeyman years he appears to have traveled extensively. Apart from absorbing the more recent developments in the Trier-Strasbourg-Ulm area, he reveals considerably Netherlandish echoes in his early alabaster *Annunciation* of 1484 (Bayerisches Nationalmuseum, Munich). His rise to fame was rapid, and in his working career he produced at least 19 complex carved wooden retables, as well as a large body of stone sculpture.

In 1490 he was commissioned to carve the high altar (now dismembered) in the parish church of Münnerstadt, and the surviving parts reveal his characteristic gentle, naturalistic style. Contrary to the

Tilman Riemenschneider: Virgin and Child; detail; limewood; full height 142cm (56in); c1490–3. Detroit Institute of Arts

current practice in Germany he delivered this retable in natural wood, but in 1503 Veit Stoss was called in to "color, paint, and gild" it. Similarly, the tender *Adam* and *Eve* commissioned in 1491 for the Marienkapelle in Würzburg (Mainfränkisches Museum, Würzburg) show his exquisite sensitivity in exploiting the natural qualities of the sandstone. This novel approach to sculpture may owe something to earlier Netherlandish sculpture, but its closest spiritual ancestors are the sculptures of Nikolaus Gerhaert van Leyden. The same sensitivity and shy spirituality is characteristic of Riemenschneider's monument to *Konrad von Schaumberg* (*c*1500; Marienkapelle, Würzburg).

Above all, Riemenschneider and his large workshop were responsible for the great series of wooden retables culminating in the *Assumption of the Virgin* in the Herrgottskirche at Creglingen near Rothenburg (*c*1505–10). In this work the natural wood surfaces are treated with consummate delicacy. In his last sculptures, such as the *Deposition of Christ* in the parish church of Maidbronn (1520–5), his wistful melancholy deepens into a new intensity, reflecting his personal sufferings in the wake of the Peasants' War.

Rietveld Gerrit 1888–1964

The Dutch architect and designer Gerrit Thomas Rietveld trained as a cabinetmaker. Before his association with the *De Stijl* group he began to work in primary forms and colors, producing his revolutionary open-construction "red and blue" chair in 1918. He joined the *De Stijl* group in 1919, with important consequences for its declared intention to unite architecture and painting. In 1923 he collaborated on an exhibition of architectural designs for the Galerie de l'Effort Moderne in Paris. His design for the Schröder house, which was built in 1924, realized *De Stijl* principles, and is still regarded as a high point in the development of modern architecture. While practicing as an architect, Rietveld continued to design furniture. His later buildings included the Dutch Pavilion at the Venice Biennale of 1953.

Rigaud Hyacinthe 1659–1743

Hyacinthe Rigaud was a French portrait painter. Trained in the Midi, he came to Paris in 1681. His highly reputed career as

Hyacinthe Rigaud: Louis XIV; oil on canvas; 277×194cm (109×76in); 1701. Louvre, Paris

a court painter began in 1688, when he painted a portrait of Monsieur, brother of King Louis XIV. He painted most people of note at Versailles, including generals, diplomats, and visiting princes. He developed a pattern for such portraits based on the elegance of Anthony van Dyck and the formality of Philippe de Champaigne. Typical military portraits show the figure in modern armor against a landscape with a distant battle. The State portraits can be typified by that of *Louis XIV* (1701; Louvre, Paris), with a tempered Baroque exuberance in its swirling draperies, complex curves, and rich color. Rigaud employed a large studio of assistants. He also painted some simple, direct portraits, which show his admiration for Rembrandt.

Rikyu Sen no 1521–92

Sen no Rikyu was a Japanese Tea Master (Tea Ceremony expert) whose influence as an arbiter of taste was unequaled. He trained in the Zen temple of the Daitokuji (Kyoto) and established the fully mature rules of taste for the Tea Ceremony. Deferred to in these matters even by the dictators Oda Nobunaga and Toyotumi Hideyoshi, he was finally forced to commit suicide by the latter, presumably because of his political influence.

Rikyu insisted on simple sobriety in architecture, in flower arrangement, and in the painting and calligraphy scrolls hung at a Tea Ceremony; and these austere tastes have persisted since his time. He also patronized the simple, very tactile Black Raku pottery of Kyoto, which became the standard tea ware.

Riley Bridget 1931–

The British painter Bridget Riley was born in London. She studied at Goldsmiths' College (1949–52) and at the Royal College of Art (1952–5), and had her first one-woman show at Gallery One in 1962. She was given a large-scale retrospective at the Hayward Gallery, London, in 1971. Riley's art, influenced at first by Victor Vasarely, has always been concerned with pattern and optical effect. She creates elaborate abstract patterns, often markedly linear in feeling, that are deliberately intended to unsettle the eyes of the spectator. The patterns often give the impression of forms vibrating—almost like objects seen from a distance in a heat haze (for example, *Fall*, 1963; Tate Gallery, London). At first she worked exclusively in black and white, but she has since added color. The designs are worked out with enormous geometrical precision, the final canvases sometimes being executed by studio assistants on the basis of Riley's *modello*.

Further reading. Lucie-Smith, E. and White, P. *Art in Britain 1969–76*, London (1970). Vaizey, M. "For the Mind's Eye", *Sunday Times*, London (July 1976). Wolfe, T. *The Painted Word*, New York (1975).

Bridget Riley: Late Morning; acrylic on canvas; 89×142cm (35×56in); 1967–8. Tate Gallery, London

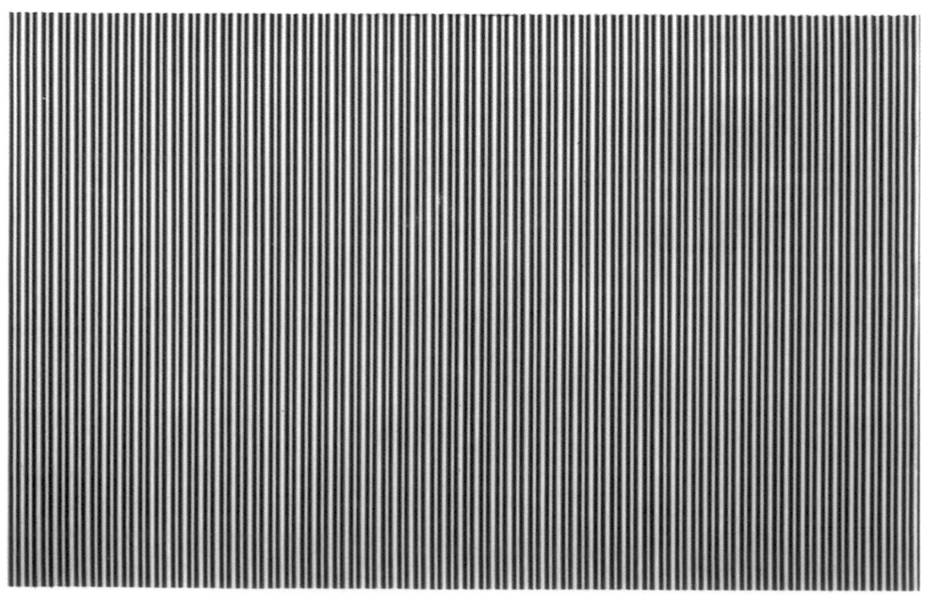

Riopelle Jean-Paul 1923–2002

The Canadian artist Jean-Paul Riopelle was born in Montreal. He began to paint his first nonfigurative pictures in 1944 and 1945, then traveled to France and Germany, and then to New York in 1946, exhibiting in the International Surrealist Exhibition of that year. In 1948 he was a cosigner of the manifesto *Refus Global*, and cofounder with Paul-Emile Borduas of the *Automatistes* group, based in Montreal. He moved to Paris in 1946, becoming a close friend of Fernand Leduc and briefly an associate of Georges Mathieu. He is considered a member of the School of Paris.

Riopelle's mature work is based on his interest in Surrealist automatism. His best known paintings rely on much use of the palette knife, and the direct application of paint from the tube—creating a mosaic surface (for example, *Encounter*, 1956; Wallraf-Richartz-Museum, Cologne). Since the early 1960s he has also been sculpting in bronze.

Rivera Diego 1886–1957

Diego Rivera was a Mexican mural painter. From 1898 to 1904 he studied in Mexico City under Santiago Rebull (1829–1902). Receiving a grant in 1907 to study in Europe, he went first to Madrid and then to Paris, becoming friends with Modigliani and Picasso among others. He also traveled in Italy, Germany, and Russia.

Back in Mexico in 1921, he received his first commission for a fresco from the new socialist government. From then on he was the acknowledged leader of the new Mexican school of painting, which concerned itself with the portrayal of Mexican history through monumental wall painting in public buildings. At intervals between the years 1931 and 1941, Rivera painted murals in New York City, San Francisco, and Detroit which provoked considerable controversy. He sought to strengthen national consciousness and solidarity by depicting man in his social and working environment (for example, *Miner Being Searched*; fresco; 1923–8; Patio of Labor, Secretariat of Public Education, Mexico City).

Further reading. Arquin, F. *Diego l ivera: the Shaping of an Artist 1889–1921*, Norman, Okla. (1971). Rivera, D. *My Life, My Art*, New York (1960). Rivera, D.

Diego Rivera: The Cafe Terrace; oil on canvas; 61×50cm (24×20in); 1915. Metropolitan Museum, New York

and Suarez, L. *Confesiones de Diego Rivera*, Mexico City (1962). Secker, H.S. *Diego Rivera*, Dresden (1957). Wolfe, B.D. *Diego Rivera: his Life and Times*, London and New York (1939).

Rivers Larry 1923–2002

Larry Rivers is an American painter born in the Bronx, New York, who studied both with Hans Hofmann and with William Baziotes. His style derived mainly from an admiration for Willem de Kooning's painting which led him out of the impasse of Abstract Expressionism. This reaction against Abstract Expressionism turned him towards both a stark realism, as in *Double Portrait of Birdie* (1955; Whitney Museum of American Art, New York), and towards a series of transcriptions of popular paintings such as *Washington Crossing the Delaware* (1953). The latter brought him close to the Pop Movement, although more in the sense of an interest in popular art as *kitsch* than in the Pop image as developed by Andy Warhol or Claes Oldenburg.

Further reading. Levy, D. et al. *Larry Rivers: Art and the Artist*, New York (2002). Rivers, L. and Weinstein, A. *What Did I Do?: the Unauthorized Autobiography of Larry Rivers*, New York (2001).

Riza *c*1565–1635

The Persian draftsman and miniaturist Riza was the son of Ali Asghar of Kashan. He received royal patronage from Shah Abbas I from the time of the latter's accession in 1587 and was in high favor during the 1590s, when he shared in the illustration of a large-scale *Shah-nama* (Book of kings) (surviving part is in the Chester Beatty Library, Dublin). By this time he was using the prefix Aqa ("Respected") but by 1606 he is said, by Qadi Ahmad, to have fallen in repute through keeping low company. By 1616 he had fallen from royal favor and was in want. Probably *c*1610, when he needed to accept private commissions, he started to use the suffix Abbasi, which may have been granted to him by the Shah.

The use of two prefixes led scholars to attribute the work of Riza to two artists, but their common identity was demonstrated in 1964 by Ivan Stchoukine.

Even after 1610 Riza continued to produce some fully colored miniatures (examples in the Hermitage Museum, St Petersburg, 1610; and Seattle Art Museum) as well as some manuscripts (examples dated 1614 formerly in the Rothschild Collection; examples dated 1632 in the Victoria and Albert Museum, London). But he was now mainly occupied with separate drawings of figure subjects, in which he had always shown virtuosity. These range from the early finished portraits of young men

Riza: A Girl with a Fan; 16×7cm (6×3in); *c*1590. Freer Gallery of Art, Washington, D.C.

and girls to later brilliant, rapid sketches in line and wash. This kind of work continued until his death in 1635, a date given on a portrait of him by his ablest pupil, Mu'in. Characteristic figure drawings are in the British Museum, London; the William Hayes Fogg Art Museum, Cambridge, Mass.; Freer Gallery of Art, Washington, D.C.; and the Bibliothèque Nationale, Paris.

Robbia Luca della 1400–82

Trained in the workshop of Florence Cathedral as a marble carver, Luca della Robbia was a major Renaissance sculptor, whose career overlapped the second half of those of Ghiberti and Donatello. He is famed for an important technical innovation: the use of vitreous glazes to color sculpture modeled in terracotta. This rendered polychrome sculpture impervious to damp, and therefore durable in external architectural settings. He worked with his nephew Andrea (1434–1525), who introduced virtual mass-production of such sculpture. Their reliefs of the *Virgin and Child*, and coats-of-arms, in glazed terracotta, abound on buildings in Tuscany and in museums (for example, Museo Nazionale, Florence; Victoria and Albert Museum, London).

Luca's first documented commission, in 1431, was a marble Singing Gallery for Florence Cathedral: its child-musicians carved in low relief are famous. He also produced other works for the cathedral authorities: five stone reliefs, to complete a series carved a century before by Andrea Pisano for Giotto's Campanile (1437–9); lunettes showing the *Resurrection* (1442–5) and *Ascension* (1446–51) to set over the Sacristy doors—his first major works in glazed terracotta; and a pair of bronze doors for the North Sacristy (1445–68).

Luca della Robbia: The Stemma of the Arte dei Medici e degli Speziali; enameled terracotta; diameter 180cm (71in); c1464–5. Orsanmichele, Florence

Elsewhere, Luca combined polychrome terracotta with marble. His first datable use of the two was for a sacramental tabernacle in S. Maria, Peretola (1441–3). He combined them again on the Federighi tomb in S. Trinità, Florence (1454). He produced several quasi-architectural projects including two for Piero de' Medici, the Chapel of the Crucifix in S. Miniato al Monte, Florence (1448), and a study in the Medici Palace (demolished; roundels from its vault now in the Victoria and Albert Museum, London). He also designed two chapels in the pilgrimage shrine of S. Maria at Impruneta near Florence and made the ceiling of the Chapel of the Cardinal of Portugal in S. Miniato, in collaboration with the Rossellino brothers (1462). Of his many reliefs in glazed terracotta inserted into architecture, the most famous are the roundels of *Apostles* in Brunelleschi's Pazzi Chapel, S. Croce, Florence (*c*1442).

Luca was an exponent of the "sweet style" in Florentine sculpture, avoiding the sort of violent emotion to be seen in the late work of Donatello. He preferred the calmer, even domestic, mood that suited his principal patrons, the Florentine bourgeois.

Further reading. Baldini, U. *La Bottega dei Della Robbia*, Florence (1965). Marquand, A. *Luca della Robbia*, Princeton (1914). Pope-Hennessy, J. *Italian Renaissance Sculpture*, London (1958). Pope-Hennessy, J. *Luca della Robbia*, Oxford (1980).

Robert Hubert 1733–1808

The French artist Hubert Robert was sometimes nicknamed "Robert des Ruines". He was a painter of landscapes both imagined and real. Born in Paris, he went to Rome in 1754 under the protection of the future Duc de Choiseul, whom he knew because his father worked for the family. He spent some time at the French Academy there, but much more important was the friendship he made with Fragonard and with the Abbé de Saint-Non. The latter was a dilettante who was to patronize both artists, and with whom they visited southern Italy and Sicily.

Robert's drawing style can be so close to that of his friend that attribution is sometimes difficult. His main claim to distinction is for his revival of the tradition of the

Hubert Robert: The Finding of the Laocoön; oil on canvas; 119×163cm (47×64in); 1773. Virginia Museum of Fine Arts, Richmond, Va

architectural and landscape *capriccio* in the manner of Giovanni Paolo Panini, a painter at the height of his fame while Robert was in Rome. Robert used a bright palette and a dashing technique; he had a large, romantic imagination, which underlined the atmosphere of the scenes he wished to represent.

The *capriccio*—the representation of real places with ruins gathered from afar, or equally of imaginary sites with real monuments or ruins—thrives on the vision of past grandeur, subjected to the picturesque action of time. Robert's views of the Villa d'Este at Tivoli, long past its efficient best by the 18th century, show a sense of the power of nature, and the pleasurably melancholic sensation of ruins. Diderot praised these elements enthusiastically when the artist returned to Paris in 1765. He became both popular and prolific, exhibiting 40 paintings and drawings at the Salon of 1769. Diderot sometimes reproached him for his sketchy manner, and his unwillingness to finish his work—but realized that this enabled the artist to make more money.

As well as depicting bizarre subjects like *Rome on Fire* (1771) or *The Grand Gallery of the Louvre in Ruins* (1796; Louvre, Paris), Robert began in later years to paint topographical views of Paris, which are now of value to architectural historians interested in that era of great change. He was interested in the notion of the museum, and in 1784 was appointed curator for the new French institution that was to educate the people in the glories of art—the Louvre. His interest in the Picturesque can be paralleled by the most forceful manner of Piranesi. His style sometimes approaches that of his rival C.-J. Vernet.

Roberti Ercole de' 1456?–96

Ercole de' Roberti was a Ferrarese painter. He was probably a pupil of Francesco del Cossa, following him to Bologna in 1470 and completing several of his paintings, including a *predella* (Vatican Museums, Rome). He succeeded Cosmè Tura as court painter at Ferrara in 1486. Although his activities are well recorded, only one painting can be authenticated, an altarpiece of 1480–1 (Pinacoteca di Brera, Milan). His many ascribed works, including a *Pietà* (Walker Art Gallery, Liverpool), show his indebtedness to Mantegna, Tura, and—in the soft, misty light effects—to Giovanni Bellini. His figures, with their expressive gestures and poses, convey intense emotions rare in the Ferrarese School. (*See* overleaf.)

Ercole de' Roberti: Portrait of Ginevra Bentivoglio; panel; 54×39cm (21×15in); c1480. National Gallery of Art, Washington, D.C.

Roberts William 1895–1980

The English painter William Roberts began his career in 1909 as a commercial artist, but his precocious talent for drawing won him a scholarship to the Slade School of Fine Art, London (1910–13). There he made increasing use of Cubist techniques, a development strengthened by a visit to France and Italy in 1913. In 1914 he joined the circle around Wyndham Lewis and signed the Vorticist Manifesto. Roberts always maintained an independent line, and his own form of mechanized abstraction developed naturally from his earlier Cubist works (for example *Study for Twostep II*, c1915; private collection).

During the First World War (spent partly as an Official War Artist) and thereafter, Roberts returned to figuration and painted groups of people engaged in communal activities. His works retained the expressive angularity of his Vorticist period; but after 1927 his figures assumed a wholesome rotundity reminiscent of Fernand Léger's classical nudes.

Rockwell Norman 1894–1978

Norman Rockwell was probably the most famous of all American illustrators. His warm, humorous depictions of everyday, small-town life in Middle America are bright, realistic and full of anecdotal detail. He created over 300 covers for the *Saturday Evening Post* and his "Four Freedoms" posters, based on a speech by F.D. Roosevelt, became some of the most familiar American images of the Second World War. With typical modesty and simplicity he wrote: "I do ordinary people in everyday situations, and that's about all I do." From the Depression to the Cold War, Rockwell provided affectionate and comforting images of an America that was innocent, untroubled and decent.

Further reading. Finch, C. *Norman Rockwell's America*, New York (1985). Gherman, B. *Norman Rockwell: Storyteller with a Brush*, New York (2000).

Rodchenko Alexander 1891–1956

Alexander Rodchenko was a Russian artist and designer, whose abstract paintings of 1915 onwards were based on simple geometric forms made using a pencil and pair of compasses. The images are often superimposed to suggest a relief structure, in contrast to the floating shapes of Malevich's Suprematism, the mystical basis of which Rodchenko rejected. In 1917 he began making constructions in wood and iron, under the influence of Tatlin. His hanging constructions of 1920, which could turn freely in space, were among the earliest sculptures to incorporate real motion, and are his most original contribution to Constructivism.

In the 1920s, Rodchenko, like most other Constructivists, rejected pure art as a parasitical activity, and concentrated on applied art and poster design.

William Roberts: The Cinema; oil on canvas; 91×76cm (36×30in); 1920. Tate Gallery, London

Auguste Rodin: The Eternal Idol; plaster; 74×40×52cm (29×16×20in); 1889. Musée Rodin, Paris

Rodin Auguste 1840–1917

François-Auguste-René Rodin was born in Paris and worked there for most of his life. After many years of hardship and neglect he was eventually recognized as the greatest sculptor of his age and, lionized by society, enjoyed international renown.

Rodin's father was a clerk in the Paris Prefecture de Police and the family was always poor. Rodin was sent away to school, however, as his uncle ran a boarding-school at Beauvais. He showed little academic ability, and at 13 returned to Paris and entered the École Impériale Spéciale de Dessin et de Mathématiques. This was known as the Petite École, because it trained craftsmen and designers rather than artists, who studied at the Grande École des Beaux-Arts. But Rodin worked diligently (one of his teachers was Horace Lecoq de Boisbaudran) and at 16 confidently expected to be accepted by the École des Beaux-Arts. He was rejected by the examining board on three successive applications. This was the first of a sequence of defeats that continued for almost a quarter of a century.

Rodin began the long series of menial tasks that were to allow him to study and do his own work at night. He attended classes held by the animal sculptor Antoine-Louis Barye (1796–1875) at the Jardin des Plantes. And he completed his first surviving sculpture, a portrait bust of his father, on which he worked for three years from 1857 to 1860.

In 1862, shocked by the death of his beloved elder sister, Maria, Rodin abandoned sculpture and entered the religious order of the Fathers of the Holy Sacrament, taking the name of Brother Augustin. But Father Pierre-Julian Eymard recognized Rodin's true vocation, sat to him for a fine portrait bust, and persuaded him to leave the Order and to return to sculpture.

For Rodin, it was a return to hardship. His great skills were employed anonymously by other, more successful, sculptors and masons. In 1864, he entered the workshop of Ernest Carrier-Belleuse, and so contributed to the sculptural decoration of many of the buildings of Paris. In the same year, his own work, the bronze *The Mask of the Man With a Broken Nose* (Musée Rodin, Paris) was rejected by the Salon. It was at this time that he met Marie-Rose Beuret; she became his mistress, bore him a son in 1866, and, in the last months of his life, became his wife.

With the outbreak of the Franco-Prussian War in 1870 Rodin was drafted into the National Guard as a corporal, but was quickly discharged because of his weak eyesight. He accepted Carrier-Belleuse's invitation to work in Brussels. After a short time, Carrier-Belleuse left Brussels, but Rodin stayed on, in partnership with the Belgian sculptor Antoine Joseph van Rasbourg (1831–1902).

Very slowly, the tide began to turn. *The Mask of the Man With a Broken Nose*, remodeled as a bust and sculpted in marble, was accepted for the Brussels Salon of 1872; and, 11 years after its original rejection, it was accepted for the Paris Salon of 1875. In 1875, Rodin visited Italy for the first time, traveling to Turin, Genoa, Naples, Pisa and Venice, as well as to Florence and Rome.

Returning to Brussels, he hired a young soldier as a model and began 18 months' work on a life-size male nude. In January 1877, at the Brussels Salon, a plaster cast of this figure held a lance and was called *The Conquered*, in tribute to the fallen of the recent War; but later that year, at the Paris Salon, it was shown without a lance and called *The Age of Bronze* (Musée Rodin, Paris). It was Rodin's first major work and aroused controversy. Despite the statue's debt to Michelangelo 1475–1564) and Donatello (*c*1386–1466), the jury in Paris was unwilling to recognize that an unknown sculptor could have produced such a work, and suspected that it had been cast directly from the flesh of its model. But its merit could not be denied; and three years later, when a bronze cast was shown at the Salon, it was awarded a third-class medal and bought by the State.

Initial response, however, was disappointing. When Rodin returned to Paris in 1877 with his mistress and son, he continued as a journeyman working for other sculptors. In 1879, Carrier-Belleuse employed him as a designer for the Sèvres porcelain factory. At home, Rodin was working on his second male nude, the striding *John the Baptist* (Musée Rodin, Paris). The statue was exhibited in plaster beside the bronze *Age of Bronze*, at the Salon of 1880, and Rodin, who was almost 40, was recognized as the supreme master he had become.

His success was sealed when, in August 1880, he was invited to design doors for the projected Museum of Decorative Arts of Paris. He was given a handsome advance, and studios in the government Dépot des Marbres. On a full-scale framework, he was soon developing an elaborate composition of several hundred figures. An early drawing shows that his original scheme followed the tradition established by Ghiberti's bronze doors for the Baptistery of Florence Cathedral, the Doors of Paradise. Rodin chose his imagery from Dante's great poem, the *Inferno;* and for this reason, and perhaps in contrast to Ghiberti's doors, his have become known as *The Gate of Hell* (now in the Musée Rodin, Paris). Rodin soon abandoned the regular panels of Ghiberti's design, in favor of a fluid open rhythm of writhing bodies recalling Michelangelo's fresco of the *Last Judgment* in the Sistine Chapel. In the center of the tympanum, where Christ in Majesty sits in the portals of Gothic churches, Rodin placed *The Thinker*, brooding over Man's folly and sin.

By 1884, the Gate was substantially complete; but when the enormous sum needed to pay for its casting was calculated, the project lapsed. In 1888 Rodin received a further advance, but the Gate remained unfinished until nine years after his death. A bronze was finally made in 1926, a monument to the artist rather than to the unbuilt museum. Rodin never really stopped work on the doors. He made alterations and additions on several occasions, and took individual motifs from it that he elaborated into separate works.

In the following decade, Rodin received a number of important public commissions, and most of them led to controversy. In 1884, the city of Calais proposed a monument to its hero, Eustache de St Pierre, the leader of the six burghers who had given themselves as hostages to the besieging English in 1347. Rodin suggested that for the same fee he should represent all six burghers. He made numerous studies, including larger-than-life nude figures for three of the burghers. For their weighty limbs and gestures of despair he drew from Michelangelo, but also from the medieval Northern sculptor, Claus Sluter (*c*1350–1406). The final version is a noble, tragic image, a blend of individual characterizations and heroic rhythms. Although the work was completed by 1889, it was not until 1895 that it was erected, and then it was not at the height that Rodin had wished, nor in the site he had intended.

He received two state commissions for a monument to Victor Hugo for the Panthéon: in 1889, and again in 1892; but neither was considered suitable for the intended site. The pedestals of his monument to the painter Claude Lorrain for the town of Nancy (1889–92), and of his monument to the Argentinian President Sarmiento in Buenos Aires were both disliked. His sketch for a monument to the painter J.A.M. Whistler (1843–1903), intended for London's Chelsea Embankment, was rejected in 1908.

But it was the commission for a monument to the French novelist Honoré de Balzac that created the greatest scandal of Rodin's career. The Société des Gens de Lettres had originally given the commission to Henri-Michel-Antoine Chapu (1833–91); but on Chapu's death, the Society's President, Emile Zola, proposed Rodin. Balzac had died in 1850 and Rodin researched into his appearance and character with great thoroughness. He read the novels, looked for photographs, visited Balzac's home town, and even had a suit made up by the writer's tailor. After numerous preliminary studies, he created a strange, contorted image of the writer's enormous maned head emerging from a loose dressing gown; contemporaries caricatured it as a performing seal. When he exhibited the plaster at the Salon of 1898, the committee of the Society declared that it was unfinished and canceled the contract. Rodin was bitterly hurt, as he considered the *Balzac* (versions in the Sculpture Garden, Museum of Modern Art, New York; Musée Rodin, Paris) to be his most important work. (The Italian sculptor Medardo Rosso claimed that Rodin had stolen the unusual idea from him.)

None of these controversies interrupted the gradual rise of Rodin's fame. In 1887, the French State commissioned a large marble version of *The Kiss* (Musée Rodin, Paris). In 1888, it awarded the sculptor with the Cross of Chevalier de la Légion d'Honneur. In 1889, he shared an exhibition with the Impressionist Claude Monet at the Galerie Georges Petit. In 1893, he was made President of the sculpture section of the Société National des Beaux-Arts. And when, in 1900, he built his own pavilion in the Place de l'Alma for the Paris World Fair his exhibition was very successful.

By now his reputation was international. In 1902, on his visit to London, the art students of the Slade harnessed themselves to his carriage and drew him in triumph through the streets. In 1903, he was made President of the International Society of Sculptors, Painters, and Gravers.

His fame had not come simply from his official commissions: rather, he had received them because of his fame. His reputation had also been created by his portraits. Bernard Shaw, whose portrait bust was made by Rodin in 1906, said, "any man who, being a contemporary of Rodin, deliberately allowed his bust to be made by anyone else, must go down to posterity (if he went down at all) as a stupendous nincompoop". After 1900, Rodin could charge whatever sum he liked for his portrait busts.

But the ultimate source of his reputation lay in the sensuous nude figures he exhibited at the Salons. For years, many of these pieces were individual motifs extracted from *The Gate of Hell. The Kiss* was originally Dante's lovers, Paolo and Francesca, on the left-hand door. But although he gave his pieces traditional titles, these were afterthoughts, and even concealed his true subject. For example, *The Fallen Angel* has also been called *The Fall of Icarus*, but as in *Metamorphoses of Ovid* (before 1896), the motif is two women passionately embracing.

Auguste Rodin: Balzac (nude study); bronze; 73×30×36cm (30×12×14in); 1893. Musée Rodin, Paris

Auguste Rodin: Cambodian Dancer; pencil and wash on paper. Musée Rodin, Paris

Rodin's imagery had been frankly sexual from the time that Camille Claudel (1856–1943) became his pupil and his mistress, in 1882. But from the beginning, his true theme had been the emotional significance of the human body, the powerful suggestiveness of a gesture, a pose, or even of a muscular rhythm. His intuition of physical rhythms enabled him to break with the sculptural stereotypes that had been handed down from the time of Bernini. He developed new forms and a new vision of the human body.

His sense of the expressiveness of his inventions led him to the odd practice of combining separate figures, or even limbs, into new combinations; he would also, in reminiscence of timeworn antique sculptures, exhibit fragments as whole works.

The foundation of his art was his prodigious skill as a modeler. He could be meticulously exact, but he worked with a fluency that gives his bronzes an uncanny surface at once like and also elusively unlike the body it represents.

He continued working until his old age. Some of his most original pieces are small sketches of dancers made after 1910. In 1914 he published a book on one of his early loves, *The Cathedrals of France*.

Further reading. Butler, R. *Rodin: The Shape of Genius*, New Haven (1993). Cladel, J. *Rodin*, London and New York (1967). Elson, A.E. *In Rodin's Studio*, Oxford (1980). Goldscheider, L. *Rodin Sculptures*, Oxford (1979). Grunfeld, F. *Rodin: A Biography*, New York (1987). Sutton, D. *Triumphant Satyr: the World of Auguste Rodin*, London (1963). Thorson, V. *Rodin's Graphics*, San Francisco (1975).

Rogers Richard 1933–

The British architect Richard Rogers is one of the leading exponents of "high-tech" architecture. He studied at the Architecture Association, London, and at Yale University. In the 1960s he and Norman Foster (together with their wives, Sue Rogers and Wendy Foster) formed the Team 4 partnership, their most important work being the innovatory Reliance Controls Factory, Swindon (1966–67), which in its uncompromising use of technology as the basis of design set the keynote of their approach. Rogers achieved international fame with his flamboyant and controversial Beaubourg or Pompidou Center (1971–77), Paris, designed with Renzo Piano (1937–). A confident assertion of functionalism, it is built with its structure clearly visible, its services (such as escalators and brightly colored ducts) arranged on the outside to leave a large interior space open. Rogers took a similar approach in his equally confident, equally controversial, Lloyd's Insurance Building in London (1979–86).

Further reading. Appleyard, B. *Richard Rogers: A Biography*, London (1986).

Romanino *c*1484–*c*1559

Gerolamo da Romano, known as Romanino, was a prolific artist, born in Brescia, the leading master of the Brescian school of Renaissance painting. His native city, situated on the border between the Duchy of Milan and the Venetian Empire, changed hands several times during the 15th and 16th centuries, and Romanino's art was subject to both Lombard and Venetian influences.

Also important was a Teutonic strain which must have reached him through the Alpine valleys to the north. Romanino was an artist of the High Renaissance, working in the same mode as Giorgione or Titian; but at times there is a squat, peasant grotesqueness about his figures, more reminiscent of Conrad Witz or Grünewald than of the Italians.

Romanino: Madonna and Child with Saints, the great altarpiece painted for S. Giustina, Padua; oil on panel; 400×262cm (157×103in); 1513. Museo Civico, Padua

He was Venetian in the central role he gave to color, in his free open brushwork, and in the importance of landscape in his paintings. But the smoky effects of light characteristic of his art were Lombard (they owed much to Vincenzo Foppa), and the particular visual qualities of the mountainous valley landscape behind Brescia were fundamental in his formation. Many of his paintings have wooded, mountain backgrounds. Often, as for example in his *St Alessandro* from the high altar of the Brescian church of that name (now National Gallery, London), the figure is seen from below, and is set directly against a vivid blue sky glimpsed through a patchwork of gray clouds. The light is stormy and the sense of space vertiginous.

Romanino used a network of loose brush strokes which convey, through their open structure, a sense of floating forms momentarily apprehended in a passing effect of light. Both his vision as a whole and his manner of recording it are, although Venetian in principle, entirely personal; they show him to be an original master of the first quality.

His career was chequered, and much of his most striking work was done for remote country villages. His early style can be seen in the great altarpiece, rich in color, texture, and largeness of form, that he painted for S. Giustina, Padua (1513; now Museo Civico, Padua). It can be seen, too, in the *Virgin and Saints* in Salò Cathedral, where the figures are placed in a stormy landscape and united with it by a tempestuous effect of light.

From 1519 to 1520 he painted in the Duomo, Cremona, continuing the cycle of frescoes begun by Boccacino and Altobello Melone. The scenes, which represent the Passion of Christ, are typical of this artist in the factual realism with which they narrate the stories; this clearly shows Northern influence, and here relates directly to Albrecht Dürer's engraved *Passion*. Romanino was, however, displaced by Pordenone, whose flashy illusionism had perhaps a more immediate appeal.

Romney George 1734–1802

The English painter George Romney was born near Dalton-in-Furness, Lancashire (now in Cumbria), and was apprenticed in 1755 to the itinerant portrait painter Christopher Steele. In the 1760s he gained prominence in London as a society portrait painter. He studied in Italy from 1773 to 1775. Shortly after returning to London, he met the poet William Hayley, who introduced him to a wide circle of literary figures and encouraged his interest in history painting. His most ambitious design in this vein, and one of the few to be realized on canvas, was *The Tempest* (now destroyed). It was commissioned by John Boydell in 1786 for his Shakespeare Gallery.

Romney remained a proficient, albeit reluctant portraitist throughout his career. In such pictures as *The Levenson-Gower Children* (1776–7; Abbot Hall Art Gallery, Kendal) he often achieved an incomparable lyricism and sensitivity. His genius as an artist, however, is more profitably measured by his oil sketches (many of which were inspired by Emma Hart, later Lady Hamilton, in the 1780s), and also by his profuse figure-drawings, which treat a wide range of horrific and sublime subjects from literature, history, and mythology.

Roriczer Matthäus *fl.* 1486–c92/5

Matthäus Roriczer was a German master mason and a member of a family of masons who were employed at Regensburg Cathedral for three generations. He is also recorded at work on other south German churches and from this experience he wrote a textbook *On the Ordination of Pinnacles*, published in 1486. It reveals, with diagrams, how medieval masons worked according to a system of proportions. Once given the size of the pinnacle base, and the intended height as a multiple of the side of the base, they had sufficient information to erect the pinnacle. Significantly, the method could be applied to constructing other elements of a church.

Rosa Salvator 1615–73

The Neapolitan artist Salvator Rosa was taught by Francesco Fracanzano, Aniello Falcone, and possibly by Jusepe de Ribera. It was in Naples that he developed his predilection for a dark palette and for fiery battle scenes and violent subject matter.

In 1635 he went to Rome, where he painted small genre scenes. Then in 1640, having angered Bernini, he moved to Florence as court painter to the Medici. Here Rosa, a brilliant conversationalist, actor, and musician, became the center of a glittering array of intellectuals, and began to write satirical poetry deriding the decadence of the court. he painted seaports

George Romney: A Lady in a Brown Dress: "The Parson's Daughter"; oil on canvas; 65×65cm (26×26in); c1785. Tate Gallery, London

and pastoral landscapes (influenced by Paul Bril and by Claude Lorrain), portraits, and macabre scenes of witches. Also, with works such as *Moral Philosophy* (Palazzo Enzelberg, Caldaro), he introduced a new type of allegorical painting.

Rosa returned to Rome in 1649, and from this date became obsessed with a desire to paint great historical compositions. His subjects were erudite and often inspired by Stoic doctrines; the influence of Poussin is clear. The theme of vanity fascinated him. In his *Democritus* (National Museum, Copenhagen) he pours bitter scorn on human achievement, while the *Humana Fragilitas* (c1657; Fitzwilliam Museum, Cambridge) is an intensely poetic meditation on the brevity of human life. At this time Rosa made his most significant contribution to landscape: his scenes are wild and desolate, the skies dark and stormy, and the twisted, shaggy trees are swept by thundery wind.

Rebellious and "savage", Rosa fascinated the 18th century. His sublime landscapes and his etchings of bandits played an important part in early Romanticism.

Salvator Rosa: Self-portrait; oil on canvas; 116×94cm (46×37in); c1641. National Gallery, London

Rosenquist James 1933–

The American Pop painter James Rosenquist was born in Grand Forks, North Dakota. He studied under Cameron Booth at Minnesota University (1952–4) and at the Art Students League, New York. While still a student he began working as an advertising billboard painter, and this became a full time occupation from 1957 to 1960. It proved the dominant influence on his paintings, which had previously been Abstract Expressionist in style. Since 1961, his style has remained relatively unchanged. He paints fragments of banal images of America, in contrasting scales, and especially in huge close-ups, derived from mass media and advertising. These are ironically and ambiguously juxtaposed, in a smooth photographic manner. Some of his paintings are extremely large (for example, *Flamingo Capsule*; Leo Castelli Gallery, New York), incorporating real objects and sheets of reflective materials. He began filmmaking in 1969.

Rosetsu Nagasawa 1755–99

The Japanese painter Nagasawa Rosetsu was a pupil of Okyo, whose ink monochrome style he learned; his works were even better than those of his master. Rosetsu's brilliant and vigorous originality in large-scale ink compositions, like the great tiger in the Okyo-Rosetsu Museum, Kushimoto, has given him the misleading label of eccentric. Much of his work is in fact done with a tightly controlled yet breathtaking technique, and in color work on silk he could paint with a clean precision rarely equalled (for example, his *Bird and Flower* handscroll in Kyoto National Museum). Rosetsu is Japan's finest animal and bird painter, imbuing his subjects—whether monkeys, tigers, toads, or sparrows—with an inner life partly humorous and partly pathetic.

Roslin Alexandre 1718–93

The Swedish born portrait painter Alex-

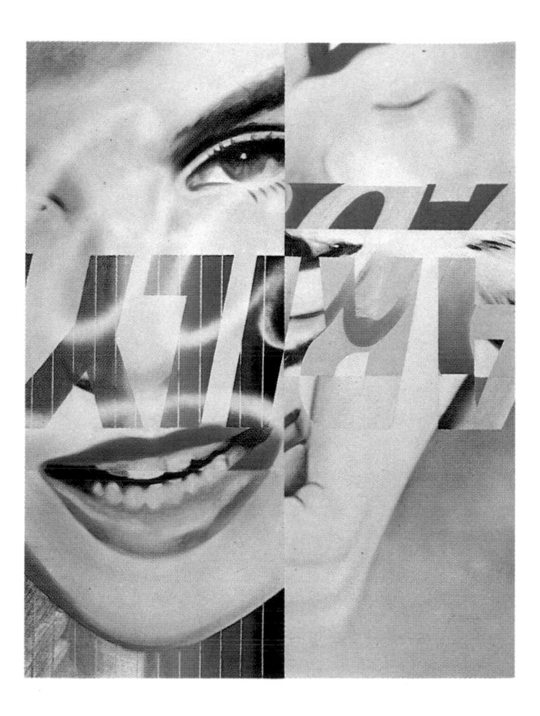

James Rosenquist: Marilyn; screenprint; 91×69cm (36×27in); 1974. Tate Gallery, London

andre Roslin worked mainly in Paris. After training in Sweden and traveling in Germany (1745–7), he went to Italy (1747–51) where he studied the portrait style of Francesco Solimena. He settled in Paris in 1752. A member of the Académie in 1753, he exhibited regularly at the Paris Salon throughout his life. His sober and sometimes stiff portraits were popular in court circles, in France and in northern European countries. Between 1774 and 1779 he traveled in northern and eastern Europe. His style lacks brilliance, wit, or excitement; but his virtues of solidity and observation maintained a steady though unfashionable reputation. His famous *Lady with a Fan* (1768; National Museum, Stockholm) is a portrait of his wife.

Rosselli Cosimo 1439–1507

Cosimo Rosselli was a Florentine painter. Though a pupil of Neri di Bicci from 1453 to 1456, he was much influenced by Benozzo Gozzoli. From 1481 to 1482 he was in Rome, painting four of the frescoes on the walls of the Sistine Chapel: these were scenes from the life of Moses and the life of Christ. At Florence he painted other frescoes, including *The Miracle of the Holy Blood* (1485–6; S. Ambrogio), and a

Cosimo Rosselli: Portrait of a Man; tempera on wood; 52×33cm (20×13in); c1481–2. Metropolitan Museum, New York

number of often large but usually conventional altarpieces. Rosselli, though competent, was never quite as good as his contemporaries, Botticelli, Perugino, or Ghirlandaio; his paintings were rather cluttered and his style lacked flair.

Rossellino brothers 15th century

The Italian sculptors Bernardo and Antonio Rossellino came from the quarry-town of Settignano. Although they were brothers, the separation in their birth dates consigned them to different generations. Bernardo (1409–64) trained Antonio (1427–79) and possibly also Desiderio da Settignano (*c*1428–64) in marble sculpture and architectural design. Bernardo's earliest known work, the facade of the Palazzo della Fraternita dei Laici at Arezzo (1433–6), shows his particular ability in combining sculpture with architecture. After executing a monument to the Florentine Chancellor Leonardo Bruni in S. Croce, Florence, and some distinguished sacramental tabernacles and other decorative sculpture, Bernardo devoted most of his time to architecture, erecting the Rucellai Palace in Florence (1446–51; designed by Alberti). He was subsequently appointed papal architect (holding the post from 1451 to 1453), built the new town of Pienza for Pope Pius II (1460–3), and ended his career as architect of Florence Cathedral.

Antonio's first signed work is a bust of Giovanni Chellini, Donatello's doctor (1456; Victoria and Albert Museum, London). Carved only three years after Mino da Fiesole's bust of Piero de' Medici (Museo Nazionale, Florence), it is one of the supreme portraits of the 15th century in Florence. Antonio collaborated with Bernardo on a number of projects, the most famous of which is the tomb-chapel of the Cardinal of Portugal at S. Miniato al Monte, Florence (1459–66), for which Luca della Robbia made the ceiling and the Pollaiuolo brothers the altarpiece. Antonio was active as a marble sculptor throughout the third quarter of the century and with Desiderio da Settignano was the principal exponent of the "Sweet" style. He specialized in reliefs, especially of the Virgin and Child, and he trained the sculptor and architect Benedetto da Maiano.

Bernardo Rossellino: monument to Leonardo Bruni; marble; c1444–7. S. Croce, Florence

Rossetti D.G. 1828–82

The Englishman Dante Gabriel Rossetti was both painter and poet. He came from a talented family: his father was a political refugee from Naples who became Professor of Italian at King's College, London; his sister, Christina Rossetti, became an important poet; and his brother, William Michael Rossetti, was an art critic. In his youth Rossetti (born Gabriel Charles Dante) vacillated between writing and painting; as no other English artist has done, with the exception of Blake, he achieved a marriage between the two arts.

After five years at King's College School, London, Rossetti joined Saas' Drawing Academy in 1841. At that time this was the traditional first step towards an artistic career; it led to a probationership and then studentship at the Royal Academy Schools. Here he met the young John Everett Millais and Holman Hunt; with four other associates they formed the Pre-Raphaelite Brotherhood in September 1848.

Although very much their inferior in painterly skill, Rossetti quickly became leader of the group: his conspicuous personality and fiery imagination inspired them in their choice of subjects for their pictures, as well as influencing their whole lifestyle and attitude to established society. Rossetti's first painting, *The Girlhood of Mary* (1849; Tate Gallery, London) was the first picture bearing the notorious initials "P.R.B." to be shown to the public. It was hung at the National Institution, which opened before the Royal Academy. This and *Ecce Ancilla Domini* ("Behold the Handmaid of the Lord"; Tate Gallery, London) were his only publicly exhibited works.

From 1851 Rossetti produced, almost exclusively, smaller works in watercolors and chalks. He found his subjects at first in the writings of Shakespeare, Dante, and Robert Browning; after 1856 he took them also from the Arthurian tales of Malory and Tennyson. These strongly worked, dramatically charged figure-scenes reflect the artist's inner life with an almost expressionist intensity. They create a world entirely different from the purely naturalistic one aimed at by Hunt and Millais, yet art historians refer to them all as "Pre-Raphaelite". Rossetti's naive style inspired the first phase of Pre-Raphaelitism in the late 1840s. It was then developed by him and imitated by admirers such as Burne-Jones and William Morris, and this new style also became known as Pre-Raphaelite; hence the confusion.

Antonio Rossellino: Giovanni Chellini; marble; height 51cm (20in); 1456. Victoria and Albert Museum, London

Rossetti was an imperious, generous, and enthusiastic man. His willingness to express himself in paint was not equaled by his facility of hand; compared to those of his friends, his works seem gauche. Yet the sheer frustration of the artist is part of their strength and magic. In them Rossetti developed a style out of naivety that influenced a whole generation; this was facilitated by the championship and protection of the critic John Ruskin. It is remarkable that Ruskin saw, and to the best of his ability nurtured, Rossetti's genius. Ruskin liked to dominate; Rossetti was beyond his control; but the critic was able to win him important new patrons among the collectors from the northern industrial towns.

As a result of Ruskin's appreciation of Rossetti's works in the press, Burne-Jones and William Morris, then graduates at Oxford, came to London in 1856 with the intention of becoming his disciples or students. This led to the decoration of the newly built Oxford Union Building Debating Hall with scenes from Arthurian legends. The young men who worked there with Rossetti, intoxicated by his charismatic influence, formed the second circle of Pre-Raphaelites, the first to have a distinctive style of its own, rather than a vague desire to challenge the Academy. The frescoes they painted quickly faded, since the ground had been most amateurishly prepared; but the ideas they formulated there lived on.

In 1861 Rossetti joined Morris and Burne-Jones as a founder-member of the

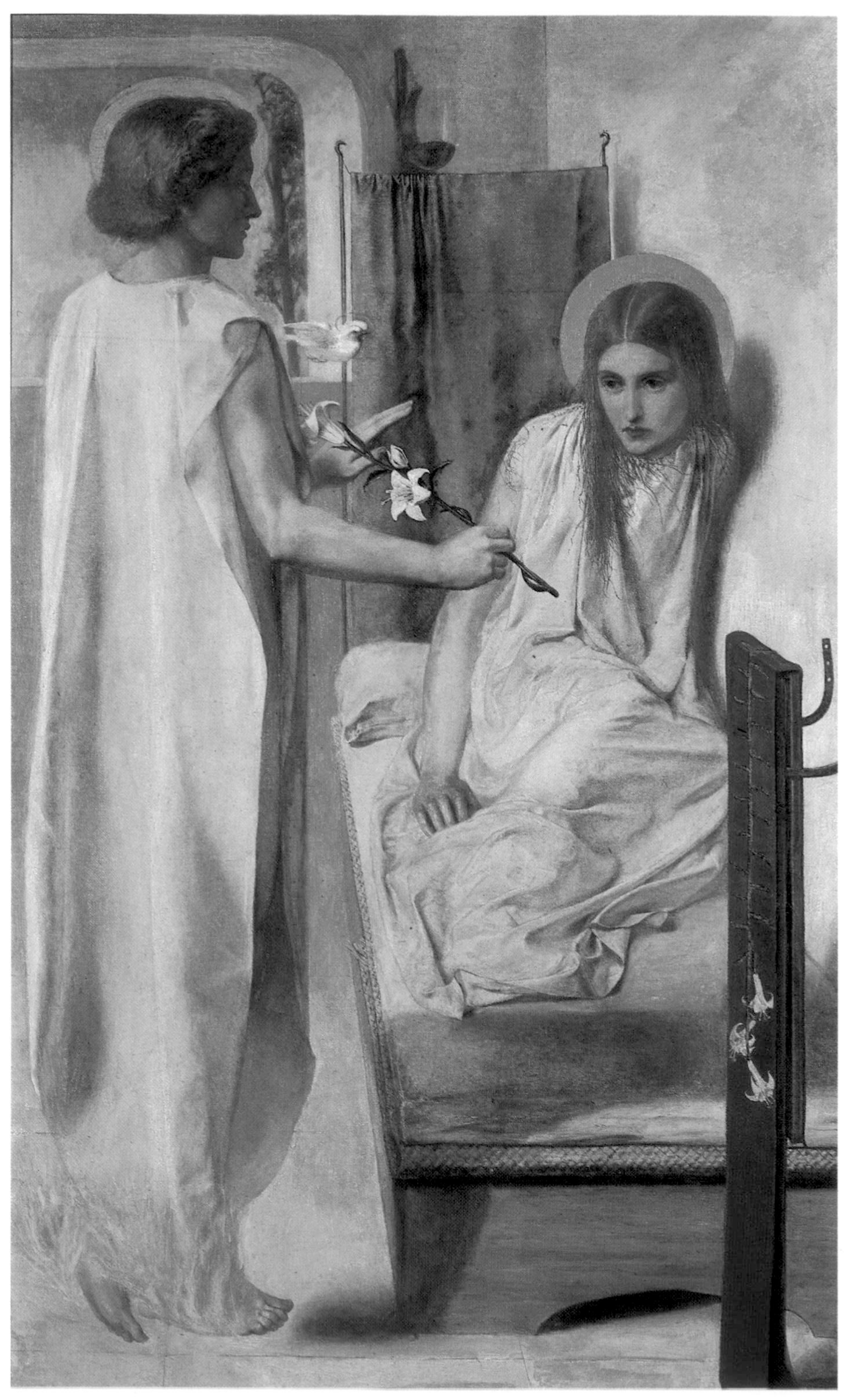

D.G. Rossetti: Ecce Ancilla Domini! (The Annunciation); oil on canvas; 74×41cm (29×17in); 1850. Tate Gallery, London

decorating firm that became known as Morris, Marshall, Faulkner and Company. The influence of their designs for furniture and tapestries, and their bold emphasis upon weighty medieval forms, shaped many of the first concepts of late Victorian aestheticism.

By the late 1850s the nervous tensions of Rossetti's earlier works began to give way to a more luxurious enjoyment of line and form. The most important model for these works was Elizabeth Siddal, with whom he lived at Blackfriars for ten years. They were finally married in 1860, and her death two years later from an overdose of laudanum was a blow from which he never recovered. He buried her with a sheaf of unpublished poems, and painted one last visionary portrait of her, as Dante's *Beata Beatrix* (*c*1863; Tate Gallery, London), perhaps his greatest work.

Those poems, which he was later persuaded to exhume and publish (as *The House of Life*, 1870), together with early writings for the P.R.B. journal *The Germ*, and translations from Dante, constitute the body of Rossetti's literary output.

After Elizabeth Siddal's death he continued to paint beautiful, idealized women, often in bust-length portraits, treated as historical or mythological figures such as Joan of Arc or Venus. A number of models posed for these works, but most of them are based on the features of either Fanny Cornforth, who lived with the artist at Cheyne Walk, or of Jane Morris, William Morris' wife, with whom Rossetti had a long and painful love affair. The pictures are frequently accompanied by verses from the artist's own pen; some explain the pictures while others are the pictures' sources of inspiration. The powerful women depicted by Rossetti relate strongly to the idea of the *femme fatale* evoked by the poet Algernon Charles Swinburne, who was included in the P.R.B. circle.

The style of these pictures is akin to the weighty classicism of George Moore, which was for a period in the 1860s an important source of ideas for many artists. Rossetti's frequent use of Japanese ephemera reflects another current phase, while his treatment of design and color is similar to that of J.A.M. Whistler and Frederick Sandys (1829–1904).

In the late 1860s his art entered its last period. Moving on to larger canvases, and working with darker colors, Rossetti painted new sinewy, swirling patterns around his symbolic figures. A work like *Astarte Syriaca* (1877; Manchester City Art Gallery) reflects his pursuit of the occult: Jane Morris' face is uplifted into a spiritual world, surrounded by the mannered forms of two attendants who press upwards against the top of the frame. The work has something of the naivety of the early watercolors, but there is also a lack of dexterity, a new attenuated curve of the lips, and a deadness in the eyes, which were not there in *Beata Beatrix*. The familiar expression of longing for love has turned bitter. There is a cruel streak in the late pictures which, with their hard, mannered forms, leads directly on to the style of Art Nouveau and the Symbolist era, especially in a work like *La Piadé Tolomei* (1881; University of Kansas Museum of Art, Lawrence, Kansas) which also uses Jane Morris as its model.

At each stage of his career, from his early student days up to the last, when he wished to withdraw from the eyes of society, Rossetti's art was a constant source of inspiration for painters both older and younger than himself. From the mid 1860s his position as a leader-figure dwindled, but the style he had encouraged continued to flourish.

At his house in Cheyne Walk, Chelsea, he gathered around him a considerable group of admirers, and a strange collection of animals; but neither of these bolstered up his deepening depressions. He became addicted to chloral. Despite late efforts to wean himself from it, the support of his friend Ford Madox Brown, and a recuperative stay at Kelmscott House with the family of William Morris, he died in a deep state of paranoia.

Rossetti's works can be seen at the Tate Gallery, London, at Manchester City Art Gallery, at the City Museum and Art Gallery, Birmingham, and in other collections.

Further reading. Doughty, O. *A Victorian Romantic: Dante Gabriel Rossetti*, London (1949). Fleming, G. *Rossetti and the Pre-Raphaelite Brotherhood*, London (1967). Gaunt, W. *The Restless Century*, London (1972). Rose, A. *The Pre-Raphaelites*, Oxford (1977).

Rosso Fiorentino 1494–1540

The Italian painter Giovanni Battista di Jacopo was born at Florence. One of the originators of Florentine Mannerism, he became known as Rosso Fiorentino. Although nothing certain is known about his training—though he acquired at this early stage a reputation for contrariness—he probably studied under Andrea del Sarto together with the painter Jacopo Pontormo; his training was certainly complete by 1513.

His first major work was the fresco of the *Assumption* (1516–17; SS. Annunziata, Florence). His innovations in style may have been encouraged by the example of Donatello's late reliefs. In his altarpiece *Madonna and Saints* (1518; Uffizi, Florence) Rosso proclaimed a counter-assertion to Florentine classicism, replacing plastic and counterpoised forms with shapes that are angular, eccentric, dissonant, and nervous. His work displayed an anticlassical fragmentation and abstraction, in which unity is governed by highly pitched emotionalism rather than by formal relationships. He continued in this manner, even to the point of violence, in such works as the *Deposition* (1521; Pinacoteca Comunale, Volterra) and *Moses and the Daughters of Jethro* (*c*1523; Uffizi, Florence). His apparently willful pursuit of the unwonted was somewhat abated during his stay in Rome from 1524, where he encountered the decorative work of Michelangelo, and of Raphael and his followers. Little remains from this Roman period, during which he gathered materials he was to use at Fontainebleau.

The Sack of Rome (1527) drove him to the provinces. His emotionalism returned to a degree verging on hysteria in his *Deposition* of 1527–8 (S. Lorenzo, Borgo San Sepolcro). By 1530 he reached Venice and there met the humanist Pietro Aretino, who recommended him to Francis I of France. In the same year he entered the king's service at Fontainebleau.

Rosso's personal cultivation as well as his skill especially favored him with the French king. Francis appointed him as his principal painter, at the head of a team of artists and artisans gathered for the decoration of the newly built enlargements to the Palace of Fontainebleau. His adjutant, from 1532, was Primaticcio. Two pictures painted in France survive, both from the last years of his life: an unfinished *Madonna and Child with St Anne* (Los Angeles County Museum of Art, Los Angeles) and a monumental *Pietà* (Louvre, Paris).

His chief works, the decorations at Fontainebleau, have been largely destroyed. The exception is the Gallery of Francis I (1534–9), which has been recently restored. Its frescoes, containing recondite allusions to Francis, are set within fantasticated stucco framing of Rosso's design. The general arrangement is covertly dependent on the ceiling of the Sistine Chapel, while a number of the details openly allude to—or wittily pervert—Michelangelo's work. This variegated and striking scheme is particularly inventive in the stucco figures and ornaments. The latter offer the first examples of strap-work, a whimsical, abstract motif which was to become commonplace of Mannerist decoration in northern Europe.

Rosso Fiorentino (attrib.): Madonna and Child. Private collection

Rosso, who lived in France "like a prince", is reported to have committed suicide.

Rosso Medardo 1858–1928

Medardo Rosso was an Italian sculptor, designer, and writer, who sought to find a plastic equivalent to the paintings of the Impressionists. Born in Turin, he moved to Milan with his family in 1870. After military service, he entered the Brera Academy, Milan, in 1882, only to be expelled the following year for disrupting classes. The next six years were spent in Milan, with brief visits to Rome, in 1883, for an exhibition of his work, and to Paris, in 1884, where he assisted the sculptor, Aimé-Jules Dalou. Rosso initially worked in clay and bronze, producing sculptures such as *The Last Kiss* (1882; now destroyed). This reflects the influence of the late-Romantic, avant-garde movement of Milan, the "Scapigliatura", with which Rosso was associated. By 1886, the year in which he executed *The Golden Age* (Galleria Comunale d'Arte Moderna, Rome), Rosso had not only adopted greater generalization in the handling of subject matter but had also employed the new technique of pouring wax over plaster. Both of these features were to characterize the rest of his work.

Rosso settled in Paris in 1889, remaining there until 1897. After a period of great physical privation, lack of recognition, and severe ill-health, he began to establish a reputation greatly helped by two exhibitions of his work held in 1893 at Charles Bodinière's Théâtre d'Application. It was here that he exchanged works with Rodin. The ensuing mutual admiration of the two sculptors has led to the suggestion that it was Rosso's influence that caused Rodin to clothe his nude *Balzac* in a dressing gown, and to alter the statue's stance.

For the last 31 years of his life Rosso lived in Italy, producing no further original work apart from the *Ecce Puer* (1907; Musée de Luxembourg, Paris). Instead he devoted his energies to traveling across Europe organizing exhibitions of his works.

Rosso rejected all dependence upon the rules of antique sculpture, such as a constantly changing viewpoint and a clearly articulated silhouette. He was influenced by Baudelaire's belief that painting could alone qualify as "Ideal Art", because it was limited to one viewpoint and hence to the presentation of a finite image. So he sought to create sculpture that would approximate as closely as possible to this end. Furthermore, he saw the form of a sculptured figure as imprecise, its edges softened by the light emanating from the space the figure inhabits, thus fusing its form with its environment. These guiding principles in Rosso's art are illustrated in his mature work, *Conversation in the Garden* (1893; Collection of Dr Gianni Mattioli, Milan).

Mark Rothko: Red on Maroon, from the series of panels in the Tate Gallery, London; oil on canvas; 267×239cm (105×94in); 1959

Roszak Theodore 1907–81

The American sculptor and printmaker Theodore Roszak was born in Poznan, Poland, and emigrated with his family to Chicago in 1909. He became an American citizen in 1919. In the late 1920s he studied at the Art Institute of Chicago, Illinois University, Urbana, Columbia University, and at the Academy of Design, New York. A fellowship for lithography enabled him to study in Europe between 1929 and 1931. He was exposed to European modernism first in Prague and then in Paris. From 1936 to 1945 he made geometric constructions in wood and plastic, while teaching at the New York Design Laboratory, guided by Laszlo Moholy-Nagy. Then he began working in welded and brazed metal, producing his characteristic sculptures with their free and often spiky forms alluding to nature. His public commissions include the eagle on the United States Embassy in London (1960).

Rothko Mark 1903–70

Mark Rothko was a Russian-born painter of the American School. He was born at Dvinsk in Russia, but in 1913 emigrated with his family to Portland, Oregon. In 1921 he went to Yale University to study the liberal arts, but left there in 1923 because of an insufficient interest in academic training. In 1925 he settled in New York and began to draw from the model. He also attended Max Weber's class at the Art Students League. He began to teach children at the Center Academy, Brooklyn, in 1929, and continued to do so until 1952. In 1933 came his first one-man show at the Contemporary Arts Gallery, New York, while from 1936 to 1937 he worked on the Works Progress Administration Federal Arts Project in New York. In 1935 he had been cofounder of "The Ten", a group of artists with Expressionist sympathies who were to exhibit together for nearly ten years. In 1945, he had another one-man show, at Peggy Guggenheim's New York gallery.

Rothko's earlier work has Surrealist overtones (for example, *Baptismal Scene*, 1945; Whitney Museum of American Art, New York). It was not until the later 1940s that his most individual and characteristic style began to emerge. At first, it consisted of shapes with ragged edges loosely composed into an Abstract composition (for example, *No. 18*, 1948, Vassar College Art Gallery, Poughkeepsie, New York; *No. 24*, 1949, Joseph Hirshhorn Museum, Washington, D.C.). During the 1950s, Rothko refined his approach. The typical Rothko canvas is upright, and contains one, two, or three rectangular (or lozenge-shaped) areas of color set against a single-color background. The edges of the areas are blurred, and there is usually a variation in the density of both the areas and the background. The effect of the best Rothkos is luminous, serene, and grave. The Tate Gallery in London owns the series of panels that Rothko had at first intended for the decoration of a New York restaurant. There are examples of his work in most of the world's leading galleries of Modern Art, including the Art Institute, Chicago, and the Museum of Modern Art, New York.

Further reading. Breslin, B. *Mark Rothko: a Biography*, Chicago (1998). Rothko, M. et al. *The Artist's Reality: Philosophies of Art*, New Haven (2004). Weiss, J. et al. *Mark Rothko*, New York (2001).

Rottmayr von Rosenbrunn J.F.M. 1654–1730

The leading early-18th-century painter active in Vienna, Johann Franz Michael Rottmayr von Rosenbrunn spent 13 years from 1675 onwards working in the studio of J.C. Loth in Venice. After his return to Austria in 1687, Rottmayr first worked for the Bishop of Passau and the Archbishop of Salzburg before settling in Vienna, probably in 1696. He was ennobled in 1704. He was the first Germanic monumental painter to break the domination of the Italian painters in central Europe, and was active in Bohemia, Moravia, and Silesia, as well as in Pommersfelden. His dark, forceful early style subsequently gave way to more open compositions painted in lighter colors.

Rouault Georges 1871–1958

The French painter and printmaker Georges Rouault was born in Paris, the son of a carpenter. At the age of 14 he served an apprenticeship in two stained-glass workshops. The depth and purity of color and the heavy black enclosing lines in medieval glass were greatly to affect his later work. He was also much influenced by Gustave Moreau, whose pupil he became in 1891. At about this time he met Matisse, and other painters who were later to be Fauves. After Moreau's death in 1898, he became curator of the Musée Gustave Moreau, Paris. In 1904, he met and was much impressed by the Catholic writer Léon Bloy.

The first unmistakable Rouault style appeared in 1903–4 in a series of "dark" gouaches devoted to acrobats, clowns, pierrots, and prostitutes. In Bloy's words, Rouault wished "to thrust at God the insistent cry of dereliction and anxiety for the orphaned multitude". Some of these were included in the Salon d'Automne of 1905. By 1908, he began his series of studies of judges and lawcourts. He also met the art dealer Ambrose Vollard who, in 1913, bought every picture in his studio and who, in 1917, provided Rouault with a room in his own house. During this collaboration with Vollard, Rouault began producing his extensive range of graphic and illustrative works, including the *Miserere* (60 etchings, completed in 1927, published in 1948), *Les Fleurs du Mal* (1926–7 and 1930s), and the 82 *Père Ubee* wood engravings and seven color etchings.

Most of his later work was concerned with religious themes. He often placed the events and parables of the New Testament in the blighted industrial suburbs of Paris. He is perhaps the last of the great religious artists.

Further reading. *Georges Rouault: Exposition du Centenaire*, Paris (1971). George, W. and Nouaille-Rouault, G. *Rouault*, London (1971). Rouault, G. and Suares, A. *Correspondance*, Paris (1960). Rouault, G. *Sur l'Art et sur la Vie*, Paris (1971). Soby, J.T. *Georges Rouault*, New York (1945).

Roubiliac L.-F. 1705–62

One of the most original sculptors of his day, the French artist Louis-François Roubiliac was born in Lyons of Huguenot parents. He is said to have served an initial apprenticeship in Protestant Dresden under Balthasar Permoser, later becoming a pupil of his fellow-Lyonnais Nicolas Coustou in Paris. At some time in the early 1730s, presumably because of his Protestant faith, he came to London, where he was to remain for the rest of his life.

He worked at first for the sculptor Henry Cheere, also of Huguenot stock, through whom he received in 1738 his first commission, for a statue of George Frederick Handel for Vauxhall Gardens (now in the Victoria and Albert Museum, London). This highly original work, blending realism with allegory, is a landmark in Rococo sculpture. It established Roubiliac's reputation and gained him a practice in portrait sculpture, in which he far outshone his contemporaries in England. It was not, however, until 1746, with his monument to Bishop Hough (Worcester Cathedral) that Roubiliac obtained a commission for a major church monument. This clever design inaugurates a series of brilliantly original monuments by Roubiliac, in which he gradually broke down the architectural dominance in English monuments. His most important early monument is that to the Duke of Argyll (1746–9; Westminster Abbey, London), in which sculptural groupings dominate the design.

Georges Rouault: Christ; stained glass; 1939–41. Musée National d'Art Moderne, Paris

In 1752 Roubiliac visited Rome, where he was deeply impressed by the monuments of Bernini. From this time, his own works become even more dramatic and sculptural. The transition can be seen in the monuments to the Duke (1750–1) and Duchess (1753) of Montagu (Warkton, Northamptonshire). His later monuments, such as those to General Hargrave and Lady Elizabeth Nightingale (1757 and 1761; both in Westminster Abbey, London) surpass in originality and drama anything produced in France at the time.

Rousseau Henri 1844–1910

The French painter Henri Rousseau was born in Laval, of petty bourgeois parents. He served in the French army (he was a clarinettist in the regimental band at Caen). He never in fact went to Mexico, as he later claimed to have done. He settled in Paris in 1869, where he eventually obtained a post as gatekeeper in the customs-house at the city gate (his nickname "Le Douanier", "The Customs Officer", rather elevates his office). In 1885, he resigned this post, took odd jobs such as painting inn-signs and devoted more time to his own painting.

Although his work was that of a primitive or "Sunday Painter", his own pretensions were to rival the Salon favorites of the day. Ironically, however, his work attracted the attention of the avant-garde: first Redon and Toulouse-Lautrec, then Alfred Jarry, and finally, in his last years, Picasso and Apollinaire. What he possessed above all was a complete confidence in the value of his painting. He once told Picasso that they were the only great contemporary artists, "I in the modern manner and you in the Egyptian."

His decision to devote his life to painting coincided with the founding of the Salon des Indépendants in 1884. In that free, juryless exhibition, he showed between three and ten paintings almost every year from 1886 to 1910. The majority were landscapes and portraits. His earliest known works are local views (for instance, of the customs house), naive in their perception of reality and in their detailed descriptiveness. But such seemingly direct reportage was followed by inventive, imaginative, and dream-like works. However obsessed he was with exact and particular detail, he was able to control his composition, subordinating what might have been a host of minute and disparate observations into a rhythmical whole.

Rousseau's famous *Jungle Scenes* and *Exotic Landscapes* were not based on his mythical Mexican experiences, but on the tropical flora and fauna that he observed in the Jardin des Plantes in Paris. Equally, the exotic creatures inhabiting these forests—monkeys, water buffaloes, hunters, and dark-skinned natives—were reproduced from photographs, or from dolls and toys (for example, *Merry Jesters*, *c*1906; Philadelphia Museum of Art). One of his last works, *The Dream* (1910; Museum of Modern Art, New York) is a memory-image of his first love reclining on a sofa in one of his imaginary jungles. Its power and conviction, its sheer convincingness as dream-reality, foretell the best of Surrealist painting. Kandinsky called Rousseau the author of "new, greater reality", the complementary pole of the "new and greater abstraction". Rousseau remains the first and the greatest of the naive or primitive painters.

L.-F. Roubiliac: George II; marble; height 79cm (31in). Collection of H.M. Queen Elizabeth II

Further reading. Alley, R. *The Art of Henri Rousseau*, Oxford (1978). Apollinaire, G. (ed. Breunig, L.C., trans. Suleiman, S.) *On Art*, London (1972). Certigny, H. *La Verité sur le Douanier Rousseau*, Paris (1961). Delaunay, R. "Mon Ami Henri Rousseau", *Les Lettres Francaises*, Paris (7 Aug. 1952; 21 Aug. 1952; 28 Aug. 1952; 4 Sept. 1952). Tzara, T. *Henri Rousseau*, Zurich (1958). Uhde, W. *Five Primitive Masters*, New York (1949). Unde, W. *Rousseau le Douanier*, Lausanne (1948).

Henri Rousseau: The Snake Charmer; oil on canvas; 169×190cm (67×75in); 1907. Musée du Jeu de Paume, Paris

Rousseau Théodore 1812–67

The French landscape painter Pierre-Etienne-Théodore Rousseau was a leading figure in the Barbizon School. Born in Paris, he studied under Neoclassical teachers; but he was more influenced by the copies he made in the Louvre of Dutch masters. He began to paint plein-air landscapes around Paris in the 1820s.

He traveled widely in the French provinces in the early 1830s, visiting the Jura, the Auvergne, and Normandy. He developed a romantic manner of sharply contrasted light and shade, using energetic brushwork (for example, *The Jetty at Granville*, 1831; Wadsworth Atheneum, Hartford, Conn.). His Salon exhibits from 1831 onwards attracted the attention of progressive critics, and he soon had influential patrons including Delacroix, George Sand, and the critic T.-E.-J. Thoré. However the academic Salon jury refused his *Descent of the Cattle* (Hendrik Willem Mesdag Museum, The Hague) in 1836; he was excluded from the Salon until 1847.

In the 1840s he began to paint more tranquil scenes in Berry and the Landes, and *c*1837 settled in Barbizon. He painted effects of weather and light (for example, *Edge of the Forest of Fontainebleau, Sunset*, 1851; Louvre, Paris). He also depicted woodland scenes, and liked to gain dramatic effects by placing trees, isolated

Théodore Rousseau: A Heath; pen, brown ink, and wash on paper; 20×28cm (8×11in). National Gallery of Scotland, Edinburgh

or in clumps, against a low skyline (for example, *The Oaks*, 1850–2; Louvre, Paris). The liberal Salon of 1849 brought his work once more into prominence, and he enjoyed a period of public and official recognition.

Though considered the Romantic landscape painter *par excellence*, Rousseau anticipated Impressionism in his dedication to plein-air painting, and in his portrayal of subtle changes of light and weather.

Rowlandson Thomas 1756–1827

Thomas Rowlandson, the English draftsman and etcher, was born in London. In 1772 he entered the Royal Academy Schools, and although he was awarded a silver medal in 1777, he had the reputation of being a capricious student. About 1774,

Thomas Rowlandson: A Club Subscription Room; pen and watercolor over pencil on paper; 32×45cm (13×18in); 1792. Victoria and Albert Museum, London

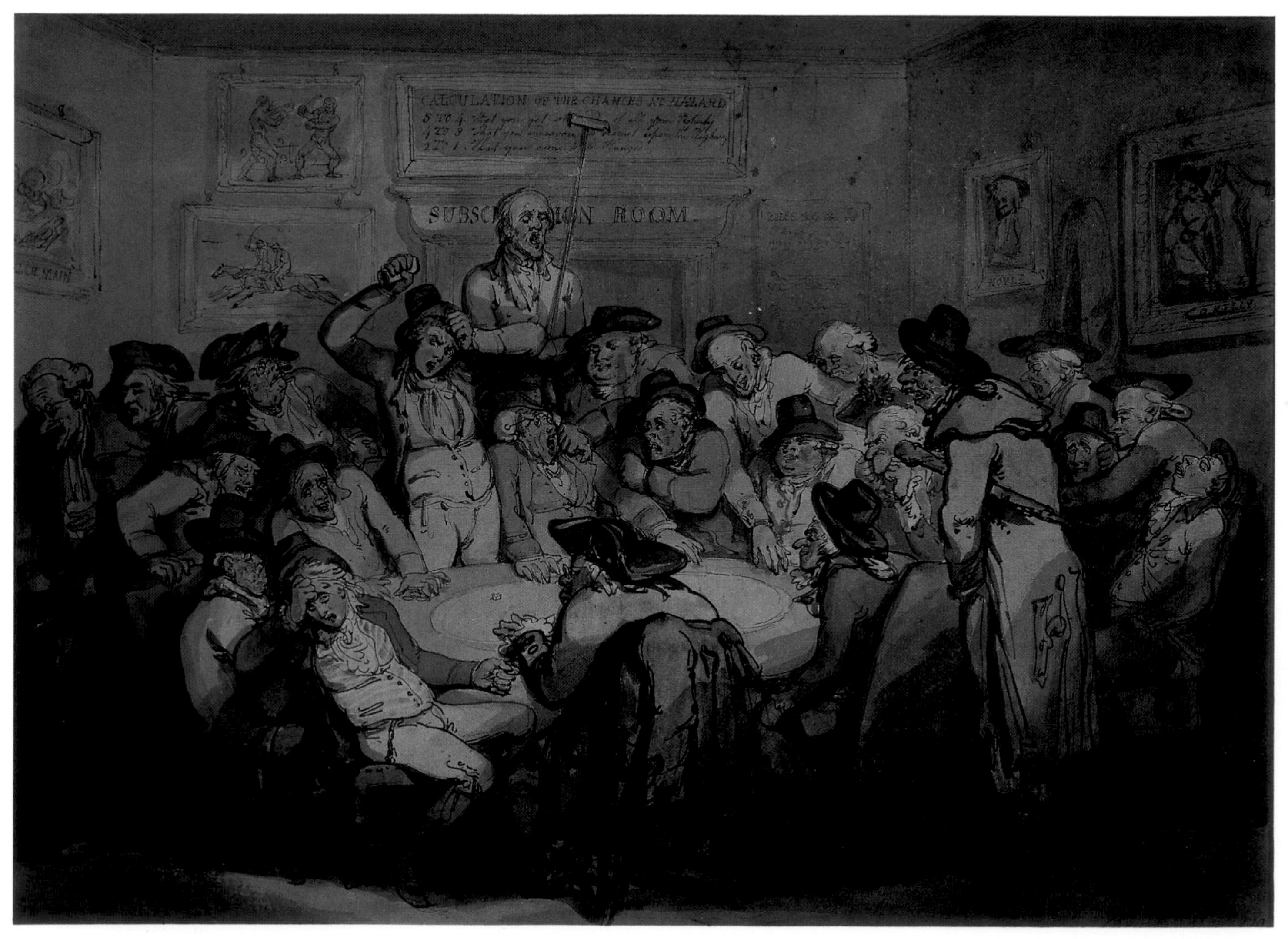

he made the first of several visits to the Continent. He exhibited watercolor drawings at the Royal Academy from 1775 to 1787, and from 1800 worked continuously for the publisher Rudolph Ackermann, for whom he illustrated *The Microcosm of London* (1808–10). *The Tours of Dr Syntax* (1818–21), and *The English Dance of Death* (1814–16).

Rowlandson's fame rests on his humorous watercolor depictions of Georgian life; however, he was a versatile artist and his repertoire of subjects included topography, rustic genre, and portraiture. His reputation has suffered from his own industriousness; yet within his prodigious graphic output there are many memorable designs. At his best, he organized large groups of figures, or described individual characters, with extraordinary facility, and with an elastic and calligraphic line that is ever varied and lively. There are fine collections of Rowlandson's drawings at the British Museum, London, the Boston Public Library, and the Huntington Library and Art Gallery, San Marino, California.

Further reading. Binyon, L. *English Watercolours*, London (1946). Falls, B. *Thomas Rowlandson: his Life and Work*, London (1949). George, M.D. *Hogarth to Cruikshank: Social Change in Graphic Satire*, London (1967). Grego, J. *Rowlandson the Caricaturist*, London (1880). Hayes, J. *Rowlandson, Watercolours and Drawings*, London (1972). Paulson, R. *Rowlandson: a New Interpretation*, London (1972).

Roy Jamini 1887–1974

Jamini Roy has been called the greatest modern Indian painter. He was able to resolve successfully the deadlock reached by the Nationalist Bengal School under Abanindranath (1861–1951) between the adoption of a pure European idiom and the self-conscious revival of ancient tradition.

Born in Bengal, he received training in the Western academic tradition at Calcutta Art School. Later he went through an inevitable sentimental revivalist "archaeological" phase, through the intervention of the Bengal School. Sensing the futility of trying to revive Ajanta or Mughal art, whose cultural values were so alien to the present age, he underwent a spiritual crisis. It was through a "great intellectual adventure" that he came to develop his highly personal style: robust, simple, at once austere and sensuous, drawing upon popular Kalighat and folk styles.

Such primitivist borrowings were not self-conscious mannerism, for he deeply loved the Santal tribes he painted. Giving up commercial paints, he went back to the use of organic pigments. Later in life he renounced an "original" contribution to art, in favor of "mass" art that was within the easy reach of ordinary people. He shared its execution with his pupils and assistants, thus making a serious social statement that sprang from deep conviction about the social function of art.

Peter Paul Rubens: The Duke of Lerma on Horseback; oil on canvas; 289×205cm (114×81in); 1603. Prado, Madrid

Rubens Peter Paul 1577–1640

Peter Paul Rubens was the greatest northern artist of the Baroque. His work was crucial to the genesis of that style, and his energy, versatility, and productivity have never been equaled in the history of art. He excelled in every kind of painting; his vast

output included altarpieces and other religious paintings, scenes from Classical history and mythology, portraits, and hunting scenes. He also produced designs for tapestry and silver, and book illustrations. He directed a large workshop, and designed and supervised the execution of many large-scale schemes of decoration. Moreover, he was a classical scholar and diplomat, and in the 1620s played an important part in international politics. The splendor of Rubens' art reflected and expressed the renewed confidence of the Roman Catholic church and the power and glory of the autocratic monarchs of the Counter-Reformation.

Rubens was born at Siegen in Westphalia. In 1587 his family returned to Antwerp where he studied painting with Tobias Verhaecht, Adam van Noort, and Otto van Veen. In 1598 he was enrolled as a master in the Antwerp Guild, and in 1600 went to Italy to study ancient and modern art. Here he entered the service of Vincenzo Gonzaga of Mantua; in the next eight years he traveled to Florence, Rome, Genoa, Venice, and Spain.

Rubens' years in Italy were crucial to his development. His knowledge of Classical civilization and literature was profound and he was inspired by the art of the Renaissance. He absorbed everything he saw in Italy, and throughout his life returned to this store of visual knowledge. He studied the glowing colors and opulence of the Venetians—of Titian (*c*1488–1576), Tintoretto (1518–94), and Veronese (1528–88)—and his sense of weight and volume clearly owes much to Michelangelo and to Classical sculpture. Among living artists he admired and copied Caravaggio, and emulated Annibale Carracci's large, bold drawings from life.

Rubens went to Spain on his first diplomatic mission in 1603. While he was there he made copies after paintings by Titian in the Spanish Royal collection. By 1608 he had already produced a series of important early Baroque masterpieces. The equestrian portrait of *The Duke of Lerma* (1603; Prado, Madrid), shows the horse head-on and boldly foreshortened. In 1606 he painted a series of portraits of the Genoese nobility. Their vitality of expression, the rustling movement and painterly surfaces of their elaborate costumes, and the terrace settings with columns and curtain, all broke with the stiffness of Mannerist portraiture and began a new tradition. The *Madonna Adored by Saints* (1607/8), the first version of an altarpiece painted for the Chiesa Nuova in Rome, heralds the Baroque; the colors and textures are decorative and glowing, the forms are powerful, and the mood ecstatic.

Rubens returned to Antwerp in 1608. In 1609 he was appointed painter to the Hapsburg Regents, the Infanta Isabella and the Archduke Albert, and in that same year he married Isabella Brant, daughter of an Antwerp lawyer. Between 1609 and 1621 an important series of paintings established him as the leading painter in northern Europe. The urgent movement and immediate sensuous appeal of his art must have amazed contemporary observers in Flanders. Rubens saw himself as heir to the great painters of the High Renaissance, and the monumentality of his work rivaled theirs.

The key works of this period were the *Elevation of the Cross* (1609–10; Antwerp Cathedral), the *Descent from the Cross* (1611–14; Antwerp Cathedral), and *The Conversion of St Bavo* (for St Bavon, Ghent, 1611–12; *modello* in the National Gallery, London). *The Elevation of the Cross* preserves the traditional triptych form; the composition of the central panel is based on a bold diagonal, and the powerfully modeled forms create a sense of violent overall movement. Rubens' early Antwerp style is restless and powerfully dramatic. This can be seen in a cycle of hunting scenes (*c*1615), and some battle paintings—*The Defeat of Sennacherib*, Alte Pinakothek, Munich, and its pendant, *The Conversion of St Paul* (1613–14; Courtauld Institute Galleries, London), and the *Battle of the Amazons* (*c*1618, Alte Pinakothek, Munich). These all show his unrivaled ability to convey in formally organized compositions the energy and power of struggling masses of men and animals. Yet his art at this period was also in a sense classical; the influence of his study of bas-reliefs and cameos is often apparent in his compositions. After 1615 he very rarely signed and dated his works.

In the 1620s Rubens was constantly involved with large-scale schemes of decoration. To fulfill these commissions he depended on the successful organization of a large workshop and on the brilliant use he made of preparatory sketches. He also began to supervise a team of engravers to popularize his work throughout Europe.

In 1620 he agreed to produce sketches for 39 canvases, to be executed with the help of assistants, for the ceiling of the Jesuit church in Antwerp (destroyed by fire in 1718). He had already painted altarpieces for the high altar. For these canvases Rubens produced two kinds of sketches: grisaille sketches, done on small panels, where the first ideas were brushed in hastily in brown tones with white highlights; and color sketches for his assistants to follow. The color sketches could also be used as contract models to show clients. He had begun to use sketches in 1605, and continued to follow variations of this procedure throughout his career; without it, the immense scope of his activity is unthinkable.

The ceiling paintings showed for the first time how deeply he had studied the great Venetian ceiling painters of the 16th century. The canvases were hung, in the Venetian manner, within wooden compartments; the individual compositions included derivations from Titian, Tintoretto, and Veronese.

Rubens also received important commissions from abroad. In 1622 Louis XIII commissioned 12 designs for tapestry of *The Life of Constantine*. Early in 1622, in 1623, and again in 1625, Rubens was in Paris to discuss and complete a cycle of paintings of *The Life of Marie de Medici* (Louvre, Paris) for the Luxembourg Palace. In this series he inaugurated a new type of political allegory. His task was not easy, as he had to commemorate several inglorious events in the life of the somewhat foolish Queen. Yet he transformed his delicate subject matter by the splendor of his allegory; ancient gods and Christian symbols work together to glorify the Queen: her birth is compared to the Nativity, and her education is presided over by the gods and goddesses of Antiquity. From 1626 to 1628 Rubens worked on designs for tapestries of *The Triumph of the Eucharist* for the Convent of the Descalzas Reales, Madrid.

The 1620s mark the climax of Rubens' Baroque style. The dramatic movement, bright light, and rhythmic force that bind the figures harmoniously together are exemplified in the *Assumption* (1626; Antwerp Cathedral) and the *Madonna and Child adored by Saints* (1628; Royal Museum of Fine Arts, Antwerp). A three-dimensional spiraling movement has re-

Peter Paul Rubens: the central panel of the St Idelfonso triptych; oil on canvas; 352×236cm (139×93in); 1630–2. Kunsthistorisches Museum, Vienna

placed the thrusting diagonals of the earlier period; Rubens' concept of dynamic movement, and his brilliantly fluent and expressive brushwork, were his most significant contributions to the Baroque.

This period was also, astonishingly, Rubens' most active time as a diplomat: he went on diplomatic missions to Spain, Holland, France, and England. His wife, Isabella Brant, had died in 1626 and Rubens was perhaps willing to distract himself with constant traveling. In 1628 he was in Spain and painted portraits of the Spanish Royal family. Accompanied sometimes by Velázquez, he again studied the Hapsburg Titians, and Titian is, in Rubens' late works, once more a profound source of inspiration.

In 1629–30, Rubens conducted peace negotiations in London. He was knighted by Charles I in 1630, and between 1630 and 1634 did paintings for the ceiling of the Banqueting House in Whitehall. These have a special importance because they are his only large decorative scheme that can still be seen in its original place. Their development may be traced through a series of exceptionally beautiful sketches. Here Rubens displayed his knowledge of classical allegory in the service of a heretic King: the theme of the ceiling was the Divine Authority of James I. As in the Jesuit ceiling, his deep indebtedness to the Venetian tradition is apparent both in the conception of the whole and in the individual canvases.

In the early 1630s Rubens was exempted from further diplomacy and in his last years enjoyed greater freedom from court duties. In 1636 he was appointed court painter to the Infanta's successor, the Cardinal Infante Ferdinand, brother of Philip IV. The Cardinal had made a state entry into Antwerp the previous year, and Rubens had supervised the lavish decorations of streets and squares. The theme was the decline in trade and other disastrous consequences of war against Holland.

Through Ferdinand, Rubens gained the contract for his last important commission, the decoration of the Torre de la Parada, Philip IV's hunting lodge near Madrid. The decorations were to include a series of scenes from Ovid and of other mythological subjects, a series of animal and hunting scenes ordered from Rubens' studio, and works by Velázquez. The mythological scenes were to be designed by Rubens himself and he did more than 50 oil sketches for them; in 1638, 112 paint-

ings, executed by assistants, were sent to Spain. Assistants played a larger part than usual in the finished products, and many are disappointing. The Torre sketches, however, are among the most spontaneous, personal, and economical of all his works; they are a warm and human interpretation of the loves of the gods.

In his last decade Rubens continued to paint the great religious themes, among them the *Adoration of the Magi* (1633–4; King's College Chapel, Cambridge) and the *St Idelfonso* triptych (1630–2; Kunsthistorisches Museum, Vienna). These works of his late style are calmer, more serene, and more radiantly spiritual than their powerfully Baroque predecessors. The *Ascent to Calvary* (c1634; Musées Royaux des Beaux-Arts de Belgique) is furiously Baroque, but the violence is tempered by the beauty of the silvery colors.

In 1630 Rubens had married the 17-year-old Hélène Fourment, daughter of a silk merchant. From this time, more of his works were painted purely for pleasure; his newfound domestic tranquillity and the beauty of his young wife inspired many of his late works. This tranquillity is the theme of a highly finished small work on panel, *Self Portrait with Hélène Fourment and his son Nicolas in their Garden* (1631; Alte Pinakothek, Munich). Beside an Italianate loggia and fountain the family enjoy their garden surrounded by tulips, orange trees, dogs, and peacocks.

Hélène Fourment also inspired his majestic renderings of the female nude. His most mellow and radiant mythological paintings, two versions of *The Judgment of Paris* (National Gallery, London, and Prado, Madrid) and also the splendid *Hélène Fourment in a Fur Wrap* (Kunsthistorisches Museum, Vienna) all date from this late period. No artist has surpassed Rubens' rendering of the sheen and glow of the surface of the skin.

In 1635 he purchased the country estate of the Château de Steen so that he could paint in peace and study landscape. His most important landscapes were all painted in the following years. They include the *An Autumn Landscape with a View of the Château de Steen* (National Gallery, London), the *Landscape with a Rainbow* (Wallace Collection, London),

Peter Paul Rubens: Hélène Fourment in a Fur Wrap; oil on panel; 175×96cm (69×38in); 1638. Kunsthistorisches Museum, Vienna

Peter Paul Rubens: Portrait of Isabella Brant; chalk and ink on paper; 38×29cm (15×11in); c1622. British Museum, London

and the *Landscape with Peasants returning from the Fields* (c1635–8; Palazzo Pitti, Florence). Rubens' landscapes, which owe much to those of his Flemish predecessor, Pieter Bruegel, start from a precise observation of the life around him: of birds, animals, fences, women carrying rakes and bundles of hay. But these details are included in compositions of solid grandeur that are controlled by Rubens' firm grasp of land masses, and irradiated by intensely romantic effects of light.

Rubens began to suffer from gout in 1627. In the late 1630s he began to have severe difficulties using his painting arm, and he died in 1640.

Further reading. Burckhardt, J. *Recollections of Rubens*, London (1950). Gerson, H. and ter Kuile, E.H., *Art and Architecture in Belgium: 1600–1800*, Harmondsworth (1960). Held, J.S. *Rubens: Selected Drawings*, London (1986). Jaffe, M. *Rubens and Italy*, Oxford (1977). White, C. *Peter Paul Rubens: Man and Artist*, New Haven (1987).

Rublev Andrei *c1370–c1430*

Andrei Rublev was a Russian painter. He entered a monastery at Zagorsk and later moved to another at Moscow, where he died. He produced both frescoes and icons; several of the latter are in museums in Moscow and St Petersburg. In Moscow Rublev collaborated with the older artist Theophanes the Greek on the icons of the iconostasis of the Cathedral of the Annunciation in the Kremlin (1405); those of the *Nativity, Baptism*, and *Transfiguration* are generally attributed to Rublev.

Although he was influenced by Theophanes in his spiritual outlook and sense of composition, his teacher was probably Prokhor of Gorodets. Rublev developed a serene style distinctly different in its classically balanced forms, controlled draftsmanship, and purer palette from the nervous and asymmetric handling of Theophanes.

In the early 15th century, Rublev also worked on the cathedral of Zvenigorod, from which several frescoes survive, for instance *St Laurus*, and also icons, for instance one of the Savior. In 1408, in the Cathedral of the Dormition at Vladmir, he painted with the monk Deniil the extensive frescoes of the *Last Judgment* and several icons, one of which is *Christ in Majesty*. About 1411 he produced what is considered his masterpiece, the icon of the *Old Testament Trinity*. In 1422 he returned to his monastery at Zagorsk, where he and Daniil executed both frescoes and icons.

Further reading. Alpatov, M. *Andrej Rublev*, Milan (1962). Antonova, V. *The Rublev Exhibition*, Moscow (1960). Lebedeva, J.A. *Andrei Rubljow und seine Zeitgenossen*, Dresden (1962).

Rude François 1784–1855

François Rude was a French sculptor whose work is Romantic in conception, but expressed with Realist accuracy. He was apprenticed to his father, a metal-worker, which gave him a strong technical grounding; he also received an academic training at the École des Beaux-Arts in Paris. He was an enthusiastic Bonapartist (see his *Awakening of Napoleon*, 1846; bronze, Fixin park, near Dijon), and spent 12 years in Belgium after the Restoration, where he had a workshop in Brussels. He sculpted a bust of the painter *J.-L. David* in exile (plaster, 1826; marble, 1831; both Louvre, Paris). His charming *Neapolitan Fisherboy* (marble, 1833; Louvre, Paris) shows the informality of his approach, while his famous *Marseillaise* (or *Departing of the Volunteers of 1792)* for the Arc de Triomphe, Paris (stone, 1836), combines expressive force with popular facial types despite its strongly classical conception.

Ruisdael Jacob van *c*1628/9–82

The painter and etcher Jacob Isaacksz. van Ruisdael is widely regarded as Holland's greatest landscapist. The son of a frame-maker and art dealer who also painted landscapes, Ruisdael may have studied under his father, and perhaps also with his uncle Salomon van Ruysdael, who influenced his early pictures. He was very precocious: the earliest dated works, views in the neighborhood of Haarlem done when he was not yet 20, show astonishing maturity, particularly in their contrasts of light and shadow and their vivid colors. Around 1650 Ruisdael visited east Holland and the regions of Germany that adjoined the Dutch border: hilly, forested areas which excited the romantic strain in him. He lived in Amsterdam from *c*1657 until his death, although he continued to travel about Holland.

Between *c*1650 and 1670 he tackled almost every kind of landscape: panoramas painted from the dunes overlooking the vast fertile plain around Haarlem, woodland scenes and the denser recesses of forests, country roads bordered by cottages and wheatfields, river scenes centered on picturesque watermills, stormy seascapes, calmer beach scenes, and pictures of villages in winter. From 1659 Ruisdael also painted a series of views of mountain streams and waterfalls inspired by the Scandinavian landscapes of Allart van Everdingen (1621–75).

Ruisdael's art is characterized by a sensitive response to the different moods of nature, whether in the elevating experience of vast, luminous panoramas of green meadows and golden wheatfields, or the image of dark, desolate winter scenes. The principal vehicle for the expression of mood in his landscapes is light and shade, particularly such dramatic and arresting devices as the fitful breaking of sunlight through massive clouds. Absence of light is also evocative, as in the melancholy forest interiors with their dead trees and stagnant pools. Many of Ruisdael's views are still recognizable, but he is not always a realist.

The conjunction of observation and imagination is illustrated by the two versions of *The Jewish Cemetery* (Gemäldegalerie Alte Meister, Dresden, and the Detroit Institute of Arts). In these paintings fictional mountains and ruins surround tombstones sketched at Ouderkerk, near Amsterdam. A degree of subjectivity is elsewhere evident in Ruisdael's majestic and powerful conception of nature—a

Jacob van Ruisdael: An Extensive Landscape with a Ruined Castle and a Village Church; oil on canvas; 109×146cm (43×57in); c1665–72. National Gallery, London

conception conveyed by giant oaks, foaming mountain torrents, and distant horizons. The question of realism is also complicated by occasional allusions to cyclical processes of decay, growth, and renewal. These are not necessarily of an explicitly allegorical kind. They are particularly evident in the *Jewish Cemetery* paintings, where a rainbow and new foliage are contrasted with such symbols of the transitoriness of life as tombs, ruins, and dead trees.

Although his influence on other Dutch artists (notably on his pupil and friend Meyndert Hobbema) was considerable, Ruisdael was much less popular in his lifetime than the painters of Italianate landscapes. There were many appreciative collectors of his work during the 18th century; but his importance was only fully recognized during the Romantic period, with the subsequent rise of naturalistic landscape in England and France during the first half of the 19th century. Works can be seen at the Hermitage, St Petersburg, the Metropolitan Museum, New York, the Rijksmuseum, Amsterdam, and the National Gallery, London.

Runge P.O. 1777–1810

Philipp Otto Runge was a German Romantic draftsman, painter, and theorist. He studied at the Copenhagen Academy (1799–1801), which was then one of the leading European centers for Neoclassicism. Under the influence of John Flaxman, William Blake, and Jacob Carstens, he developed a strong linear style, especially in his drawings. In 1801 he transferred to the Dresden Academy, hoping to find there a more profound approach to art, but he was disappointed. This, together with his failure in the Weimar Art Competition in 1801, caused him to question the whole basis of classical art and to seek inspiration in the literature of the Romantics (works by Tieck, Novalis, and Wackenroder), and the mystics (Jakob Böhme, etc).

He concluded that since art was the product of a particular age and country and the expression of the artist's inner self, a new art-form was needed to reflect the spiritual upheavals of the age. Landscape should supersede history painting, since idealistic philosophy had shown nature to be an extension of man's mind. Likewise, a revival of Christian art was required, not in its traditional historical form, but as the revelations of nature itself, interpreted by the divine spark within the artist.

P.O. Runge: Self-portrait; chalk on paper; 55×43cm (22×17in); 1801/2. Hamburger Kunsthalle, Hamburg

This mystical pantheism found its greatest expression in his cycle *Die Tageszeiten* ("The Times of the Day"; drawings, 1802–3; engravings, 1805). Here, in four highly symmetrical, decorative compositions, Runge used an interrelated flower-and-child symbolism to represent the light or darkness at Morning, Noon, Evening, and Night. Several layers of meaning, involving Christian and cosmic symbolism, lie beneath this; but the detailed, linear style and complex allegorical framework fail to make them sensuously expressive. Color was needed. Runge devoted several years to color research (including a correspondence with Goethe), and in 1810 published his treatise *Die Farbenkugel* ("The Spheres of Color").

After his return to Hamburg in 1803, Runge took painting lessons, and painted several important portrait groups (for example, *We Three*, 1803; *The Artist's Parents*, 1806; both Hamburger Kunsthalle, Hamburg). In their stern realism and lack of idealization these works show the influence of Runge's Copenhagen teacher, J. Juel, and his Dresden mentor, A. Graff. But Runge's innovations lie in his almost plein-air treatment of landscape and his ability to combine an intense immediacy with symbolic meaning.

In 1808 Runge painted the first version of *Morning*, and in 1809 the second and larger version (both in Hamburger Kunsthalle, Hamburg). The greater visual impact of the paintings compared with the drawing is due not only to the use of color but to the replacement of symbols by a real landscape. Runge had intended to paint even larger mural versions of all four *Tageszeiten* so as to create a total artistic environment, but ill health prevented this and he died in Hamburg in December 1810.

Ruskin John 1819–1900

The English critic, author, and artist John Ruskin was the most original and influential art theorist of his time. Born of prosperous parents (his father was a sherry merchant), he profited early from frequent trips to Italy. His experience of grand foreign scenery, coupled with a close, often scientific, study of nature formed the basis of his aesthetic. His early enthusiasm for the works of J.M.W. Turner widened this response.

Modern Painters, published between 1843 and 1859, began as a justification of Turner's vision; it became, in the course of five volumes, a general survey of art. The success of this, together with *The Seven Lamps of Architecture* (1851) and *The Stones of Venice* (1854), established Ruskin as a leading critic of the age.

In 1851 he became involved with the Pre-Raphaelites, defending their works in letters to *The Times*, and also in *Academy Notes*, a personal review of each year's display at the Royal Academy (1855–9). Ruskin's intervention on the behalf of Millais, Hunt, and Rossetti marks a turning point in their fortunes. In 1848 Ruskin married Effie Gray; she left him to become Millais' wife in 1854, but despite family battles, Ruskin continued to support Millais' work. He was also personally involved in Rossetti's life, giving him financial support, and winning him important patrons. In 1854, Ruskin began teaching drawing at the Working Men's College, and encouraged Rossetti to join him.

Ruskin exhibited at the Old Water Colour Society from 1873 to 1883; he completed over 2,000 drawings. His work consists mainly of watercolor and pencil studies of rocks, trees, plants, and architectural details.

In the 1860s he became increasingly involved with social problems, and his later writings are mainly economic and philosophical. In 1869 he was made Slade Professor at Oxford, and founded a drawing school there. He passed his last years at

John Ruskin: The Glacier des Bossons, Chamounix; bistre and brown wash on paper; 33×47cm (13×19in); 1849. Ashmolean Museum, Oxford

Brantwood on Lake Coniston, mentally troubled and often deeply depressed.

The best of Ruskin's critical writing is fired by a deeply personal response: his description of his visit to the Tintorettos in the Scuola di S. Rocco, Venice, is noteworthy. His passages in appreciation of the oils and watercolors of J.M.W. Turner remain unsurpassed.

Russell Morgan 1886–1953

Morgan Russell was a member of an American movement in Parisian painting called Synchromism, which was close to Cubism and Orphism. Born in New York, Russell trained first as an architect, and then with Robert Henri in New York. He absorbed the art of Monet and Cézanne in Paris; from 1908 to 1909 he worked as an assistant to Matisse, to whom he had been introduced by Gertrude Stein. His paintings, such as *Synchromy* (oil; *c*1913; Museum of Modern Art, New York) and *Synchromy in Orange: To Form* (oil; 1913–14; Albright-Knox Art Gallery, Buffalo, N.Y.), are dense essays in the style of Delaunay. Despite vigorous polemics on the part of the American group, it is unlikely that their color theory and practice predated that of Robert Delaunay and Franz Kupka.

Ruysdael Salomon van *c*1600–70

Salomon Jacobsz. van Ruysdael was a Dutch painter of realist landscapes and seascapes; he came from Haarlem, and was an uncle of the more famous Jacob van Ruisdael. His early works show the influence of Esaias van de Velde; but those from *c*1630 to 1645 are more in the monochromatic style of the slightly older Jan van Goyen, and there are also similarities of motif. Ruysdael is best known for calm, expansive pictures of rivers and estuaries. These are usually cool in color, make use of diagonally receding compositional axes, and have low viewpoints and horizons. His most characteristic motifs are ferries, sailing boats, and fishermen.

After the mid 1640s, Ruysdael introduced more compact and prominent features (such as groups of trees and windmills) into his paintings, and these served to integrate more fully the two main components of his work: land and sky. In the later 1640s and 1650s he used stronger color, and introduced more emphatic contrasts of light and shade. During this period he painted several seascapes, some of which are in a less usual vertical format. Ruysdael also painted some village scenes and winter landscapes with skaters.

Ryder Albert 1847–1917

The American painter Albert Pinkham Ryder was born in New Bedford, Mass., and moved with his family to New York in 1870. He was largely self-taught, although

Salomon van Ruysdael: Drawing the Eel; oil on panel; 75×106cm (30×42in); c1650. Metropolitan Museum, New York

he did study for a while at the National Academy of Design. He started by painting landscapes, but from *c*1880 he turned for inspiration to literary sources such as the Bible, Chaucer, Shakespeare, and the 19th-century Romantic poets. He is perhaps best known for his pictures of marine subjects (for example, *Toilers of the Sea*, 1884; Metropolitan Museum, New York). These are often shown by moonlight, and are painted in a very thick, sometimes even turgid technique. Between 1877 and 1896 Ryder traveled extensively in Europe but he was little influenced by the great tradition of European painting. His work sets him apart from the conventional schools of his day, just as his own somewhat eccentric character drove him to live the life of a hermit.

Albert Ryder (attrib.): Night and Clouds; oil on panel; 31×22cm (12×9in). Saint Louis Art Museum, Saint Louis, Mo.

Rysbrack John 1694–1770

John Michael Rysbrack was a Flemish sculptor who worked in England. He was born and trained in Antwerp, but in 1720 moved to England, and remained there for the rest of his life. Heir to the restrained Baroque of Francesco Duquesnoy, he developed a strong affinity with Roman sculpture, and was the sculptor most perfectly in tune with the English taste of the 18th century. He established a good and lasting practice in portrait sculpture, in which he excelled, and in monuments. He became the leading provider of monuments of his time in England, collaborating at first with the architect James Gibbs, and later with William Kent. More talented than his main rival, Peter Scheemaeckers, Rysbrack was so well established in English favor that he survived competition with the more brilliant and showy Louis-François Roubiliac, whose influence can, however, be seen in his later works.

S

Saarinen Eero 1910–61

The Finnish architect Eero Saarinen, son of the architect Eliel Saarinen (1873–1950), was born at Kirkkonummi. The family emigrated to the United States in 1923. Eero studied in Paris (1929–30) and at Yale University (1931–4) before briefly returning to Finland in 1935. From 1937 until after the Second World War he worked in partnership with his father. In 1949 he won the competition for the Jefferson National Expansion Memorial in St Louis, Mo. (completed in 1965).

The first significant works in Saarinen's brief career date from after his father's death in 1950. Initial designs for General Motors Technical and Research Center at Warren, Michigan, were done under Eliel's direction in the late 1940s, but the final project, with its highly individual water tower, is unquestionably Eero's work. The influence of Mies van der Rohe's plan for the Illinois Institute of Technology can be seen in Saarinen's solution for the General Motors complex: a number of glazed, box-like units assembled in interesting combinations around a large central lake.

He was not for long to remain a follower of van der Rohe. Surprise is the keynote of a career marked by what has been called a "bewildering eclecticism". There is little continuity between the various breathtaking achievements that came after General Motors. The Kresge Auditorium (1953–5) for the Massachusetts Institute of Technology, the Yale University Hockey Rink (1953–9), and the two airport schemes for which he is perhaps best known, the TWA Terminal, Kennedy Airport, New York (1956–62), and Dulles Airport, Washington, D.C. (1958–63), show Saarinen experimenting with dramatic forms to enclose vast interior spaces. In the case of the airport buildings, Saarinen confronted and attempted to solve some of the increasingly sophisticated problems connected with air travel.

Further reading. Saarinen, A.B. (ed.) *Eero Saarinen and his Works: a Selection of Buildings dating from 1947 to 1964*, London and New Haven (1968). Saarinen, E. *The City: its Growth, its Decay, its Future*, Cambridge, Mass. (1965). Temke, A. *Eero Saarinen*, New York (1962).

Andrea Sacchi: Hagar and Ishmael in the Wilderness; oil on canvas; 96×92cm (38×36in); c1630. National Gallery of Wales, Cardiff

Sacchi Andrea 1599–1661

The Italian painter Andrea Sacchi was born in Rome; he was a representative of the classical tendency in Roman painting of the mid 17th century. He was taught by Francesco Albani in both Rome and Bologna. He was in Rome again from 1621 and remained there for most of his life. From 1625 to 1627 he painted *St Gregory and the Miracle of the Caporal* (Vatican Museums, Rome) for St Peter's, a painting that shows his Raphaelesque manner and the restriction on the number of figures he used in a composition: only six. He developed this restrained approach in *The Vision of St Romuald* (c1638; Vatican Museums, Rome).

Artistically, Sacchi was the opposite of Pietro da Cortona, with whose work his has often been compared. Both artists were employed by the Barberini, and their differing approach to decorative fresco painting may be seen in the Palazzo Barberini, Rome. Here Sacchi painted *The Allegory of Divine Wisdom* (1629–33) which, muted in color, is composed of only 11 figures, and contrasts with Cortona's crowded *Divine Providence* (1633–9) in the same building. Sacchi's later works in Rome include *St Anthony of Padua Raises a Dead Man* (c1638; S. Maria della Concezione), *Stories of St John the Baptist* (1640–9; S. Giovanni in Fonte), and *The Death of St Anne* (1649; S. Carlo ai Catinari). With Poussin and Algardi, Sacchi maintained the classical tradition in the Baroque period; his later work leads directly towards the weightiness of the paintings of his pupil Carlo Maratti.

Further reading. Harris, A.S. *Andrea Sacchi: Complete Edition of the Paintings*, Oxford and Princeton (1977). Wittkower, R. *Art and Architecture in Italy: 1600–1750*, Harmondsworth (1973).

Sadiqi Beg 1533–1610

The Persian artist Sadiqi Beg was a soldier, poet and biographer, draftsman, and miniaturist. Born in Tabriz, he was a pupil of Muzaffar Ali. He was in the service of Shah Isma'il II (ruled 1576–7) and of Shah Abbas I from 1587 to 1598 as head of the Royal Library in Qazwin. His style was dynamic and colorful, his character overbearing, and his criticism outspoken. So he fell from office in 1598, his last royal work being on a large *Shah-nama* which survives in part in the Chester Beatty Library,

Dublin. In 1593 he was presented, probably by his pupils, with a book of fables, the *Anwar i-Suhayli* (private collection). This is illustrated with 107 miniatures attested as "prepared for Sadiqi Beg, the Rarity of the Age". Some scholars believe these to be by Sadiqi himself, but they seem to be the work of several hands.

Saenredam Pieter 1597–1665

The Dutch painter Pieter Jansz. Saenredam specialized in church interiors, although he also produced topographical views of architectural exteriors (for example, *The Old Town Hall of Amsterdam*, 1657; Rijksmuseum, Amsterdam). He sometimes depicted the interiors of churches in Amsterdam and elsewhere in Holland, but his views were more often of the Gothic churches in Utrecht and his native Haarlem. The development from his preliminary sketches to his finished oil paintings was usually a lengthy process, involving the preparation of detailed perspective drawings and other diagrams, with reference to architectural plans and measurements. The final result was invariably an accurate transcription of the view presented, although modifications were occasionally made for compositional reasons. In this respect his work differs from that of earlier architectural painters, in which the buildings tended to be imaginary structures.

Saenredam's paintings are of much more than architectural interest. Their colors are cool, delicate, and restful; there is a sensitivity to the effects of pale light reflected from whitewashed walls, and a subtle evocation of the stillness and silence enclosed beneath great vaults. The complex and harmonious geometry of flat, carefully balanced tones and colors Saenredam created from the architectural members and sparse decorations of Protestant church interiors looks forward to the formalism of certain 20th-century paintings.

Pieter Saenredam: The Buurkerk at Utrecht; oil on panel; 60×50cm (24×20in); 1644. National Gallery, London

Sagrera Guillen 1375?–1454

The Spanish sculptor Guillen Sagrera may have been born in Majorca. He was sculptor and architect to the Court of Aragon, although after 1420 his center of activity was Majorca. The figures of St Peter, St Paul, and a bearded man in Palma Cathedral are good examples of his work. His dramatic, almost Burgundian style is even better represented by the archangel on the facade of the Lonja, or Commercial Exchange, of Palma—a building he was contracted to construct in 1426. In 1447 he was called to Naples by Alfonso the Magnanimous, to build the main hall of the Castel Nuovo; he died in Naples before the work was completed.

Saint-Gaudens Augustus 1848–1907

Augustus Saint-Gaudens was the most noted American sculptor of the late 19th century. As a boy he was apprenticed to a cameo-cutter, and studied at Cooper Union and the National Academy of Art and Design (both in New York), and at the École des Beaux-Arts in Paris. He established himself as a sculptor in New York in 1875, becoming famous both for his monumental sculptures (for example, his monument to Admiral Farragut, 1880; Madison Square Garden, New York), and for his bas-relief decorations. Saint-Gaudens belonged to one of the leading groups of late-19th-century American artists and architects, a circle that included Henry Hobson Richardson, Stanford White, and the painter John La Farge. A memorial collection of his works was made in Cornish, New Hampshire, after his death (the Saint-Gaudens National Historical Site).

Further reading. Cortissoz, R. *Augustus Saint-Gaudens*, Boston, Mass. (1967). Saint-Gaudens, H. (ed.) *The Reminiscences of Augustus Saint-Gaudens* (2 vols.), New York (1913). Taft, L. *The History of American Sculpture*, New York (1930).

Salviati: An Episode in the History of the Farnese Family; c1549–63. Palazzo Farnese, Rome

Salviati 1510–63

The Italian artist Francesco de' Rossi was known as Salviati; he was a leading Florentine Mannerist painter of the mid 16th century. Trained by Andrea del Sarto, he was active in Rome by 1530 under the protection of Cardinal Salviati, from whom he took his name. His mature style shows a typically Mannerist range of sources: it is reminiscent of works by both Raphael and Michelangelo but is endowed, however, with a new elegance, artificiality, and complexity. He specialized in large-scale multifigured mural decorations, usually packed with learned allegory and archaeological detail. He spent his career traveling restlessly between Florence and Rome; he also visited northern Italy from 1538 to 1541, and Fontainebleau in 1554.

Sánchez Coello Alonso 1531–88

The Spanish painter Alonso Sánchez Coello was born at Benifayó, Valencia. He was taken to Portugal when young and later sent to study under Anthonis Mor van Dashorst in Flanders. By 1555 he was in Castile, where he became court painter to Philip II and produced an extensive series of royal portraits in a stiff, Mannerist style with superbly rendered details of dress (examples in the Prado, Madrid; the Escorial, near Madrid; and Hampton Court Palace, London).

Although his reputation rests firmly on his portraits, Sánchez Coello also painted religious compositions, including many full-length pairs of saints over the minor altars of the monastery church at the Escorial (1580–2) and *The Martyrdom of St Sebastian* (1582; Prado, Madrid).

Sánchez Cotán Juan 1561–1627

The Spanish painter Juan Sánchez Cotán was born at Orgaz. At Toledo he studied under Blas del Prado (*c*1545–*post* 1592) and created the typical Spanish still-life composition; this consists of a few simple objects—mainly vegetables—spread out in precisely calculated rhythmical arrangement in a window opening or niche, or hanging on strings from above. Signed examples of his work are in the Museum of Art, San Diego and in the Hernani Collection, Madrid.

In 1603 Sánchez Cotán joined the Carthusian order as a lay brother and thereafter painted only religious compositions, sometimes in a tenebrist style. However, these works never rivaled his earlier still-life masterpieces, for example his *Still Life* of *c*1600 in the San Diego Museum of Art.

Sandby brothers
18th and 19th centuries

The British artists Paul Sandby (1725/6–1809) and his brother Thomas (1721–98) were important figures in the development of English landscape painting in watercolors. They worked in the Military Drawing Office of the Tower of London, and after 1745 were employed as draftsmen on a survey of the Scottish highlands. Thomas, who was not so accomplished as his brother, specialized in architectural details.

Paul worked extensively in Wales. He produced numerous landscape paintings that were remarkable for their spontaneity rather than for the conventions associated with the Picturesque. His varied technique included thin washes as well as work in gouache, and he also introduced the aquatint process to England. His landscapes were much admired by Thomas Gainsborough (1727–88).

Paul Sandby: A Milkmaid in Windsor Great Park; pen and watercolor; 30×24cm (12×9in); c1765–70. British Museum, London

Sangallo family
15th and 16th centuries

The Florentine Sangallo family was a large one and played a leading role in Italian architecture from the 1480s until the death of Antonio the Younger in 1546. Their practice was built around a family system and often several members were involved in the same commission, as at the Villa Madama and S. Giovanni dei Fiorentini, in Rome. Their work included the whole range of architecture, including military architecture.

Giuliano (1445–1516) and Antonio the Younger (1483–1546) were perhaps the most distinguished members of the family. Giuliano's virtuoso performance in the 1480s, at the Villa of Poggia a Caiano, the fortress of Volterra, and the church of S. Maria delle Carceri, Prato, was most impressive. On his death in 1516, his mantle passed to his nephew Antonio the Younger; the stylistic contrast between them was that of the Quattrocento against the Cinquecento. Antonio the Elder (1455–1535), another uncle, also became more popular after his brother Giuliano's

Juan Sánchez Cotán: Still Life; oil on canvas; 69×85cm (27×33in); c1600. San Diego Museum of Art

Giuliano da Sangallo (architect): the gran salone of the Villa of Poggia a Caiano, Florence; c1485

death, producing his major works in the house of Montepulciano and the beautiful church of the Madonna di S. Biagio (1518–28; near Florence). Antonio the Younger, as a Florentine, enjoyed the patronage of the Medici pope Clement VII, and in 1520 he succeeded Raphael as *capomaestro* at St Peter's, Rome. He produced for this building a series of designs which culminated in the final model of *c*1534, engraved by Antonio dall'Abacco; this made an ambiguous compromise between a centralized and a longitudinal plan. Here, as at the Palazzo Farnese and S. Giovanni dei Fiorentini, his work was overtaken by the more dynamic style of Michelangelo. A vast collection of drawings by Antonio and by other members of the Sangallo family survives in the Uffizi at Florence.

Further reading. Clausse, G. *Les San Gallo*, Paris (1900–2). Giovannoni, G. *Antonio da Sangallo il Giovane* (2 vols.), Rome (1959). Loubouski, G.K. *Les Sangallo*, Paris (1934). Severini, G. *Architetture Militari di Giuliano da Sangallo*, Pisa (1970).

Sanmicheli Michele 1484–1559

Michele Sanmicheli was a Veronese architect, trained in Rome in the circle of Bramante, whose major works are in Venice and in his native city. He was, with Sansovino, one of the most original architects working in north Italy in the first half of the 16th century, and did more than anyone else to acclimatize the classical style to the Venetian *terra firma*. Earlier north Italian architects, like Gian Maria Falconetto at Padua, had shown a somewhat timid and archaeological approach to classicism. Sanmicheli's architecture, by contrast, is plastic, vigorous, and highly imaginative. It gives an expressive and often specifically North Italian cast to the tradition of Bramante.

Early in his career, from 1509, Sanmicheli worked as architect to Orvieto Cathedral and advisor on papal fortifications. It was thus that he acquired his thorough knowledge of Classical and High Renaissance Roman architecture. Returning to north Italy by 1530, he embarked on a series of palace designs for his native city; they span his whole career and define the aims of his architecture. With their two-storied facades, the lower story rusticated, they are based on Bramante's Palazzo Caprini (the so-called House of Raphael). But they play complex variations upon it. These range from the Palazzo Bevilacque —with its complicated articulation of interlocking orders, its dramatic juxtapositions of solid and void, and its rich sculptural detail—to the more austere Palazzo Canossa, which has only a single order of half columns and shows a more restrained approach to surface texture.

The changes in Sanmicheli's facades are sometimes thought to reflect the general development of 16th-century Italian architecture, from the fantasy and elaboration of early Mannerism, in the 1530s and 1540s, to a more correctly classical style in the 1550s. But all Sanmicheli's architecture aims at giving imaginative expression to the function of the building, and the differences may equally be seen as varied interpretations of a central intention: that of displaying the grandeur and importance of the palace itself, and of the family who built it.

The same may be said of Sanmicheli's fortress architecture. Like most Renaissance architects, he built fortifications, and by 1530 was officially employed for this purpose by the Venetian Republic. His works are extensive, and are made particularly expressive by the use of very heavy rustication. His gateways, the Porta Nuova (1533–40), and the Porta Palio (*c*1555–60) in Verona, and the Castello di S. Andrea del Lido on the Venetian Lagoon, confront the onlooker with a firm statement of their intentions. In the most refined of them, the Porta Palio, we see a stylistic feature characteristic of Sanmicheli's architecture. It is a tendency to treat the facade in layers, cutting away sections of a wall to show another section behind it, often of a different texture. He also projects the facade outwards by means of pilasters, columns, and sculptural detail. This gives a great richness of light and shade to his architecture. The style can be seen in his Palazzo Grimani on the Grand Canal, Venice, where the forceful order of columns seems almost like a freestanding screen in front of the great arched windows behind.

Individual effects of this kind give Sanmicheli's buildings an air of inventive fantasy, which often seems to come from a fusion of Roman with North Italian modes. This is particularly true of his churches. Both the Pellegrini Chapel, attached to S. Bernardino, Verona, and the Madonna di Campagna outside the city, are centralized buildings in the tradition of North Italian votive chapels; but they are brought up to date by reference to Roman models: the Pantheon and Bramante's Tempietto. In the interior of the Pellegrini Chapel, the architectural articulation is richly complex, with its elaborate layers, discrete touches of color, and richness of texture in the individual features such as striated columns. It recalls the coloristic exuberance of 15th-century Lombard architecture, for example, Amadeo's Colleoni Chapel in Bergamo. It was Sanmicheli's mission to give the ornate and highly decorative tradition of north Italian architecture a new and more disciplined expression, through the classical vocabulary of the 16th century.

Further reading. Lagenskiöld, E. *Michele Sanmicheli, the Architect of Verona*, Uppsala (1938). Puppi, L. *Michele Sanmichele*, Padua (1971).

Sano di Pietro 1406–81

The Sienese painter and miniaturist Ansano di Pietro di Mencio was known as Sano di Pietro. He founded his style upon that of Sassetta (1392–1450), and concentrated on pleasing decorative effects. He was a popularizer of the Sienese preacher S. Bernardino (fresco, 1450; Palazzo Pubblico, Siena) and creator of the half-length Virgin with half-length saints and angels (Metropolitan Museum, New York). His work is easily recognizable by the sharp facial features of his figures, their large almond eyes, heavy forms, and hard outlines. He was a repetitious painter, but seems to have been popular with his contemporaries; his charm compensates for his rather monotonous style.

Sanraku Kano 1559–1635

The Japanese painter Kano Sanraku was the founder of the Kyoto branch of the *Kano* School. He was a retainer of the family of the dictator Hideyoshi, who apprenticed him to Kano Eitoku. Sanraku decorated Hideyoshi's Momoyama castle after his teacher's death. Although he was less brilliant than Eitoku, his technique was sound, and he embodies the change from the Momoyama style to the gentler early Edo manner.

This can be seen in the sliding doors of the Samboin, Hideyoshi's retreat at the Daigoji Temple, Kyoto, where waving grasses are set against gold-leaf backgrounds in elegantly complex patterns. It is also evident in the more famous set of doors at the Daikakuji Temple, Kyoto, where he sets big clumps of red or white peonies on a gold leaf ground, the foreground varied by a few simple rocks shaded in green. The ink outline is firm but not dashing, and the whole has the deceptive simplicity of the best Japanese decorative work.

However, Sanraku did not forget the boldness of his master's style. The room he decorated in the Nijo Palace, Kyoto, has a huge cypress tree spread across many panels, done with great grandeur but with a breathing liveliness which contrasts with the equally big but static pine compositions painted by the young Tan'yu in the same palace.

Sanraku continued the *Kano* ink-painting tradition, doing figure compositions on Chinese Confucian themes for the government, and also painting ink landscapes in a soft cursive style. In his last years his work took on the more tortured mood of a new age. He became a pioneer of distorted, leaning rock shapes and conflicting lines, which he passed on to his pupil Kano Sansetsu.

Sansetsu Kano 1590–1651

The Japanese painter Kano Sansetsu was the pupil of his adoptive father Sanraku. After the calm naturalism of the early Edo period, his work reflects the more tortured unnatural atmosphere that characterized the period of Japan's isolation from the outside world. In particular he adopted his master's tendency for conflicting pictorial planes. In the beautiful rooms of the Tenkyuin (*c*1635; Myoshinji Temple, Kyoto), the rocks are sloped and hatched to point in three different directions, and in the great *Plum Tree and Pheasant* composition, all pretence at naturalism is abandoned. His ink painting, also extremely skilled, showed the same tendencies to decorative drama. After the death of Sanraku, Sansetsu became head of the *Kano* School in Kyoto.

Sano di Pietro: The Madonna and Child; gold ground on panel; 60×46cm (24×18in). Private collection

Sansovino Andrea *c*1467–1529

The Italian sculptor Andrea Contucci da Monte Sansovino was born in the Tuscan town of Monte San Savino or Sovino whence he derived his surname. He modeled altarpieces in terracotta in his native town. This bears out Vasari's statement that he was trained by Antonio Pollaiuolo, for the latter was primarily a modeler. Sansovino, however, found his *métier* in marble carving, which he probably learned in Florence, perhaps in the workshop of the Ferrucci family. He showed his prowess in his first documented commission in

Florence, the Corbinelli family altar in S. Spirito (1485–90). He was admitted to the sculptors' guild in 1491, and was then sent by Lorenzo de' Medici as an artistic emissary to Portugal, where he spent nine years.

Sansovino reappeared in Florence at the turn of the century and undertook two major commissions: a pair of marble statues (*Madonna and Child* and *St John the Baptist*), to complete a series in Genoa Cathedral left unfinished at the death of Civitali (1501), and a group of the *Baptism of Christ*, for the eastern doorway of the Baptistery in Florence (1502–5). Work on these was interrupted by a call to Rome in 1505, and it was not until 1569 that they were finished and erected, by Vincenzo Danti. The four marble statues from these two commissions are the epitome of High Renaissance sculpture in Florence, equivalent to paintings by Fra Bartolommeo (1472–1517) or Mariotto Albertinelli (1474–1515).

The sculptor was summoned to Rome by Pope Julius II to carve a pair of elaborate marble tombs in the choir of S. Maria del Popolo, for the Cardinals Ascanio Sforza and Basso della Rovere. They are designed like ancient Roman triumphal arches, containing eight nearly life-size statues, including the effigies. The angels and virtues are subtle variations on the classical themes of standing or seated female figures, and are

Andrea Sansovino: The Holy Family, a detail of Adoration of the Shepherds; marble; c1520–4. Basilica della Santa Casa, Loreto

some of the best High Renaissance sculptures. In 1512 Sansovino followed this success with a group of the *Virgin and Child with St Anne* (S. Agostino, Rome), deriving his composition from Leonardo's versions of the subject (cartoon in the National Gallery, London).

From 1513 until the end of his career Sansovino was in charge of the important Papal commission for a sculptural complex to be built in the Basilica della Santa Casa at Loreto. He carved two of the large narrative reliefs (1518–24)—the *Annunciation* and the *Adoration of the Shepherds*. He also supervised a group of younger sculptors, including important manifestations of the High Renaissance spirit, unaffected by the Mannerism that others were deriving from the later work of Raphael and Michelangelo.

Sansovino Il 1486–1570

Jacopo Tatti, called Il Sansovino, was a High Renaissance sculptor and architect. He was born in Florence and trained in Rome by Andrea Sansovino, whose name he took. Before the Sack of Rome in 1527 he worked both there and in his native city, developing from his master a fluent, elevated style that was based on the grace and harmony of Raphael, rather than on the *terribilità* of Michelangelo. His *Madonna del Parto*, a Virgin and Child enthroned in a spacious, Bramantesque niche in S. Agostino, Rome, is close in style to Raphael's frescoed Isaiah in the same church. Like its model, it gives a gentler and more harmonious cast to the monumental figure-style that Michelangelo had evolved on the Sistine Chapel ceiling. The same is true of his *St James* for Florence Cathedral. This was carved during his stay there from 1511 to 1513, from a block originally intended for Michelangelo himself.

Jacopo Sansovino also worked as an architect in Rome. His work strives after an ideal balance between sculptural and architectural forms, seeking to translate into three dimensions what Raphael had achieved in paint in the Stanze of the Vatican.

In 1527, as a result of the Sack of Rome, Sansovino went to Venice. He had intended to go on to France, but the *Signoria* employed him to give advice on S. Marco, and in 1529 he was given an official position as architect to the Venetian Republic. He survived a temporary disgrace, when the vault of his new library collapsed, and held the post until his death.

Il Sansovino: St John the Baptist; marble; height 120cm (47in); c1554–6. S. Maria Gloriosa dei Frari, Venice

As the first architect and sculptor to work in a High Renaissance style in Venice, he formed Venetian 16th-century taste in these fields. His major buildings—the Library, the Mint, the Loggetta for the Campanile of St Mark's, and the now-destroyed church of S. Geminiano at the end of Piazza S. Marco—were the first to give classical form to the city.

The settled political climate of Venice, her prosperity, self-confidence, and pride, formed an excellent basis for the development of the temperate and harmonious classicism of Sansovino's style—a style further enriched by the specifically Venetian experience of light and color.

This is apparent above all in the new

Library, one of the masterpieces of the High Renaissance. (The building was begun in 1537, and completed after Sansovino's death.) The long loggia of the Library faces those of the Doges' Palace on the other side of the Piazzetta. Its two-storied facade is lower than the three stories of the palace opposite. But Sansovino provides a contrast to the sheer, coloristically patterned surface of that 15th-century building, with his exceptionally deeply cut, sculpturally enriched structure; this is thrown into such rich and vibrant relief by the light that its weight perfectly matches the flat facade opposite. Most of the motifs are Roman, but the sensuous richness of the whole is Venetian. It is as original, in its way, as the pictorial style of Titian.

The neighboring Loggetta (1537–40), with its delicate use of colored marbles, again gives northern expression to central Italian ideas. Here, with bronze statues in niches elegantly incorporated into the design, Sansovino gives perfect expression to that harmonious relationship between sculpture and architecture which he had already sought in Rome. This ideal harmony is entirely in keeping with the iconography of the Loggetta, which, through figures such as Peace and Apollo, glorifies the harmony and virtues of the Venetian State.

Sansovino also worked in bronze in S. Marco, notably on the reliefs of the Sacristy door. He formed 16th-century Venetian tomb design through his Venice monument in S. Salvatore (1556–61); and he carved the colossal statues of Mars and Neptune which give the Sala dei Giganti of the Doges' Palace its name. With his friends Titian and Pietro Aretino, he became during the middle of the 16th century something of an arbiter of Venetian artistic taste.

Further reading. Howard, D. *Jacopo Sansovino: Architecture and Patronage in Renaissance Venice*, Yale (1975). Mariacher, G. *Il Sansovino*, Milan (1962). Tafuri, M. *Jacopo Sansovino e l'Architettura del 1500 a Venezia*, Padua (1969).

J.S. Sargent: Carnation, Lily, Lily, Rose, oil on canvas; 174×154cm (69×61in); 1885–6. Tate Gallery, London

Sargent J.S. 1856–1925

John Singer Sargent was an American painter of portraits and landscapes. He was born while his parents were visiting Florence, and was educated in France, Italy, and Germany. He studied at the École des Beaux-Arts in Paris under Carlos Duran, and first exhibited at the Salon in 1877. His early portraits attracted harsh criticism in both London and Paris. His portrait of *Madame X (Madame Gautreau*, 1884; Metropolitan Museum, New York) caused a famous scandal in Paris, which provoked his move to London. He established a studio at Tite Street, London, and began a series of popular child portraits, the best known of which is *Carnation, Lily, Lily, Rose* (1885–6; Tate Gallery, London). He was perhaps equal to Joshua Reynolds (1723–92) and Thomas Gainsborough (1727–88) as a stylish portrait painter of his own era. The reputation that he established bridged the Atlantic. He was made a Royal Academician in 1897, he decorated Boston Public Library (1890–1921), and was appointed an official British War Artist in 1918.

Sarrazin Jacques 1588–1660

The most important French sculptor of the mid 17th century, Jacques Sarrazin, trained initially under Nicolas Gullain before spending the period from 1610 to *c*1617 in Rome. In Italy he worked at Frascati for Giacomo della Porta, and after his return the influence of the classicizing Roman style is evident. A more personal manner is apparent in his first royal commission—the decoration of Jacques Lemercier's Pavillon de l'Horloge, at the Louvre, Paris (1636). His caryatid figures on the attic story clearly derive from firsthand study of the Antique, and may claim to be the earliest examples of French classicism in sculpture. From 1642 to 1650 he directed the decoration of the Château de Maisons, Paris, for François Mansart. His last work was the monument to Henri Bourbon, Prince of Condé, in the church of St Paul, St Louis (begun in 1648, finished in 1663, and moved to Chantilly in the 19th century where it stands in the Musée Condé). It anticipates the Louis XIV style in its peculiar mixture of classicism and the Baroque. The style established by Sarrazin was to dominate the sculpture of Versailles for the next two decades.

Sassetta 1392–1450

Stefano di Giovanni, known as Sassetta, was the most important Sienese painter of the 15th century. He was probably born in Siena, and was certainly at work there by 1426. His first great work was an altarpiece for the Arte della Lana in Siena (1423–6), of which parts survive in Siena (Pinacoteca Nazionale), Budapest (National Gallery), the Vatican (Museums), and elsewhere. In 1426, he was working for Siena Cathedral, and the following year made a drawing for the baptistery font. He continued his architectural work, and in 1440 he made designs (which were not used) for the circular west window of the cathedral.

At first, Sassetta worked in an International Gothic style, much influenced by Taddeo di Bartolo. In his seven *Scenes from the Life of St Anthony Abbot* (*c*1436; some panels in National Gallery of Art, Washington, D.C., for example, *The Meeting of St Anthony Abbot and Paul the Hermit*), the influence of French illumination seems clear, placing the scenes far away from anything to do with ordinary life. Sassetta's art—and that of his contemporaries—is characterized by an intense awareness and imitation of the forms of the previous century. Whereas Florence was very conscious of the newness of her artistic style, and vaunted the break with the past occasioned by Masaccio and Donatello, Siena carried on using the gold backgrounds, brightly painted forms, and unreal settings until the end of the century.

Sassetta and his fellows did not, however, avoid absorbing some influence from Florence, seen, for example, in his splendid *Madonna of the Snows* (1430–2; Contini-Bonacossi Collection, Florence). Painted

Sassetta: St Francis renounces his Earthly Father; a panel from an altarpiece; 88×53cm (35×21in); c1437–44. National Gallery, London

for the Chapel of S. Bonifazio in Siena Cathedral, it depicts in the *predella* the miracle by which the plan of a church was marked out on the ground by a fall of snow. The carved and gilded scallops of the wooden frame overhang the painting as if it were formed of figures within an actual tabernacle; but there is little perspective, and the Virgin's robe is draped on to the floor in a slow elaboration of luscious folds. The saints at the back on either side are likewise flat and decorative. But the figures of the Baptist and St Francis of Assisi at the front are completely different. They are kneeling, and the artist has taken pains to indicate how the garment forms taut creases over the knees—and to impose those knees and also the slowly gesticulating hands almost into our space. In this work Sassetta has grafted the manner of Masaccio on to the traditionalism of Siena.

More characteristic of his style is the panel of the *Madonna and Child Crowned by Two Angels* (*c*1445; Frick Collection, New York), a late work in which a Virgin with all the sinuous delicacy of a Virgin by Simone Martini floats in a golden heaven, clutching her child warmly to her face. A similar gesture enlivens his *Madonna and Child with SS. John the Baptist, Michael, Nicolas and Margaret* (*c*1437; S. Domenico, Cortona). In this painting, the figures are not set within one unified space, as in *Madonna of the Snows*, but are separated from the central section by Gothic colonnettes, each housed within its own scalloped arch. Again, there is a distinction between the figure-styles: all the saints are flat and decorative, symbols of another world rather than elevated heroes from our planet, whereas the Virgin and the foremost of the two angels have some solidity—an indication of Florentine contact. Even after Sassetta's time, Florentine influence continued to pervade Sienese art in the work of painters like Matteo di Giovanni and Francesco di Giorgio.

Roelandt Savery: Alpine Landscape; black and red chalk with pale blue wash on paper; 40×39cm (16×15½in). British Museum, London

Sassoferrato 1609–85

Giovanni Battista Salvi, called Sassoferrato from his birthplace, was active mostly in Rome and Umbria. He was one of a small group of painters in Rome who rejected the excitement and vivid color of the Baroque and sought instead a rigorous purity of design, and cold, clear colors. Sassoferrato's works are strikingly archaic, and reach for inspiration beyond Domenichino to the 15th century; they suggest a kind of 17th-century Pre-Raphaelitism. He painted some portraits of ecclesiastics, but most of his works are of sacred subjects. His many altarpieces and small devotional paintings of the Madonna and Child had widespread popular appeal.

Sassoferrato: Self-portrait; oil on canvas; 38×33cm (15×13in). Uffizi, Florence

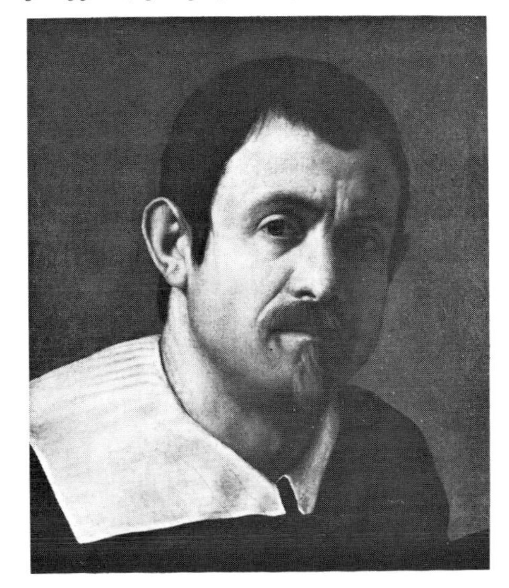

Saura Antonio 1930–1998

The Spanish painter Antonio Saura began to paint in 1947, during a long illness. From 1953 to 1957 he lived in Paris. In 1956 he exhibited at the Spanish Museum of Contemporary Art in Madrid, and in 1957 became a founder member of the "El Paso" group of painters and writers, along with Rafael Canoger, Luis Feito, and Manolo Millares. Early in his career he came under the influence of Surrealism, but by the late 1950s his work was concerned with an expressionistic, almost abstract, portrayal of figures (for example, *Crucifixion*; triptych; oil on canvas; 1959–60; Joseph Hirshhorn Museum, Washington, D.C.). From 1953 he used only black and white in his paintings, tempered later by the addition of brown contrasts. Saura moved towards more cartoon-like work with strongly emotional, political, and social subjects concerned to condemn the outrages done to man.

Savery Roelandt 1576?–1639

The painter Roelandt Savery was born at Courtrai of mixed Dutch and Flemish background. In 1591 he settled in Amsterdam, where he was probably taught by his brother. His combination of elegant artificiality and precise observation is characteristic of Flemish art in the early 17th century. He was most famous for his flower pieces—vast bouquets of an infinite variety of species set in niches. He specialized, too, in fantastic landscapes, crowded with exotic birds and animals. His work was influenced by Gillis van Coninxloo (1544–1607)—his many details are meticulously rendered, and the landscapes are sharply divided into planes of color (for example, *The Garden of Eden*, 1623; Kunsthistorisches Museum, Vienna). About 1604 he was called to Prague by Rudolph II; in 1619 he settled in Utrecht.

Savoldo Girolamo 1480?–1548

Giovanni Girolamo Savoldo was a Brescian painter, who settled in Venice *c*1520. He had visited Florence, where he must have seen the works of Michelangelo, and the grandeur of his large, monumental figures surely comes from this experience. In his *St Jerome* in the National Gallery, London, we can see the massiveness of the limbs and the expressive largeness of hands and feet. This is a feature common in Savoldo, and reminiscent of Michelangelo's *David*.

The ideal nobility of Savoldo's saints is always tempered by an earthy realism. They are peasants, and their garments, although they fall in grand, simplified folds, are homespun. This earthiness is typical of the Brescian school—we find it also in Romanino—and is one of the qualities that distinguishes Savoldo's style from Venetian painting proper. It is present even when, as in the *St Jerome*, he paints in a thoroughly Venetian manner, constructing his landscape in planes of intense blue in the manner of Titian.

Savoldo's chief contribution to the history of painting was a new apprehension of light. His settings are almost always dark, and he loved to paint the moment of dusk, when the local colors of the foreground forms stand out sharply against encroaching darkness.

This *contre nuit* (as opposed to *contre jour*) device is the main effect in his paintings. It is often enhanced by additional contrasts between different kinds of natural and artificial light—a fire, a candle, the remains of a sunset sky, moonlight, or the visionary light emanating from some spiritual being—as can be seen in the *St Matthew and the Angel* in the Metropolitan Museum, New York.

Girolamo Savoldo: St Mary Magdalen approaching the Sepulcher; oil on canvas; 86×79cm (34×31in). National Gallery, London

Such paintings evoke an intense, poetic mood and Savoldo was certainly influenced by Giorgione; but his careful recording of specific realistic effects is in the Lombard tradition. He influenced the later styles of his contemporaries Titian and Jacopo Bassano, and played an important role in the later 16th century in forming the artistic style of his fellow countryman, Caravaggio.

Johann Schadow: Self-portrait; height 41cm (16in); c1794. Nationalgalerie, Berlin

Scamozzi Vincenzio 1552–1616

The Italian architect Vincenzio Scamozzi is best known as the successor to Palladio and an early exponent of Palladianism. He completed several of Palladio's commissions, notably the Teatro Olimpico in Vicenza (1579–80; completed in 1583). The contrast between his style and Palladio's is shown in the more severe and geometric classicism of the Villa Pisani a Rocca (*c*1576), itself a chaste variation of Palladio's Villa Capra at Vicenza. In imitation of his master, he published in 1615 *L'Idea dell'Architettura Universale*, a longer, more detailed, but less effective version of Palladio's *I Quattro Libri*. About 1613 he sold a large collection of his drawings and those of Palladio to the Earl of Arundel and to Inigo Jones, which enormously advanced the standing of classical architecture in England.

Schadow Johann 1764–1850

Johann Gottfried Schadow was the greatest German Neo-classical sculptor, and a distinguished draftsman and graphic artist. He studied in Italy, where he befriended Antonio Canova, before returning to his native Berlin as court sculptor in 1788. His best period was from 1788 to 1797, when he produced the *Quadriga of Victory* for the Brandenburg Gate (1793), the double-portrait of *Princesses Louisa and Frederica of Prussia* (1797; Staatliche Museen, Berlin), and the statue of *General von Zieten* (1794). The latter was one of the first German monuments to a man who was not a ruler. He made a study-tour of French equestrian statues in northern Europe during 1791 and 1792, in preparation for a memorial to Frederick the Great; the commission was later canceled. From 1800 he depended chiefly on private commissions. He was Director of the Berlin Academy from 1816.

Scheemaeckers Peter 1691–1781

Peter Scheemaeckers was a Flemish sculptor who worked in England. Born in Antwerp, the son of a sculptor, he went to London at some time before 1721; he made his career there, retiring to Antwerp in 1771. By 1725 he had set up a practice in monumental sculpture in partnership with the Walloon Laurent Delvaux, with whom he went to Rome in 1728, to study Classical sculpture. Returning alone in 1730, Scheemaeckers became one of the most successful sculptors in England. He was more prolific than his rival Michael Rysbrack, whose prices he undercut, but he was less talented and flexible, and some of his work is mechanical and repetitive. In 1741 he briefly eclipsed Rysbrack with his monument to Shakespeare (Westminster Abbey, London).

Scheerre Herman *fl. c*1403–19

The illuminator Herman Scheerre was probably of Rhenish origin. He became master of a prominent English workshop early in the 15th century, with his associates, exercised a profound influence on native manuscript and illumination. Only one work bears his full signature: a small miniature of *St John the Evangelist*, in a simple select Missal (*c*1403–5; British Library, London). He may be identifiable with Herman Lymnour, who, in 1407, witnessed a London will connected with Cologne legatees. Certainly Scheerre's style shows affinity with the Cologne panel-painter known as the "Veronica Master". During 1388–9, William Duke of Gelder, close ally of Richard II, employed "Herman of Cologne"; this artist assisted Jean Malouel with work for the Duke of Burgundy in Dijon, between 1401 and 1403, and was in Paris, at court, in 1419. It seems probable that these Hermans are one and the same.

Scheerre was a versatile master-artist, rather than simply an illuminator. Although comparatively few miniatures are attributable to his hand with certainty, he brought a new approach to painting in England. He was no portraitist, but his figures convey a spiritual quality, with pallid faces and deep-set black eyes: their drapery is uncomplicated, the coloring harmonious and glowing. A courtly motto links a number of manuscripts like a workshop signature: *Omnia leuia sunt amanti. Si quis amat non laborat.* Part of this appears in the magnificent Great Bible (completed *c*1410; British Library, London) which employed many artists, English and foreign. The first illuminated initial of the Breviary made for Archbishop Chichele (*c*1408–14? Lambeth Palace, London), contains the second part of the motto, continuing *Quod Herman*.

The Bedford Hours and Psalter (*c*1419?; British Library, London) was commissioned for John Duke of Bedford, the younger son of Henry IV. It excels in variety; the rich border decoration includes fashionable French motifs. "Herman" is written in two line-endings. After this splendid work was finished Herman Scheerre apparently left England, but his School continued to produce manuscripts in a similar, if debased, style.

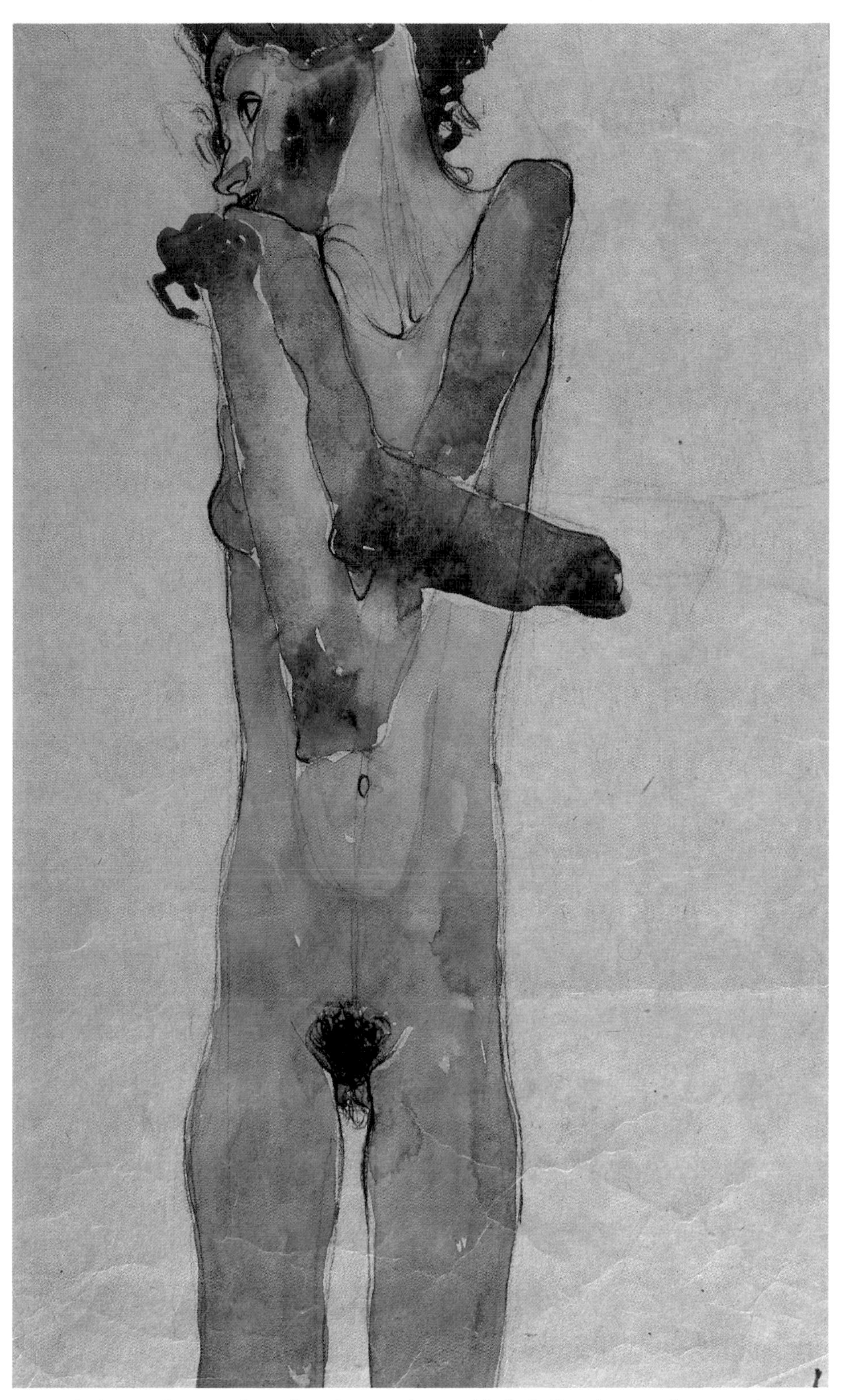

Egon Schiele: Standing Female Nude with Crossed Arms; black chalk and watercolor; 45×28cm (18×11in); 1910. Graphische Sammlung Albertina, Vienna

Schiele Egon 1890–1918

The Austrian painter Egon Schiele was born at Tulln, Lower Austria. After an unsatisfactory school career, he entered the Vienna Academy of Fine Arts in 1906. He soon came into contact with the avant-garde and exhibited at the second (*Internationale*) *Kunstschau* of 1909.

Gustav Klimt, whom Schiele met in 1907, had a formative influence upon his early work. Their admiration was mutual and Klimt was aware of the younger artist's powers of draftsmanship. Schiele quickly shook off his influence, and that of *Jugendstil* in general, and went on to produce oil paintings, watercolors, and drawings of great nervous intensity and an aggressive linear energy, often erotic in content. Sexuality was a theme that pervaded much radical Viennese thought and art of this time (for instance the works of Otto Weininger, Sigmund Freud, and Klimt), and Schiele's studies of nude girls and of his own body are no exception. They are explicit but at the same time tortured images of humanity, a fact that led people to label his work "Expressionist".

Just before and during the First World War, Schiele painted a series of major portraits, psychologically penetrating works such as the portraits of *Johann Harms* (1916; Solomon R. Guggenheim Museum, New York), *Albert Paris von Gütersloh* (1918; Minneapolis Institute of Arts), and *Edith Seated* (1917–18; Österreichische Galerie, Vienna). He also created some semiallegorical paintings, of which *The Family* (1917; Österreichische Galerie, Vienna) is the most forceful and moving. Schiele died in the notorious influenza epidemic of 1918—the year that also claimed Otto Wagner and Gustav Klimt, and saw the collapse of the old world of Austria-Hungary.

Further reading. Mitsch, E. *The Art of Egon Schiele*, London (1975). Vergo, P. *Art in Vienna 1898–1918*, London (1975). Whitford, F. *Egon Schiele*, London (1981). Wilson, S. *Egon Schiele*, Oxford (1980).

Schlemmer Oskar 1888–1943

The German painter and sculptor Oskar Schlemmer studied painting at Stuttgart under Holzel, and taught at the Bauhaus from 1920 to 1929 as form master in the metal and sculpture workshops. His most important contribution was as director of the stage workshop (1923–9). His designs for the *Triadisches Ballet* (performed in Stuttgart in 1922, and at the Bauhaus in 1923, to music by Paul Hindemith), accorded with his ideas of synthesis and universal art. He explored form and movement, reducing figures to precise profile, frontal, and rear positions. His Bauhaus staircase (Dessau, 1933) unified painting with architecture. He taught at Breslau (1929–32) and in Berlin (1932–3), before being classified as "degenerate" by the Nazis in 1933.

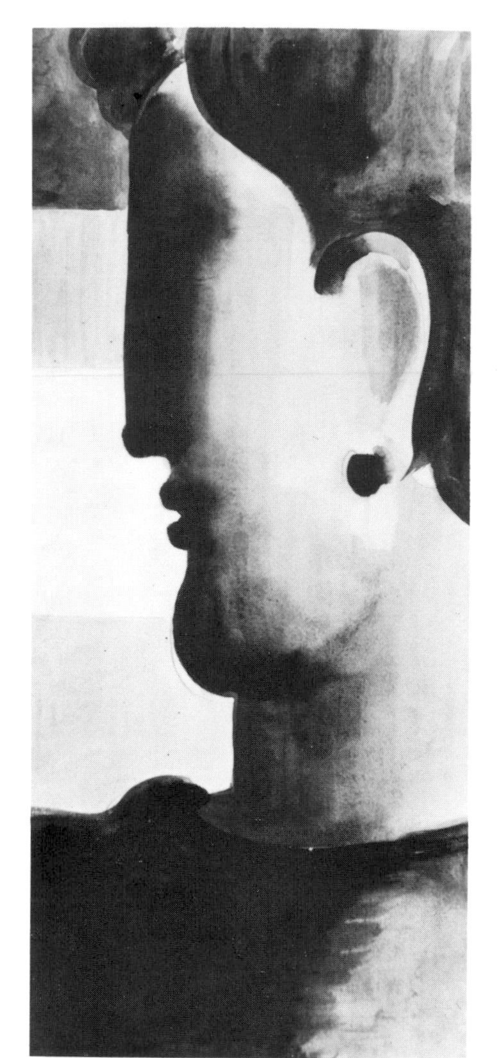

Oskar Schlemmer: A Head in Profile; watercolor over pencil on paper; 40×18cm (16×7in); 1931/2. Collection of Mrs Tut Schlemmer, Stuttgart

Schlüter Andreas *c*1660–1714

Trained in Danzig, the German architect and sculptor Andreas Schlüter is first documented as working on the decorative sculpture of the Krasiński Palace in Warsaw (1689–93). In 1694 he arrived in Berlin. His early work there is confined to sculpture, including the keystones for the Arsenal, commissioned in 1696. In the same year he began the bronze statue of *Frederick III* (1696–1709; Schloss Charlottenberg, Berlin). Between 1700 and 1706 he was the genius presiding over the commissions of Frederick III, including the ambitious, monumental Royal Palace in Berlin. His late style was revealed by his Kamecke house (1711–12; Berlin, destroyed). In 1714, after the death of his royal patron, he moved to St Petersburg, dying there in the same year.

Schmidt-Rottluff Karl 1884–1976

The German painter Karl Schmidt-Rottluff was born at Chemnitz, Saxony. He was an architectural student at Dresden, and founded the *Brücke* group in 1905 together with Fritz Bleyl, Erich Heckel, and Ernst Kirchner. After 1905 his paintings and graphics reflect the influence of Post-Impressionism, and also that of Emil Nolde, with whom he worked in 1906 (for example, *Self-portrait*, 1906; Stiftung Seebüll Ada und Emil Nolde, Seebüll). Unlike his *Brücke* colleagues he concentrated on landscapes, but in 1912 his expressive color brought him to the brink of Expressionist abstraction. His spiky figure paintings combined African influences in a semi-Cubist idiom (for example, *Woman Resting*, 1912; Staatsgalerie, Munich). Proscribed by the Nazis, he returned to Berlin after the war and taught art from 1947 in Berlin as a Professor at the Academy of Fine Arts.

Further reading. Brix, K. *Karl Schmidt-Rottluff*, Leipzig (1972). Dube, W.-D. *The Expressionists*, London (1972). Grohmann, W. *Schmidt-Rottluff, Aquarelle und Zeichnungen*, Munich (1963). Schmidt-Rottluff, K. "Brief über Munch und die Brücke", *Die Schanze*, Munich (1951).

Below: Karl Schmidt-Rottluff; Still Life. Private collection

Right: Martin Schongauer: Madonna in the Rose Bower; panel; 201×112cm (79×44in); 1473. Church of St Martin, Colmar

Schongauer Martin c1430–91

Descended from a patrician family of Augsburg, the German artist Martin Schongauer was best known in his lifetime as a painter, but his influence and his posthumous fame stem from his copper engravings. He was the son of a goldsmith who settled in Colmar c1440, and his name appears in the matriculation book of Leipzig University in 1465. Vasari records an old tradition that the young Schongauer studied under Rogier van der Weyden; he certainly knew the latter's *Last Judgment* Altarpiece in the hospital at Beaune. In 1469 he was mentioned as living in Colmar, but unlike his father he does not seem to have acquired citizenship there before his departure for Breisach.

Nothing certain is known about Schongauer's training as a painter. It seems probable that he studied under the minor Colmar painter Caspar Isenmann, who was himself greatly influenced by Netherlandish painting. No engravings can be dated to before 1465, but three drawings by Schongauer are dated 1469, and another 1470. These are clearly early works, and in them he is revealed to be the heir to the upper Rhine graphic tradition (that of Master ES and the Master of the Playing Cards).

His early *Adoration of the Magi* is inspired by Rogier van der Weyden's *St Columba* Altarpiece, a work which was then in Cologne (now Alte Pinakothek, Munich), and his early *Madonna and Child with the Parrot* is partially based on the *Madonna and Child* by Dieric Bouts (National Gallery, London). Although his technique has its origins in the Upper Rhine, the detailed treatment of the subject matter and the impeccable finish of his engravings stem from the sophistication of Netherlandish painting.

Presumably Schongauer traveled widely; his first known group of ten prints was executed shortly after 1470. His early work is characterized by vigorous and slightly uncoordinated hatching, as well as by vertical uprights to his initial "M"; his technical evolution parallels his stylistic development. In his mature years, the delicate hatching and soft transitions of light and shade have a poetic reticence and reach a climax in his late *Annunciation*. In the mature and late engravings, the uprights of the "M" in his initials are splayed. Although Schongauer initialed all his engravings and many drawings, no paintings that can be connected with him are signed, and only the *Madonna in the Rose Bower* is dated (1473; St Martin, Colmar).

In 1488, Schongauer moved to nearby Breisach to paint the enormous *Last Judgment* frescoes in the cathedral (these are now in ruinous condition). He died there in 1491, probably of the plague. The young Albrecht Dürer traveled to Breisach to visit him. He arrived after Schongauer's death, but acquired some of his drawings. The technical sophistication and clarity of Schongauer's forms deeply impressed Dürer, and the bizarre inventions of his *Temptation of St Anthony* engraving fascinated artists as different as Hieronymus Bosch and Michelangelo.

Schoonhoven Jan 1914–1994

The Dutch painter Johannes Jacobus (Jan) Schoonhoven was born in Delft. He studied at the Hague Academy from 1932 to 1936. Since 1946 he has worked for the Dutch Post Office. From 1957 to 1959 he was a member of the Netherlands Informal Group, and in 1960 he was a cofounder of "Groupe Null".

From 1940 to 1956 his works consisted of figurative drawings and gouaches inspired by Paul Klee. In 1957 he made his first formal, Abstract reliefs in papier-maché which continued the linear and organic divisions of the picture surface of the earlier works. The white reliefs he made from 1960 onwards consisted of squares and rectangles, serial in form, gradually becoming more precise. Later, by using cardboard, he introduced inclined planes that produced changes in light and shade. All his reliefs—whether rectangular, in concentric circles, or spiral in form—are divided into identical, repeated elements, allying him to Minimal art. His freehand drawings display the same properties.

Schwitters Kurt 1887–1948

The German artist and poet Kurt Schwitters founded the Dadaist movement *Merz*. Born in Hannover, he studied art there and in Dresden. Towards the end of the First World War, abstract and expressionist tendencies emerged in his paintings, but his earliest independent works date from 1918–19, when he made his first collages and *Merz*-pictures. (The term *Merz* was derived from the name of a bank—*Kommerz und Privat Bank*—while making a collage from its newspaper advertisements, and was ultimately applied by Schwitters to all his art activities and to the magazine he founded in Hannover in 1923.)

The *Merz* pictures are composed entirely from rubbish—including wire, string, rags, newspaper, and tickets—which Schwitters had lovingly rescued. Although they are abstract in form, the choice of collage material ensures that many suggest identifiable themes or scenarios. His poems were composed into rhythmic patterns in a similar manner, from banal phrases, scraps of sentences, and fragments of words. The *Merz* pictures represent an implicit attack on the notion that art can be made only from fine materials, by someone possessed of special technical and creative gifts.

It was his insistence that *Merz* was an art, not an anti-art movement, together with his indifference to politics, that earned him the hostility of the leader of Berlin Dada, Richard Huelsenbeck, who debarred Schwitters from Dada activities in Berlin. But Schwitters had been friendly with Raoul Hausmann, a leading Berlin Dada artist, since 1918; he accompanied him on a Dada lecture tour to Prague in 1921, and his magazine, *Merz* (1923–32), was openly sympathetic to the Dada movement.

In 1922 he toured Holland with Theo van Doesburg. His subsequent *Merz* pictures—although still assembled from detritus—show the influence of *De Stijl* in their more rectilinear, less expressionistic compositions. In 1923, he began to work seriously on the conversion of his family home in Hannover into a complete *Merz* environment; over the years he transformed it into a series of grotto-like chambers by the accretion of an immense variety of objects. This, his first and most elaborate *Merzbau* (Merz house), was destroyed during the Second World War.

Increasingly involved in abstractionist and constructivist circles, Schwitters collaborated with El Lissitzky on various advertising projects in the mid 1920s, experimenting in a radical way with layout and typography. In 1932 he joined the *Abstraction-Création* group. Many of his *Merz* collages and constructions of this period reflect these contacts in their severe and simple compositions.

A refugee from Nazi Germany, Schwitters settled in Lysaker, near Oslo, in 1937, and there began work on a new *Merzbau*. (It, too, was destroyed—in 1951.) When the Germans invaded Norway in 1940, he fled to England. He spent a period in internment camps, and later lived in

Kurt Schwitters: interior view of the first Merzbau, Hannover; 1923–6; destroyed

London where he was welcomed by avant-garde artists; he finally settled in Ambleside in the Lake District. There he began work on a third *Merzbau*, but it was far from completion when he died.

Schwitters' ultimate ambition was to create a "total work of art". This *Merz-Stage* was never realized, but his collages and constructions have exerted a considerable influence on many artists since the War.

Further reading. Ades, D. *Dada and Surrealism Reviewed*, London (1978). Richter, H. *Dada: Art and Anti-Art*, New York (1965). Schmalenbach, W. *Kurt Schwitters: Leben und Werk*, Cologne (1967). Steinitz, K. *Kurt Schwitters: a Portait from Life*, Los Angeles (1968). Tzara, T. "Merz Master: Kurt Schwitters 1887–1948", *Portfolio*, New York (Spring 1964).

Scopas 4th century BC

The Greek late Classical sculptor and architect Scopas came from Paros. He worked primarily in marble, and was active on the mainland as well as in east Greece and Samothrace. Around the middle of the 4th century he collaborated with Bryaxis, Leochares, and Timotheus in the sculptural decoration of the Mausoleum at Halicarnassus. While in Asia Minor, he carved one of the elaborate columns of the Temple of Artemis in Ephesus. For Cnidos he executed an *Athena* and a *Dionysos*—works that were obscured by the glory of the *Aphrodite* of Praxiteles.

Scopas was the architect, and presumably supervisor of the sculptures, of the Temple of Athena Alea at Tegea. He also carved the marble statues of Asclepius and Hygeia on either side of the cult statue of Athena Alea in the *cella*. The temple was perhaps built after the Mausoleum; it was Doric, and had interior semidetached Corinthian columns with capitals of an individual design. The east pediment was decorated with *The Calydonian Boar-hunt*, the west with *The Battle of Achilles and Telephus*. The surviving heads of heroes offer an indication of Scopas' style: cubic, with deep-set eyes and half-open mouths, they are violently twisted to express emotion (examples in the Archaeological Museum, Tegea, and the National Museum, Athens).

The pathetic aspect of his art has long been emphasized. A *Maenad* in frenzy grasping a kid she had just killed was praised in verse and prose. We also hear of two statues of *Longing* (Pothos), one possibly copied in the figure of a winged effeminate boy, his body and gaze directed upwards and to the left, a goose at his feet.

His *Herakles* in Sicyon may be the prototype of the Lansdowne *Herakles* (J. Paul Getty Museum, Malibu, California), a Classical composition indebted to Polycleitos. Another Classical type attributed to Scopas is the *Meleager*, perhaps adapted by him from the east pediment of the temple in Tegea.

Scorel Jan van 1495–1562

The Dutch painter Jan van Scorel (or Schoorel) was born at Schoorl and studied at Amsterdam. Between 1519 and 1525 he traveled extensively through Germany, the Holy Land, and Italy, where he served for a time as conservator of the papal collections in Rome under the Dutch pontiff, Hadrian VI. He settled in Utrecht, where he became a canon. His *Rest on the Flight into Egypt* (1530; National Gallery of Art, Washington, D.C.) is highly Italian in format and style, with a classical mountainous landscape. The Madonna's dress is reminiscent of that of Michelangelo's *Madonna and Child* sculpture at Bruges (Notre-Dame). His portraits are more conventionally Northern, but with lively

Jan van Scorel: Alpine Landscape; pen and brown ink on paper; 21×16cm (8×6in); c1518. British Museum, London

characterization (for example, *Agatha van Schoonhoven*; Galleria Doria Pamphili, Rome).

Scott Tim 1937–

The English sculptor Tim Scott was born in London. He studied at the Architectural Association, London (1954–5), and with Anthony Caro at St Martin's School of Art, London (1955–9). From 1959 to 1961 he worked in Paris at the Le Corbusier-Wegenscky atelier. He has taught sculpture at St Martin's since 1962.

Since 1961, when he abandoned his cast-plaster techniques, Scott has favored combinations of contrasting materials. In the early 1960s he used painted fiberglass or wood and glass to create simple but eccentric shapes whose color emphasized mass. From 1965 until the early 1970s he used colored acrylic sheets bolted to steel tubing to create large, open groups of flat planes. Smaller works constructed from clear acrylic sheets or blocks joined by steel elements, were followed in 1974 by sculptures in forged steel and bars, and later, by large, rugged works in steel and wood.

Scott William 1913–89

The British painter William Scott was born at Greenock, Scotland. He studied at the Belfast College of Art (1928–31) and at the Royal Academy in London (1931–5). For four years, from 1942 to 1946, Scott served in the Army and did no serious painting. His early work reveals the influence of both Cézanne and Picasso. His *Colander, Beans and Eggs* of 1948 (Albright-Knox Art Gallery, Buffalo) reveals a strong interest in the flat, abstract qualities of shape and form. This continued as the basis of Scott's vision: a variation on some domestic theme, usually a simple still life, so treated that the main emphases fall on color, shape, and design (for example, *Deep Blues*, 1970–1; artist's collection).

Sebastiano del Piombo
c1485–1547

The Italian painter Sebastiano Luciani was called "del Piombo" from his keepership of the Papal seal, a sinecure for official artists that was conferred on him in 1531. He was a Venetian by birth, and his career until 1511 was closely paralleled by that of his near-contemporary, Titian. Like him, he passed from the studio of Giovanni Bellini to that of Giorgione, and participated in the completion of at least one unfinished work of that master's, the *Three Philosophers* (Kunsthistorisches Museum, Vienna). In 1511 he accepted an invitation to go to Rome and remained there, except for a visit to Venice during 1528/9, for the rest of his life.

His earliest certain works were a pair of organ shutters, of *St Lewis* and *St Sinibald* (1507–8; S. Bartolommeo a Rialto, Venice). These reflect the impression made on him by Giorgione's fresco figures on the Fondaco dei Tedeschi (now the main post office in Venice) and are painted with an extreme delicacy, and sensibility to subtleties of light and color, that derive from Giorgione. The altarpiece of *S. Giovanni Crisostomo and other Saints* (1509; S. Giovanni Crisostomo, Venice), and the unfinished *Judgment of Solomon* (c1510/11; Bankes Collection, Kingston Lacey, Dorset) show a monumental classicism beyond anything in Giorgione's authenticated work.

After his move to Rome, Sebastiano became a close friend of Michelangelo. It is widely accepted that some preliminary drawings for two of his major works are from Michelangelo's hand. The works are *The Raising of Lazarus* (c1517–19; National Gallery, London), painted for Narbonne Cathedral in rivalry with Raphael's *Transfiguration*, and the fresco of *The Flagellation of Christ* (1520–4; S. Pietro in Montorio, Rome). *The Raising of Lazarus* is a handsome picture, but the handling seems depressingly coarse and heavy.

Vasari regarded him as a portrait painter, and a number of powerful portraits have come down to us. The *Portrait of a Lady* (*c*1512; Staatliche Museen, Berlin) still retains much of the delicacy of his Venetian work, and a particularly fine example of his later style is the *Birth of the Virgin* (1532; S. Maria del Popolo, Rome).

Further reading. Dussler, L. *Sebastiano del Piombo*, Basel (1942). Hirst, M. *Sebastiano del Piombo*, London (1981). Palluchini, R. *Sebastiano Viniziano*, Milan (1944).

Sebastiano del Piombo: Portrait of a Lady; poplar panel; 76×60cm (30×24in); c1512. Staatliche Museen, Berlin

Segal George 1924–2000

Born in New York City, the American artist George Segal studied at Coopers Union, the Pratt Institute of Design, and Rutgers University. During the late 1950s he worked as a painter in an Abstract Expressionist style. Then in 1961 he turned to sculpture, making figure sculptures by taking plaster casts from life. Though rough, unfinished and starkly white, these fully dressed, life-size figures (reminiscent of the petrified figures from Pompeii) have an uncanny presence, and often evoke a mood of loneliness and isolation. Segal's stated concern is with the "presence of man in daily life" and he uses real objects to provide an everyday setting for his figures, who are captured performing the routine actions of anonymous, uneventful lives. In *The Diner* (1964–6; Walker Art Center, Minneapolis), for example, a stool, counter and coffee machine are used to create a setting for a waitress and a seated customer. From the mid 1970s he created part figures—concentrating, for example, on the head and an arm—and began experimenting with bright colors.

Further reading. Pachner, J. *George Segal: Bronze*, New York (2004). Tuchman, P. *George Segal* (Modern Masters Series, Vol. 5), New York (1983).

Seghers Hercules 1589/90–*c*1635

Little is known of the life of Hercules Seghers, the first of the great 17th-century Dutch landscapists, and only about 15 of his paintings survive. He was born in Haarlem, and studied in Amsterdam under the Flemish-born landscapist Gillis van Coninxloo (1544–1607). Thereafter he worked in several Dutch centers, and may also have visited and worked in Flanders. His work seems to have found few buyers, and the artist died in poverty.

Seghers' paintings contain elements from 16th-century Flemish landscapes and also those of the German painter Adam Elsheimer (1578–1610), but they are otherwise highly individual works in which realistic detail is contained within visionary conceptions of awesome grandeur. His landscapes are typically horizontal, panoramic views of desolate valleys surrounded by vast mountain ranges. The few tiny figures emphasize the sense of solitude, and also underline the depth of space and the majesty of nature. A dramatic note is frequently added by the powerful interplay of light and shade in the sky and on land. Seghers' landscape paintings influenced the work of Philips Koninck, and also the landscapes of Rembrandt (who owned eight of Seghers' paintings).

A few of Seghers' paintings represent actual places (for example two views of Rhenen in the Staatliche Museen, Berlin), but it is fantasy that predominates in his work. Fantasy is also particularly characteristic of the artist's 50 or so etchings. In these the realistic detail found in paintings of mountain ranges and other motifs (which suggest that Seghers may have journeyed through the Alps) is subordinated to the unearthly appearance of wastelands filled with cold, crumbling rocks and water-filled craters. The power and individuality of Seghers' disturbingly eerie conceptions is such that his exploitation of traditional motifs (like the decaying pines of Danube School artists) is not at first apparent. The influence of Seghers' etchings is found in the prints of Jacob van Ruisdael rather than in those of Rembrandt, although the latter actually bought and reworked one of the artist's original copperplates. As an etcher, Seghers is historically important for his technical experiments, notably his use of colored inks, paper, and linen, and for his practice of tinting individual proofs. His prints have been admired by a number of 20th-century Surrealist artists.

Segonzac André Dunoyer de 1884–1974

The French painter and etcher André Dunoyer de Segonzac was born at Boussy-St-Antoine in the Île de France. He achieved international success between the Wars with paintings of the countryside of the Île de France and Provence. His somber browns and dark greens, and his vigorous use of the palette knife, owe much to Courbet. He views nature as a setting for leisure and repose. Figures are depicted boating or resting; the latter are sometimes mythological in style and are given a monumental quality by the use of foreshortening. He was acclaimed by conservative critics for presenting an undogmatic and characteristically French alternative to advanced art.

Semon Master *fl. c*500 BC

The Semon Master was a Greek gem-engraver. He is named for a gem in the Staatliche Museen, Berlin, showing a naked girl stooping to fill her jar at a fountain; the name Semon inscribed on it may be that of the owner. He is the best of the conventional late Archaic engravers, well able to combine the finest of Archaic patterning with decisive anatomical study on a small scale. He worked on scarabs and scaraboids of various colored quartzes, and the number of gems attributed to him and found on Cyprus suggests that he may have had his studio there for a time. The attributed stones include several with winged figures—Eros seizing a girl (Metropolitan Museum, New York), a sphinx with a youth (British Museum, London), a griffin with a youth (Museum of Fine Arts, Boston), and a winged, man-faced bull (British Museum, London) which might be a Hellenized version of the Persian monster. A larger gem in the Museum of Fine Arts, Boston, has a subject rare for this date: a mythological study of Achilles killing the Amazon Queen Penthesilea.

Semper Gottfried 1803–79

The German architect and theoretician Gottfried Semper studied first law and then mathematics. He began his architectural studies in Munich with Friedrich von Gärtner (1792–1847), who influenced him towards classicism. A stay in Paris in 1826 further strengthened his interest in the architecture of Antiquity. Between 1830 and 1832 he visited Naples, Pompeii, Sicily, and Greece. In late 1833 he met the great German classical architect K.F. Schinkel in Berlin. At this time his attention turned towards the use of color in architecture, and in 1834 he published his first theoretical work, *Vorläufige Bermerkungen . . . (Provisional Remarks on the Polychrome Architecture and Sculpture of Antiquity*). His first buildings were erected in Hamburg in 1834.

In the same year he was appointed Professor of Architecture at the Dresden Academy. The first famous building he designed was the Dresden Opera House (1837–41), which has been described as one of the epoch-making buildings of the 19th century. In accordance with his ideas on the polychrome architecture of Antiquity, his intention was a synthesis of all the arts of the decorator. Semper and Richard Wagner were friends, and it was intended that Semper be given the commission for designing the Festspielhaus in Munich. Caught up in the political activities of 1848, the Year of Revolutions, he was exiled in 1849 for his part in the May uprisings. He subsequently lived in Paris, England, Switzerland, and Vienna, and died in Rome.

His major theoretical work, *Der Stil* ("Style"), was published in 1860 during a Renaissance revival. In it he praises Roman architectural achievement above that of the Greeks, and especially emphasizes its realism—a style suitable for both churches and railroad stations. The book also advances a materialistic theory for the genesis of an art based on utilitarian purpose, raw material, and technology. The impact of these ideas was to be felt in early contributions to the Modern period.

Sergel Johan 1740–1814

The Swedish Neoclassical sculptor Johan Tobias Sergel first worked for ten years under the French sculptor P.-H. Larchevêque. Between 1767 and 1778 he lived in Rome, where he met John Henry Fuseli and J.-A. Houdon. During his stay there Sergel was influenced by Antiquity, and by the work of Raphael, Michelangelo, and the Carracci. His most successful sculpture, of mythological groups, was made in Rome, but in 1778 he was recalled to Stockholm against his will, to become a portrait sculptor. Sergel's sculpture combines Neoclassical ideals with closely observed realism.

Serlio Sebastiano 1475–1554

Sebastiano Serlio was an Italian architect and decorative artist who worked in the circle of Peruzzi and Raphael in Rome. He left the city some time *c*1527. He was in Venice in 1528, and there began publication of a series of books on architecture planned as a complementary set of eight volumes. These are his chief claim to posterity. The idea of such a work evidently sprang from his association with Peruzzi, who had intended to produce some sort of publication on Classical architecture before his death in 1536. Serlio was the spiritual heir to this project, and several of his drawings were closely derived from those of his master. His third book, which appeared in 1540 with a dedication to Francis I of France, resulted in his arrival in Paris in 1541. He remained there, in court favor, until Francis' death in 1547, and thereafter eked out a living in France until he died at Lyons in 1554.

Serra Richard 1939–

The works of the American sculptor Richard Serra, who has worked almost exclusively with metal, combine Minimalism and Environmental sculpture. Born in San Francisco, he studied at Berkley and Yale, and then in Paris and Florence. In his early works there is often an element of precarious balance—in *One-Ton Prop (House of Cards)* (1968–69; Saatchi Collection, London) sheets of lead are leant against one another to form a cube. Later works, often constructed for a specific site, typically feature huge, gently curved sheets of untreated steel imbedded in the ground, Serra's intention being to create a "field force... so that space is discerned physically rather than optically". One such work—*Tilted Arc* (1981), a sheet of steel 37m (120ft) long by 3.7m (12ft)—became the object of a bitter controversy when city officials had it removed from its site in Foley Square, New York, with politicians challenging the public funding of the arts, and the arts community defending artists' creative freedom.

Further reading. Foster, H. *Richard Serra (October Files)* Boston, Mass. (2000).

Sérusier Paul 1864–1927

Paul Sérusier was a French artist and theorist, and the intellectual leader of the Nabis. He was born in Paris, and studied at the Académie Julian. Visiting Pont-Aven, Brittany, in the summer of 1888, he was introduced by Emile Bernard to Gauguin, under whose tutelage he painted *The Talisman* (1888; Collection of J.F. Denis, Alençon). This was a brilliantly colored evocation rather than a literal transcription of a landscape. It became the pictorial manifesto for Sérusier's Académie Julian friends (Pierre Bonnard, Édouard Vuillard, Maurice Denis, Ker-Xavier Roussel, and Paul Ranson) who banded themselves together to form the Nabis. During the 1890s Sérusier was engaged in such "Nabi" activities as theater design (including designs for Alfred Jarry's play *Ubu Roi*, 1896), book illustration, and mural decoration. He also met Jan Verkade, a painter of the School of Beuron, under whose influence he became a Theosophist and embarked upon a search for an art based upon sacred proportions and color relationships. He published the fruits of these researches in *ABC de la Peinture* (1922).

Paul Sérusier: Melancholia; oil on canvas; 71×57cm (28×22in); c1890. Collection of Mlle H. Boutaric, Paris

Sesshu 1420–1506

The Japanese painter Sesshu was also known as Toyo. He was the greatest master of the Chinese-inspired ink monochrome style, and is considered by many of his countrymen to be their greatest artist. Like all the painters of that period who worked in pure ink he was a Zen monk, and his work is partly a conscious exploration of the nature of reality.

Sesshu was born in Bitchu Province, near modern Okayama. He returned to live in western Japan later in his life, thus creating a precedent for great artists to work away from the capital. He was a pupil of Shubun at the Sokokuji Temple in Kyoto, then the center of Zen painting in the ink monochrome style. From Shubun he learned the subtle use of graded washes, which had originated in the Southern Sung school.

During the years 1467 to 1469 he visited China to seek more advanced masters, but he found none whom he considered worthy among the then-dominant Che School. However, the effect of his stay can be clearly seen in the four great landscape hanging scrolls of the seasons (Tokyo National Museum), which were done in China. They have the architectural power and rational organization that came naturally to even the weakest Che School painter, but which was rarely achieved by the more emotional and decorative genius of the Japanese.

The majestic mountain landscapes of China, and no doubt the study of original Sung and Yuan period masterpieces in Peking, gave his later work a detached elevation. This is expressed in concise, exact ink strokes, to which ink washes are an adjunct, rather than of the essence—as they are among his contemporaries such as Bunsei, Gakuo, or Soami.

After his return, Sesshu traveled widely in Japan. Some of his later works show an admirable fusion of Japanese sentiment and detail with Chinese rational power—a synthesis never achieved by the later, Chinese-inspired *Kano* and *Nanga* schools. His masterpiece is the long handscroll of the four seasons (Mori Collection). This depicts a continuous, changing panorama, complex in detail but integrated in overall design, the brushwork varied almost in the manner of orchestration. Most of the individual details are Japanese, especially the series showing water with fishing boats. No other Japanese painting gives such a sense of intellectual power expressed through the brush.

Late in life, Sesshu developed from the depths of his confidence very abbreviated styles, where a few controlled but violent-seeming splashes of ink, and a few light washes, can suggest great mountains and vast distance (for example, *Haboku Landscape* or *Ink-Splash Landscape*, 1495; Tokyo National Museum). Even more startling is the *Snowy Landscape* (Tokyo National Museum) where the line of the side of a cliff is arbitrarily extended into the sky, like a crack in ice. No other Zen artist distorted apparent reality with such breathtaking and assured violence.

Sesson Shukei 1504–89

Shukei Sesson was an independent Japanese artist who painted in the Zen manner. An admirer of Sesshu, he followed his example by working in the provinces; his studio is preserved in Miharu, in the rugged northeast of Japan. The harshness of the area is reflected in the howling winds, scudding boat, and tongued waves of his famous ink sketch *Wind and Waves* (Nomura Collection, Kyoto), and in *The Immortal Lu Tung-pin on a Dragon in a Storm* (private collection). His technique was assured; but the directness and roughess of his approach, which is essentially Zen in spirit, tends to hide it. He had some followers, but was too individualistic to be greatly influential.

Seurat Georges 1859–91

The French painter Georges-Pierre Seurat was the leader of the Neo-Impressionist group. Born in Paris in 1859, he studied briefly at the École des Beaux-Arts (1878–9). He made many drawings after antique sculpture (for example of the Parthenon frieze), Renaissance masters (such as Piero della Francesca), and Ingres; he also did life drawings, often of a Holbeinesque naturalism. During his military service in Brest (1879–80), he drew more everyday subjects in his sketchbook.

On his return to Paris, he continued to draw, often using conté crayon on heavy-texture ("Michallet" or "Ingres") paper, from which he obtained an astonishing range of texture and tone. Almost 500 drawings exist; from 1882, their subject matter was taken from the fields, from Parisian street-scenes, and from the urban poor, in which Daumier's influence can be detected. He also drew scenes from the circus and the café concert (the composition somewhat influenced by the work of Degas). Seurat deeply admired Rembrandt and Goya. From all these sources, he evolved a consciously considered, classical—and ultimately classic—style of drawing: it was a rigorously thought-out system rationally applied. His drawings alone would guarantee Seurat's place among the great artists.

In addition, he pondered deeply the problems of color. From early youth, he had been engrossed in scientific color theory. By 1881, he had read treatises on optical science by Michel-Eugène Chevreul, Ogden Rood, and Hermann von Helmholtz; these eventually enabled him to move towards a systematic, methodical, and carefully analyzed application of color and brush stroke. He also looked hard at the paintings of Delacroix, as can be seen in his detailed color analyses of three of Delacroix's paintings. His early paintings were generally of small format, often on panel; most of them depict fragments of landscape around Paris. They show the influence of the Barbizon painters and, by 1882, of Impressionism. A drawing of his painter-friend, Edmond-François Aman-Jean, was accepted at the Salon in 1883.

In the spring of 1884, his large composition, *Bathing at Asnières* (reworked c1887; National Gallery, London), measuring 79 by 118 in (201 by 300 cm), was shown at the inaugural exhibition of the Salon des Artistes Indépendants. He

Georges Seurat: A Small Man by a Parapet or The Invalid; oil on panel; 25×16cm (10×6in); 1881–2. Rothbart Collection, New York

met Signac in 1884; in the following year, Camille and Lucien Pissarro were converted to the Neo-Impressionist movement. At the last Impressionist exhibition in 1886, Seurat exhibited *Sunday Afternoon on the Island of the Grande Jatte* (1886; Art Institute of Chicago). This was an Impressionist subject *par excellence*, but the Impressionist technique was scientifically rationalized into a regular, dot-like brush stroke, and the seemingly haphazard Impressionist slice-of-nature was given a geometrically structured base. The picture created a scandal.

Divisionism and Pointillism were publicly denounced. Young Symbolist poets and critics—Félix Fénéon and Gustave Kahn in particular—wrote enthusiastically in their defence. At the exhibitions of the Salon des Artistes Indépendants, and in smaller venues like dealers' galleries, the group of artists who gathered around Seurat and Signac gave the movement a vital cohesiveness that lasted from 1886 until Seurat's death in 1891. Some of them were also invited to exhibit with Les Vingt in Brussels, and this helped to establish a group of Belgian Neo-Impressionists.

Seurat's own path, however, was masterfully and often secretively single-minded. He continued to draw; he continued to print small *pochades*; but fundamentally he aimed to produce at least one large "statement-picture" every year. He also painted a series of canvases that resulted from his summer stays in the Channel coast—Grandchamp (1885), Honfleur (1886), Port-en-Bessin (1888), Crotoy (1889), and Gravelines (1890). In these pictures an organized, finely filtered observation is married to an introspective, melancholic mood that is sometimes relieved by witty outbursts: for example, the "frozen" fluttering flags in *Sunday, Port-en-Bessin* (1888; Kröller-Müller Museum, Otterlo).

One further preoccupation found increasing outlets in his last works: his theory of the emotional character of linear directions. This was based to a large degree on the quasi-scientific writings of a brilliant young aesthetician, Charles Henry, whom both Seurat and Signac befriended. The theory is apparent in several of Seurat's "statement-pictures". These include *La Parade* ("Invitation to the Side-show", 1887–8; Metropolitan Museum, New York), which also reveals the workings of the system of proportion known as the Golden Section, and *Les Poseuses* ("The Models", small version 1888; on loan to the Alte Pinakothek, Munich), which incidentally plays a skillful variation on the theme of picture-within-a-picture. In *Le Chahut* (1889–90; Kröller-Müller Museum, Otterlo) and *La Cirque* (1890–1; Musée du Jeu de Paume, Paris), the deliberately achieved stylization clearly gave a strong impetus to the emergence of Art Nouveau, especially through the Belgian *confrères* in Les Vingt.

Although Seurat himself wrote little, a few of his letters survive; one of these, to the writer Maurice Beaubourg (28 August 1890), provides a summary of his technique and his aesthetic. He was jealous of his discoveries, and it was left to Fénéon and Signac to explain them publicly. His secrecy extended to his private life. When Seurat died suddenly of angina in 1891, not even his closest friends were aware of his relationship with Madeleine Knobloch, who had borne him a son. She had been the model in his only large portrait, *Jeune Femme se Poudrant* (1889–90; Courtauld Institute Galleries, London).

Seurat is the epitome of the artist as laboratory scientist: analyzing, questioning, and seeking, fanatical and emotionally tense. He sought what he considered to be the universal laws of nature, and of art. His approach was essentially conceptual and rational, but it was never exclusively so. His method never dries up into a repetitive and lifeless formula, as happened to some of his lesser followers. Elements of his art have influenced the Fauvists, the Cubists, and the more geometrical exponents of Abstract art.

Further reading. Dorra, H. and Rewald, J. *Seurat*, Paris (1960). Hauke, C.M. de *Seurat et Son Oeuvre* (2 vols), Paris (1961). Herbert, R.L. *Seurat's Drawings*, New York (1963). Homer, W.I. *Seurat and the Science of Painting*, Cambridge, Mass. (1964). Russell, J. *Seurat*, London (1965).

Severini Gino 1883–1966

The Italian painter Gino Severini was born in Cortona, but lived in Paris from 1906. He signed the 1910 *Technical Manifesto of Futurist Painting* and was instrumental in bringing Futurism to Paris, London, and Berlin. He also introduced the Futurists to Cubism. He acknowledged the ideals of Futurism, but his paintings are decorative rather than aggressive (for example, *The Dynamic Hieroglyph of the Bal Tabarin*, 1912; Museum of Modern Art, New York), and he often aimed at reproducing the dynamics of movement and sensation. In the 1920s and 1930s Severini did many

Gino Severini: Still Life with "Lacerba"; papier collé, gouache, ink, and charcoal; 50×60cm (20×24in); 1913. Musée d'Art et d'Industrie, St-Etienne

murals and mosaics in Italy, France, and Switzerland. After he had published *Du Cubisme au Classicisme* in 1921, his style became Neoclassical, though he still experimented with Cubism.

Shafi Abbasi *fl.* 1630–74

Shafi Abbasi was a Persian draftsman and designer, the son of Riza. He imitated his father's work and signature, especially in an album from the Sarre Collection (Freer Gallery of Art, Washington, D.C.). His most original work was as a designer for textiles based on flower and bird studies, some of which derived from English engraved pattern books. The suffix Abbasi indicates that he must have served Shah Abbas II who reigned from 1642 to 1666, but by the latter date Shafi was at the court of the Mughal Emperor, where he died. Other works by him are in the St Petersburg Public Library, the Bibliothèque Nationale, Paris, and the Cleveland Museum of Art.

Shahn Ben 1898–1969

Ben Shahn was a Russian-born painter of the American school. His family emigrated to the United States in 1906. While studying at various New York colleges Shahn worked as a lithographer's assistant. In 1927 and 1929 he visited Europe, where he was deeply impressed by the work of the early Italian masters. Their "naivety" became part of his own very personal style, which he applied to subjects of serious social significance. Perhaps his best known works are the gouaches inspired by the Sacco and Vanzetti case (*The Passion of Sacco and Vanzetti*, 1931–2; Whitney Museum of American Art, New York). He often worked in tempera. His compositions are characterized by figures with enlarged heads in settings inspired by, but remote from, the world around him (for example, *Liberation*, 1945; private collection). Shahn was also involved in various large-scale decorative schemes, such as the frescoes in the Post Office, Bronx Central Annex, New York (1938–9), and the mural in the Washington Social Security Building (1940–2).

Further reading. Anreus, A. *Ben Shahn and the Passion of Sacco and Vanzetti* Piscataway, N.J. (2001). Chevlowe, S. *Common Man, Mythic Vision*, Princeton, N.J. (1998). Greenfeld, H. *Ben Shahn: an Artist's Life*, New York (1998). Kao, D. M., Katzman, L. and Webster, J. *Ben Shahn's New York: the Photography of Modern Times*, Cambridge, Mass. (2000). Pohl, F. K. and Shahn, B. *Ben Shahn*, Beverly Hills, Calif. (1993). Shahn, B. *The Shape of Content*, Cambridge, Mass. (1972).

Sharaku Toshusai *fl.* 1794–5

The Japanese artist Toshusai Sharaku was the greatest master of the *Kabuki* actor print, combining psychological subtlety with rare forcefulness of design. He is the most mysterious figure in Japanese art. He began making his 200 or so known prints in 1794, and they were published for only about ten months, into 1795. Nothing is known of his life or identity. His greatest prints are head-and-shoulders portraits of actors in specific roles, done with thick, flexible lines, and bright patches of color. They almost always have a plain background, often of mica, which emphasizes their artificiality. Yet they suggest both a dramatic moment in a play and the psychology of the actor.

Toshusai Sharaku: Nakamura Konozo and Nakajima Wadgemon in Character; woodblock print; 38×23cm (15×9in); 1794. British Museum, London

Shaw Norman 1831–1912

The British architect Richard Norman Shaw was born in Edinburgh. He was articled to a London architect, won the Royal Academy Gold Medal and Traveling Studentship (1854), and published his sketches of continental Gothic buildings (1858). He succeeded Philip Webb as George Street's assistant, and in 1862 set up his own practice in London with William Eden Nesfield.

During the six years of this association, Shaw designed two churches (including the English church in Lyons, 1868) in a bold, early Gothic style, but he soon showed a preference for house design. He perfected a picturesque "manorial" type of country house (for example Leyswood, Sussex, 1868; and Grim's Dyke, Harrow, 1872) with tile hanging and half-timbering, far more ebullient than Webb's buildings. These did much to establish Shaw's international reputation.

For the many domestic and commercial buildings in London that he designed during the 1870s and 1880s, Shaw adopted an early-18th-century town-house style (generally, although inaccurately, called "Queen Anne"). At first he interpreted this most exuberantly (as in New Zealand Chambers, Leadenhall Street, 1872), but he later used decorative details more sparingly. He developed a versatile manner of building in red brick. This was suitable not only for the many artists' houses he built in Hampstead and Kensington, but also for the varied buildings of the first garden suburb (Bedford Park, begun 1875), and for larger buildings such as the Albert Hall Mansions (1879).

Shaw worked in this manner for some time, but gradually his enthusiasm for its picturesqueness waned; this can be seen in his more ordered designs for No. 170 Queen's Gate, London (1888), and Bryanston, Dorset (1890). He was by now one of the elders of British architecture. The formality of these buildings was the prelude to a period of overt classicism and monumentality, which Shaw adopted and which culminated in his designs for Regent Street and the Piccadilly Hotel, London (1905).

Sheeler Charles 1883–1965

The American painter and photographer Charles Sheeler was born in Philadelphia, where he studied under William Chase at the Pennsylvania Academy (1903–6). He saw works by modern French artists during a stay in Paris from 1908 to 1909, and showed in the Armory exhibition in 1913. In 1912 he took up photography. His commercial work for *Vogue* and *Vanity Fair* (1923–32) and the Ford Motor Company, particularly photographs of the River Rouge plant (1927), ensured his international reputation. Following the death of his friend and associate Morton Schamberg, Sheeler moved to New York in 1919. By the early 1920s his range of themes and his approach—from near abstraction to intense realism—had been defined. His paintings of the city, industrial landscape, and machinery, such as *Upper Deck* (1929; William Hayes Fogg Art Museum, Cambridge, Mass.), contrast with his depictions of interiors and farm buildings, such as *Bucks County Barn* (1932, Museum of Modern Art, New York), but all may be considered outstanding examples of Precisionism.

In 1939, the year his biography was published, Sheeler had a retrospective exhibition at the Museum of Modern Art, New York. Throughout his career he alternated between photography and painting, but in both media he concentrated on structured, formal compositions with clearly defined features. His photographs were often the basis for, or an influence on, his paintings, especially in the "double exposures" of the early 1950s such as *Architectural Cadences* (1954; Whitney Museum of American Art, New York).

Charles Sheeler: Upper Deck; oil on canvas; 74×56cm (29×22in); 1929. William Hayes Fogg Art Museum, Cambridge, Mass.

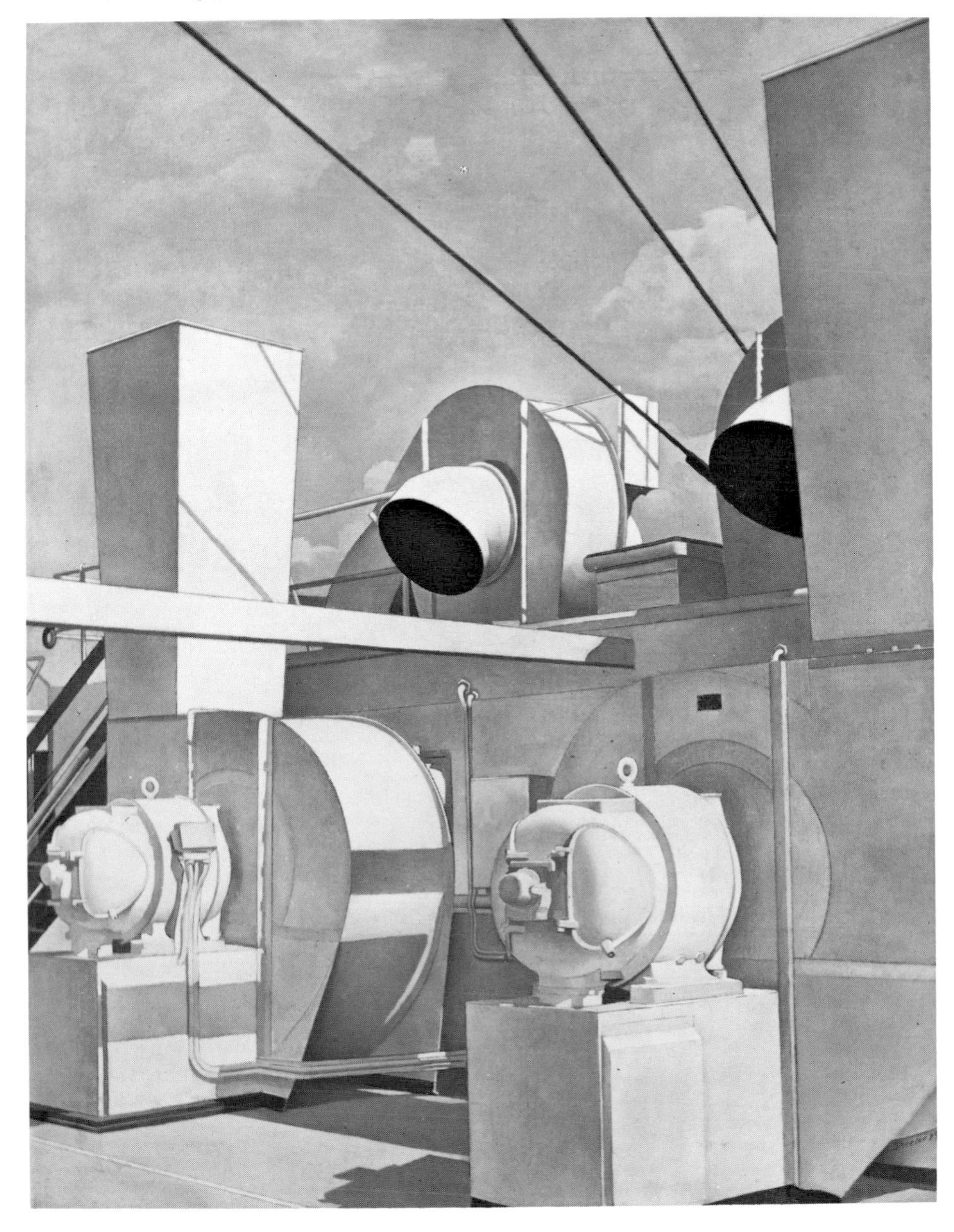

Shen Chou 1427–1509

The Chinese painter Shen Chou was a native of Wu Hsien (today's Suchow), Kiangnan. The son of a landed family he was well educated. Just as he was about to take up an official career his father died. He remained at home, first for mourning and then to care for his mother, and never took up the career for which he was qualified. He became a painter and poet. He was the inspiration of the Wu School of painters, who felt themselves in contrast with, and sometimes in opposition to, the Che School of Chekiang, which consisted mostly of Academy and Court artists.

Shen Chou was a typical scholar-painter. By instinct an eclectic, he worked in many styles throughout his life. His position as a scholar-gentleman was such that he would have had access to many old masters; he was also personally popular with his contemporaries. There is a strong individual character to his works, which were often painted from his own experience. Many of his landscapes show places on his estate, and record specific occasions (for example, *Walking with a Staff*, Palace Museum Collection, Taichung) or feelings (for example, *Poetona Mountain*, Kansas City Album, William Rockhill Nelson Gallery, Kansas City, Mo.) which require the use of words. This use of simple poetry with a painting is beautifully done. Like all of Shen Chou's work, it shows a direct approach, unique to Far Eastern painting.

His handling of ink and color is both bold and sensitive. He follows the scholar's wish to handle his brush in an "unprofessional" style which will, nevertheless, show his undoubted knowledge of the old masters. His composition is inventive and daring, but in no way mannered, so that his paintings often appear very simple. His painting was highly thought of throughout the later periods of Chinese art, and was an inspiration to Shih T'ao (1630–1707) and some of the later-18th-century independent painters.

Many of Shen Chou's paintings have survived, often in handscroll and album leaf format, in ink or color on paper. His later work, from a period when he followed the ink style of Wu Chen, is still much admired. (*See* overleaf.)

Shen Chou: Returning Home in the Autumn; ink and slight color on paper; 38×61cm (15×24in); c1495–1500. William Rockhill Nelson Gallery, Kansas City, Mo.

Shih T'ao 1630–1707

The real name of the Chinese painter Shih T'ao was Chu Tao-chi. He came from Honan, and was a relative of the Ming royal house. He retired to a monastery at the fall of the dynasty, but it is not recorded that he became a monk. After a period of wandering he finally settled in the Yangchow area. He was a well-educated intellectual, who was also a serious and individual painter. "When asked if I paint in the manner of the Southern School or Northern School, I reply with a laugh that I do not know whether I am of a School or the School of me, I paint in my own style".

Shih T'ao was a romantic painter who built upon his eclectic training, but who stressed the need to look at and to experience Nature. He also found inspiration in literature. His *Peach Blossom Valley* handscroll (Freer Gallery of Art, Washington, D.C.) is acutely evocative and displays something of the eclectic spirit that was very much alive in his day. Despite his independence of spirit, Shih T'ao was not out of touch with his fellow artists, and corresponded both with Chu Ta and with Wang Shi-min. He was engrossed in painting: he experimented with brushwork, with the use of color, and with composition, displaying such vitality that artists are building upon his work to this day.

Shih T'ao's range was enormous. It varied from large works on silk (which he disliked doing, and which must have been commissioned) through all sizes of work on paper, both in monochrome and in color, which he used to great atmospheric effect. His brushwork has a marvelous strength, although it is often delicate. In contrast to the works of Chu Ta, the paintings of Shih T'ao are in an additive style. He builds up his landscapes, covering the bones, however thinly, to create a sense of texture, light, and atmospheric distance.

Shiko Watanabe 1683–1755

A Japanese painter of the *Rimpa* School, Watanabe Shiko trained as a *Kano* artist, then changed to the style of Ogata Korin. His work combines *Kano* inkwork with Korin's brilliant decorative style, but adds a feeling for the real world that foreshadows Okyo's naturalism (he did a sketchbook of birds, that was copied by Okyo). His crowded screens, for example, *Flowers and Grasses of the Seasons* (Hatakeyama Collection) have a joyous exuberance lacking in the work of other *Rimpa* artists. His screens of the *Yoshino Cherry Blossom* (private collection) and his *Iris* screens (Cleveland Museum of Art) have the simple effectiveness of Korin or Sotatsu.

Shiseki So 1712–86

So Shiseki was a Japanese painter of the Nagasaki school who specialized in detailed bird-and-flower painting in the Chinese style. Born in Edo (Tokyo), he went to Nagasaki c1740 and studied under Kumashiro Yu, who had learned from the emigré Chinese artist Shen Nan-p'in. Later he studied under another Chinese artist, known in Japanese as So Shigan, from whom he adopted his new family name. Shiseki took the Nagasaki style back to Edo, where he popularized it in woodblock books, and also taught it, notably to Shiba Kokan and Tani Buncho. Shiseki added native sensuousness, poetry, and oblique design to his rather literal Chinese models.

Shohaku Soga 1730–81

Soga Shohaku was an eccentric and rebellious Japanese painter. He studied with the *Kano* School, but later claimed to be a *Soga* School artist, having adopted the dynamic *Soga* ink line. Little is known of his life, but the inscriptions on his paintings show that he worked in many different places. His favorite subjects were Chinese Buddhist and Taoist figures. These were usually painted with violent movement and grotesquely distorted faces (notably in the large hanging scrolls of *Kanzan* and *Jittoku* in the Kyoto National Museum). Most of his work is in ink monochrome. His landscapes can be surprisingly soft, but some are remarkable for their Cubist tendencies, the mountains being drawn as pure oblongs.

Shoi Iwasa 1578–1651

The Japanese painter Iwasa Shoi is better known as Matabei; he has been called, incorrectly, the founder of the *Ukiyoe* School. In fact, he was a *Tosa*-trained artist. Like his contemporaries Sotatsu and Jokei, he developed the traditional native styles into something both more dynamic and more decorative. His handscrolls, such as *Tokiwa in the Mountains* (Atami Art Museum, Atami), are vigorous in detail, often crowded, yet superbly organized; they convert the traditional *Tosa* cloud-bands into subtly shaded bands of mist. His faces have great vigor, and are distinguished by a strongly projecting chin. Shoi was also a master of dashing ink monochrome portraits, and also did decorative screens.

Shubun *fl.* c1420–c65

Shubun was a Japanese painter in the Chinese pure-ink style. The first major

Japanese artist in this school, he probably learned from Josetsu at the Sokokuji Temple in Kyoto; this was the headquarters of the government academy, and he later became its director. In the 1420s he visited Korea, which was apparently his principal source for the Chinese styles; it was here that he developed his interest in spatial depth. He was a Buddhist sculptor, and a painter of traditional images. He also painted many vertically constructed landscapes which were extremely influential, especially on Sesshu. No one surviving painting is certainly by his hand, but there is a consistency in the style of those works attributed to him.

Shunsho Katsukawa 1726–93

The Japanese painter and print designer Katsukawa Shunsho is the best-known member of the Katsukawa school, which specialized in prints of the *Kabuki* theater. He learned from Shunsui, the founder of the school, and also from the neo-*Kano* painter Sukoku. He is perhaps the most skillful of all the painters in the pure *Ukiyoe* style, combining strong composition, detailed and sensuous execution, and lyrical charm, as in *Airing Books* (Freer Gallery of Art, Washington, D.C.). In middle life he began to design prints of *Kabuki* actors (often in diptychs or triptychs), with a new realism and great subtlety of character, and an original use of simple blocks of powerful color. He is also notable as the teacher of Katsushika Hokusai.

Joannes Siberechts: Landscape with Rainbow (Henley-on-Thames); oil on canvas; 81×103cm (32×41cm); c1690. Tate Gallery, London

Siberechts Joannes 1627–c1703

The Flemish painter Joannes Siberechts was born in Antwerp, but worked in Italy from 1648 to 1649. He painted peaceful landscapes with peasants and animals; his best pictures show fords and flooded roads, with carts, that suggest the influence of Rubens. Between 1672 and 1676 he lived in England, where he traveled extensively and pioneered the "portrait" of the English country house. He painted views of Longleat as early as 1675 and of Chatsworth in 1694. For Sir Thomas Willoughby he also painted landscapes of English scenery which show, for the first time in English art, a real awareness of the English countryside.

Katsukawa Shunsho: An Interrupted Letter, frontispiece to "The Common Cuckoo"; woodblock print; 20×36cm (8×14in); 1788. British Museum, London

Sickert Walter 1860–1942

The English painter and printmaker Walter Richard Sickert was born in Munich. His father, an artist, was Danish, and his mother was Anglo-Irish. He was brought to England in 1868, educated at King's College, London, and, after a short period on the stage, studied briefly at the Slade School of Fine Art (1881–2). He then became a pupil of J.A.M. Whistler, and in 1883 met Degas in Paris. Whistler and Degas were the seminal influences on his work. In the 1880s and 1890s, he produced a series of music-hall pictures which explored fresh subject matter in late Victorian art, revealing new compositional devices and a mastery of low-toned color

(for example, *The Old Bedford*, c1897; Walker Art Gallery, Liverpool). For over 40 years, Sickert haunted Dieppe, observing its street architecture and depicting obsessively the medieval church of St Jacques. He has been called the "Canaletto of Dieppe"; but he banished ceremony and circumstance from his evocations of the Channel port.

In 1888 he joined the New English Art Club; in 1889, he helped organize an exhibition of the Club's more radical wing under the title of "The London Impressionists". His drawings and paintings were reproduced in *The Yellow Book*. He held his first one-man show in 1895. In the same year—and again in 1896—he visited Venice, producing a series of low-toned views that were not always of the tourist spots. From 1899 to 1905 he lived abroad, mainly in Dieppe and Venice. He held one-man shows in Paris in 1900, 1903, and 1907, also exhibiting there in the artists' societies. Had he chosen to stay in France, he could have continued to build up his reputation.

Instead, he returned to London in 1905, and gathered round him a new band of associates, including Harold Gilman and Spencer Gore; together they formed the Camden Town Group in 1911. He provided the group's theoretical justification and acted as its practical mentor. From a series of figures and nudes seen in fairly confined interiors, which he produced on his last stay in Venice from 1903 to 1904, Sickert evolved his characteristic Camden Town style. Based to a large extent on drawings, Impressionist in its fine observation of *contre-jour* effects, and asserting strong painterly qualities, this style marked the high point of his art.

Sickert had already written articles, reviews, and essays during the 1880s and 1890s; from 1908 to 1914, his literary output was virtually uninterrupted. He wrote about art from the inside, and was pungent and polemical, witty and idiosyncratic. He was also a prolific printmaker. In his late paintings, his palette lightened considerably, as can be seen in the series *Echoes*, based on Victorian illustrations.

Further reading. Bacon, W. *Sickert*, London (1973). Beil, I. *Victorian Artists*, London (1967).

Left: Walter Sickert: Boredom (Ennui); oil on canvas; 152×112cm (60×44in); c1914. Tate Gallery, London

Paul Signac: The Port of St Tropez; oil on canvas; 65×81cm (26×32in); 1899. Musée de l'Annonciade, St Tropez

Siferwas John *c1360–post 1421*

John Siferwas was an English illuminator of manuscripts. His workshop enlivened book-illumination during a period of changing styles and may have contributed to wall paintings in the Chapter House of Westminster Abbey. The Siferwas family was prominent in Herefordshire during the 14th century. John was ordained an acolyte at Farnham in 1380, and became a Dominican at Guildford Priory. His signature appears in two manuscripts: a massive missal executed for the Benedictine Abbey of Sherborne, Dorset (1396–1407; Collection of the Duke of Northumberland, Alnwick Castle), and a Gospel Lectionary (c1408; British Library, London) ordered as a gift for Salisbury Cathedral by John, 5th Lord Lovell of Tichmersh. A remarkable self-portrait shows Siferwas, wearing the Dominican habit, presenting the book to Lord Lovell.

The highly decorated Sherborne Missal measures 21 by 15 in (53 by 38 cm) even after an unfortunate trimming of the edges. The patrons of the work were Richard Medford, Bishop of Salisbury, and Robert Bruynyng, Abbot of Sherborne, both of whom are frequently depicted in its pages. Many birds are beautifully painted and named, and indicate a close connection with a late-14th-century sketch book (in the Pepys Library, Magdalene College, Cambridge). This is evidently an atelier pattern-book, with human and animal figures. Pages of realistic birds recall the Sherborne Missal, and may be by Siferwas.

The great *Crucifixion* page in the Sherborne Missal, painted in the Italian style, is masterly though overcrowded. Drama is conveyed by rhythmic compositional stresses, but the faces of the mourning group lack the sensitivity of a painter like Herman Scheerre (*fl.* c1403–19). It has been suggested that the Italianate-English retable in Norwich Cathedral influenced the stye of Siferwas, and his ornate costumes are certainly similar. One assistant signed his name "Johannes" in the Marco Polo Manuscript (c1410; Bodleian Library, Oxford). He inherited the fantastical garments and headgear, with a cruder Siferwas style. Johannes apparently joined Herman Scheerre's workshop early in the 15th century, continuing the tradition in the absence of later known works by John Siferwas.

Signac Paul 1863–1935

The French painter and theorist Paul Signac was a close friend of Georges Seurat, and a propagandist for Neo-Impressionism. He was born in Paris, of well-to-do parents. His early paintings (*c*1880–4) show the influence of Monet and Armand Guillaumin. He met Seurat in 1884; both artists showed in the Salon des Artistes Indépendants, a juryless exhibiting society founded in Paris in May 1884. Signac introduced Pissarro to Seurat in 1885: the result was a strong group of Neo-Impressionist artists who showed at the last Impressionist exhibition and at the Salon des Indépendants of 1886.

From then until Seurat's death in 1891, the discoveries of the new movement were articulated and expanded. After 1891, Signac saw himself increasingly as the personification of Neo-Impressionism. The most lasting result of this was his book, *D'Eugène Delacroix au Neo-Impressionistes*, published in Paris in 1899, which influenced Matisse and Derain.

In Signac's own paintings, his early Impressionist phase was followed by his main Neo-Impressionist period (1884–1900), in which he exemplified the theoretical basis of the movement. His subject matter included views of Paris, of the Seine, of the Channel coast, and of the south of France. He settled in St Tropez in 1893. After 1900, the pointillist dots were enlarged into brush strokes that were predominantly square. He painted most of the harbors in France in this style (he was a keen yachtsman). He admired J.M.W. Turner, and the Dutch artist J.B. Jongkind, about whom he published a monograph in 1927. Signac's watercolors, more freshly convinced and spontaneously painted than his oils, show the influence of these two artists.

Signac maintained his allegiance to the Salon des Indépendants until his death, fulfilling the office of President with enthusiasm and tenacity.

Luca Signorelli: Portrait of Dante; fresco; 1499–1504. S. Brizio Chapel, Orvieto Cathedral

Signorelli Luca *c*1450–1523

The Italian painter Luca Signorelli was born in Cortona. Little is known of his early years, but his surviving works support Vasari's claim that Piero della Francesca first taught him to paint. The pattern of Signorelli's career is similar to that of his teacher's. He, too, became an important provincial artist, who, though he visited Florence, set up a *bottega* in his small native town. During the half-century of Signorelli's activity, from *c*1470 to 1523, he produced a great many paintings; these were mostly for churches in and around Cortona, but also for important churches in more distant places, such as Loreto, Rome, and Orvieto.

In his early works, Signorelli was an important innovator who infused fresh dynamism into the monumental, sculptural style he had learned from Piero della Francesca. His *Flagellation of Christ* (*c*1480; Pinacoteca di Brera, Milan) and the Vagnucci Altarpiece (1484; Museo dell'Opera del Duomo, Perugia), show that he cultivated a new style at once grand and lively, as did his Florentine contemporaries Sandro Botticelli and Leonardo da Vinci. Signorelli is also important because he built upon the achievements of Antonio Pollaiuolo to develop a plausible formula for depicting the body in movement, and extending its expressive range.

Signorelli's frescoes in the S. Brizio Chapel (1499–1504; Orvieto Cathedral) secured his fame as a master of the nude figure. In eight large scenes Signorelli turned the Last Judgment into a narrative that begins with *The Preaching of the Anti-Christ* and ends with *The Crowning of the Blessed in Paradise*. Nude figures abound—twisted into *grotteschi* in the dadoes, contorted to express emotions of violent fear, pain, or joy in the Apocalyptic scenes. Those powerful, often brutal male nudes influenced not only Michelangelo but also, much later, Delacroix, Cézanne, and Max Beckmann.

Further reading. Kury, G. *The Early Work of Luca Signorelli 1465–1490*, New York (1978).

Siloe Gil de *fl.* 1475–*c*1505

Little is known of the origins or life of Gil de Siloe, one of the greatest sculptors of the Iberian peninsula, save that he was almost certainly Flemish by birth and training, and was possibly a native of Antwerp. It can only be said with certainty that by 1475 he was established in Burgos, and that his highly individual style was already well-formed and confident. By 1498 he was a property owner in Burgos. The apparent ending of his activities soon after the beginning of the 16th century suggests that he died *c*1505. He had one known son, Diego de Siloe, the architect of Granada Cathedral.

The works of Gil de Siloe are few, and are confined to the region of Burgos. At the time of his rather abrupt appearance in 1475, he was working on the tomb of Bishop D. Alonso de Cartagena in Burgos Cathedral. His two altarpieces in the cathedral may date from around the same period. His finest works were executed in the Cartuja de Miraflores between 1486 and 1499: there were the tombs of Juan II of Castille and Isabel of Portugal (1486), and of their son Don Alfonso (*c*1489). His masterpiece was the high altar of the same church (*c*1499), made with the collaboration of Diego de la Cruz. His last commission seems to have been the tomb of the page Juan de Padilla, in the monastery of Fresdelval (*c*1503).

The distinctive style of Gil de Siloe may reflect his northern origins. His delight in intricate but solid values, and especially in fabrics and embroidery, recalls the pleasure in textures to be found in Flemish painting. His concern with the expression of minute detail has invited comparison with gold- and silverwork, and is clearly related to the tastes that generated Plateresque architecture.

The tomb of Juan and Isabel is exceptionally complex. The richly dressed figures, separated by a grille of great intricacy and each with an equally intricate canopy, lie side by side on a geometrical base in the form of an eight-pointed star; they are attended by the Virtues and Old Testament figures. The monument to their son occupies a separate position on the wall; the boy kneels in prayer in the confines of a richly ornamental niche.

These works were executed in alabaster, but the high altar of Miraflores, in gilded wood, demonstrates the flexibility of Gil de Siloe's art. The work is dominated by an immense Christ, flanked by St Peter and St Paul. Yet, as with the tomb of Juan and Isabel, profusion is controlled by a strict geometrical and human structure. What might, in the hands of a lesser sculptor, have been a mass of sugary ornament, is always kept in check by an underlying strength of line. However great his delight in the richness of the superficial, Gil de Siloe was wholly conscious that his subject was the human form.

Simone Martini 1280/5?–1344

Simone di Martino, called Simone Martini, was an Italian painter of the Sienese school. His first certain work, the *Maestà* (1315) in the Sala del Mappamondo of Siena Town Hall or Palazzo Pubblico, suggests an apprenticeship in the studio of Duccio. It also reveals a knowledge of Florentine painting, both in the logical and unified treatment of space and light, and in specific features such as the kneeling angels bearing flower bowls at the foot of the Virgin's throne, derived directly from those in Giotto's *Ognissanti Madonna*. In this painting there are still clear Byzantine features, but during the course of Simone's career these are replaced by a feeling for line, decoration, and form which is derived rather from French Gothic art.

This French Gothic influence was introduced through a variety of channels, of which the French court in Naples was an important one. The King of Naples, Robert of Anjou, summoned Simone to Naples before 1317. He commissioned the artist to depict him kneeling at the feet of his elder brother, St Louis of Toulouse, who had abandoned the secular for the monastic life and resigned his dynastic rights and duties to Robert (*St Louis of Toulouse Crowning Robert of Anjou, King of Naples*; Museo e Gallerie Nazionali di Capodimonte, Naples). The *predella* panels show scenes from the life of St Louis, and in them for the first time the perspective of all five scenes is unified around a central axis.

By 1320 Simone had returned to Tuscany, painting altarpieces that are now in Pisa and Orvieto. In 1333 he signed and dated a panel painting depicting the *Annunciation* (Uffizi, Florence); according to the inscription, this was painted in partnership with his brother-in-law Lippo Memmi da Siera. Here the figure of the Virgin, suddenly disturbed by the Angel, is surrounded by an agitated line tracing the outline of her drapery, and her emotion is conveyed largely by means of this line.

At some time in the 1320s or 1330s Simone painted murals in the Chapel of St Martin in the Lower Church of St Francis at Assisi. As the result of another State commission, he depicted the figure of the commander of the recently victorious Sienese army, Guidoriccio da Fogliano (*c*1328), on the wall facing his *Maestà* in the Palazzo Pubblico, Siena. In these works Simone shows himself to be a skilled landscape painter, within the admitted limitations of the time.

The artist's last years were spent in Avignon, the seat of the Papacy for much of the 14th century. Petrarch, whom the artist met there, thanked him for a portrait of his beloved Laura in two Sonnets datable to before November 1336. This literary reference securely places Simone's first visit to Avignon before that date, although Sienese records put his final departure from Siena in late 1340. It also records, by referring to Simone's exact depiction of Laura's features in the now-lost portrait, Simone's interest at an early date in the precise imitation of facial features. His main works in Avignon, murals painted in the cathedral there, survive only fragmentarily although their appearance is known through copies. Simone, or more probably some French follower of his, has been held responsible for the highly ornamental hunting scenes decorating the walls of the Guardaroba in the Palais des Papes.

Among the surviving works from this time are the small but exquisite panel depicting *The Holy Family* (Walker Art Gallery, Liverpool), the six panels of the Antwerp Passion Polyptych (1340s; Royal Museum of Fine Arts, Antwerp, and Staatliche Museen, Berlin), and the frontispiece to Petrarch's copy of Virgil's *Aeneid* (Pinacoteca Ambrosiana, Milan). As in the Uffizi *Annunciation*, the later panel paintings make considerable dramatic use of the surrounding outline silhouetting the figures against the rich golden background. But the linear element in Simone's paintings never predominates to the exclusion of his sophisticated interest in spatial construction.

It was the combination of these talents, linear and spatial, together with an ability to imitate nature and to render and balance colors (inherited from Duccio), that ensured that his work would influence and inspire many later artists. In Italy and more especially in France, the school of miniaturists that developed in the Burgundian court during the 14th century often found their models in works by Simone.

Further reading. Edgell, G.H. *A History of Sienese Painting*, New York (1932). Paccagnini, G. *Simone Martini*, Milan (1955).

Sinan 1491–1588

Sinan was the greatest Ottoman architect, at a time when building was that culture's major form of artistic expression. He was born in 1491 in Kayseri, Anatolia. He was of Greek parentage, but was brought up in the Janissary school as a Muslim and a soldier. He fought in Rhodes (1520), and in the Hungarian campaign that culminated in Suleyman's great victory at Mohacs (1526). During this period Sinan served as a military engineer; he won notice from the Sultan for skilled bridging of the Danube and was promoted to the rank of captain. It was at this time that he first displayed his administrative gifts.

He was appointed Master of the Works in 1538 and held this post for 50 years, until his death in his 97th year. He remained a skilled military engineer as well as an architect. In 1539 he built his first mosque, at Aleppo, and in 1541 his first *türbe* (tomb chamber) for Barbarossa, at Besiktas on the Bosphorus. This was of classical octagonal form, in Marmara marble. At Usküdar, on a difficult site between shore and hillside, he built a mosque and madrasa for the Sultan's daughter Mihrimar, wife of Rustam Pasha (1548). It was erected on a podium, with a double portico facing towards the sea.

His greatest accomplishment was the building of the great complex round the Sultan's own mosque: *türbe*, bath house, caravansaries, and seven colleges, the whole completed in seven years by 1557. Here he showed his liking for the austere, with a limited use of tiles, but with clear articulation into 16 sections rising to a high dome with two semidomes and two great arches, as at St Sophia (Istanbul). The tiles used here in the mihrab and the *türbe* of Roxelana (1558) are superb examples of Iznik red and blue floral designs. Even more splendid are the tiles that cover the interior of the mosque of Rustam Pasha (1561), the building raised above the podium as an octagon set in a square.

His masterpiece is the great mosque at Edirne, built for Selim II. This was conceived in 1569, when Sinan was 78, and finished in 1575. Here the architect shows his genius in the organization of space and his skillful use of contrasts in stone and tiles, all with the finest detail.

Siqueiros David 1898–1974

The Mexican mural painter David Alfaro Siqueiros was born in Chihuahua and studied at the Academy of San Carlo in Mexico City. He played an active role in the revolutionary and economic struggles of his time as well as in the Mexican mural renaissance along with Orozco and Rivera. From 1919 to 1922 he traveled and studied in Belgium, France, Italy, and Spain. In 1932, and again in 1940, he was banished from Mexico because of his revolutionary politics. In 1936 he organized the Experimental Workshop in New York which was attended by Jackson Pollock.

Siqueiros was a technical innovator and attempted to revolutionize the materials, tools, and compositional forms of mural painting. This involved the use of spray guns and plastic paints, and led him to create the "New Realism" (with Surrealist elements), in order to convey his revolutionary message (for example, *Revolution against the Dictatorship of Porfirio Diaz: The Strike in Cananea*; pyroxilin; 1957; National History Museum, Mexico City).

Further reading. Charlot, J. (ed.) *An Artist on Art* vol. 2, Honolulu (1972). Charlot, J. *The Mexican Mural Renaissance 1920–5*, London and New Haven (1963). Reed, A.M. *The Mexican Muralists*, New York (1960). Rodriquez, A. *A History of Mexican Mural Painting*, London (1969). Siqueiros, D. *Art and Revolution*, New York (1975).

Sisley Alfred 1839–99

The Impressionist painter Alfred Sisley had English parents, but was born in Paris and spent his childhood there. He was in London from 1857 to 1861, preparing for a commercial career, and apparently studied the work of J.M.W. Turner and John Constable at that time. In 1862, having decided to become a painter, he entered the Paris studio of Charles Gleyre, where he met Monet, Renoir, and Frédéric Bazille. These friendships shaped the direction of his career.

In the later 1860s, he worked in the tradition of the Barbizon School landscapists, painting forest and village scenes in comparatively subdued color. One of these, *Avenue of Chestnut Trees near the Celle-Saint-Cloud* (Southampton Art Gallery) was shown at the 1868 Salon. In 1869 he began to paint Parisian scenes, and in 1870 exhibited at the Salon two small, informal views of the Canal Saint-Martin in Paris (*View of the Canal Saint-Martin*, Musée du Jeu de Paume, Paris; *Barges on the Canal Saint-Martin*, Sammlung Oskar Reinhart "Am Römerholz", Winterthur). These paintings are varied in brushwork and focus on atmospheric qualities; in many ways they anticipate the characteristic Impressionist landscapes of the early 1870s.

Between 1872 and 1880, Sisley lived mainly in the countryside west of Paris, around Marly and Louveciennes. In 1872, he worked with Monet at Argenteuil, and in 1874 spent four months in England, painting at Hampton Court. He exhibited in the first three Impressionist group exhibitions, in 1874, 1876, and 1877. More than any of the other Impressionists, he limited himself to landscape painting. He harnessed the varied touch and sensitivity to atmosphere of his 1870 canal scenes to the depiction of the Seine Valley, its villages and its countryside.

The paintings he did between 1872 and 1876 are of moderate size (rarely more than 30 in or 75 cm across), and show great responsiveness to the variety of natural lighting and textures. They share many features with Pissarro's work of 1871 to 1873. In these works Sisley sets off small, crisply painted accents against softer and broader areas of paint, to create subtle and carefully organized rhythms and patterns, as in *The Road to Sèvres* (1873; Musée du Jeu de Paume, Paris). Sometimes the rhythms are bolder, as in *The Weir at Molesey near Hampton Court* (1874; National Gallery of Scotland, Edinburgh). Like the other Impressionists, Sisley began in the early 1870s to introduce an increasing range of color to his landscapes; blues, in particular, are used to express shadow, and foliage is conveyed by a great variety of greens.

Later in the 1870s, Sisley began to adopt busier, more broken brushwork all over the picture, to animate the whole canvas —as in *The Seine at Suresnes* (1877; Musée du Jeu de Paume, Paris). In 1880 he moved to the area around Moret, near the junction of the Seine and Loing rivers, southeast of Paris and near the forest of Fontainebleau. Here he lived and painted for the rest of his life, in increasing seclu-

Alfred Sisley: View of the Canal Saint-Martin, Paris; oil on canvas; 50×65cm (20×26in); 1870. Musée du Jeu de Paume, Paris

sion; he traveled to paint only in 1894 (to Normandy) and 1897 (to the South Wales coast). In his later works, the touch is sometimes coarser and the color less sensitively used than in his best paintings of the 1870s, but at times his elaborate paint surfaces rival the richness of Monet's.

Further reading. Cogniat, R. *Sisley*, New York (1978). Shone, R. *Sisley*, New York (1979).

Škréta Karel 1610–74

A member of the aristocratic family of Šotnovský z Závořice, the painter Karel Škréta left Bohemia in 1628 to live with his mother in Saxony. As a Protestant, he spent ten years in exile, mostly in Italy, where he received his artistic training. He became a Catholic, and by 1650 was established as the leading painter in Prague. His portraits are distinguished by a sober realism expressed with extreme economy of color and strong chiaroscuro. The same qualities are apparent in his remarkable cycle depicting *The Legend of St Wenceslas* (1641–3; Mělník Castle). His later altarpieces, however, are more emotional and dramatic.

Sloan John 1871–1951

The American painter John Sloan was the leader of the group known as The Eight (of 1908), and of the Ashcan School in New York. He worked as a journalist in Philadelphia from 1871 to 1891, teaching himself to draw and to etch during these years. Encouraged by Robert Henri, he began to paint in 1897. Sloan was an illustrator, painter, and etcher, and organizer of the group exhibitions of the Ashcan School. He was a leading figure in the realist attack on the academy system's control of taste and patronage in America. Sloan's art was based on sympathetic observation rather than exposure or satire. It was at its best in his etchings, and in his paintings of the New York scene such as *Dust Storm, Fifth Avenue* (oil on canvas; 1906; Metropolitan Museum, New York) and *McSorley's Bar* (oil on canvas; 1912; Detroit Institute of Arts). (*See* overleaf.)

John Sloan: Southwest Art; oil on canvas; 53×64cm (21×25in); 1920. Collection of the Anschutz Corporation, Denver, Colo.

Slodtz family 17th and 18th centuries

The sculptor René-Michael Slodtz (1705–64) was also known as Michel-Ange Slodtz. One of the five sons of the sculptor Sebastien Slodtz (1665–1726), a Flemish-born sculptor and a former pupil of Girardon who settled in Paris, René-Michael won first prize for sculpture at the Académie in 1726, then left for Rome in 1728, returning in 1746. In Rome he developed a style that was full-bloodedly Baroque, yet sensitive to the germs of Neoclassicism. His chief Roman works were the St Bruno (for a niche at the crossing of St Peter's, Rome), and a bust for the tomb of Nicolas Vleughels in S. Luigi dei Francesi, Rome (1736; Musée Jacquemart—André, Paris). The monument to Archbishops La Tour d'Auvergue and Montmorin, (in St Maurice, Vienna) are among his other important works.

The *St Bruno* employs a variety of Baroque effects with consummate skill. The composition is at the point of apparent fragmentation—the saint's refusal of the crozier and miter of a bishopric, proffered by a child-angel, is expressed as much by the agitated twist of the drapery as by the gesture itself. The Montmorin monument (1740–4), and the monument to Languet de Glergy in St-Sulpice, completed in Paris in 1753, are equally Baroque. They borrow from Bernini not only their partly narrative, partly symbolic conception, but also the polychromy of differing metals and marbles. In sharp contrast is the Capponi Monument, S. Giovanni dei Fiorentini, Rome. Dating from the early 1740s, it shows Slodtz equally at home in a less rhetorical, more seriously classicizing style.

His brothers Sebastian-Antoine (*c*1695–1754) and Paul-Amboise Slodtz (1702–58) were also sculptors. They followed their father into the *Menus-Plaisirs du Roi*, producing *pompes-funèbres* and other ephemeral displays for the Court. Of the the two, only Paul-Amboise was a sculptor of merit, although his work is usually minor and decorative.

Sluter Claus *c*1350–1406

Claus Sluter was a Netherlandish sculptor whose career in the service of the Dukes of Burgundy left a permanent imprint on Burgundian art, and whose profound realism heralded a new phase in the art of northern Europe. His surviving works are concentrated in Dijon, where he was one of a number of distinguished artists engaged by Philip the Bold, Duke of Burgundy, to embellish the Carthusian monastery (the Chartreuse de Champmol) that he founded to house the tombs of the Burgundian dukes. The monastery was attacked during the French Revolution and later demolished, but the portal with Sluter's sculptures, and the remains of his monumental fountain in the large cloister remained *in situ*, and were incorporated into the design of the hospital built on the site. The ducal tombs were restored, and are now in the Musée des Beaux-Arts, Dijon.

Sluter's early career is obscure. Most of our information about him comes from the Burgundian archives, where he is documented from March 1385 until his death early in 1406. Various spellings of the name occur, but the form "Claus Sluter" was used by the artist himself for the design of his seal. He was born in Haarlem, in the county of Holland, but gravitated to Brussels, where he was inscribed in the stonemasons' guild *c*1380. He probably acquired some reputation in Brabant and Flanders at this time, and some of his contemporaries in the stonemasons' guild later came to work under his direction in Dijon. But apart from some statuettes of prophets from the Town Hall of Brussels (now in the Musée Communal de Saint-Lambert-Woluwe) no known surviving work relates very closely to his mature style.

In 1385 Sluter went to Dijon to join the workshop of Jean de Marville, who was then chief sculptor to the Duke of Burgundy. On Marville's death in 1389 he assumed contol of the workshop and was designated *valet de chambre* to the Duke. All the works stamped by his very individual style date from this time onwards. Apart from a few excursions made on behalf of the Duke (to Paris in 1392, to Mehun-sur-Yèvre in 1393, and to Dinant and Malines in 1395) he remained in Burgundy. A major work, known to have been done by him at this time but now lost, was the very original decoration of the château of Germolles (1396), where the Duke and Duchess were portrayed at its entrance in a pastoral scene.

The background to all Sluter's Burgundian activity was the sculpture for the Chartreuse de Champmol. Two of the major works associated with him at the Chartreuse were begun before he himself was in control of the workshop. The architectural framework of the Duke's tomb had already been completed, and the portal of the church (consecrated in 1388) had been built to a design by the Duke's architect Drouet de Dammartin. This was probably done in consultation with Marville, and was probably intended to include only three sculptures—standing figures of the Duke and Duchess, on either side of a *trumeau* figure of the Virgin. Sluter's dynamic transformation of this Parisian formula shows the independence of his creative approach. Huge consoles jut out and beyond the architectural framework, disregarding the limitations of the original design, to support additional figures of St John the Baptist and St Catherine. The two saints bend forward to present the kneeling figures of the Duke and Duchess to the Virgin. The drama of the presentation is intensified by the way in which the saints appear almost to surge forward towards the Virgin; she looks at the Child, who in turn looks up to where there was once a canopy of angels. The exaggerated scale of the saints in comparison to the Virgin suggests a type of stage perspective, in which the down-to-earth realism of the Duke and Duchess supply the human elements in a transcendental happening.

From 1395, Sluter was involved in the planning and execution of one of his greatest works. The *Puits de Moise* or *Well of Moses* is only a part of the monumental fountain that once dominated the large cloister of Chartreuse, which was also the monks' cemetery. It originally served as the hexagonal base for a tall Calvary—the whole being conceived as a "Fountain of Life". Only fragments of the Calvary, including the torso of Christ, survive (Musée Archéologique, Dijon). But the hexagonal base with its figures of six prophets (who predict the inevitability of the Crucifixion), and the angels (who mourn the sacrifice on the symbolic Mount Golgotha), are among the great sculptures of all time. Each of the prophets (Moses, David, Jeremiah, Zachariah, Daniel, and Isaiah) is interpreted with unprecedented realism, and with a psychological penetration that was only to be equalled later by Rembrandt. The fountain as originally painted and gilded must have been spectacular. Its deep religious significance and spiritual power were recognized by the granting of indulgences to pilgrims who visited it in the 15th century.

Although the tomb of Philip the Bold had been one of the first monuments to occupy Marville's workshop, Sluter seems to have been reluctant to bring it to a speedy completion. When the Duke died in April 1404, only two mourning figures (or *pleurants*) had been completed. They were the forerunners of the now-famous funeral procession that now surrounds the tomb. Sluter's own death in January 1406 undoubtedly frustrated the wishes of John the Fearless to have his father's tomb completed within a period of four years. But the final conception bears every mark of Sluter's personality, and it seems likely that his nephew, Claus de Werve, who finished the tomb by 1410, followed his uncle's designs.

As the tomb stands today the effigy of Philip is a modern restoration, but the *pleurants* survived the Revolution, and are remarkable for the range and depth of their expression. Sluter's idea of surrounding the tomb with a solemn liturgical procession was not new, but every detail of the procession is permeated by a new realism and a new sense of drama. Even when the facial expressions are concealed beneath heavy mourning garments, the attitudes of the figures and the fall of drapery can still emanate a profound emotional effect.

Sluter was a medieval artist with the

Claus Sluter: David and Jeremiah, two of the six prophets on the base of the Well of Moses; stone; 1395–1406. Musée Archéologique, Dijon

individuality of a Renaissance personality, and the patronage of Philip the Bold enabled him to express this. Contemporary painters and sculptors, caught in the decorative artificiality of the International Gothic style, found in his work the inspiration to explore for themselves a more deeply realistic approach to the problems of art.

Further reading. David, H. *Claus Sluter*, Paris (1951). Finn, D. *Claus Sluter*, London (1991). Liebreich, A. *Claus Sluter*, Brussels (1936). Monget, C. *La Chartreuse de Dijon* (3 vols.), Montreuil-sur-Mer and Tournai (1895–1905). Quarré, P. *La Chartreuse de Champmol*, Dijon (1960). Quarré, P. *Les Pleurants des Tombeaux des Ducs de Bourgogne*, Dijon (1971).

Smith David 1906–65

The American sculptor David Smith was born at Decatur, Indiana. He studied art first (by a correspondence course) at the Cleveland School of Art, and then at Ohio University (1924–5). In the summer of 1925, he worked in the steel frame assembly department at the Studebaker plant. The experience contributed to his lifelong skill as a worker in metal, and also left him with an equally long-lasting affection for machinery.

In 1926 he moved to New York, where he studied painting at the Art Students League of New York (1926–32). It was during this period that he became familiar with Cubism, which was to exert a considerable influence on his development. He also saw in a magazine reproductions of welded-steel sculpture by Picasso. Smith produced his first welded-steel piece in 1932; and throughout the 1930s and 1940s he created a whole series of sculpture in which the influence of both Picasso and Julio Gonzalez is apparent (for example, *Star Cage*, 1950; University of Minnesota, Minneapolis; *Aerial Construction*, 1936; Joseph Hirshhorn Museum, Washington, D.C.).

During the Second World War, he worked in a locomotive factory. The scale of the engines influenced his sculptural thinking and led, many years later, to the series of sculptures by which he will perhaps be best remembered. These are the very large-scale, freestanding pieces that he produced in the machine shop of his farm at Bolton Landing, New York State. They are sometimes still markedly linear in character (for example, *Sentinal IV*, 1957; private collection).

The most striking of them, which were to influence the general development of Minimal art in America, are those of the so-called *Cubi* series. They are made out of cubes and cylinders of stainless steel, polished and then abraded; they are often balanced one on top of another in a seemingly precarious manner (for example, *Cubi XIX*, 1964, Tate Gallery, London; *Cubi XVII*, 1963, Dallas Museum of Fine Arts). Smith, who was the most original American sculptor of his generation, was killed in an automobile accident in 1965.

Further reading. Carandente, G. et al. *David Smith in Italy*, Milan (1995). Merkert, J. *David Smith: Sculpture and Drawings*, Munich (1986). Pachner, J. *David Smith Photographs 1931–1965*, New York (1998). Smith, C. et al. *The Fields of David Smith*, London (1999). Wilkin, K. *David Smith*, New York (1984). Wilkin, K. *David Smith: Two into Three Dimensions*, Miami, FL (2000).

Matthew Smith: Lilies in a Vase; oil on canvas; 74×53cm (29×21in); 1913–14. City Art Gallery, Leeds

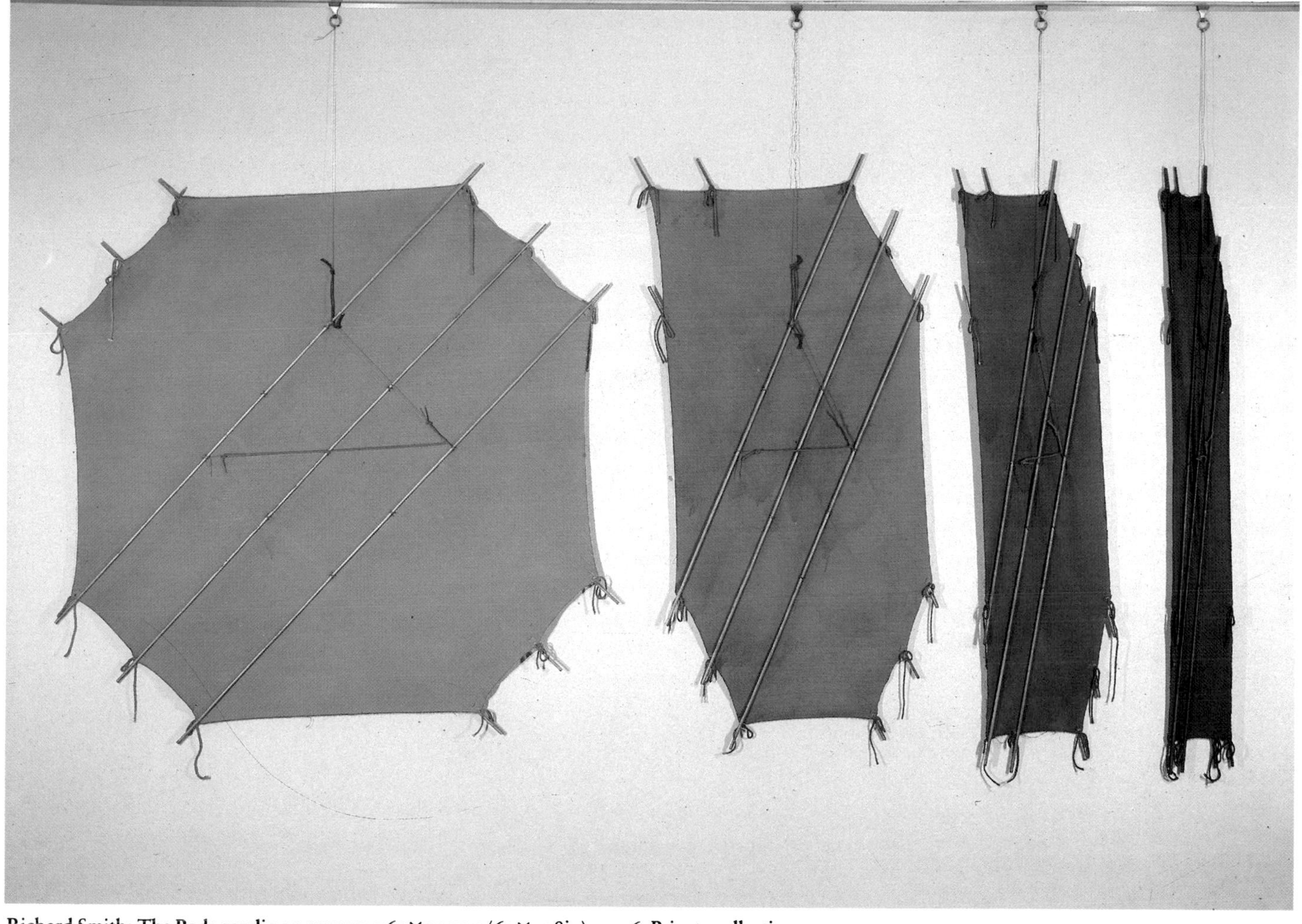

Richard Smith: The Pod; acrylic on canvas; 160×325cm (63×128in); 1976. Private collection

Smith Matthew 1879–1959

The English painter Sir Matthew Smith studied at the Manchester School of Art (1900–4), and the Slade School of Fine Art (1905–7), but drew his real inspiration from France. Between 1908 and 1912 he spent most of his time in Pont-Aven, Étaples, and Paris, slowly imbibing the influence of Gauguin and Matisse (he spent a month at Matisse's school). The resultant works, painted when he was back in London (for example, *Nude, Fitzroy Street, No. 1*, 1916; Tate Gallery, London), are related to paintings by the Camden Town artists, but are more Fauve in color. This boldness also characterizes the Cornish landscapes he painted in 1920. Thereafter his colors became less strident and took on a subdued sensuosity that matched the baroque richness of his nudes and still lifes.

Smith Richard 1931–

The English painter Richard Smith was born in Letchworth, Hertfordshire. He studied at Luton School and the St Albans School of Art (1948–54) and at the Royal College of Art (1954–7). He taught mural decoration at Hammersmith College of Art, London (1957–8), and spent the years 1959 and 1960 on a Harkness Fellowship in the United States. He taught at St Martin's School of Art (1961–3) and has held various teaching posts in the U.S.A. (1965–8). He was a prize winner at the Venice Biennale in 1966 and at São Paulo in 1967.

From 1961 to 1969 most of Smith's paintings were based on advertising images. In the early 1960s his loosely and elegantly painted pictures in heraldic colors were succeeded by large three-dimensional shaped relief paintings inspired by billboards. Smith's interest in the constructed supports then led to very long paintings made up of complicated modular sections, with blurred, spray-painted imagery, such as *Riverfall* (1969; Tate Gallery, London). In the early 1970s he reacted against the complexity of his earlier work and began painting on loosely stretched canvas on light, aluminum tube, in which strings and ties are left visible. These paintings may be in series or may combine two or more overlapping canvases. Smith has also made prints on the same theme using folded card or paper with ribbons.

Smith Tony 1912–80

The American sculptor, painter, and architect Tony Smith was born in South Orange, New Jersey. He studied part-time at the Art Students League, New York (1935–6), and at the New Bauhaus, Chicago (1937–8). In the following year he worked on architectural projects under Frank Lloyd Wright. Between 1940 and 1960 he designed houses, and also monuments that were not in fact built. He spent the years 1953 to 1955 in Germany. He taught at Bennington College, Vermont (1958–61), and at Hunter College, New York (1962–6).

Most of his work before 1960 was architectural, though he did some paintings and reliefs during the late 1930s that were influenced by Georges Vantongerloo. In 1961 he produced his first sculptures (for example, *Gracehoper*; Detroit Institute of Arts). These were constructed from pure geometrical modules, sliced, beveled, and truncated, and combined according to classical ratios with an architectural sensibility. Massive and austere, these intuitively controlled forms separate him from most Minimalist sculptors with whom he tends to be identified. In the late 1960s his structures became more complicated, based on multifaceted solids and repeated modules. His works originate as paper maquettes and plywood mock-ups, which are later executed in steel, welded bronze, or marble.

Smithson Robert 1938–73

Robert Smithson, the American "land" artist, writer, and visionary theorist, was born in New Jersey. He studied part-time at the Art Students League, New York (1953–6), and then at the Brooklyn Museum School. In the mid 1960s his sculptures were associated with Minimalism, but a group of transitional works, the *Mirror Displacements* and *Non-sites*, led him to make the large earth-works for which he is best known. Notable among these are *Spiral Jetty* (1970; Utah), a spiral of earth created in the Great Salt Lake, and *Amarillo Ramp* (1973; Texas). The latter work was completed after Smithson had been killed in a plane crash on the site. Few of his many large earthwork proposals were carried out.

Snyders Frans 1579–1657

Frans Snyders was a Flemish painter of animals and still-life subjects. He worked in Antwerp on his return from a visit to Italy between 1608 and 1609. He painted animals and still-life details in the pictures of Rubens and Jacob Jordaens. Rubens, in turn, painted the figures in a number of Snyders' hunting scenes. These are pictures of boar and stag hunts which, like those of fighting animals, contain exuberant color and vigorous movement. The vitality and freedom of style in these works was extended to Snyders' cornucopian still lifes. These blend the meticulous realism of the flower and fruit paintings of Pieter Bruegel the Younger (by whom Snyders was trained) with both formal and literal movement—the latter through the inclusion of animated cats, dogs, and birds.

Soami *c*1470–1525

Soami, also known as Shinso, was a Japanese ink painter who specialized in landscape. He was the third of the "three -amis", his father and grandfather being the painters Geiami (1431–85) and Noami (1397–1471). Although all were ink painters, none were Zen devotees. They came from the artisan class whose names often ended "-ami" to indicate their belief in the savior Buddha Amida. All three painters worked at cataloging the Shogun's collection of paintings and *objets d'art* (nearly all of which were Chinese). Their influence as arbiters of taste probably caused the takeover of the Academy by the non-Zen *Kano* School.

Little is known of Soami's life, though a good many of his paintings survive. He is best known for his "wet" style, but he could paint in a number of other manners. His versatility was derived from his study of the Shogun's Chinese collection, which he viewed in an aesthetic and nonreligious way. This is a very important transition in Japanese painting. His *Viewing a Waterfall in the Lu Mountains* (*c*1508; private collection) is done in the "square style" with firmly angled rocks and mountains and straight hatching, but the middle ground is filled with vaporous mists, giving an almost sensuous feeling of distance. This "hard and soft" mixture is very Japanese, and became a feature of the *Kano* School.

His greatest work is certainly the set of sliding doors of *c*1513 from the Daisen'in (Daitokuji Temple, Kyoto), now mounted as hanging scrolls. It is a great panorama

Il Sodoma: St George and the Dragon; panel; 138×98cm (54×38in); c1516. National Gallery of Art, Washington, D.C.

done in wet wash (much influenced by Southern Sung) with almost no outline, combining grandeur with a credibly Japanese scale. Similar works with a feeling of total fluidity are the sixfold screens in the Metropolitan Museum, New York.

Sodoma Il 1477–1549

Together with Peruzzi and Beccafumi, Giovanni Antonio Bazzi, known as Il Sodoma, was one of the leading painters of early-16th-century Siena. Trained in his native Vercelli, he arrived in Siena by *c*1503, apparently already conversant with the Milanese works of Leonardo. He worked in Rome in 1508, and again from 1516 to 1518, as a large-scale decorator under the patronage of Agostino Chigi. He was only superficially influenced by the mature Raphael; and despite a certain response to Florentine Mannerism and to the art of Beccafumi, in his later career, after *c*1520, his style increasingly reverted to its provincial roots.

Solimena Francesco 1657–1747

Francesco Solimena, the Italian painter of the early Rococo, was born in Nocera. He was the leading Neapolitan painter during the first half of the 18th century. Having arrived in Naples by 1674, he was influenced by Luca Giordano, particularly in the frescoes of the sacristy of S. Paolo Maggiore, Naples (1690). After 1692 the influence of Mattia Preti is also discernible, and thereafter a darker color range is employed in his works: this quality is typical of his style. There are important frescoes of his late period in Naples, in S. Maria Donnaregina, S. Domenico Maggiore, and the Gesù Nuovo.

Sonderborg 1923–

The Danish-German artist Kurt R. Hoffmann, known from his place of birth as Sonderborg, was originally trained for a business career. He decided, however, to become a painter and attended the Landeskunstschule in Hamburg (1947–9). In 1951 he visited Italy. He studied graphics with S.W. Hayter in Paris in 1953 and became a member of the "Zen 49" group (1956–7). He began teaching at the Academy of Art in Stuttgart in 1965. From 1969 to 1970 he taught at the College of Art and Design in Minneapolis.

Automatism, speed, and movement are basic to Sonderborg's work. Through a drip technique, and the use of many different tools for scratching and digging at the surface of his canvases, he aims to catch fleeting impressions (for example, *13.11.58/2107–2156*; gouache; 1958; Museum Bochum, Bochum).

Sophilos *fl.* *c*580–570 BC

Sophilos was an Athenian painter and potter. He is the first black-figure artist whose name is known, from four inscribed vases; three of these are signed by him as painter and one as potter.

His early career emerged from the old-fashioned school of Athenian artists,

Francesco Solimena: Dido Receiving Aeneas and Cupid Disguised as Ascanius; oil on canvas; 207×310cm (81×122in); 1720s. National Gallery, London

headed by the Gorgon Painter, whose major preoccupation was with the animal frieze style that they had learned from their rivals in Corinth. This involved covering the vase with numerous horizontal zones of animals (interspersed with florals), coursing monotonously round the pot. An *amphora* from Vourva (now in the National Museum, Athens) represents one of his many unsigned pieces decorated in this diehard style. The troop of animals and mechanical florals—weary and debased versions of the Gorgon Painter's more thoughtful and meticulous compositions—characterize the early achievement of Sophilos as a leading exponent of the conventional.

His important contribution to the history of black-figure painting came only after he had relegated the animal parades to an unobtrusive position on his vases. This done, he applied himself wholeheartedly to decorating vases with scenes from myth. A fragment of a *dinos* found in Thessaly (now in the National Museum, Athens) reveals Sophilos as an enterprising, if clumsy, proponent of early narrative art. The animals make an appearance on the lip and lower frieze; but the artist's prime concern is to depict a chariot race, with an animated team of horses galloping past a stand packed with gesticulating spectators. The artist proudly claims responsibility for the questionable draftsmanship—the vase is inscribed "Sophilos painted me". He goes on to say that this is no common race, but rather an excerpt from the *Iliad*.

A *dinos* resting on its own stand and signed by Sophilos as painter (British Museum, London), further illustrates his commitment to myth. Animals and florals occupy eight horizontal zones, while the upper frieze contains the main subject: the arrival of divine guests at the wedding festivities of Peleus and Thetis. The guests proceed round the vase to the house of the bridegroom, who stands before its closed doors, wine-cup in hand. There are fragments of another *dinos*, depicting the same scene and signed by Sophilos as painter, in the National Museum, Athens. The next painter to illustrate the celebrated wedding feast was Sophilos' younger and more fastidious follower, Kleitias, whose volute-*krater* is a true masterpiece of narrative painting: the animals are banished to a single subsidiary frieze, and five zones are devoted entirely to myth. This work, known as the François Vase, is in the Museo Archeologico, Florence.

Sophilos occupied a key position in Attic painting, as the last of a generation of animal frieze painters, and a pioneer in the formation of Greek narrative art. Although his enthusiasm as a story-teller usually surpassed his talents as a draftsman he had clearly paved the way for successors such as Kleitias.

Sosen Mori 1747–1821

The Japanese animal painter of the Edo period, Mori Sosen, worked mainly in Osaka. He learned painting from a *Kano* artist, but was clearly influenced by the naturalism of Okyo, though he was never his pupil. He became a specialist in painting monkeys, deer, and other furry animals. He is said to have studied wild monkeys in the mountains for three years. His animals are extraordinarily alive, whether done in the minute, detailed brushwork of his early style, or in the more free and dashing hand of his last years. Numerous forgeries have detracted from his reputation. His descendants (all called Mori), Yusen, Tessan, and Ippo, continued Sosen's tradition.

Sotatsu Tawaraya *fl. c*1600–30

The Japanese painter Tawaraya Sotatsu was the founder of the *Rimpa* School, influencing almost all movements after his time. The facts of his life are little known. He worked as a fan-painter in Kyoto, but rose to work for the court. As a producer of fine decorated papers for calligraphy, he absorbed much of Kyoto's old courtly culture. He met the great designer and calligrapher Hon'ami Koetsu, for whose elegant writing he painted under-designs in gold and silver.

Sotatsu excelled in works that needed careful placing—decorative screens and fans. He took to its highest level the Japanese genius for brilliant off-center composition. In his screens of *bugaku* dancers, for example (Daigoji Temple, Kyoto), the figures are placed thinly on a plain gold background, with no apparent organization, and yet with perfect effect.

He pioneered a new boldness of color and line. Simple, bright colors are often applied in thick patches, as in his screens *God of Thunder* and *God of the Winds* (Kenninji Temple, Kyoto) and shapes are reduced to pure ornament. In his *Genji* screens (Seikado Foundation, Tokyo) the round, green hills are linked into one sweeping thrust that runs diagonally across the six leaves. On his wooden doors in the Yogen'in, Kyoto, he made a virtue of necessity, producing on his massive elephant a line so thick that it became decorative in itself. He also popularized a technique of dropping one color on to another while the first was still wet (*tarashikomi*), and an original style of ink monochrome-painting where the ink was used sensuously, as if it were color.

Soto Jésus 1923–

Jésus Rafaël Soto, the Venezuelan optico-kinetic painter and musician, was born in Ciudad Bolivar. He studied at Caracas School of Fine Art (1942–7). After a period as Director of the Maracaibo School of Fine Art (1947–50), he moved to Paris. In 1954 he formulated the concepts of Kineticism, with Yaacov Agam and Jean Tinguely.

Between 1950 and 1952, influenced by Mondrian and the Constructivists, Soto made relief paintings of repeated geometrical elements and paintings of colored dots inspired by serial music. The paintings he did on superimposed sheets of clear plexiglass consisted of single colored motifs; dots and lines were his first exploitation of the "moiré effect", followed by spirals against striped grounds. In the early 1960s his informal, irregular constructions of twisted wires were succeeded by paintings in which metal plaques and rods appear to vibrate. Later reliefs made with moving elements led, in 1969, to "penetrables": sculptures of hanging rods, through which spectators may pass.

Soufflot Jacques 1713–80

The French architect Jacques-Germain Soufflot was the son of a provincial lawyer. He studied architecture in Rome between 1731 and 1738. His first major commission was the huge Hotel-Dieu, Lyons, begun in 1741. This made his reputation, and in 1749 he was chosen by Mme de Pompadour to accompany her brother, M. de Marigny, to Italy to prepare him for the office of *Surintendant des Bâtiments*. If this tour marks the birth of French Neoclassicism, Soufflot was to bring the style to maturity with the Panthéon in Paris. Designed as the Church of Ste-Geneviève in 1757, and unfinished at his death, it is Soufflot's masterpiece. Perhaps surprisingly, many of the structural techniques are borrowed from Gothic architecture. Soufflot did not attempt to conceal this fact, advocating in 1762 the combination of Greek orders with the admirable lightness of Gothic buildings. His later buildings, the École de Droit (1771–83), and garden buildings at the Château de Menars (begun in 1767) are less important.

Soulages Pierre 1919–

The French painter Pierre Soulages was born at Rodez. He developed an interest in local Romanesque and prehistoric art, and began painting while still at school. He visited Paris from 1938 to 1939 and there saw exhibitions of work by Cézanne and Picasso. In 1941, after serving in the French army for two years, he began work as a vineyard laborer. For the rest of the Occupation, until he settled in Paris in 1946, he did no painting, but he met Sonia Delaunay and became interested in Abstract art.

His first nonfigurative paintings, done in 1947, were graphically linked black brush strokes on a light ground. Rigorous avoidance of extra-pictorial references led to larger, denser, and more gestural forms. Later, blues, reds, and browns appear in his work, but the main architectonic structures are invariably black. The ground may be obliterated, or lights may permeate interlaced forms, but spatial readings of depth are always apparent. Soulages has designed for the theater, and since 1952 has also made etchings. His works are owned by many public collections around the world, including the Nationalgalerie, Berlin, the Musée National d'Art Moderne, Paris, the Art Institute of Chicago, and the Okara Art Museum, Kurashiki.

Soutine Chaim 1893–1943

The Russian painter Chaim Soutine spent most of his painting life in France. He was born near Minsk, the tenth son of a poor Jewish tailor who intended him to be a bootmaker. He attended art school at Vilna from 1910 to 1913, then from 1913 to 1918 he lived in Paris in extreme poverty. He paid his first visit to Cagnes, on the Mediterranean coast, in 1918, and the following year went to Céret in the Pyrenees. He spent much time in each of these places, until 1925. In 1922, he found a lavish patron in the American collector Dr Albert C. Barnes; from this time, the relationship guaranteed him some financial security. In the early 1930s, he spent several summers near Chartres. The German occupation forced Soutine, as a Jew, to leave Paris. He moved to Touraine, but a stomach ulcer compelled him to return to Paris for an operation. He died in August 1943.

His early work in Paris was mainly still life. He also occasionally painted single figure portraits. The main influences on his work were Cézanne, Van Gogh, and his friends Marc Chagall and Amedeo Modigliani. His southern landscapes were dense and somber: claustrophobic and almost two-dimensional at Céret, but more open, lighter, and airier at Cagnes. In paintings of both places, the landscape forms are turbulent and the brush strokes violent. His later landscapes of the Île de France are more controlled, but still belong to a kind

Pierre Soulages: Painting; oil on canvas; 194×130cm (76×51in); 1957. Musée National d'Art Moderne, Paris

Stanley Spencer: The Resurrection, Cookham; oil on canvas; 274×549cm (108×216in); 1923–7. Tate Gallery, London

of Slav-Jewish Expressionism. His best known single-figure portraits are of pastry cooks, page boys, valets, and waiters. Among his still lifes is a series done in 1925–6 influenced by Rembrandt's *The Flayed Ox* (1655; Louvre, Paris), for example *Side of Beef* (1925; Albright-Knox Art Gallery, Buffalo) and *Carcass of Beef* (*c*1925; Minneapolis Institute of Arts).

Spencer Stanley 1891–1959

The English painter Sir Stanley Spencer was born at Cookham, Berkshire. From 1908 to 1912 he studied at the Slade School of Fine Art, where his gift for drawing was strengthened by the teaching of Henry Tonks. From the beginning, Spencer's works showed a bold naiveté of vision that was the result of both study (particularly of the Italian Primitives and the Post-Impressionists) and a strong individuality. His experiences in the First World War heightened the visionary qualities of his work, and led to the murals he painted for the Memorial Chapel, Burghclere (1926–32). In these and in other paintings (for example, *The Resurrection, Cookham*, 1923–7; Tate Gallery, London) Spencer expressed his religious belief that all mankind's mundane activities partook of the life eternal. In furtherance of this awareness he also preached sexual liberation, and painted several works whose explicit sexuality prefigures that of Francis Bacon and Lucian Freud.

Further reading. Carline, R. *Stanley Spencer at War*, London (1978). Robinson, D. (ed.) *Stanley Spencer 1891–1959*, London (1976). Robinson, D. *Stanley Spencer: Visions from a Berkshire Village*, Oxford (1979). Rothenstein, E. *Stanley Spencer*, London (1962). Rothenstein, J. (ed.) *Stanley Spencer, the Man: Correspondence and Reminiscences*, London (1979). *Stanley Spencer, R.A.*, London (1980).

Spinello Aretino *c*1345–1410

The Italian painter Spinello Aretino came from Arezzo, but he probably trained in Florence. His earliest documented work is a *Madonna* (1385; William Hayes Fogg Art Museum, Cambridge, Mass.). His most important surviving works are the sacristy frescoes in S. Miniato al Monte, Florence (*c*1387). Comparison of these with the work of Agnolo Gaddi (for instance his frescoes of *The Legend of the Cross* in the choir of S. Croce, Florence, *c*1380) suggest that Agnolo might have been his teacher. The significance of Spinello's work is that it clearly restates the principles of Giotto (1266–1337). In his paintings, large, bulky figures move with monumental deliberation within simple compositions, sometimes backed by an architecture in almost-convincing perspective. Masaccio (1401–?28) must have learned much from Spinello's work.

Spinello Aretino: a detail of the scene St Benedict Expels the Devil from One of his Monks; fresco; c1387. Sacristy of S. Miniato al Monte, Florence

Spranger Bartholomaeus

1546–1611

The Flemish painter Bartholomaeus Spranger was the son of an Antwerp merchant. He studied under several local artists, including Jan Mandyn, Frans Mostaert, and Cornelis van Dalem, but his true apprenticeship was served in many years of travel through France and Italy. He is recorded at Paris, Lyons, Milan, and then at Parma, where the sensuous forms and colors of Correggio were to have a profound effect upon him.

By 1567 he was in Rome, where he stayed for several years. Most of his paintings for Roman churches are lost, but a *Last Judgment* painted for Pius V survives (now in the Museo Civico, Turin). He worked in the Zuccaro workshop for the Farnese family at Caprarola. In 1575 he was at the Imperial court at Vienna, and he finally settled in Prague in 1581 at the court of the Emperor Rudolf II. He married the daughter of a Prague jeweler.

As a result of his extensive travels, Spranger's style marks a highpoint of the International Mannerist style of the 16th century. His elongated, elegant forms, and bright, jewel-like colors are perhaps closest in type to the figure-style of the School of Fontainebleau. Works for Rudolf II such as the *Minerva Conquering Ignorance* (*c*1591; Kunsthistorisches Museum, Vienna) meet the demands of a circle of Court *cognoscenti*; they also convey the strong hint of eroticism demanded by the Emperor himself. The dark backgrounds of his pictures allow a highly contrived lighting, which accentuates the sweeping curves of figures and drapery.

Spranger's most successful religious works are those that give the opportunity for a flamboyance of dress and pose, as in the *Adoration of the Magi* (National Gallery, London). His influence was widespread in northern Europe, mainly through engravings after his work by Hendrick Goltzius (1558–1617).

Squarcione Francesco 1397–1468

Francesco Squarcione was an Italian painter of the Paduan school. In 1423 his profession was "tailor and embroiderer", and he is first mentioned as a painter in 1429. From the many paintings mentioned in documents, only two certain works survive: the Lazzara Altarpiece (1449–52; Museo Bottacin e Museo Communale, Padua) and a signed *Madonna and Child*, also from the Lazzara family (Staatliche Museen, Berlin). The first of these is a polyptych, set within an elaborate Gothic frame, and with a surface richness similar to the work of the Vivarini. The Madonna shows a Tuscan influence (specifically that of Donatello), with the Virgin's face in sharp profile and the Child standing on a marble parapet before her.

Squarcione is chiefly important as the master of a large number of painters, including Andrea Mantegna. An early biographer records the artist's youthful travels through Greece and Italy, and his collection of sculpture, but the two works described above make no reference to such antiquarian interests.

Staël Nicolas de 1914–55

Nicolas de Staël: Figure by the Sea; oil on canvas; 130×162cm (51×64in); 1952. Kunstsammlung Nordrhein-Westfalen, Düsseldorf

Nicolas de Staël was a French painter born in St Petersburg, Russia. Forced to flee after the Bolshevik coup of 1917, he was orphaned and grew up in Belgium. He studied with M. van Haelen at the Academy of Fine Arts in Brussels (1932–3). He visited Holland, and also Paris, where he was impressed by the work of Cézanne, Matisse, Braque, and Soutine. Between 1934 and 1938 he traveled and lived in Spain, North Africa, and Italy, before returning to Paris. After military service in the Foreign Legion (1939–40), he lived in Nice until 1942. He returned to Paris in 1943, and there, the following year, became a friend of Georges Braque. He obtained French nationality in 1948, and then traveled widely (1949–53), settling in Antibes in 1954.

De Staël's paintings are known for their luminous color, which was often laid on with a palette knife. His work in the early 1940s was abstract and geometric in design. It gradually shifted to a freer abstraction, and then—by the early 1950s—to figurative compositions of still lifes, figures, and seascapes (for example, *Le Bateau*; oil on canvas; 1954; Scottish National Gallery of Modern Art, Edinburgh).

Stankiewicz Richard 1922–83

The American sculptor Richard Stankiewicz was born in Philadelphia. He studied at the Hans Hofmann School, New York (1948–50), and in Paris under Fernand Léger and Ossip Zadkine (1950–1). In 1967 he became Professor of Art at New York State University, Albany, and settled in Massachusetts. Stankiewicz was a leading "junk" sculptor in the 1950s. He used mostly discarded machine parts such as pipes, gearwheels, cogs, boilers, and springs, to make witty parodies of human and animal figures, such as *Kabuki Dancer* (Whitney Museum of American Art, New York). In the 1960s the sculptures became lighter and nonreferential. Even more refined sculptures followed, made of fewer parts in limited forms such as "I-beams" and cylinders.

Steen Jan 1626–79

The Dutch artist Jan Steen painted humorous scenes showing the recreations of the middle and lower classes. His pictures are invariably categorized as genre, but they are often more complex, containing allusions to old proverbs and sayings. In this respect his mildly satirical work continues a tradition of which Hieronymus Bosch and Pieter Bruegel the Elder are two of the best-known exponents.

Steen was born in Leiden, the son of a brewer. He may have studied at Haarlem under Adriaen van Ostade and also at The Hague under the landscapist Jan van Goyen, in whose style he painted a few landscapes, and whose daughter he married. His *Game of Skittles* (*c*1660–3; National Gallery, London) reveals a more lyrical treatment of the kind of subject earlier popularized by both Ostade and Adriaen Brouwer. Steen simultaneously tackled portraits and biblical subjects (both of which are given genre-like treatment), but he is now best known for his tavern scenes and depictions of popular

festivals. In Haarlem during the 1660s he painted a number of pictures of this kind, full of animation and vitality. Notable among them are *The World Upside Down* (1663; Kunsthistorisches Museum, Vienna) and several versions of *The Feast of St Nicholas*. The paintings from this period are full of differentiations of character and expression in the figures. This, together with the profusion of detail, the multiplicity of incident, the frequent proverbial or literary basis, and an occasional theatrical element, requires them to be "read" rather than simply experienced as a visual whole. Subjects of this kind are complemented by a number of pictures of doctors' visits (to love-sick girls), and music lessons in respectable bourgeois settings. These are more tranquil works, which exhibit Steen's wide thematic range.

During his later years, when Steen combined the profession of painter and innkeeper at Leiden, he turned to a more idyllic vein, depicting scenes of amorous dalliance placed in park settings. These works look forward to the early 18th century *fête champêtre* paintings of Watteau. Steen apparently never gained popular esteem during his lifetime; he died with 500 unsold pictures in his house.

Steer Philip 1860–1942

The English painter Philip Wilson Steer was born in Birkenhead, Cheshire. He studied in Paris from 1882 to 1884, but without mastering the French language or familiarizing himself with avant-garde French painting. In 1886, however, after his return to London, he became a founder-member of the New English Art Club; this was a society led by Walter Sickert, which tried to import into English painting the lessons of Manet, Degas, and Monet.

Steer's landscapes of the late 1880s and early 1890s were beach scenes at Walberswick, often with young girls or children. They created a sharply individual note, in which high-keyed color, robust handling, and unexpected viewpoints aimed towards exciting new directions. In the same period, his figures in interiors were caught in offbeat, arbitrarily cut compositions, which he would also apply to his portraits (for example, *Mrs Cyprian Williams and her Children*, 1890–1; Tate Gallery, London). He held a one-man show at the Goupil Gallery, London, in 1894; he received critical support from D.S. MacColl, George Moore, and Walter Sickert; his work was illustrated in *The Yellow Book*; and he exhibited with Les Vingt in Brussels.

Left: Jan Steen: Game of Skittles; oil on panel; 33×27cm (13×11in); c1660–3. National Gallery, London

Philip Steer: The Beach at Walberswick, Suffolk; oil on canvas; 60×76cm (24×30in); c1889. Tate Gallery, London

When Steer reached his mid 30s, his inventive searching began to flag. He never married. His life took on a repetitive pattern—he spent his summers in various parts of England and Wales, and his winters in London, where he taught at the Slade School of Fine Art from 1893 to 1930. His style became increasingly eclectic, echoing in turn the styles of François Boucher, of John Constable, and of Thomas Gainsborough. The handling in some of his landscapes showed an awareness of Adolphe Monticelli. He was an accomplished watercolorist, but his style became increasingly insular, accepting neither Post-Impressionism, nor any of the 20th-century art movements. He relapsed into an agreeable but fundamentally unadventurous picture-making that lasted from about 1910 until the mid 1930s, when blindness forced him to stop painting.

Stefano da Zevio *c*1375–1451

Stefano da Zevio was a painter from Zevio, near Verona; he was also known as Stefano di Giovanni da Verona. He was a pupil of Altichiero (*fl.* 1369–90), and an exponent of the International Gothic style. His works have been described as "illuminated manuscripts on a larger scale". The *Madonna in the Rose Bower* (Museo di Castelvecchio, Verona) is typical of his works. They show the artist's fascination with the pretty details of nature, but lack any interest in pictorial depth of mass. This courtly style derives from Gentile da Fabriano. Vasari (who mentions Donatello's wonderment at the beauty of Stefano's work) says he was a pupil of Agnolo Gaddi, in Florence.

Stefano della Bella 1610–64

The Florentine etcher Stefano della Bella was early influenced by the art of Jacques Callot (1592–1635). As court artist to the Medici Dukes he etched scenes of lively popular holidays and of the lavish spectacles of Florentine court life. After a stay in Rome, he spent 11 years in Paris (1639-50), where his style absorbed something of the freer atmospheric effects of Rembrandt and the Dutch landscapists. He then returned to Florence. His etchings are technically superb—he produced over 1,000—in a subtle mixture of etching, drypoint, and engraving.

Steinbach Erwin von *fl.* 1277–1318

Erwin von Steinbach was a German master mason, eulogized by Goethe (in his essay "Von Deutscher Baukunst", "On German Architecture", published in *Von Deutscher Art und Kunst*, "On German Nature and Art", 1773). His name appears in documents and inscriptions at Strasbourg Cathedral where he designed the west facade, begun in 1277. He is probably the author of the surviving drawing, now known as "B", which was copied in the construction of Strasbourg Cathedral up to the level of the second gallery, where the design changes. The facade has been analyzed to prove the strict geometric basis for its plan, but it is chiefly remarkable for the skeletal effect of the freestanding tracery that covers Erwin's work. The style suggests that he was influenced by French Gothic architecture, such as the facade of Reims Cathedral, and the church of St Urbain at Troyes.

Frank Stella: Sinjerli Variation I; fluorescent acrylic on canvas; diameter 305cm (120in); 1968. Private collection

Stella Frank 1936–

The American painter Frank Stella was born at Malden, Massachusetts. He studied painting at Phillips Academy, Andover, with Patrick Morgan, and also at Princeton with William Seitz and Stephen Greene. Since 1958 he has lived in New York. Although his earlier work has obvious links with Abstract Expressionism, he shared his contemporaries' distrust of that movement's potential self-indulgence.

The canvases Stella painted in the late 1950s, worked out in terms of stripes and patterns, are already characterized by the bold clarity of color and design that distinguishes his later and better known pictures. Since the early 1960s, the geometrical basis of his paintings has become even clearer; he uses many different shapes, sometimes cut out. The individual stripes of color are defined by hard edges. His color is often fluorescent in effect, creating a suggestion of hard, shiny machine-made surfaces.

Stella Joseph 1877–1946

The American painter Joseph Stella was born in Italy. In 1897, a year after arriving in New York, he enrolled at the Art Students League. He began his artistic career as an illustrator, but after two visits to Europe (1909–10, 1911–12), where he met Henri Matisse and the Futurist painter Carlo Carrá, he concentrated on painting. Works by him were included in the Armory Show in 1913. His paintings from this period were in the Futurist idiom (for example, *Battle of the Lights, Coney Island*, 1913–14; Yale University Art Gallery, New Haven, Conn.). Later he developed his personal, more structured, illusionistic style, which was half abstract and half precisionist (for example, *Brooklyn Bridge*, 1917–18; Yale University Art Gallery, New Haven). In the early 1920s he made a group of very original Abstract collages. He continued to paint until his death in 1946.

Further reading. Jaffe, I.B. *Joseph Stella's Symbolism*, New York (1994).

Still Clyfford 1904–81

Clyfford Still, born in Grandin, North Dakota, was one of the earliest and most consistent of the American Abstract Expressionist painters. Unlike most of the group, he was not a New Yorker; he lived in the city only from 1950 to 1961. He made a single radical break with tradition in 1941 while doing war work in Oakland, California, far removed from the intellectual ferment of wartime New York. His paintings of this period demonstrate the formula of all his mature work. They reject the shallow, structured space of Cubism, and the literary overtones of Surrealism, in favor of a flat two-dimensional surface of almost-romantic, jagged shapes and colors (for example, *1957–D No. 1*, 1957; Albright-Knox Art Gallery, Buffalo).

Furthur reading. *Clyfford Still: Thirty-three Paintings in the Albright-Knox Art Gallery*, Buffalo, N.Y. (1966). Hess, T.B. "The Outsider". *Art News*, New York (December 1969). McCaughey, P. "Clyfford Still and the Gothic Imagination", *Artforum*, New York (April 1970).

Clyfford Still: 1953; oil on canvas; 236×174cm (93×69in); 1953. Tate Gallery, London

Stimmer Tobias 1539–84

The Swiss decorative artist Tobias Stimmer was born at Schaffhausen; his surviving work there includes the painted facade of the Haus zum Ritter (1568–70), now in the Museum zu Allerheiligen, Schaffhausen. Its illusionistic architecture, with mythological figures and cartouches, was much influenced by similar facade painting done by the Holbein workshop at Augsburg and Basel.

Stimmer spent later years in various German towns. He designed woodcut illustrations to biblical and Classical texts printed at Strasbourg, and decorated the astronomical clock at Münster (1571–4). He also did the ceiling paintings for the banqueting hall of the Castle of Baden-Baden (1578–9), which prefigure the German Baroque style. He was also noted for his large portraits, intimate in mood (for example *Jakob Schwytzer*, 1564; Öffentliche Kunstsammlung, Kunstmuseum Basel).

Stomer Matthias 1600–*post* 50

Matthias Stomer was a Dutch painter whose Caravaggesque manner is related to that of the artists of the Utrecht School. He is, deservedly, much less well known than his teacher Gerrit van Honthorst, whose style he imitated. After working in Utrecht in the 1620s, Stomer traveled in Italy: he is first recorded there in Rome, and subsequently in Naples. The remainder of his working life appears to have been spent in southern Italy and Sicily.

Stoss Veit *fl.* 1477–1533

A painter and printmaker as well as one of the greatest German sculptors of the late Gothic era, Veit Stoss was born at Horb in Swabia. Estimates of his birth date vary (from *c*1438 to *c*1447), but the first documented information is that in 1477 he resigned his citizenship of Nuremberg and moved with his family to Krakow. It can be deduced on stylistic grounds that his roots lie in the Upper Rhine area; he seems to have been influenced in particular by Nikolaus Gerhaert van Leyden. It is not known how long he had spent working in Nuremberg, but he must have been an experienced master by 1477 when he received the commission for the huge *Death of the Virgin* Altarpiece in the church of the Virgin at Krakow (completed 1489).

During nearly 20 years of activity in Krakow he also executed the red marble tomb of King Casimir IV Jagiello in Krakow Cathedral (1492), and other tombs at Włocławek and Gnesen. He returned to Nuremberg in 1496 a rich man, but lost his fortune through bad investments. He was convicted for forgery in 1503, and lost his rights as a citizen.

He carved the Volckamer memorial in the church of St Sebald, Nuremberg; it has three reliefs, and is signed and dated 1499. The *Christ Crucified* in St Lawrence, Nuremberg, dates from the same period (*c*1500). During 1503–4 he painted and gilded the figures in Tilman Riemenschneider's high altar for the parish church of Münnerstadt and added painted wings (now dismembered). In about 1508 the carved frame for Dürer's *Holy Family and Saints* was produced in his workshop.

His pair of figures of *Tobias and the Angel* were given to the Dominican church in Nuremberg in 1516 (Germanisches Nationalmuseum, Nuremburg) and the great *Annunciation* group for St Lawrence, Nuremberg, was carved in 1517–18. Among his important late works, the *Crucifix* in St Sebald, Nuremberg, was executed in 1520. The Reformation prevented the delivery of the *Altar of the Virgin* that had been intended for the Carmelite church in Bamberg (1520–3; unfinished and now in Bamberg Cathedral). Stoss died in 1533, having lost his sight.

The over-life-size figures in Krakow depicting the *Death of the Virgin* are polychromed and gilded. Their expressive qualities mark a high point in German late Gothic sculpture, and in the tomb of King

Casimir IV the veined, dark red marble is effectively used to evoke emotion. The Volckamer reliefs in St Sebald, Nuremberg, strike a more restrained note; the effect is entirely sculptural, since they were not polychromed. But in the brooding figure of St Andrew (*c*1505?) in the choir of the same church, the highly expressive, contorted folds reveal the intense spiritual energy of Veit Stoss' later sculptures.

Street George 1824–81

The English architect George Edmund Street was born at Woodford, Essex. He designed his first churches during the years 1845 to 1849 while he was working as an assistant to Gilbert Scott. He joined the Ecclesiological Society (as did Butterfield), was deeply religious, and was greatly interested in Gothic architecture. He had a preference for boldly massed forms, and the exploitation of the color or texture of building materials. The Village School at Inkpen, Berkshire (1850), is a characteristic early work; and St James the Less, Westminster (1860) with its simple brick tower is among the most famous of his many churches. Street's major secular work, the Law Courts, London, was still being built when he died.

Strozzi Bernardo 1581–1644

The Italian artist Bernardo Strozzi, born in Genoa, was the best and most influential painter working there in the early 17th century. From 1595 to 1597 he studied under the Sienese artist, Pietro Sorri. About 1597 he entered the Capuchin order. Although he remained a priest, from *c*1610 he was allowed to work as an artist, in order to support his destitute mother.

His early work shows the influence of Tuscan Mannerism, both in composition and in the delicate high-keyed colors. Around 1615 he developed a more expressive and naturalistic style. He responded to the works of Rubens that could be seen in Genoa, to the genre scenes produced by the Flemish artists working there (for example, *Old Woman at the Mirror*; private collection), and to paintings by visiting Caravaggesque artists. Strozzi's robust religious style has strong genre elements, and a new range of browns and reds and ruddy flesh tones; an example is the powerful *St Augustine washing Christ's Feet* (Museo dell' Accademia Ligustica di Belle Arti, Genoa). Between *c*1615 and 1620 he produced a group of genre paintings. The most famous of these are *The Cook* (*c*1612; Palazzo Rosso, Genoa) with its elaborate still life, and *The Pipers* (Palazzo Rosso, Genoa), in which the figures surge forward with Rubensian vitality. He also painted frescoes and portraits.

Bernardo Strozzi: Old Woman at the Mirror (An Allegory of Vanity); oil on canvas; 132×108cm (52×43in). Private collection

In 1631 he settled in Venice, and shortly afterwards painted *Doge Francesco Erizzo* (Kunsthistorisches Museum, Vienna). He became one of the city's leading portrait painters. His admiration for the work of Veronese (1528–88) was unlimited. Among his important mythological and religious works are his *Rape of Europa* (National Museum, Poznan), and his *Martyrdom of St Sebastian* (*c*1635/6; S. Benedetto, Venice). They demonstrate how skillfully he continued the decorative and painterly qualities of the great 16th-century Venetian tradition.

Further reading. Milkovich, M. *Bernardo Strozzi: Paintings and Drawings*, Binghamton, N.Y. (1967). Mortani, L. *Bernardo Strozzi*, Rome (1966). Tietze, H. (ed.) *Three Baroque Masters: Strozzi, Crespi, Piazzetta*, Baltimore (1944).

Stuart Gilbert 1755–1828

The American painter Gilbert Charles Stuart was born in the colony of Rhode Island, of Scottish parentage. He came to London in 1775, and from 1777 to 1782 was a pupil of Benjamin West, one of the leading history painters of the day. Stuart stayed in London until 1787; he then lived for a period in Dublin before returning to America in 1793. He set up a studio in New York, and later worked in Philadelphia. There he painted several portraits of *George Washington*, which were much duplicated in his studio, and which are probably his best-known works. From *c*1805 until his death he lived in Boston.

Stuart's main practice was as a portrait painter. He combined a fluent sense of composition—influenced by what he had seen in London of the work of Thomas Gainsborough, Joshua Reynolds, and George Romney—with a straightforward approach to character. *Mrs Richard Yates* (1793–4; National Gallery of Art, Washington, D.C.), which shows a middle-aged lady seated at her needle-work, is among the finest of his portraits. The key images of George Washington are the so-called "Vaughan" portrait (1795; National Gallery of Art, Washington, D.C.), the "Athenaeum" Portrait (1796; Museum of Fine Arts, Boston), and the "Lansdowne" Portrait (1796; Pennsylvania Academy of the Fine arts, Philadelphia).

Gilbert Stuart: George Washington (the "Atheneum" portrait); oil on canvas; 122×94cm (48×37in); 1796. Museum of Fine Arts, Boston

Stubbs George 1724–1806

George Stubbs was an English animal and portrait painter. He was acknowledged during his lifetime as a master of the sporting picture, but the full scope of his talents has only recently been recognized. Born in Liverpool, he had little formal training in art. From the early 1740s until his departure for Italy in 1754, he studied anatomy in northern England while supporting himself by portraiture. He stayed only briefly in Rome, finding its artistic heritage of little interest. From 1756 to 1758 he lived in relative seclusion in Lincolnshire, where he dissected horses and made detailed anatomical studies. His *Anatomy of the Horse*, published in 1766 with his own text and illustrations, is one of the great achievements of 18th-century natural history.

By 1760 Stubbs had settled in London. His horse portraits and hunting and racing pictures were immediately popular, and the next decade was the most productive of his artistic career. To this period belong such masterpieces as *The Grosvenor Hunt* (1762; Trustees of the Grosvenor Estate, London), *Gimcrack on Newmarket Heath* (1765; private collection), and the remarkable series of paintings of mares and foals. His earliest painting of a wild animal, the clinically observed *Zebra* (*c*1760–2; Paul Mellon Center for British Art, Yale University, New Haven), was followed shortly afterwards by the first of his animal paintings that depict the mortal combat of horses and lions. This last series anticipated specific themes that would be more fully exploited by the next generation of Romantic artists, both in England and in France.

Between 1770 and 1790 Stubbs complemented the successes of the previous decade with many of his most original conversation pieces and genre subjects. He also turned his inquisitive mind to experiments with printmaking techniques, and enamel painting on large ceramic plaques that were specially manufactured by Josiah Wedgwood. His second major investigation, *A Comparative Anatomical Exposition of the Structure of the Human Body with that of a Tiger and a Common Fowl*, was begun towards the end of his life. Although the book was never published, 142 delicate chalk and pencil studies for the illustrations have survived (Paul Mellon Center for British Art, Yale University, New Haven).

Further reading. Egerton, J. and Taylor, B. *George Stubbs: Anatomist and Animal Painter*, London (1976). Gaunt, W. *Stubbs*, Oxford (1977). Sparrow, W.S. *George Stubbs and Ben Marshall*, London and New York (1929). Tattersall, B. *Stubbs and Wedgewood: Unique Alliance between Artist and Potter*, London (1974). Taylor, B. *Stubbs*, London (1975).

Sugai Kumi 1919–1996

The Japanese painter Kumi Sugai was born in Kobe, and studied at the Osaka School of Art (1927–32). Little is known of his early work. He moved to Paris in 1952, where his reputation as one of the School of Paris tachist painters soon developed. His Abstract paintings of the 1950s were based on Oriental forms, painted in strong but luminous colors. Later he began to use quite different, linear forms with brighter

George Stubbs: Whistlejacket; oil on canvas; 325×259cm (128×102in); 1761–2. Private collection

colors expressing energy and tension but carefully controlled. In 1968 he was included in the Japanese pavilion at the Venice Biennale and began to live in Tokyo again. During the 1970s he abandoned his earlier expressive, Abstact style, in favor of a slick, mechanical finish. This later work apparently expresses the conflicts between traditional and modern Japan. Sugai is also a notable printmaker.

Suger of St-Denis 1081–1151

Abbot Suger of St-Denis figures prominently in the history of medieval art, as a patron who commissioned the first Gothic building, sponsored a new type of portal design, and stimulated the development of stained glass windows and metalwork. In 1122 he was made Abbot of the royal abbey of St-Denis (now a suburb of Paris). He was a friend and advisor to two kings, Louis VI and Louis VII, also acting as Regent during the Second Crusade in 1146. Between 1137 and 1140 he added to the old Carolingian Abbey a two-towered west front which incorporated three portals with column-figures; it was the first time that such a feature had been used on a large scale in France. During the same period, the Italian sculptor Niccolò experimented with a similar portal design. Many features of Suger's portals are Italian, but it is not known whether the column-figures were invented in Italy or in France.

During the years 1140 to 1144 Suger built the choir of the abbey. This was the first Gothic structure in Europe, and one that was to have an enormous influence on the subsequent history of architecture. He was not the designer of this revolutionary building, but he had the foresight to allow the architectural experiment to be carried out.

Suger left an account of his work, devoting most space to a description of the metal objects he commissioned. These included altar frontals, a large cross, vessels of various kinds, candlesticks, and reliquaries—all made from precious materials and studded with jewels. Some of these still survive, and demonstrate that Suger was quite justified in using Ovid's phrase, "Materiam superabat opus" ("the workmanship surpassed the material"), when praising them. Suger also describes in some detail the stained glass windows he commissioned to be made "by the exquisite hands of many masters from different regions". Several of these also survive. It has been claimed that Suger invented some new iconographic representations, for instance the "Tree of Jesse", but these claims have since been disproved.

Further reading. Panofsky, E. *Abbot Suger on the Abbey Church of St Denis and its Art Treasures*, Princeton (1946).

Sullivan Louis 1856–1924

Louis Henry Sullivan was the most inventive member of the Chicago School of Architecture, and the first major American architect concerned with the aesthetics of the skyscraper. More than 100 of his most important city buildings were produced between 1879 and 1895, while he was in partnership with Dankmar Adler. These include the Auditorium Building, Chicago (1866–89), the Wainwright Building in St Louis (1890–1), and the Guaranty Building, Buffalo, New York (1894–5). Sullivan wanted to combine new techniques of construction and installation with a relevant and original decorative scheme. His writings, *Kindergarten Chats* (1901) and *Autobiography of an Idea* (1922), although subjective and frequently obscure, proclaim the stylistic and functional integrity in the commercial skyscraper. Among his pupils was the prominent architect Frank Lloyd Wright.

Graham Sutherland: Devastation 1941: an East End Street; watercolor, gouache, pen and ink; 65×114cm (26×45in); 1941. Tate Gallery, London

Sultan Muhammad *fl. c*1520–*c*40

Sultan Muhammad of Tabriz, instructed the young Shah Tahmasp before his accession in 1524, and became head of his library. He must have both planned and contributed to the major royal manuscripts, including the "Houghton" *Shah-nama* of *c*1520–30 (Metropolitan Museum, New York, and private collections) and the British Library *Khamsa* of Nizami of 1539–43. There are two works signed by him in each manuscript. According to contemporaries, his masterpiece in the *Shah-nama* was *The Court of Gayumars* and this work can be identified in the "Houghton" manuscript. His training was at the Court of the Aqqoyunlu, but he was an artist with progressive ideas, as evidenced by his signed *Court Feast*; this work is in a *Hafiz* that was made for Sam Mirza, brother of the Shah, in about 1527. Sultan Muhammad's son Mirza Ali also joined the royal painting staff.

Sutherland Graham 1903–80

Graham Sutherland was an English landscape painter and portraitist. After abandoning an engineering apprenticeship, he went to Goldsmiths' College, London (1921–6), where he studied engraving. While there he became friends with the engraver F.L. Griggs, who shared Sutherland's enthusiasm for the work of Samuel Palmer (1805–81). This interest is reflected in the rich, dark etchings of pastoral subjects that Sutherland produced between 1925 and 1931. Palmer's romantic view of nature helped to stimulate Sutherland's imagination, but it also had a restricting effect. When the print market collapsed, he turned to landscape painting.

He taught himself to paint landscapes by copying objectively from nature, but in his drawings and watercolors he allowed his imagination freer rein. This approach (inspired by Paul Nash's poetic landscapes and *objets trouvés*) became dominant after his first visit to Pembrokeshire in 1934. He was captivated by the extraordinary richness of organic forms, and by the unexpected dramas of the landscape, and his paintings show this. They are romantic in mood, and Palmer's twilight colors linger on, but they are also often highly abstracted; his tree and rock forms have an anthropomorphic, malignant quality that presages his postwar creations.

During the Second World War Sutherland sketched armament factories and bombed cities as an Official War Artist: the experience heightened his Dantesque vision of the world, and renewed his interest in mechanical forms. In 1944 he was commissioned to paint a Crucifixion for St Matthew's Church, Northampton. This, his first major figure-painting, led to a renewed interest in anthropomorphic imagery. He saw Christ's crown of thorns as a "paraphrase" of the tortured human body. The related paintings of thorn trees and heads are more general metaphors of the underlying unity between Man and the natural world; and the hybrid, metamorphic forms that he developed in the 1950s (for example, *Head III*, 1953; Tate Gallery, London), express the predatory nature of all living things.

Although these works represent Sutherland's greatest contribution to postwar art, he is known popularly for his portraits, and for his tapestry of *Christ in Glory*, designed for Coventry Cathedral (1952–61). In both, he has shown that it is possible to give meaning to a debased genre, provided the artist is totally honest and committed.

Further reading. Cooper, D. *The Works of Graham Sutherland*, London (1961). Hayes, J. *The Art of Graham Sutherland*, Oxford (1980). Sackville-West, E. *Graham Sutherland*, Baltimore and London (1955). Sanesi, R. *Graham Sutherland*, Milan (1979). Tassi, R. *Graham Sutherland: Complete Graphic Work*, London (1978). Tassi, R. *Graham Sutherland: Parafese della Natura e Arte e Altre Corrispondenze*, Parma (1979).

T

Tacca Pietro 1577–1640

Pietro Tacca was a Florentine sculptor who worked during the period of the transition from Mannerism to the Baroque. The most distinguished of Giovanni da Bologna's pupils, he played an important role in the execution of the various equestrian monuments undertaken by his master in his late career. Tacca was particularly adept at working in bronze on a scale larger than life, and as official sculptor to the Medici Grand Dukes, he was responsible for two of the gigantic tomb statues of Ferdinand I and Cosimo II in the Cappella dei Principi, S. Lorenzo, Florence (1627–34). Among his independent equestrian statues, that of *Philip IV* of Spain in the Plaza de Oriente, Madrid (1634–40), is remarkable for its successful introduction of the motif of the prancing horse.

Pietro Tacca: Slave; bronze; c1615–23. Piazza dalla Darsena, Leghorn

Taiga Ike no 1723–76

Ike no Taiga was a Japanese painter and calligrapher; he was one of the greatest masters of the *Bunjinga*, or scholar-painter's art. Born in Kyoto, he was educated at the Manpukuji Temple, where he learned Chinese-style calligraphy and acquired an interest in Chinese painting. As a young man he earned his living by painting fans, often with designs taken from Chinese painted manuals. He became famous for finger-painting—no mere party trick, as his great series of screens of *Five Hundred Rakan* (Manpukuji Temple, Kyoto) show. Finger-painting taught him his characteristic economy of means.

He traveled widely in Japan and transferred the Chinese idealistic landscape style to real views, as in his set of 12 ink landscapes (Kawabata Collection, Kamakura). He became so famous that his widow Gyokuran (1728–84), herself an original painter, set up the Taigado Museum in Kyoto in his memory. This may have been the world's first one-man art museum.

Taiga's styles were many, original, and unconventional. His techniques ranged from the simple monochrome album *Eight Views of the Hsiao-Hsiang* (Kumita Collection, Tokyo), each plate consisting of a few lines, to the refined and detailed album *Ten Conveniences and Ten Pleasures*, done with Yosa Buson, in which he shows his skill as a colorist. He could create dashing ink sketches, like the handscroll *Scenes of Mutsu Province* (Shimosaka Collection, Tokyo), or highly polished works such as his screens *Landscapes with Pavilions* (Tokyo National Museum), done in ink and splashes of bright color on gold. He also studied Western perspective, and adapted it to Chinese styles, thus extending the expressive range of his painting.

Taikan Yokoyama 1868–1958

The Japanese painter Yokoyama Taikan was the leading formulator of the Nihonga style. He entered the Tokyo School of Fine Arts in 1889, and in 1896 joined the theorist Okakura Tenshin, who inspired him to seek a new style of traditional painting. This was achieved by combining Western space, perspective, human naturalism, and some shading, with the bright colors, clear outline, and sense of design of *Yamatoe*.

The style is fully mature in his figure screens *Master Five Willows* (1912; Tokyo National Museum) and most splendid in *Cherry Trees at Night* (1929; Okura Shukokan Museum, Tokyo). Taikan also practiced virtuoso ink-painting without outline, notably in the landscape handscroll *The Wheel of Life* (1923; National Museum of Modern Art, Tokyo).

Talenti family 14th century

Francesco Talenti (*c*1300–69?) and his son Simone (*c*1340/5–81?) were Florentine architects. Francesco is first recorded in 1325 working in a minor capacity under Lorenzo Maitani at Orvieto Cathedral. In 1343 he succeeded Andrea Pisano as *capomaestro* of Florence Cathedral.

During the 1340s and 1350s he completed the Campanile, which had been started by Giotto in 1334 and continued by Andrea Pisano up to the second main cornice. Francesco adopted a more obviously Gothic style, with tracery windows and gables adorned with crockets. The whole is richly decorated with colored marble. The spire was never built.

While work on the Campanile proceeded, he drew up a scheme for the cathedral, which was accepted in 1357. This scheme was an enlargement of Arnolfo di Cambio's original plan. In the same year Francesco won the competition for the detailed design of the nave piers. In 1364 he was discharged from his post as *capomaestro*, though he was recalled in a much reduced capacity in 1366. The years 1366 and 1367 saw a revision of the plans amid many commissions and much public debate; Francesco took only a very minor part in all of this. Nevertheless the present interior—a very parochial Gothic style compared with contemporary building north of the Alps—is essentially the work of Francesco.

Simone Talenti was also involved in work for the cathedral. He helped his father to carve the prototype pier capital, and submitted (unsuccessfully) a design in the competitions of 1366–7. He was *capomaestro* briefly in 1376, and held a similar post at the church of Orsanmichele in Florence from 1379. From 1376, together with Taddeo Ristori and Benci di Cione, Simone oversaw the building of the Loggia della Signoria, employing a pier style similar to that of the Cathedral.

Tamayo Rufino 1899–1991

The Mexican painter Rufino Tamayo was born in Oaxaca in 1899, and studied at the Academia de Arte de San Carlos in Mexico City (1917–21). The most important influence on his art was his contact with Pre-Columbian and native artistic traditions, as a teacher of ethnographic drawing at the National Museum of Anthropology, Mexico City (1921–3). He experienced mainstream European art in New York and Paris, and his paintings are a synthesis of traditional Mexican styles with Cubist-derived figuration. In his Expressionist pictures of the 1940s and 1950s, such as *Animals* (1941; Museum of Modern Art, New York) he was influenced by Picasso. Since the late 1950s his single and paired figures have tended to depict archetypal and timeless themes; his colors and surface textures play an integral part in the expressive qualities of his work. He painted murals for the Palace of Fine Arts in Mexico City and the UNESCO headquarters in Paris, among others.

Tanguy Yves 1900–55

Yves Tanguy, a French Surrealist painter, was born in Paris. After several years in the Merchant Navy and in the Army he settled in Paris, and became a friend of the poet Jacques Prévert. In 1923, inspired by a painting by Giorgio de Chirico, he decided to become a painter. He joined the Surrealists in 1925. He was completely self-

Yves Tanguy: The Invisible Ones; oil on canvas; 99×81cm (39×32in); 1951. Tate Gallery, London

taught, and his earliest work is naive in execution and vision.

In 1927, he developed a precise and illusionistic style which altered little in later years (for example, *Mama, Papa is Wounded!*, 1927; Musum of Modern Art, New York). His mature work evokes a tangible but imaginary landscape, reminiscent of beach, desert, or sea-bed (for example, *Four Hours of Summer, Hope*, 1929; private collection). The deeply receding space is inhabited by three-dimensional biomorphic forms—owing much to Arp, Miró, and Picasso—which threateningly overcrowd the space of his late work. Restrained in color, his work combines a modern, abstract form-language with a labored, academic style.

Further reading. Tanguy, K. *Yves Tanguy: a Summary of His Works*, New York 1963).

Tan'yu Kano 1602–47

The Japanese painter Kano Tan'yu was the last great master of the *Kano* School. He was born in Kyoto, the son of Kano Takanobu (*ob.* 1618) and grandson of Kano Eitoku. With his brothers Naonobu (1607–50) and Yasunobu (1613–85) he was educated by Kano Koi (*ob.* 1636), who made them masters of the ink monochrome medium.

Tan'yu soon attracted official attention. At the age of 20 he was appointed painter to the Edo government, receiving a house at Kajibashi, and moving to the new capital. Thereafter, though much of his work continued to be in western Japan, his school was known as "Kajibashi Kano". His many official commissions included the decoration of the Nijo and Imperial palaces (Kyoto), and of Nagoya and Edo castles.

Like most great Japanese artists, Tan'yu painted well in many different styles. He is less successful as a decorative artist than as an ink-painter; his huge, many-paneled compositions of hawks on pine-trees in the Nijo palace are dull, compared with Sanraku's room there. Yet his folding screens of the *Four Seasons* from the Myoshinji Temple (Kyoto) have a charm equal to anything of the period, and his handscroll on the founding of the Toshogu Shrine is a masterpiece of delicate color in a *Tosa* idiom.

His strength lies in his ink-painting for temples, especially in his great landscapes suggested in a few strokes and washes. Tan'yu's reputation reached such heights that later *Kano* artists spent much time copying his more academic works, to the great detriment of Japanese painting.

Antoni Tàpies: Gray Ocher LXX; oil on canvas; 262×196cm (103×77in); 1958. Tate Gallery, London

Tàpies Antoni 1923–

The Spanish painter and sculptor Antoni Tàpies was born in Barcelona. He read law at Barcelona University from 1943 to 1946, but as an artist he was largely self-taught. From 1945 to 1947 he made collages and impasted paintings. In 1948 he was a cofounder of *Dau al Set*, a late Surrealist group. During 1950 he lived in Paris on a French Government scholarship. After geometrical paintings and studies in pure color, he returned in 1953 to earlier techniques using plaster, collage, and graffiti; he explored the formal qualities of banal materials, and incorporated real objects into his work. His later paintings are on or appear actually to be walls, doors, and windows. He made his first sculptures in 1970. Tàpies' work ranges from strongly gestural pure painting, through the random juxtaposition of common objects and materials, to contrived symmetrical images. He has also made murals, stained glass, and graphics.

Further reading. Permanyer, L. *Tàpies and the New Culture*, New York (1986).

Tassi Agostino *c*1580–1644

Agostino Buonamici Tassi was a painter of large-scale mural decorations in Baroque Rome. After an early career in Florence, where he was trained in the tradition of stage design, he returned to his native Rome, and then became a specialist in secular decoration involving perspective illusionism. Most of his major *quadratura* schemes in Roman palaces were executed in collaboration with important figure-painters such as Giovanni Lanfranco, Carlo Saraceni, Orazio Gentileschi, and Guercino. Tassi occasionally included within his decorative schemes landscapes and seascapes in the manner of Paul Bril (1554–1626), which were in turn to influence Tassi's pupil, Claude Lorrain.

Tatlin Vladimir 1885–1953

Vladimir Tatlin was a Russian artist who entered the Moscow School of Painting, Sculpture, and Architecture in 1910. Probably through Natalia Goncharova, his work was influenced by icon painting, especially in its use of color and flat curvilinear rhythm. But his greatest formative experience was his short visit to Paris in 1913, where he saw Picasso's Cubist constructions.

In late 1913 Tatlin began his "painting reliefs". These used what he termed "real materials [tin, wood, glass, plaster] in real space"; even at this early stage, they were more radical than the Cubist examples. The flat background of the relief imposed limits on real space. In 1915 he constructed the "corner relief", suspended on a wire attached to the walls in the corner. Now planes could move freely in all directions, released from the constraints of frame and background. He made studies of individual materials, and later used this "culture of material" in his teaching.

After the Bolshevik Revolution in Russia, Tatlin was appointed head of the Moscow section of the Department of Fine Arts (1918), which commissioned his project for a monument to the Third International. A large wooden model was exhibited in 1920, but the monument itself was not erected. Hugely ambitious, it was to have been twice the height of the Empire State Building. Its intention was both symbolic and functional: to house the many activities of the Revolutionary Government. His design consisted of three basic shapes constructed in glass—hemisphere, pyramid, and two cylinders—all revolving at different speeds. They were to be suspended on an asymmetrical axis within an iron spiral framework.

During the 1920s he designed practical objects such as workers' clothes. Another project was a self-propelled glider, based on a close study of insects and birds. He was for a time influential in the Constructivist movement in Russia and the West.

Further reading. Zhadova, L. (ed.) *Tatlin*, London (1988).

Tchelitchew Pavel 1898–1957

The Russian painter and stage designer Pavel Tchelitchew was born in Kaluga, Moscow. As a youth, he was influenced by the Romantic book illustrations of Gustave Doré and Mikhail Vrubel. He attended the Academy at Kiev and received encouragement from Léger's pupil, Aleksandra Exter. Tchelitchew lived in Berlin (1921–5) before settling in Paris, where he reacted against Abstract art and became a member of the group later known as the Neo-Romantics. He was much influenced by the early work of Picasso, painting clowns and acrobats, and often employing blue as the main color. He settled in America in 1934, but died in Rome.

Tchelitchew designed the scenery and costumes for Diaghilev's *Ode* (1928), and continued as a stage designer throughout the 1930s and 1940s. Much of his best work is Surrealist in mood and character

Vladimir Tatlin: Counter Relief 1915; wood and metal; 69×83×79cm (27×33×31in); a reconstruction. Private collection

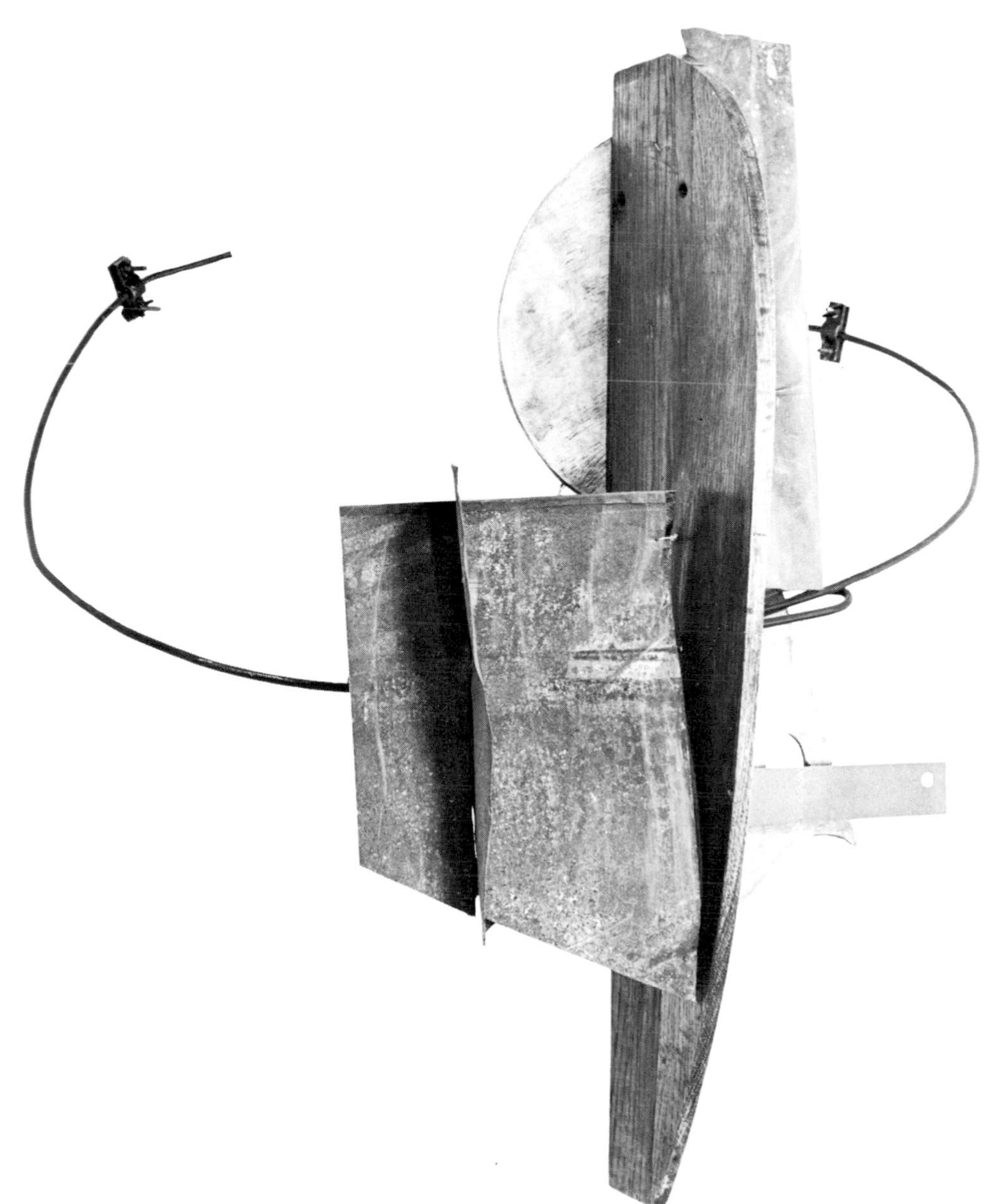

(for example, *Leaf Children*, 1939, and *Hide and Seek*, 1940–2; both Museum of Modern Art, New York). It was weakened by a certain theatrical artifice, an elegance tinged with *kitsch*, which he was never entirely able to banish from his art. He is often more interesting as a portrait painter, especially in the portraits of his friend, the poet Edith Sitwell (1937 version in the Tate Gallery, London).

Teniers David, the Younger

1610–90

The Flemish genre painter David Teniers the Younger was the most famous member of a family of artists. Born in Antwerp, he was probably trained by his father, David Teniers the Elder (1582–1649). He painted a wide range of subjects (including civic guard processions, landscapes, religious themes, and representations of the Witches' Sabbath) but is chiefly known for pictures of peasant life and some paintings of guardroom scenes. His work from the 1630s shows the influence of Adriaen Brouwer's low-life scenes, although it lacks Brouwer's vitality and coarseness. He later expanded his themes to include multi-figured depictions of rustic revelry, full of lively and amusing incident.

From 1651, Teniers was employed in Brussels as court painter by the Regent of the Netherlands, Archduke Leopold Wilhelm. His duties involved compiling a catalog of the Archduke's picture collection (published with engraved plates in 1660), and painting views of the galleries in which this collection was hung. Teniers made several small copies of paintings in the collection, notably of those by Venetian artists, but this practice had no visible effect on his other work. During these years in Brussels he also acted as an art dealer. The quality of Teniers' work declined in his later years, during which he relied much more than before on assistants.

Pavel Tchelitchew: The Composer Igor Markevitch and his Mother; oil on canvas; 91×74cm (36×29in); 1930. Tate Gallery, London (on loan from the Edward James Foundation)

Tenniel John 1820–1914

The English artist and draftsman Sir John Tenniel studied in London at the Royal Academy Schools and at Chipstone Street Life Academy. He joined *Punch* in 1850 as the magazine's second cartoonist. He became first cartoonist in 1864, and held the post until 1901. His political works won great respect for their fairness as well as their draftsmanship. He excelled in drawing beasts and allegorical figures, and his history paintings and serious illustrative work are also noteworthy. But it is usually for his illustrations to Lewis Carroll's *Alice's Adventures in Wonderland* (1866) and *Through the Looking-Glass and What Alice Found There* (1871) that he is remembered today. Tenniel was knighted in 1893.

Terborch Gerard 1617–81

Gerard Terborch (or ter Borch) was a Dutch genre and portrait painter. His early genre paintings show guardroom scenes, but he later abandoned these in favor of small pictures of genteel, expensively dressed Dutch families enjoying their leisure (for example, *The Concert*, *c*1675; Staatliche Museen, Berlin). These pictures are characterized by a minutely detailed technique, a limited color range of grays, blacks, and blues, and careful rendering of the textures of such materials as silk, satin, and velvet. The subtlety of Terborch's psychological relationships and the refined textures of his draperies are seen in *The Fatherly Admonition* (1654–5; Staatliche Museen, Berlin). The picture was long thought to represent a bourgeois family incident, but is in fact a depiction of a brothel scene.

David Teniers the Younger: A View of Het Sterckshof near Antwerp; oil on canvas; 82×118cm (32×46in); c1646. National Gallery, London

Terborch appears to have been fairly wealthy, and he traveled widely in Europe. In 1648 he was in Germany, where he painted one of the very few 17th-century Dutch representations of contemporary history: *The Swearing of the Oath of Ratification of the Treaty between the Dutch and the Spanish at Münster, 15 May, 1648* (National Gallery, London). This painting, which measures only 18 by 23 in (46 by 58 cm), contains over 50 full-length portraits. Few of the works Terborch saw on his travels influenced his style, although knowledge of Velázquez' paintings in Madrid is evident in a number of small full-length portraits.

Terbrugghen Hendrick
*c*1588–1629

The Dutch painter Hendrick Terbrugghen (or ter Brugghen) was the most important member of the Utrecht School. Born in Deventer, he is believed to have spent ten years in Italy as a young man, perhaps arriving in Rome as early as 1604. There he may have met Caravaggio, whose paintings had a decisive influence on him. His earliest surviving works, which date from after his return to Utrecht, sometimes echo Caravaggio's subjects, depicting such themes as *The Calling of St Matthew* (*c*1617; Nouveau Musée des Beaux-Arts, Le Havre). They frequently use Caravaggist chiaroscuro which, in Terbrugghen's paintings, creates rather hard, sculptural forms and throws sharply defined detail into relief.

Although Terbrugghen never completely abandoned Caravaggism, in his later work light falls more softly on figures and objects, conveying a more subtle sense of their forms and textures. Together with the rejection of harsh, raking light effects, there is a preoccupation with reflected light. This is particularly noticeable in such half-length single-figure genre paintings as the poetic *The Flute Player* (1621; Gemäldegalerie Alte Meister, Kassel). In these and in some later religious paintings the cool, clear colors, pale silvery tonality, and an air of silence and stillness look forward to Vermeer and the Delft School.

Terbrugghen was admired by Rubens, but he was much less well-known in his day than other Utrecht artists such as Gerrit van Honthorst, and was neglected until the present century.

Tessai Tomioka 1835–1924

The Japanese painter Tomioka Tessai was well-known in the West for the racy and individualistic style of the works he did in his old age. Born in Kyoto, he was deeply learned in Confucian and Taoist classics, Buddhist literature, and native Shinto studies, serving at times as a Shinto priest. He studied various painting styles, but finally developed a very strong neo-Chinese manner, specializing in the use of transparent color washes over a richly black and nervous line. His work exploits the traditional humor in the Chinese Immortals and Buddhist divinities. In the last 20 years of his life he produced many thousands of works, some of great power, but some merely eccentric.

Tessin family 17th and 18th centuries

The Swedish architect Nicodemus Tessin the Elder, lived from 1615 to 1681. He was born at Stralsund in Sweden, and trained as an architect under Simon de la Vallée. In 1651 and 1652 he toured Europe, and in 1661 was appointed City Architect of Stockholm, becoming one of the leading Baroque architects in Sweden.

His chief work is Drottningholm Palace (begun in 1662), built in an eclectic Baroque style which borrowed elements from Italy, France, and Holland. His other works include Kalmar Cathedral (1660) and Göteborg Town Hall (1670).

His son, Nicodemus Tessin the Younger (1654–1728), succeeded him as the leading Swedish architect, completing his father's work at Drottningholm. He traveled to England, France, and Italy between 1673 and 1680. His major building is the huge Royal Palace at Stockholm (begun 1697), which shows a knowledge of Bernini's unexecuted project for the Louvre. His son, Carl Gustavus Graf von Tessin (1695–1770), was an important patron of French 18th-century artists.

Further reading. Josephson, R. *L'Architecte de Charles XII, Nicodeme Tessin à la Cour de Louis XIV*, Brussels and Paris (1930). Kommer, B.R. *Nicodemus Tessin der Jungere und das Stockholmer Schloss*, Heidelberg (1974). Wiegert, R.-A. and Hern-Marck, C. *Les Relations Artistiques entre la France et la Suide 1693–1718: Nicodeme Tessin le Jeune et Daniel Cronstioni, Correspondance*, Stockholm (1964).

Testa Pietro 1611–50

Born in Lucca, the Italian artist Pietro Testa was in Rome by 1630; after a brief period in the studio of Domenichino he studied with Pietro da Cortona. His paintings and etchings, light and delicate in touch, were influenced by Titian's Bacchanals and by Poussin's lyrical reinterpretations of them.

Later in his career Testa's style became more classical and he concentrated almost exclusively on etching—a medium he considered most suitable for the expression of complex philosophical speculations. His compositions were crowded with emblematic and erudite symbolism. Testa's learning was in conflict with his melancholy temperament, and it is almost certain that he drowned himself in the Tiber.

Theodoric Master *fl.* 1348–86

Master Theodoric was an isolated figure in Bohemian painting of the 14th century. His surviving works are concentrated in the Chapel of the Holy Cross in the castle of Karštejn near Prague. He is recorded as court painter in Prague in 1359, with a house on the Hradčany, which he still owned in 1368. The dating of the decorations in the Chapel of the Holy Cross presents a number of problems.

The chapel was consecrated in 1357, and again in 1365. Master Theodoric was named as the artist responsible in 1367, when he was rewarded by the Emperor Charles IV. No other evidence is available to indicate whether the cycle of panels representing the *Crucifixion*, the *Man of Sorrows*, and 127 half-length saints, angels, and prophets, was executed between 1357 and 1365, or between 1365 and 1367.

Since the style of the panels by Master Theodoric marks such a sharp break with the earlier, Italian-inspired phase of Bohemian painting under Charles IV, the dating of 1365–7 is marginally the more probable. It is conceivable, however, that the differences in style between the inner and outer areas of the chapel are due to differences in date of execution, rather than to the employment of a studio assistant. Certain points of contact can be noted with the work of Master Bertram of Hamburg, but these are apparently generic rather than specific, and no direct links can be postulated.

The evolution of the style of the Master Theodoric can be satisfactorily explained in terms of Bohemian manuscript illuminations. Master Theodoric turned away from the earlier interest in relating figures to spatial constructions, by concentrating his entire attention on the physical bulk of the figures, and by allowing them to create their own space. His figures share a consistent canon of proportions, with massive heads set on short, thick necks, and fleshy faces and hands. Their draperies often extend over the integral frames, while the same diapered gold grounds extend over both.

These stylistic quirks reinforce the hypothesis that the Master Theodoric owed his origins, at least, to Bohemian miniature painting. However, outlines had little significance for him. Instead, the figures are built up of delicate transitions in tone, with occasional brilliant colors; the overall effect is one of extreme softness.

Master Theodoric appears to have been a technical innovator: his paint medium is close to oil paint, and in the *Holy Cross* cycle he exploited its relatively slow-drying characteristics. No other paintings can be attributed to him. Although he was a forerunner of the Soft style, his influence on Bohemian painting was very limited.

Theodorus of Samos 6th century BC

Theodorus of Samos was a Greek architect and artist, around whom legends grew up. He is an early example of the versatility that was probably common among Greek artists. With Rhoecus he planned the largest temple in the Greek world—the Temple of Hera on Samos. He was also consultant engineer for the Temple of Artemis at Ephesus.

As a sculptor, Theodorus had the reputation of being one of the first to cast major statuary in bronze. An anecdote tells how, by using Egyptian canons of proportion, he collaborated in the production of a statue with Telecles, who made one half in Samos while Theodorus made the other half in Ephesus. It was he who made the famous signet ring "encased in gold and made of an emerald", for Polycrates, tyrant of Samos. Polycrates threw the ring away, to demonstrate his renunciation of his most treasured possession and forestall the envy of the gods at his good fortune; the ring was returned in the belly of a fish.

Theophanes the Greek
*c*1340–*c*1410

Theophanes the Greek was a Byzantine painter active in Russia. Probably born in Constantinople, he decorated about 40 churches there and in Russia, whither he emigrated in the 1370s. His only surviving frescoes are in the church of the Transfiguration in Novgorod (1378). They include the *Old Testament Trinity* (the three Persons of the Trinity, represented by the three angels entertained by Abraham).

His style was highly influential in Novgorod, where painters of his school decorated St Theodore Stratelates (*c*1380s), and the church of Volotovo (1380s). In Moscow, where he collaborated with Andrei Rublev, Theophanes painted two palaces, and three churches (in 1395, 1399, and 1405). A large icon of the *deesis* (1405) (the Virgin and John the Baptist flanking Christ as intercessors in the Cathedral of the Annunciation, Moscow) is attributed to him from this period.

Theophanes worked boldly, creating intense portraits with a silvery and terracotta palette and distinctive white linear highlights. The vigor of his style reflected his manner of painting as recorded by a contemporary: "No one ever saw him looking at models ... he seemed to be painting with his hands, while his feet moved without rest."

James Thornhill: a detail of the Painted Hall in Greenwich Hospital, London (Royal Naval College); 1708–27

Theophanes the Greek (attrib.): The "Virgin of the Don" Ikon; c1380. State Tretyakov Gallery, Moscow

Theophilus *fl.* early 12th century

The priest and craftsman Theophilus may have come from north Germany. He was the author of one of the most valuable texts to have survived from the earlier Middle Ages: the treatise on the arts entitled *De Diversis Artibus*. It contains instructions on the techniques employed in the arts in three parts, the second of which is incomplete. The first section is on painting, the second on glass working and enameling, and the third, the longest and most detailed, on goldsmith's work and bronze casting. It describes the refining of precious metals, how to make tools and dies, how to chase and emboss, how to design open and cast work, altar plate, frontals, bookcovers, reliquaries, and secular work like saddles and horse-trappings; it even gives detailed instructions for making an organ and casting church bells.

The earliest copy of the text to survive has been dated to the first half of the 12th century, and has at its beginning "Theophilus qui et Rugerus". This has led to the identification of the author as Roger of Helmarshausen, who is also known by a documented portable altar made in 1100 AD for Henry of Werl, Bishop of Paderborn. Dedicated to SS. Kilian and Liborius, it is now in Paderborn Cathedral. The techniques employed on this small altar provide almost an inventory of those described in Theophilus' text.

Because the internal evidence of the text also points to an early 12th-century date, and to a probable north German provenance, the identification of Theophilus as Roger is now often accepted, although it cannot be finally proved. Other work has been attributed to Roger, including the portable altar from the Abbey of Abdinghof, now in the Franciscan church, Paderborn, and the Gospels from Helmarshausen, in the Cathedral Library, Trier.

Roger's style of hard, linear Byzantine forms, with the human figure vividly articulated by panels of drapery, is probably derived from provincial Italian sources. It had an important influence in lower

Saxony until the end of the 12th century, especially at Hildesheim (Shrine of St Godehard; *c*1132) and at Fritzlar (chalice, church of St Peter; *c*1180).

Thornhill James 1676–1734

Sir James Thornhill was the only native artist to practice the Baroque style of decorative painting in England. His first major work was in the dome of St Paul's Cathedral, London, (1715–17), a reinterpretation of Raphael, but painted without the illusionistic bravura of the French Baroque. He reached his maturity with the walls and ceilings in the Painted Hall at Greenwich Hospital (1708–27), where he painted modern subjects in an allegorical manner, carried out in an Italianate illusionistic style. Thornhill also worked at Hampton Court (1717). He competed successfully with his many European rivals working in England, such as Louis Laguerre and Sebastiano Ricci, both of whom influenced his style.

Thornton John, of Coventry

fl. early 15th century

John Thornton of Coventry was an English glass-painter. His east window at York Minster (1405–8) contains scenes from Genesis, Exodus, and The Revelation of John, with individual figures above and below. Here he introduced a style of glass-painting new to York, which probably derived from the school working at Oxford and Winchester. The fine draftsmanship of his figures, in the International Gothic style, and the dramatic qualities of his extensive narrative scenes dominated York glass-painting for the following 50 years. He may also have supervised the painting of the *St William* window in York Minster (1422), and the *Fifteen Last Days* window in All Saints, North Street, York (*c*1410).

Thorvaldsen Bertel *c*1770–1844

Bertel Thorvaldsen was a Danish Neoclassical sculptor. He studied at the Royal Academy in Copenhagen with Johannes Wiedewelt and Nicolai Abildgaard. In 1797 he arrived in Rome, where he lived in a studio formerly occupied by John Flaxman. During his early years in Rome Thorvaldsen became an intimate of leading Neoclassicists, particularly Asmus Carstens and the Danish scholar Jörgen Zoëga. The artist's interest in Antiquity was fundamental to his sculpture, but he suffered from the overwhelming influence and rivalry of Antonio Canova.

Thorvaldsen developed a style of sculpture more severe and monumental than that of his great Italian contemporary. Canova himself considered that Thorvaldsen had founded a totally new style when he viewed the Dane's first large work, *Jason with the Golden Fleece* (1803–28, Thorvaldsen Museum, Copenhagen). It was bought by the rich Dutch banker Thomas Hope; his patronage, and that of other collectors interested in Neoclassicism, enabled Thorvaldsen to remain in Italy for most of his life.

He met many artists in Italy whose interest paralleled his own. They included J.-A.-D. Ingres, Joseph Koch, and John Gibson as well as the German Nazarenes, whose paintings and drawings Thorvaldsen often bought for his own collection. The sculptor's popularity increased, and he specialized in portrait busts, including one of his patron *Thomas Hope* (1817; Thorvaldsen Museum, Copenhagen).

In 1819 Thorvaldsen visited Denmark. He was received as a national celebrity and undertook several commissions to portray members of the Danish royal family. He moved to a large studio in Rome in 1822 and stayed in the city until 1838. After the deaths of Canova and Flaxman he was the greatest Neoclassical sculptor in Europe. His typical style is a static, heavy representation of Antiquity, but his drawings are lively and accomplished.

Tiepolo family 18th century

The Italian painter Giambattista Tiepolo (1696–1770) was the most important practitioner of the Rococo style in Italy during the 18th century. He combined the Venetian coloristic tradition of Titian and

Bertel Thorvaldsen: Briseïs Being Led away from Achilles; marble; height 116cm (46in); 1803. Thorvaldsen Museum, Copenhagen

Veronese with the art of Roman Baroque illusionism. He was born in Venice, and trained under Gregorio Lazzarini; his early work was influenced by the chiaroscuro manner of Federico Beneovich and Giambattista Piazzetta. He gradually moved away from these masters towards an independent, coloristic style, as in *The Sacrifice of Isaac* (1716; Chiesa dell'Ospedaletto, Venice).

With the return of Sebastiano Ricci—another influence on his work—to Venice in 1717, Giambattista turned towards Veronese's work for inspiration. His first monumental work, the *Madonna of the Carmelites and Saints* (1720–2; Pinacoteca di Brera, Milan) shows this influence in the open arrangement of figures, a compositional device he was to develop further. In his first ceiling decoration, *The Power of Eloquence* (1725; Palazzo Sandi, Venice), figures are seen foreshortened but their form is still suggested by means of light and shade rather than by pure color; a large expanse of sky sets off the figures.

The two masterpieces of Giambattista's early career are the decorations of the Cappella del Sacramento (1726; Udine Cathedral), and for Diomisio Dolfino's Palazzo Arcivescovado (formerly the Palazzo Dolfin) Udine (1726–7/8). The *Judgment of Solomon* in the latter shows the degree of luminosity he was able to obtain through modeling his figures by color alone, instead of using conventional chiaroscuro.

In 1731 Giambattista was commissioned to decorate the Palazzo Casati (now Dugnani) in Milan, returning to Venice in 1732. From then until his departure for Spain in 1760 he dominated Venetian painting. His decorative virtuosity was extraordinary, and his invention prodigious, as he covered huge areas of wall and ceiling with grandiose mythological or religious scenes. One of the most important works of his middle years is *The Institution of the Rosary* (1737–9; S. Maria dei Gesuati, Venice). The painting is Veronesian in its color and in its foreshortening; the fully-modeled figures emerge from a luminous background towards the spectator. Two other notable paintings from this period are *The Sacrifice of Melchizedek* and *The Gathering of the Manna* (1738–40; parish church of Verolanuova, Brescia).

In *St Simon Stock receiving the Scapular* (1740; Scuola dei Carmini, Venice), painted on canvas and placed in the center of a ceiling, most of the scenographic accessories that appeared so plentifully in the Gesuati ceiling have been abolished. The main theme is reduced nearly to its essentials. Color helps to unify the painting by evoking atmospheric luminosity. The most ambitious decoration of Giambattista's middle years in Venice was the painting of the *salone principe* of the Palazzo Labia, executed in 1743 in collaboration with Girolamo Mengozzi Colonna, who painted the architectural sections. *The Banquet of Cleopatra* is the most famous of its scenes; here the protagonists are portrayed with such realism that their presence is almost palpable.

Giambattista Tiepolo: The Banquet of Cleopatra; fresco; approx. 650×300cm (256×118in); 1743. Palazzo Labia, Venice

On 12 October 1750, Giambattista accepted the invitation of Prince-Archbishop Charles Phillip of Greiffenclau to decorate the dining-hall of his new palace, the Fürstbischöfliche Residenz in Würzburg. Later that year he arrived at Würzburg with his sons Giandomenico and Lorenzo Tiepolo. The two large scenes, *The Marriage of Barbarossa* and *The Investiture of Bishop Harold* are not framed with a painted architectural surround, but are set within actual stucco, which performs an abstract and decorative function. The treatment of the scenes themselves is also strongly illusionistic. Between 1752 and 1753 Giambattista painted the fresco above the stairway representing *Olympus*.

In 1753 Giambattista was back in Venice, where he painted *The Martyrdom of St Agatha* (Staatliche Museen, Berlin). One of his most complex works, it reveals the coloristic intensity of his late style. This magniloquence is also to be seen in the frescoes depicting mythological scenes from works by Tasso, Ariosto, and Virgil in the Villa and Foresteria of the Counts of Valmarana, Vicenza. These works date from the year 1757. Giambattista was assisted by Giandomenico, who decorated five of the rooms of the Foresteria. The last major work of Giambattista's late Venetian period was the ceiling of the *gran salone* of the Palazzo Pisani, Stra (Venice).

Giambattista was invited by Charles III of Spain to decorate the new Royal Palace in Madrid. He arrived on 4 June 1762, together with his sons Giandomenico and Lorenzo. Anton Raphael Mengs, the leader of the Neoclassical reform of European painting, was already in the city. In the Royal Palace, Giambattista painted three ceilings. *The Apotheosis of Spain* in the throne room, signed and dated 1764, is the most ambitious of these, but it also reveals the artist's declining powers. Giambattista died in Madrid on 27 March 1770. Faced with the competition of Mengs' purist approach, his exuberant Rococo had already begun to seem unfashionable.

The painter Giandomenico Tiepolo (1727–1804) was born in Venice. He worked as assistant to his father, Giambattista, and was deeply influenced by him, but did not possess his sublime vision, and was more attracted towards the realistic representation of contemporary life. Giandomenico's hand many be distinguished from that of his father, in the frescoes at Valmarana, by its more naturalistic style. Giandomenico was active as a printmaker, and 177 etchings by him are known. He was also a prolific draftsman. Among his independent works are the *Stations of the Via Crucis* (1748–9; Oratorio del Crocifisso, S. Polo, Venice), and *St Oswald prays for the Cure of a Sick Boy* (parish church, Merlengo). He went to Würzburg and Madrid with his father, and returned to Venice after the latter's death in 1770. There he found that the artistic atmosphere was much changed, and that his old-fashioned style, based on that of his father, was not in great demand.

Further reading. Knox, G. *Catalogue of Tiepolo Drawings in the Victoria and Albert Museum*, London (1960). Levey, M. *Giambattista Tiepolo: His Life and Art*, New Haven (1986). Morassi, A. *G.B. Tiepolo: his Life and Work*, London (1955). Rizzi, A. *The Etchings of the Tiepolos*, London and Milan (1971). Shaw, J.B. *The Drawings of Domenico Tiepolo*, London (1962).

Tinguely Jean 1925–1991

The Swiss sculptor Jean Tinguely was born at Fribourg and studied at the School of Fine Arts in Basel. In 1945 he began to construct in wire, metal, paper, and wood, and in 1948 experimented with motorized movement. In Paris, where he moved in 1953, Tinguely developed his "meta-mechanical" technique, which included the introduction of random and surprise elements into his constructions. In 1960 he founded, with Yves Klein and others, the *Nouveau Réalisme* movement.

There is much humor and irony in Tinguely's bizarre machines: the anarchic spirit of Dada lies behind his work. His fascination with the machine—his awareness of its obsolescence as well as its usefulness—led to a series of events in which his works exploded in a frenzy of self-destructive energy. The most famous of these took place in 1960 at the Museum of Modern Art, New York.

Tino da Camaino c1295–c1337

The Sienese sculptor Tino da Camaino was probably the pupil of Giovanni Pisano. His early work is in Pisa, where he was working by 1311 (and possibly as early as 1306). He was commissioned in 1315 to make the tomb of the Emperor Henry VII, of which only fragments survive (Camposanto, Pisa). He worked in Siena from 1319 to 1320. He probably spent the years 1321 to 1323 in Florence, making the tomb of Cardinal Orso (Florence Cathedral). From 1323 he lived at Naples, probably at the request of King Robert of Anjou, where he made the tomb of Margaret of Hungary with Gagliardo Primario (S. Maria Donna Regina, Naples), as well

Jean Tinguely: fragment from Homage to New York; painted metal; 204×224cm (80×88in); 1960. Museum of Modern Art, New York

Tino da Camaino: Charity; marble; height 127cm (50in); c1321–3. Museo Bardini, Florence

as the tomb of Mary of Valois (S. Chiara, Naples; 1333–7) and others. His influence on Neapolitan sculptors was extensive.

Tino's style derives from that of Giovanni Pisano, whose manner he helped to spread. But his work can have an additional solemn massiveness which at first sight relates to the classicism of Nicola Pisano. There is also the impression of contact with Giotto's example. The two artists surely met while Giotto was working in Naples from 1329 to 1333, but Giotto's influence on Tino's style must have taken place earlier.

Tintoretto Il 1518–94

The Italian artist Jacopo Robusti is always known by the nickname of "Il Tintoretto", "The Little Dyer", from the profession of his father. Second only to Titian, Tintoretto was the leading painter in Venice in the second half of the 16th century.

In *La Vita di Giacopo Robusti detto Il Tintoretto* ("The Life of Giacopo Robusti called Tintoretto"; 1648) Carlo Ridolfi states that Tintoretto spent a short time as a boy in Titian's studio, but that Titian expelled him through jealousy of his promise. He also tells us that Tintoretto wrote on the wall of his studio the motto: "The drawing of Michelangelo and the coloring of Titian". This is probably apocryphal, but reflects the fact that Tintoretto was deeply affected by contemporary developments outside Venice, in northern and central Italy. In particular, his work shows the influence of Parmigianino as well as of Michelangelo. Tintoretto possessed copies of Michelangelo's Medici Chapel statues, and drew them from many angles.

The achievement of Tintoretto cannot, however, be expressed in any neat academic formula of eclecticism. His powerful

Il Tintoretto: St George and the Dragon; oil on canvas; 158×100cm (62×39in); c1558. National Gallery, London

imagination dictated dynamic compositions which he was able to realize on canvas through a unique mastery of light, and a brilliant technique of drawing directly with his pigment.

His earliest surviving work, *Apollo and Marsyas* (1545; Wadsworth Atheneum, Hartford, Conn.) was painted for a ceiling in the house of Pietro Aretino. It already shows his brilliance of handling but is rather flat and unexciting in design. It is in two pictures of the end of the decade, *The Last Supper* (1547; S. Marcuola, Venice), and *The Miracle of the Slave* (1548; Gallerie dell'Accademia, Venice) that we first encounter his genius. In this 1547 version of *The Last Supper*, Tintoretto places the figure of Christ in the conventional position in the center of the far side of the table, but four of the Apostles are seated at the near side, and some are rising to their feet, giving movement to the whole composition. In *The Miracle of the Slave*, St Mark hurtles down from the sky in bold foreshortening, the executioner displays his broken hammer to his master, and agitated spectators cling to the columns at the left. The color is strong, but clear and light, and the execution incisive and direct. Tintoretto's technique of building up forms through a series of clearly defined brush strokes is particularly well demonstrated in *The Four Evangelists* (1552; S. Maria Zobenigo, Venice).

At about the same time he produced *The Presentation of the Virgin* (*c*1552; Madonna del Orto, Venice). This picture originally formed the outer side of the organ shutters, and it is designed to be seen from below. Our gaze travels up the flight of curved steps to the point where Mary stands before the High Priest, silhouetted against the sky, while mysterious elders watch her from the shadows on the left. The emotive and symbolic character of the representation contrasts with the ordered rationalism of Titian's version of this subject (1534–8; Gallerie dell'Accademia, Venice).

Tintoretto's decoration of the choir of the same Gothic church of the Madonna del Orto survives intact, with its great canvases of *The Worship of the Golden Calf* and a *Last Judgment* on the side walls, reaching up into the pointed lunettes of the vault (*c*1560; Madonna del Orto, Venice). Comparison of the *Judgment* with the altar wall of the Sistine Chapel shows how little the fundamentals of Tintoretto's style, with its contrasts of light and shade and its recession into depth, owes to Michelangelo's example.

Il Tintoretto: Self-portrait; detail; oil on canvas; full size 61×51cm (24×20in); c1588. Louvre, Paris

Shortly after his decoration of the Madonna del Orto, Tintoretto added two canvases to the series of the *Miracles of St Mark* which he had begun with *The Miracle of the Slave* in 1548: *The Finding of St Mark's Body* (*c*1562; Pinacoteca di Brera, Milan) and *The Transport of the Body of St Mark* (*c*1562; Gallerie dell'Accademia, Venice). These two paintings are distinguished by their deep perspective settings. In both, but especially the latter, this violent recession heightens the emotional impact of the picture.

The whole of the interior of the Scuola di San Rocco in Venice was decorated by Tintoretto between 1564 and 1587, and the decoration survives intact. Here, as nowhere else, we can appreciate the breadth of Tintoretto's genius. The canvas of *Christ before Pilate* (1564–6) shows the elongated, pale figure of Christ movingly isolated against the dark architecture. The *Ascension* (1576–81), with its rhythmical pattern of the cutting edges of the angels' wings in its upper part, and the open meadow with the Apostles below, is a splendidly imaginative creation. *The Flight into Egypt* (1583–7), with its extended landscape, reminds us how far Tintoretto anticipates the developments of the following century.

Almost all the pictures mentioned so far have been religious in content. They are paralleled by a less extensive, but equally impressive, series of mythological paintings such as *The Origin of the Milky Way* (*c*1582, National Gallery, London). Another series of four paintings includes the *Bacchus and Ariadne* (1578; Sala del Anticollegio, Doges' Palace, Venice). He also painted historical scenes both for the Venetian Doges' Palace (Library) and for the Gonzaga family at Mantua (now in the Alte Pinakothek, Munich).

The great *Paradise* in the Sala del Maggior Consiglio in the Doges' Palace was begun after 1588 when Tintoretto was 70. It could only be carried out with the help of numerous assistants, and does not realize his idea as effectively as the sketch made for the original competition (1579; Louvre, Paris). A masterpiece of his last years is *The Last Supper* (1592–4; S. Giorgio Maggiore, Venice). With its receding diagonal perspective, it contrasts strikingly with this first version at S. Marcuola.

He was widely employed as a portrait painter, but his portraits lack the humane authority of Titian's and this remains a minor branch of his activity. However, his late *Self-portrait* (*c*1588; Louvre, Paris) is profoundly human, and at the same time splendidly abstract. Its icon-like quality is a reminder of the Byzantine substructure of all Venetian painting.

Tintoretto's son, Domenico (1562–1637), assisted him in his later work, and also worked independently. A daughter, Marietta, was also a painter.

Further reading. Berenson, B. *Venetian Painters of the Renaissance*, London and New York (1897). Bernardi, C. and Vecchi, P. de *L'Opera Completa di Tintoretto*, Milan (1970). Newton, E. *Tintoretto*, London (1952). Parlucchini, R. *La Giovanezza del Tintoretto*, Milan (1950). Pittaluga, M. *Il Tintoretto*, Bologna (1925). Rossi, P. *Jacopo Tintoretto*, Venice (1973). Tietze, H. *Tintoretto: the Paintings and Drawings*, London (1948).

Tissot James 1836–1902

The French painter James Tissot was born in Nantes. He went off to Paris in 1856 and became a friend of J.A.M. Whistler and Degas. He departed from his initial romantic-medieval style (seen, for example, in *The Two Sisters*, 1864; Louvre, Paris) and inaugurated a highly salable line in pictures of ladies wearing contemporary, exotic, and historical costumes. In

James Tissot: The Henley Regatta of 1877; oil on canvas; 46×95cm (18×37in); 1877. Leander Club, Henley-on-Thames

London, where he lived from 1871, his polished depictions of fashionable society (for example, *Ball on Shipboard*, 1874; Tate Gallery, London) soon gained middle-class popularity. On the death of his much-portrayed mistress in 1882, Tissot returned to Paris and took up spiritualism. His *Life of Christ* paintings (begun in 1886) received enormous acclaim for their factual quality (derived from studies and sketches made in the Holy Land, most of which are now in the Brooklyn Museum, New York). In 1896 he published the first volume of the *Tissot Bible*, illustrated with 865 compositions.

Titian *c*1488–1576

The Venetian painter Tiziano Vecellio is known in English as Titian. Contemporary sources indicate possible dates of birth as widely separated as 1473 and 1490. His earliest documented work is of 1511. He was born in the Alpine valley of Cadore and brought to Venice as a boy, where he was placed with the painter and mosaicist Sebastiano Zuccato. He passed through the studios of Gentile and Giovanni Bellini, and became associated with Giorgione *c*1507, completing a number of works that were left unfinished at Giorgione's death in 1510.

Titian remained based on Venice throughout his life, but worked for numerous outside patrons such as the Dukes of Ferrara, Mantua, and Urbino, the Emperor Charles V, his son Phillip II of Spain, and Pope Paul III. He visited Rome from 1545 to 1546 and Augsburg from 1548 to 1549 and again in 1550. He excelled as a painter of religious and mythological scenes and as a portraitist.

It is impossible to exaggerate Titian's importance in the history of Western painting. It was he, more than any other artist, who drew together the achievements of the earlier Renaissance and transmitted them to future generations as a living tradition. Unlike some other figures of the High Renaissance, he was essentially and exclusively a painter. The actual pigment plays as positive a part in the creation of his works as the marble does in Michelangelo's sculptures. Titian's feeling for the tangibility of pigment may owe something to his early contact with the art of mosaic. From Giovanni Bellini he would have learned the liberating possibilities of the oil technique.

Titian's earliest paintings, dating from the first decade of the century, such as *The Gipsy Madonna* (Kunsthistorisches Museum, Vienna) follow Bellinesque types of design, but are distinguished by their freedom of handling and rich texture. The earliest of his altarpieces is the relatively small one, now in the sacristy of S. Maria della Salute in Venice, of *St Mark Enthroned*. The flanking saints, Cosmas and

Titian: The Tribute Money; oil on poplar panel; 75×56cm (30×22in); c1516. Gemäldegalerie Alte Meister, Dresden

Damian, Roche and Sebastian, are those invoked against the plague, and the picture is usually linked with the epidemic that carried off Giorgione in the autumn of 1510. The symmetrical disposition of the figures follows the traditional pattern. But the architecture is asymmetrical, and, by a bold stroke, the head of the principal figure is placed in shadow so that it is silhouetted against the light cloud behind.

This silhouetting reappears in the head of the central apostle in the great *Assumption of the Virgin*, painted for the high altar of S. Maria dei Frari between 1516 and 1518. In other respects, there is little in the quiet dignity of the *St Mark* to prepare us for this amazing work. Mary is borne up on a cloud crowded with boy angels, in a red robe, against an orange glory of light; the Father seems to take material form under our eyes as he prepares to receive her. The apostles, earth-bound, strain towards her and show her as humanity transfigured. This work, painted when he was probably around 30, is a masterpiece, and sets Titian at once in the company of Leonardo, Michelangelo, and Raphael. He was to reach this level again, and by very different routes, but he could not surpass it.

We find this dramatic style in a very different context in the votive altarpiece of the Pesaro family, also in S. Maria dei Frari, painted between 1519 and 1526. Here Titian fused two earlier types: the votive picture, in which the donor kneels on one side before the holy figure enthroned on the other, and the conventional, centrally enthroned Madonna with saints. He produced a splendid asymmetrical but balanced design, which was to influence the future development of the altarpiece in Venice. It has been suggested recently that the great columns in the background of the painting, which echo the piers of the nave of the Gothic church, are a later modification of Titian's original design. This theory is certainly mistaken. Titian's dramatic approach to altarpiece design culminated in the narrative scene of *The Death of St Peter Martyr*, painted for the church of SS. Giovanni e Paolo between 1528 and 1530. The picture was destroyed by fire in 1867.

Parallel with this development of religious themes we find a series of allegorical and mythological pictures. If *Fête Champêtre* in the Louvre, Paris, had been established as Titian's work it would be among the earliest of these. But its dreamy, indeterminate mood is remote from Titian's affirmative nature; it seems more probable that it is in part, if not wholly, the work of Giorgione. By contrast, the rich, incisive, and eloquent *Sacred and Profane Love* (*c*1515; Museo e Galleria Borghese, Rome) is the essence of Titian. It may be seen as the secular prelude to the *Assumption* begun in the following year, and is hardly less of a masterpiece.

Titian: The Venus of Urbino; oil on canvas; 120×165cm (47×65in); 1538. Uffizi, Florence

At about the same time, Titian began his series of Bacchanals for the Duke of Ferrara: *The Worship of Venus* and *Bacchanal of the Andrians* in the Prado, Madrid, and *Bacchus and Ariadne* in the National Gallery, London. The latter was completed in 1523. Its feeling for form and movement is close to the *Assumption* but is contained here in a frieze-like composition reminiscent of antique sculpture.

Bacchanal of the Andrians is probably the last of the series. It may be compared to another, smaller religious work, the *Entombment* in the Louvre, Paris, painted at about the same time for the Duke of Mantua. In his portraits of this period Titian gradually abandoned the restraint of his *Portrait of a Man* (National Gallery, London). This still used the containing parapet of the previous century, and may be dated, on grounds of costume, to *c*1512. He progressed towards the free movement of his *Man with a Glove* (1523; Louvre, Paris).

In the 1530s Titian's style became quieter. The *Presentation of the Virgin* (1534–8) still occupies the place for which he painted it in the Scuola della Carità, Venice, now part of the galleries of the Accademia. The picture reflects the Venetian tradition of civic pageantry and architectural fantasy (to be found about 40 years earlier in the work of Gentile Bellini and Carpaccio). It introduces us to a more subdued palette than that of the 1520s. For his *Venus of Urbino* (1538; Uffizi, Florence) he set the goddess awake, on a bed in a shaded room, with a lapdog and female attendants—no longer a goddess but a lovely woman.

Titian's first contacts with Charles V are commemorated in the full-length portrait of *Charles V with a White Dog* (1532–3; Prado, Madrid). Painted in Bologna in 1533, it is a sublime translation of the mediocre work done by Charles' Austrian court painter in the previous year. The portrait of *The Duke of Urbino* (Uffizi, Florence), painted at the same time as the Venus, is a dramatic presentation of the Duke in armor, as commander of a Papal league against the Turks. This probably reflects the martial spirit Titian infused into the great historical canvas of *The Battle of Cadore*. He was working on this at the time, for the Hall of the Greater Council in the Doges' Palace. The hall was destroyed by fire in 1577. Had Titian's work survived, it might have furnished a clear link with the work of the previous decade.

As early as the *Assumption*, Titian's work had shown knowledge and understanding of contemporary developments in central Italy, but it is not until his work of the 1540s that we begin to feel this as a determining influence. He was friendly with the sculptor and architect Jacopo Sansovino, who had come to Venice after the Sack of Rome in 1527. Titian had also known Giulio Romano and his work in Mantua, and he met Giorgio Vasari, who was in Venice in the early 1540s. We see the fruits of these contacts in such works as the ceiling panels now in the sacristy of S. Maria della Salute, painted between 1542 and 1544, with their more defined drawing, muted color, and bold use of foreshortening. Somewhat similar features distinguish the *St John the Baptist* in the Gallerie dell'Accademia, Venice, and *The Crowning with Thorns* of 1542–4 in the Louvre, Paris.

From 1545 to 1546 Titian made his only visit to Rome. The most important result of his stay is the *Danaë* in Naples (1545–6; Museo e Gallerie Nazionali di Capodimonte). In this painting Titian is measuring himself against Michelangelo, and has adopted for his figure a pose closely related to that of Michelangelo's *Notte* and his *Leda*. According to Vasari, Michelangelo admired the way this picture was painted, but regretted that the Venetian painters' training in drawing was imperfect.

This decade saw Titian's greatest achievements in portraiture. The trio *Clarissa Strozzi* (1542; Staatliche Museen, Berlin), *A Young Englishman* (1545; Pitti Palace, Florence), and *Paul III* (1546; Museo e Gallerie Nazionali di Capodimonte, Naples) shows childhood, manhood, and old age marvelously typified and at the same time individualized. Similar qualities distinguish the great group-portrait of *The Vendramin Family* (1543–7) in the National Gallery, London. The Pope wanted to establish Titian permanently in his service in Rome, but the painter rejected his offers and came to rely increasingly on the patronage first of the Emperor, and then of his son, Phillip II of Spain.

In 1548 Titian was summoned to the Imperial court at Augsburg, where Charles V was settling the affairs of Germany after the defeat of the Protestant princes at Mühlberg in the previous year. Titian was employed on the portraits of the principal actors in these events, and particularly on the equestrian portrait of *Charles V as the Victor of Mühlberg*, now in the Prado, Madrid. This splendid composition provided the model from which, in the next century, the great equestrian portraits by Rubens, Anthony van Dyck, and Velazquez were to derive.

Titian had one more commission for the Emperor: the painting of the Imperial family in adoration of the Trinity (1551–4), known as *La Gloria* and now in the Prado, Madrid, which the Emperor took with him on his retirement from the world in 1556. The vertical composition with its screen of figures shows the impression made on Titian by Michelangelo's *Last Judgment* (Sistine Chapel, Vatican, Rome) but the functions of light, color, and pigment show how very differently he understood the painter's task.

At about the same time as he undertook this picture, Titian began a series of mythological paintings for Philip II. These are less frieze-like in composition than the Ferrara *Bacchanals*, and contain fewer figures on a larger scale. Their more open eroticism perhaps reflects a chord common to painter and patron. These works are distinguished by increasingly free handling of pigment and an overall use of broken color. The *Diana and Actaeon* of 1559 (on loan to the National Gallery of Scotland, Edinburgh, from the Duke of Sutherland) has a complex design in depth which may be contrasted with the frieze-like character of the *Bacchus and Ariadne*. We may also contrast the looser definition of forms in the *Diana and Actaeon*, and the more unified, less contrapuntal use of color.

The *Europa* (1559–62; Isabella Stewart Gardner Museum, Boston), finished a little later, is a singing, shimmering harmony of blue, silver, and pink. By contrast, the grim and vengeful picture of *The Death of Actaeon* in the National Gallery, London, which must have been painted *c*1559 is superficially almost monochrome in its effect, but is made up of the subtlest mingling of browns, greens, and reds. Similar but more silvery effects are seen in *Nymph and Shepherd* (1570; Kunsthistorisches Museum, Vienna). In the design for this, one of his last pictures, Titian seems to have gone back to the work of Giorgione, the companion of his youth. *The Flaying of Marsyas* (1570; Archiepiscopal Palace Museum, Kroměříž), another work probably in his studio at the time of his death, shows, like *The Death of Actaeon*, a sense of cruelty which seems to have formed part of Titian's understanding of the world.

Parallel to these mythologies is a splendid series of religious works, such as the swirling silvery *Annunciation* in S. Salvatore, Venice (early 1560s), and the recreation of the Louvre's *Crowning with Thorns* in terms of flickering lights and broken color. This painting (1570) is now in the Alte Pinakothek, Munich, and must have been among the last canvases on which he worked.

The whole of Titian's career seems to be summed up in the *Pietà* (1570–6) in the Gallerie dell'Accademia, Venice. He intended it for the altar in front of which he wished to be buried. The picture was unfinished at his death, and was tactfully completed by his pupil Palma Giovine. The scene is set before a symmetrical architecture, as in the altarpieces of his master, Giovanni Bellini. The central niche has a shimmering mosaic which may recall his apprenticeship with Sebastiano Zuccato. The gesture of the Magdalene recalls that of Sacred Love in *Sacred and Profane Love* (Museo e Galleria Borghese, Rome), and the central group of Mary and her Son derived from Michelangelo's *Pietà* in St Peter's, Rome. But Titian's *Pietà* points forward as well as looking back. This is the inheritance that Rubens, born in 1578 two years after Titian's death, was to take up and hand on to the future.

Further reading. Crowe, J.A. and Cavalcaselle, G.B. *Titian: his Life and Times* (2 vols.), London (1881, reprinted 1978). Hope, C. *Titian*, London (1980). Pallucchini, R. *Tiziano* (2 vols.), Florence (1969). Panofsky, E. *Problems in Titian, mostly Iconographic*, London and New York (1969). Wethey, H.E. *The Paintings of Titian* (3 vols.), London and Oxford (1969–75).

Tobey Mark 1890–1976

The American painter Mark Tobey was born at Centerville, Wisconsin. His formal artistic training was restricted to a series of Saturday classes at the school of the Chicago Institute of Art (1908). He moved to New York in 1911 and worked there as a fashion designer and interior designer, and then did the same in Chicago, until 1917. In that year he had his first one-man show at Knoedler's, exhibiting charcoal portraits of a fashionable kind. He had already been impressed by the Armory Show, as well as striking up an acquaintance with Marcel Duchamp, but his own artistic aims were still confused.

In the months after the end of the First World War, Tobey became a convert to the Bahai faith, which preaches "A oneness of mankind, an indivisible reality that does not admit of multiplicity". He settled in Seattle (1922–30), but at the beginning of the Depression moved to England; until 1938, his base there was the advanced educational center at Dartington Hall, Devonshire.

Although Tobey had begun as a representational artist, he gradually moved towards a highly personal form of Abstract art. His development was influenced by his newly found religious faith, and by the art forms of the Far East (which he visited in 1934), especially calligraphy. He also became fascinated by Japanese woodcuts and American Indian art. A painting like *Broadway* (1936; Metropolitan Museum, New York) shows Tobey's art at a transitional stage: the perspective is still traditional, and it is possible to make out details of traffic and architecture, but the strongly textured calligraphic style is already beginning to absorb the forms into its own abstract scheme.

By the mid 1940s, the change to abstraction was complete. Tobey's mature style, with its elaborate buildup of tiny calligraphic signs and gestures, and its creation of effects that are both luminous and serene in appearance, can be seen in, for example, his painting *New York* (1945; private collection).

Further reading. Cage, J. et al. *Sounds of the Inner Eye*, Washington, D.C. (2002).

Mark Tobey: Shadow Spirits of the Forest; tempera on paper; 48×63cm (19×25in). Kunstsammlung Nordrhein-Westfalen, Düsseldorf

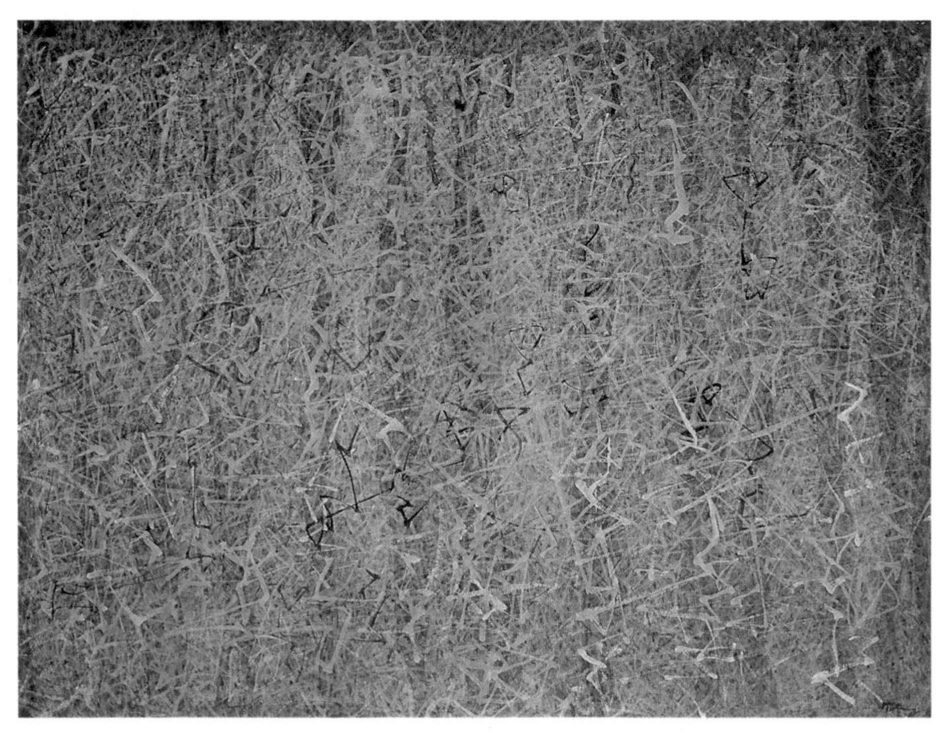

Togan Unkoku 1547–1618

The Japanese painter Unkoku Togan was the founder of the Unkoku School. A Kyushu man of a Samurai family, he first studied with Kano Shoei (1519–92). Later he studied the style of Sesshu (1420–1506), with such success that he became official head of the Sesshu line, inherited the master's Unkokuan studio in western Honshu, and, moreover, adopted the name Unkoku.

Togan's greatest works are the set of ink monochrome sliding doors in the Daitokuji Temple, Kyoto; they are grave in feeling, soft yet detailed, and weighty in execution. Like his contemporary, Yusho, he favored the "boneless" style of figure-painting. His school continued into the 19th century with ink-painting in the Sesshu style.

Tohaku Hasegawa 1539–1610

The Japanese painter Hasegawa Tohaku was the founder of the Hasegawa School.

Above: Hasegawa Tohaku: Pine Woods; detail of a screen; full size 160×355cm (63×140in); c1570. Tokyo National Museum

He studied in the school of Sesshu and claimed to be his artistic heir, although this was disputed by Unkoku Togan. His talents as an ink-painter, however, did not need the authority of Sesshu behind them. Little is known of Tohaku's early life, but it is clear that he had access to Chinese paintings of the Southern Sung dynasty and the Zen works of Mu Ch'i.

His pair of screens depicting pines in the mist (Tokyo National Museum) represent the final absorption of Chinese techniques into a Japanese subject. The great foreground trees loom dimly in the smoky morning, and those further away almost disappear into the gray wash, with astonishing control. So real is this very Japanese scene that, on close inspection, the viewer is surprised by the powerful artifice of the ink work. Other mist-dominated, almost "empty" works, are the monkey and bamboo screens from the Sokokuji Temple, Kyoto. Tohaku was also a master of combining ink and gold washes.

He also attempted the Momoyama decorative style with great success, being the only challenger to Eitoku and his *Kano* successors. The sets of sliding doors at the Chishakuin, Kyoto, were done with his son Kyuzo (1568–93). They represent trees and plants of the four seasons done in ink and colors against gold leaf. Tohaku's naturalism in the famous maple-tree decoration, *Autumn* (Chishakuin, Kyoto), is allied with delicate coloring, powerful line, and dynamic composition to make it possibly the greatest of Momoyama screens.

Tomlin Bradley 1899–1953

Bradley Walker Tomlin, the American painter of the New York School, was born in Syracuse, New York. He studied painting at Syracuse University (1917–21) and then moved to New York, where he lived until his death. He worked as an illustrator, but his independent paintings took on a semi-Abstract, synthetic Cubist appearance. In the late 1940s, under the influence of his Abstract Expressionist contemporaries, he began to develop his mature Abstract style. This was initially calligraphic, with ribbon-like marks over a uniform ground. But his most memorable paintings resemble light colored petals; they consist of squared brush strokes floating over darker layers of loosely painted ground.

Tommaso da Modena 1325–79

Tommaso da Modena was an Italian painter. His style, unlike that of his fellow Modenese artist Barnaba da Siena, was thoroughly up-to-date; it may reflect a training in a center such as Bologna, and the influence of Siena. Much of his work looks like that of a miniaturist working on a large scale, and the confident, naturalistic figure-style is often at odds with the uncertain handling of perspective in surrounding details.

Most of Tommaso's work is to be found not in Modena, but further north, in Treviso. He is recorded there between

Below: Tommaso da Modena: Albertus Magnus, one of the Forty Dominican Worthies; fresco; c1352. S. Niccolò, Treviso

1349 and 1358, and painted frescoes in several Trevisan churches. His chief monument is the decoration of the chapter house of the Dominican church of S. Niccolò (frescoes signed and dated 1352). The subject matter, portraits of *Forty Dominican Worthies*, might have been repetitive and dull, but Tommaso enlivened the figures with many touches of characterization and detail, such as a pair of spectacles balanced on a nose, or the sharpening of a quill pen. On a pillar in the nave of the same church is a fresco of *St Jerome in his Study*, which cleverly adapts the subject to the curved picture surface. S. Margherita, Treviso, contains frescoes of *The Life of St Ursula*; these are believed to be by Tommaso, although the attribution has been questioned.

On the evidence of two signed panel paintings in Karlstein Castle, Prague, one of which includes St Wenceslas, it seems likely that Tommaso actually visited the city, which was then a considerable international center of court patronage. This is likely to have been late in his career, after his documented activity in Modena; he was painting in his native town between 1358 and 1368, but little of his work there has survived.

Toorop Jan 1858–1928

Born in Java, the Dutch painter Jan (Johann Theodorus) Toorop was a link between the late-19th-century avant-garde circles of Brussels, Paris, London, and Holland. He studied first in Amsterdam (1880–2), and then in Brussels (1883–5), where he met James Ensor and the poet Émile Verhaeren. In 1885 he was elected a member of Les Vingt for which he later organized two Dutch exhibitions (in 1891 and 1892). He traveled to Paris, and to London, where he met J.A.M. Whistler, and was impressed by the applied art of William Morris.

After he settled in The Hague in 1890, Toorop's painting moved from a socialist-inspired neo-Impressionism to the Symbolist, early Art Nouveau style of *The Three Brides* (1893; Kröller-Müller Museum, Otterlo). The works of Oscar Wilde provided some of his subject matter; Aubrey Beardsley, William Morris, and Javan shadow puppets were the prototypes for his use of two-dimensional space, his silhouetted figures, and his stylization of natural objects to create an abstract pattern. Toorop was converted to Roman Catholicism in 1905, after which his painting became more traditional in style, and almost entirely devoted to religious subjects.

Torel William 13th century

William Torel was an English goldsmith. His gilded bronze effigies of Queen Eleanor and her father-in-law, Henry III (1293; Westminster Abbey, London) represent the earliest use in England of the *cire perdue* process for casting life-size figures. They were commissioned by Edward I for the Chapel of Edward the Confessor in the Abbey, in imitation of the French royal tombs at St-Denis. Although they are related in form to earlier English stone effigies, their delicate, idealized faces and rippling draperies are characteristic of the sophisticated style of Edward's court school. A second effigy of Queen Eleanor, made—probably from the same model—for Lincoln Cathedral, was destroyed in 1641.

Torres-Garciá Joaquin 1874–1949

The Uraguayan painter Joaquin Torres-Garciá was born in Montevideo. Between 1891 and 1934, when he returned to settle in his native city, he traveled extensively abroad. He went first to Spain; as a student, in Barcelona, he made contact with the Catalan architect Gaudí, who made a deep impression upon him. After a decade in Brussels (1900–10) Torres-Garciá returned to Spain. Ten years later he went to New York (1920–2), then to Italy (1923), and finally to France, where he stayed until 1932.

In Paris, Torres-Garciá was a founder member of the *Cercle et Carré* group of International Constructivists. Despite such geometrical-abstract tendencies, his work has affinities with Paul Klee's, and even with certain of the Surrealists', such as Joan Miró. Like them, Torres-Garciá was interested in the idea of painting as a language of signs, and sought inspiration in primitive art.

Joaquin Torres-Garciá: Design with an Alien Figure; oil on canvas; 89×53cm (35×21in); 1931. Private collection

Torrigiano Pietro 1472–1528

Pietro Torrigiano was an Italian sculptor. He trained at Florence in the Medici sculpture collection under Bertoldo di Giovanni (*c*1490), and specialized in modeling statuettes and busts in terracotta. He was exiled from Florence by 1492, for breaking Michelangelo's nose in a quarrel. He went to Rome and produced a number of busts, three of which are now in the Ospedale di S. Fina, San Gimignano. In 1511 he contracted to make the tomb, in bronze and marble, of Lady Margaret Beaufort, and in 1512 that of King Henry VII and his Queen; both works are in Westminster Abbey, London. His terracotta busts of *Henry VII* (Victoria and Albert Museum, London) and of *Henry VIII* and *Bishop Fisher* (Metropolitan Museum, New York) also date from this period. After executing private commissions, and beginning a tomb for Henry VIII and Katherine of Aragon (1519), he went to Spain; there he modeled in terracotta a *Virgin and Child* and a *St Jerome* (Provincial Museum of Fine Arts, Seville). Torrigiano's sculpture is typical of the Florentine High Renaissance, evolving from the work of Benedetto da Maiano and Verrocchio, but not affected by Michelangelo. It played a crucial role in bringing Renaissance art to England.

Torriti Jacopo *fl.* 1287–92

Jacopo Torriti was an Italian painter and mosaicist. He is known for a signed mosaic in the apse of S. Giovanni in Laterano, Rome (*c*1291) and the mosaic of *The Coronation of the Virgin* in S. Maria Maggiore, Rome (*c*1296). The Lateran

Jacopo Torriti: The Coronation of the Virgin; mosaic; c1296. S. Maria Maggiore, Rome

work was, itself, probably a reworking or imitation of an original of the 4th or 5th century AD—demonstrating one of the sources of his style. In the mosaic of *The Coronation of the Virgin* in S. Maria Maggiore his manner is basically Byzantine. The mosaic resembles the work of Pietro Cavallini, and contains some naturalistic details from late Roman works; but it never attains the vigor of Cavallini, or his sense of monumentality.

Torriti may have worked on the fresco decoration of the Upper Church of St Francis at Assisi (c1290–2). The scenes of *The Creation* clearly recall the style of his Roman work, but the attribution has been disputed.

Toulouse-Lautrec Henri de

1864–1901

Henri de Toulouse-Lautrec was a French painter, printmaker, and poster artist. Born in Albi into the aristocratic family of Toulouse-Lautrec Monfa, he divided his early years between the family estates and school in Paris. His health was delicate, and he broke both femurs, one at 14, one at 15. These injuries left him with a normal torso, but stunted legs. He showed an early capacity for drawing and painting, and was encouraged by the animal painter René Princeteau (1843–1914). In 1882 he entered the atelier of Léon Bonnat, a strict academic teacher; he worked conscientiously and devotedly, and produced many drawings after the model. In 1883 he moved to Cormon's atelier, where he met Émile Bernard and Vincent van Gogh.

Among the influences on his early paintings were Manet, J.A.M. Whistler, and the Impressionists in general, but he reserved his greatest admiration for Degas. The influence of Japanese prints is also clear. In 1885 he finally settled in Paris; from then until his death, he was to observe urban life, especially that of the circus, theater, dance-hall, and brothel. His important paintings include the *Equestrienne of the Fernando Circus* of 1888, *At the Moulin Rouge* of 1892 (both Art Institute of Chicago), and the *Salon in the Rue des Moulins* of 1894 (Musée Toulouse-Lautrec,

Henri de Toulouse-Lautrec: The Salon in the Rue des Moulins; pastel; 112×133cm (44×52in); 1894. Musée Toulouse-Lautrec, Albi

Albi). He became a master of summary characterization, of tellingly abbreviated spatial effects, of the laconic line, and of heightened, non-naturalistic color. Most of his paintings were done with thinned oil-paint on unprimed cardboard; some were works in their own right; others, however, were rapid studies for his pictures and his posters.

It was in 1891 that Toulouse-Lautrec produced his first poster for the Moulin Rouge. Its large size, its eye-catching play of flattened and exaggerated shapes (for instance the continuous black silhouette of the onlookers in the background), and its simple and direct use of color revolutionized the art of the poster, transforming it from the Rococo-inspired extravaganzas of Jules Cheret into the immediacy of Art Nouveau. Toulouse-Lautrec designed some 31 posters: in each, his exploitation of the resources of color lithography was skillful, idiosyncratic, and assured.

He began using lithography as early as 1885, but his greatest period of production was during the 1890s, coinciding with his work on the posters. Many of his lithographs were produced as series by the rapidly expanding print publishers. Among them are *Le Café Concert* (1893), 16 lithographs of the performer Yvette Guilbert (1894; text by Gustave Geoffroy), followed by a further set of the same (1898), *Elles*, a set of 11 lithographs (1896), and *Les Histoires Naturelles* of Jules Renard (1899).

Throughout his career, Toulouse-Lautrec used pastel and watercolor with brevity and wit. During a period of convalescence in a clinic in 1899, he worked on a series of drawings of the circus. His last paintings show a trend towards Expressionism, both in mood and in color.

Further reading. *Adheman, J. Toulouse-Lautrec: his Complete Lithographs and Drypoints*, New York (1965). Caproni, G. and Sugana, G.M. *L'Opera Completa di Toulouse-Lautrec*, Milan (1969). Cooper, D. *Henri de Toulouse-Lautrec*, London (1955). Toulouse-Lautrec, H. (ed. Goldschmidt, L. and Schimmel, H.) *Unpublished Correspondence*, London (1969).

Toyokuni Utagawa 1769–1825

Utagawa Toyokuni was a Japanese print artist of the *Ukiyoe* school. He was the true founder of the Utagawa figure-style which dominated the field for nearly a century. His master Toyoharu trained him in the *Ukiyoe* tradition and actually founded the Utagawa School. The style was characterized by a long face, hatchet chin, and tortured expression; although it suited heroic works, it killed the tradition of prints of beautiful women.

In his earlier years, Toyokuni had emulated the beauties of Utamaro and Eishi with some success, but his real talent was for the portrayal of actors, either full-length, or half-length, or "large head". In his last years, commercial considerations seemed to overcome his artistic scruples.

Traini Francesco *fl.* 1321–63

The Italian painter Francesco Traini came from Pisa. He is known both from documents and from a signed panel painting of *St Dominic* of 1345 (Museo Nazionale di S. Matteo, Pisa). This came from the same church as a panel painting of the Dominican *St Thomas Aquinas in Glory* (S. Caterina, Pisa) that can be attributed to him. It is clear from these two panels that Traini was strongly influenced by the Sienese painter Simone Martini (1280/5–1344), who painted an altarpiece in Pisa in 1320, and by the Lorenzetti. In 1321 we first hear of Traini in connection with the frescoes of the Camposanto, Pisa. Although it is still a matter of controversy, it seems likely that Traini painted the frescoes there of *The Triumph of Death, Last Judgment, Hell*, and *Legends of Hermits*. These were formerly dated to about the 1350s, but it is now believed that they were painted earlier.

The frescoes reflect the fear of God's judgment, which was so prevalent in the middle of the 14th century. The *Last Judgment* is accompanied by a vision of Hell far more dominant than any glimpse we are given of Paradise. In *The Triumph of Death*, Traini uses the emotional, Gothic elements of Sienese art to emphasize the cruel indifference of Death. The crippled and blind call out for deliverance from life, but Death instead strikes out at a group of young men and ladies enjoying a life of courtly pleasure.

The Camposanto frescoes have been damaged by war and the passage of time, but underneath them have been revealed *sinopie* of great beauty; these give a rare opportunity to study this usually hidden aspect of the art of the 14th-century painter.

Trdat of Armenia *fl.* 972–1036

The Armenian architect Trdat worked for the Bagratid court of Ani. His work marks a Renaissance of Armenian architecture. Although he used church plans and decorative elements from 7th-century Armenia, he made important modifications to the earlier style. He applied the pointed arch and the rib and colonnette in clustered piers, in vaulting, and in blind arcades to produce an effect resembling that of the Gothic architecture that came a century later.

His first commission was the cathedral of Argina (972–91). His renown is demonstrated by his employment in Constantinople to repair the damaged dome of S. Sophia (989). This direct contact with Byzantine architecture apparently left little

Above: Utagawa Toyokuni: The Festival Offerings; woodblock print; 38×25cm (15×10in); c1789. Private collection

Below: Francesco Traini: St Dominic and Scenes from his Life; panel; 1345. Museo Nazionale di S. Matteo, Pisa

mark on his subsequent work. For the cathedral of Ani (988–1000) he reused the 7th-century Armenian "cross in rectangle" plan which featured a dome supported by four piers. The church of St Gregory of Gagik (1001–10), also at Ani, is based on the aisled-tetraconch church of Zvartnots at Vagharchapat (641–61). A third church at Ani, the Holy Savior (1036), has a similarly centralized design.

Troost Cornelis 1697–1750

Cornelis Troost was a painter of the Dutch bourgeoisie in early-18th-century Amsterdam. He is associated with the development of the increasingly fashionable "Conversation Piece": a group portrait in which sitters are shown in their domestic setting and engaged in conversation, the playing of music, or some other leisurely or cultured activity. He also painted a number of humorous genre pictures, notably the series of five "NELRI" paintings in The Hague (Royal Museum of Art, Mauritshuis), which illustrate the debauchery accompanying a reunion supper party. Despite the absence of any moralizing intent, this type of work (done in pastel and gouache) earned Troost the designation of the "Dutch Hogarth". Troost, like William Hogarth (1697–1764), was interested in the theater. He painted pictures of contemporary theatrical performances, and also designed scenery for Amsterdam's municipal theater.

Cornelis Troost: The Dilettanti; oil on canvas; 66×56cm (26×22in); 1736. National Gallery of Ireland, Dublin

Trumbull John 1756–1843

The American painter and diplomat John Trumbull left his homeland in order to study under Benjamin West in London. During a visit to Paris he saw works by J.-L. David and Charles Lebrun and fell under their influence. On his return to the United States he painted scenes from the American Revolution. He made a second visit to London (1794–1804) as a commissioner for the Jay Treaty. Between 1816 and 1837 he worked on four of the eight canvases that decorate the interior of Capitol Rotunda, Washington. He played a leading role in the American Academy of Fine Arts, and was president of it from 1816 to 1835. He painted many portraits and modern history pictures, and also a fine group of American landscapes, mainly waterfalls.

Tucker William 1935–

The English sculptor William Tucker was born in Cairo. He read history at Oxford University (1955–8), then studied sculpture at the Central School of Art and Design and at St Martin's School of Art, London (1959–60). In 1961 he began teaching sculpture at Goldsmiths' College and at St Martin's School of Art. From 1968 to 1970 he was Gregory Fellow at Leeds University. He published *The Language of Sculpture* in 1974.

From 1960 Tucker worked with cut and welded iron, and created wood sculptures and reliefs. This led him to a concern with volume, contour, and symmetry; he began to use combinations of plaster, wood, polyester, and metal. From 1962 to 1969, his use of color added formal definition to his work. In 1964 he made symmetrical fabricated steel and fiberglass pieces, with repeated elements; later he turned to various permutations of a few cylindrical units. In 1970 he reacted against his former style, and made several series of works in wood, steel tubes, and bars; these were open, linear, complex, and intuitively constructed.

Tung Ch'i-ch'ang 1555–1636

The Chinese painter Tung Ch'i-ch'ang was a native of Hua T'ing. He was a successful graduate who rose to become an official in the Board of Rites, before retiring to live on his family estates. He was an accomplished painter with impeccable technique, and a great admirer of many old masters, particularly of Mi Fei (1051–1107) and Ni

John Trumbull: The Declaration of Independence, Philadelphia, 4 July 1776; oil on canvas; 51×76cm (20×30in); 1786–1819/20. Yale University Art Gallery, New Haven

Tsan (1301–74). His analytical nature led him to explore the construction and composition of landscape painting. He was a scholar of great erudition, and defined landscape in terms of the paintings of the old masters devoid of vulgarity or sentimentality, of spiritual significance. His own works follow the academic, eclectic tradition to which he was devoted.

With a group of artists known as the Nine Friends, but most notably with Mo Shih-lung, he undertook the study and classification of painting. The group's object was to point the right path for painting. They judged from a moral standpoint not only the painters of the past, but also their contemporaries. At the close of the Ming Dynasty, painting was moving towards a greater diversity of style. The Wu and Che schools had polarized two of the contrasting styles of the previous periods. Tung wished to point out the pitfalls of what he regarded as the superficialities of the Che School, and the painting from which it derived, which he termed the "Northern School". The corollary to this was his wish to evaluate the great line of landscape artists whose work had been inherited by the scholar painter tradition, described by Tung as the "Southern School".

Tung seems to have been the first art historian to do more than list and grade artists, and his classification is extremely perceptive. Unfortunately his strictures rather than his constructive comments have been remembered, and have sometimes inhibited lesser artists. After his day, the movement toward diversification continued; his classification, although preserved and still used, does not readily apply to many great works produced in the 17th century and later.

As a painter, Tung Ch'i-ch'ang shows a certain gracelessness, but he is an unusual Chinese painter in that he is above all a theoretician. His large compositions appear to be mere skeletons of Chinese classical painting. Explicitly working out the structure, he builds ever more convoluted mountains which strain the mechanisms of both surface and recessional composition. There is no place in Tung's large works for nuance or atmosphere. These are not abstractions, but they are analytical, and have the fascination of a complex structure. In his album leaves and his less formal painting one sees another side to this versatile artist. His small paintings are almost romantic in style; they are not original, but are more easily appreciated than his large compositions.

Tung Yuan *fl.* 947–70

The Chinese painter Tung Yuan came from the Chiangnan. He was called to the Court of the Southern T'ang during the Five Dynasties, and worked there for Li Hou-Chou, his ruler and patron. He held office as a court painter, and was a master of many styles. Tradition has it that he painted landscape in color in the style of Li Ssu-hsun, and that his figure-painting was meticulous and magically lifelike. It was his ink landscape painting, however, that established his reputation. He is said to have followed Wang Wei, and to have developed a style of soft ink tone, in which—according to contemporary critics—"only at a distance the object is clear". He created atmospheric effects of mist and rain and storm. Very little painting can be attributed as representative of his style. His immense influence on Chinese landscape painting rests on his depiction of soft southern landscape, in which a distant range of hills juts forward in a spur reaching to the foreground. He was also known for his fine painting of the trees, often making a group of contrasted trees form a focal point in a mountain landscape. This feature of his work was later to become an artistic cliché.

Tura Cosmè *c*1430–95

The Italian painter Cosmè Tura became the first great master of the Ferrarese school. He is recorded in the service of Duke Borso d'Este of Ferrara from 1451; in the following year he became a salaried employee, continuing as court painter until 1486, when he was succeeded by Ercole Roberti. A will made by Tura in 1471 shows that he had accumulated sufficient wealth to provide for the building and decorating of a church, and to bequeath a large sum of money to the poor of Venice. But less than 20 years later, in 1490, he described himself to Duke Ercole d'Este as poor, sick, and unable to work or support himself. The fashion for his idiosyncratic style of painting had evidently passed.

Tura's work for the Ferrarese Court (which included many items other than panel or mural painting) has mainly disappeared. That which survives shows that the most important influence on his style came from Padua, from the Squarcionesque painters, and from Mantegna and Donatello. In addition, Piero della Francesca's lost frescoes in Ferrara were certainly influential. His stylistic development cannot be accurately traced because of the scarcity of dated or datable works. Paintings that probably date from early in his career include *Madonna with the Sleeping Child* (Gallerie dell'Accademia, Venice), the dismembered altarpiece from the Ferrarese church of S. Maria della Consolazione (Musée Fesch, Ajaccio, and Italian public and private collections), and *Allegorical Figure* (National Gallery, London).

The Roverella Altarpiece (National Gallery, London) can be dated fairly precisely to 1474. In it we see many of the characteristic features of Tura's style, such as the wiry outline surrounding his firmly modeled figures, in which surfaces reflect rather

Cosmè Tura: Virgin and Child Enthroned (The Roverella Altarpiece); panel; 239×102cm (94×40in); c1474. National Gallery, London

than absorb light. We also notice his use of bright, flickering colors and of rich decorative details, most of which are derived directly from natural phenomena—especially shells, fish, and fruit. These are the distinguishing features of the Ferrarese school, which flourished during the second half of the 15th century and which included manuscript illuminators as well as panel painters. Other works by Tura, such as the damaged frescoes of the *Months* (Palazzo Schifanoia, Ferrara) and the *Lamentation* from the Roverella Altarpiece (Louvre, Paris), show the artist's abilities both in narrative painting, and in the depiction of pain and passion.

Turnbull William 1922–

The Anglo-Scots sculptor and painter William Turnbull was born in Dundee. He studied at the Slade School of Fine Art, London (1946–8), and then lived in Paris (1948–50). He worked at the Central School of Arts and Crafts, London, as a visiting instructor in Experimental Design (1952–61) and as a teacher of sculpture (1964–71). Since the late 1940s, his sculpture and paintings have emphasized cool simplicity and directness through a repetition of elements. His early stick or line sculptures led, through heads and masks, to stark, upright bronze "idols" and permutation pieces made of bronze and wood. His emphasis upon the vertical continued in the painted steel tube and zigzag sculptures that he made in the mid 1950s. Until the late 1970s his sculptures were permutations of identical elements, either upright on bases or lying, in metal, perspex, and wood. As a painter, he first produced Dubuffet-like heads, and tachist monochrome works. Later, pure color began to predominate, used in flat planes with borders or stripes, in one or two colors.

William Turnbull: Head; bronze; height 20cm (8in); 1955. Collection of Mr D. Blinken, New York

J.M.W. Turner: A Scene on the Loire; body color and watercolor on blue-gray paper; 14×19cm (5½×7½in). Ashmolean Museum, Oxford

Turner J.M.W. 1775–1851

Joseph Mallord William Turner, born in London, was probably the greatest of all British painters, and the greatest landscape painter of the Romantic movement. Though firmly rooted in the academic traditions of the 18th century, his development was unmatched and his range covered all fields, including portraiture.

Turner's earliest artistic activity is said to have been the coloring of prints, which were sold in his father's barbershop. His first signed and dated watercolors were painted in 1786, and his first sketches from nature, in the "Oxford" sketchbook, probably dated from 1789 (British Museum, London). He became a pupil of the architectural topographer Thomas Malton (1748–1804) *c*1789 and entered the Royal Academy Schools the same year.

His first exhibit at the Royal Academy, the crude watercolor of *The Archbishop's Palace, Lambeth* (Indianapolis Museum of Art), was in 1790. In 1791 he began a series of annual sketching tours in Britain which provided material for highly accomplished topographical watercolors intended for exhibition, for landed patrons, or for engravings. These were in the traditional technique of the "tinted drawing": first a pencil outline, then monochrome washes establishing the broad areas of light and shade, and finally the local color, still restrained in tone.

From *c*1794 to 1797 Turner spent the winter evenings, together with Thomas Girtin and others, copying drawings by J.R. Cozens and other artists for the famous art connoisseur and collector Dr Monro. This introduced him to a different watercolor tradition, that of generalized, idealized landscapes. Although these depicted recognizable places, they conveyed atmosphere and mood in a freer technique than that of the earlier, topographical works. In 1799, the diarist Joseph Farington recorded that Turner had "no systematic process for making drawings ... By washing and occasionally rubbing out, he at last expresses in some degree the idea in his mind".

In 1796 Turner exhibited his first oil painting, *Fishermen at Sea* (Tate Gallery, London). This is a moonlight scene with

J.M.W. Turner: Snow Storm: Hannibal and his Army Crossing the Alps; oil on canvas; 145×236cm (57×93in); exhibited in 1812. Tate Gallery, London

contrasted warm light from a lamp in the manner of C.J. Vernet, P.J. de Loutherbourg, and Joseph Wright of Derby. In other oils of the later 1790s, such as *Buttermere Lake, a Shower* and *Morning amongst the Coniston Fells, Cumberland* (both Tate Gallery, London), the strongest influence is that of Richard Wilson, but Turner already surpasses his masters in the subtlety of his effects of weather and time of day—an interest echoed in his titles.

Turner was elected an Associate of the Royal Academy in 1799, and a full member in 1802. This early success was accompanied by a determined effort to make his mark with large pictures challenging the Old Masters. *The Fifth Plague of Egypt*, exhibited at the Royal Academy (R.A.) in 1800 (now Indianapolis Museum of Art), rivals Poussin; *Bridgewater Sea-piece* (or *Dutch Boats in a Gale*, R.A. 1801; private collection) brought new energy to the marine tradition that had been introduced into Britain in the 17th century by William van der Velde and his son.

In 1802, Turner's first journey abroad took him to the Savoy Alps. In Paris he visited the Louvre, where he made detailed studies of the Old Masters. His 1803 exhibits included the Titianesque *Holy Family* (Tate Gallery, London). Other works shown that year combined his ambitions more directly with the record of places seen. Among them were *Calais Pier* (National Gallery, London), based on his stormy crossing of the English Channel, the Poussinesque *Château de St Michael, Bonneville, Savoy* (Paul Mellon Center for British Art, New Haven, Conn.), and the Claudian *Festival upon the Opening of the Vintage at Maçon* Sheffield City Art Galleries). A later example is *Snow Storm: Hannibal and his Army Crossing the Alps* (R.A. 1812; Tate Gallery, London), which combines his experience of the Alps with a dramatic storm he experienced in Yorkshire, a picture inspired by the Romantic interest in Hannibal (the series is described in Mrs Radcliffe's *The Mysteries of Udolpho*, 1794) and by David's *Napoleon Crossing the St Bernard Pass* (1800; Versailles). *Crossing the Brook* (R.A. 1815; Tate Gallery, London) is an Italianate, Claudian view of the Tamar Valley in Devonshire. The two grand Claudian port scenes, *Dido Building Carthage* (R.A. 1815; National Gallery, London) and *The Decline of the Carthaginian Empire* (R.A. 1817; Tate Gallery, London), are early examples of Turner's preoccupation with the rise and fall of empires, and show the relevance of his painting to contemporary affairs.

His *Liber Studiorum* ("Book of Studies") engravings of landscapes categorized as "Historical", "Mountainous", "Pastoral", "Marine", "Architectural", or "Epic Pastoral", and issued in parts from 1807 to 1819, illustrate Turner's range, and his consciously didactic approach. At the same time, he continued sketching from nature; he produced more intimate landscapes for exhibition, lighter in tone and more atmospheric than his grander historical landscapes. The key works in this development are *Sun Rising through Vapour* (R.A. 1807; National Gallery, London), which also reflects Dutch models, and several groups of sketches on the Thames. Some of these are in pencil and watercolor, as in *The Thames from Reading to Walton* sketchbook (*c*1806–7; Tate Gallery, London); others are among his rare sketches from nature in oils, both on small mahogany panels and on larger canvases (these probably also date from *c*1806–7).

The more intimate style he developed appears in commissioned views of houses, such as the pair showing Tabley: *Tabley, the Seat of Sir J.F. Leicester, Bart.: Windy Day* (R.A. 1809; University of Manchester) and *Tabley the Seat of ... Calm Morning* (R.A. 1809; Petworth House, Sussex), *Petworth* (Petworth House, Sussex), and *Somer-Hill* (R.A. 1811; National Gallery of Scotland, Edinburgh). He also employed it in views of less specific locations, such as *Ploughing Up Turnips, near Slough* (1809; Tate Gallery, London) and *Dorchester Mead, Oxfordshire* (1810; Tate Gallery, London). The most considerable group of watercolors was that done for Walter Fawkes, in and around his Yorkshire home, Farnley Hall, between 1809 and 1818 (most of them are still at Farnley Hall). Similar in mood, though rather more finished, were the watercolors done for series of engravings, beginning with *The Southern Coast*, published from 1814 to 1826. In these works Turner's precise sense of locality extended to the depiction of the economic activities typical of each place.

In 1817, after the final defeat of Napoleon, Turner went abroad again, to the Low Countries, partly to gather material for *The Field of Waterloo* (1818; Tate Gallery, London). His journey resulted in a renewed interest in Dutch painting, particularly in the work of Aelbert Cuyp (1620–91); this led to a series of large pictures of harbors, beginning with the *Dort* (R.A. 1818; Paul Mellon Center for British Art, New Haven, Conn.). On the same trip Turner went up the Rhine as far as Mainz. He filled sketchbooks with small studies (in the Turner Bequest in the Tate Gallery, London), on the basis of which he completed, within three months, 51 finished watercolors (examples in the British Museum, London).

Turner's first visit to Italy, long anticipated in his paintings, occurred in 1819. He did a large number of drawings and watercolors in Venice, and in and around Rome and Naples; Venice in particular produced a new purity and delicacy in his colors. But in the next five years he only exhibited four oil paintings, the lightweight *What you Will*, a pun on Watteau (R.A. 1820; Collection of Sir Michael Sobell, Englefield Green, Surrey), and three large Italian subjects: the artistic manifesto *Rome from the Vatican* (R.A. 1820; Tate Gallery, London), *The Bay of Baiae, with Apollo and the Sybil*, a grand panoramic landscape that set the pattern for several later works (R.A. 1823; Tate Gallery, London) and *Forum Romanum* (R.A. 1826; Tate Gallery, London).

However, it was in the later 1820s that Turner painted the first of the oil sketches, or unfinished pictures, that are now among his most admired works. One group is associated with Petworth House, where the unconventional Third Earl of Egremont even gave Turner a studio. Sketches of *c*1828 show Petworth Park and neighboring places such as Chichester Canal, more finished versions of which remain at Petworth. Also associated with Petworth, but probably dating from the mid 1830s, are the partly Rembrandt-inspired interiors such as *Music Party, Petworth* (*c*1835; Tate Gallery, London) and *Interior at Petworth* (*c*1837; Tate Gallery, London). These grew out of a group of small figure scenes done in body-color on blue paper—a technique developed from the drawings in pencil, pen and white chalk on blue paper, done while Turner was staying with the architect John Nash on the Isle of Wight in 1827.

On that visit Turner also painted another group of delightful oil sketches. He used some of them for two pictures of *East Cowes Castle, the Regatta Beating to Windward* (R.A. 1828; Indianapolis Museum of Art) and *Starting for their Moorings* (R.A. 1828; Victoria and Albert Museum, London). All of these sketches were painted on two large rolls of canvas (only cut into separate pictures in 1905). This extraordinary procedure saved having separate stretchers, and made for ease of transport; Turner used the method again on his second visit to Italy (1828–9).

This second Italian visit was extremely productive of finished oil paintings, three even being exhibited at Rome: *Orvieto* (1828; reworked 1830; Tate Gallery, London) *Vision of Medea* (1828; Tate Gallery, London), and *Regulus* (1828, reworked 1837; Tate Gallery, London). All were exhibited again back in London, but only after considerable reworking. One of the oil sketches painted in Rome was used for *Ulysses Deriding Polyphemus* (R.A. 1829; National Gallery, London).

The remarkable feature of Turner's reworking was that, from as early as 1815, much of it was done after the paintings had been hung on the walls of the Royal Academy or the British Institution. It took place during the so-called Varnishing Days, which were allowed to members for

J.M.W. Turner: Petworth: Playing Billiards; watercolor on paper; 140×190cm ($5\frac{1}{2}$×$7\frac{1}{2}$in); c1827–30. Tate Gallery, London

minor adjustments necessitated by accidents of placing or lighting. Of *Orvieto* and *Pilate Washing his Hands* (R.A. 1830; Tate Gallery, London), a critic wrote that it was "difficult to define their subject" when they were first sent in; and of *The Burning of the House of Lords and Commons, 16 October 1834* (R.A. 1835; Philadelphia Museum of Art) E.V. Rippingille wrote that it was, when sent in, "a mere dab of several colors and 'without form and void', like chaos before the Creation". These and similar accounts show that what are now regarded as perhaps Turner's greatest works, the ethereal watercolor-like studies such as *Norham Castle, Sunrise* (c1835–40; Tate Gallery, London) are the chance survivors among oil sketches intended for later completion as pictures for exhibition.

In 1833 Turner exhibited *Bridge of Sighs, Ducal Palace and Custom-House, Venice: Canaletti Painting* (R.A. 1833; Tate Gallery, London), a typical tribute to an earlier painter. It was probably not until later the same year that he returned to Venice, for the first time since 1819. The Venetian pictures he continued to exhibit until 1837, and again from 1840 (the year of his third and last visit) until 1846, were among the most popular of his later works. His early aristocratic patrons had died, or had withdrawn support because of the hostile criticism of the connoisseur Sir George Beaumont. His chief patrons were now mainly *nouveau-riche* manufacturers or dealers. The critics, increasingly baffled by his later style, continued, however, to be impressed by the sheer impact of his work: "gorgeous" and "extravagant" are their most common adjectives. In 1843, Turner found a new champion with the publication of the first volume of John Ruskin's *Modern Painters*.

Turner's later output showed an increasing range of subjects and formats. There were industrial scenes such as *Keelmen heaving in Coals by Night* (R.A. 1835; National Gallery of Art, Washington, D.C.) and four pictures of *Whalers* exhibited in 1845 and 1846; one now in the Metropolitan Museum, New York, the others in the Tate Gallery, London). Pictures pairing ancient and modern Italy and Rome (*Ancient Italy, Ovid Banished from Rome*, R.A. 1838, private collection; *Modern Italy, the Pifferari*, R.A. 1838, Glasgow Art Gallery and Museum; *Ancient Rome ...*, R.A. 1839, Tate Gallery, London; *Modern Rome, Campo Vaccino*, R.A. 1839, private collection) led on to pairs, square or octagonal in shape, of contrasted coloring. These include *Peace—Burial at Sea* and *War—the Exile and the Rock Limpet* (R.A. 1842; both now in the Tate Gallery, London) and the experiments stimulated by reading Charles Eastlake's translation of Goethe's *Theory of Colours (Shade and Darkness—the Evening of the Deluge*, R.A. 1843, and *Light and Colour (Goethe's Theory)—the Morning after the Deluge—Moses Writing the Book of Genesis*, R.A. 1843; both Tate Gallery, London).

From c1840 Turner's compositions became rather less disciplined, his colors more broken, and his handling more fragmentary. In his best works the effect is more brilliant than ever, as in *Slavers Throwing Overboard the Dead and the Dying—Typhoon Coming On* (R.A. 1840; Museum of Fine Arts, Boston), *Snow Storm—Steam-Boat off a Harbour's Mouth* (R.A. 1842; Tate Gallery, London), and the apocalyptic *Angel Standing in the Sun* (R.A. 1846; Tate Gallery, London) perhaps intended as a deliberate "last work". In 1847 and 1849 he exhibited three pictures; all were from early in the century, though he repainted two of them. In 1850, in a final effort, he exhibited four pictures on the perennial theme of Carthage. In the exhibition of 1851 he showed nothing, and on 19 December of that year he died.

One great exception to this decline was the series of late Swiss watercolors. In 1842 and 1843 he painted 15 particularly highly finished examples on commission, including the *Red, Blue*, and *Dark Rigis* (National Gallery of Victoria, Melbourne, and private collections). He continued to paint further subjects until at least 1846.

During his lifetime, and for the rest of the 19th century, Turner was admired for his finished works. Only in the 20th century have the riches of his unfinished oils and watercolors become known, through the gradual bringing to light of the Turner Bequest, acquired by the British Nation as the result of his confused and disputed will. It is possible that Turner would have wanted to be judged solely on what he himself defined in his will as his "finished works". An essential part of these was their moral content, often based on mythological, historical, or literary sources—though he had received little academic education, and his reading was enthusiastic rather than thorough. It is a great part of his achievement that he was able to enlarge the repertoire of his early Academic masterpieces to include scenes of less specific storms, fires, and glowing light, in which he gave expression to the forces of nature and their importance for mankind.

Further reading. Butlin, M. and Joll, E. *The Paintings of J.M.W. Turner,* rev. ed., New Haven (1987). Butlin, M., Wilton, A., and Gage, J. *Turner 1775–1851*, London (1974). Gowing, L. *Turner: Imagination and Reality*, New York (1966). Hamilton, J. *Turner: A Life,* New York (2003). Lindsay, J. *J.M.W. Turner: his Life and Work*, London (1966, reissued 1971). Wilton, A. *The Life and Work of J.M.W. Turner*, London (1979).

Twachtman John 1853–1902

John Twachtman was an American Impressionist painter who, with Childe Hassam, Theodore Robinson, and J. Alden Weir was part of the American Ten Exhibition in 1898. American Impressionists were among the most popular painters at the turn of the century, yet their art generally placed more emphasis on subject matter than on purely visual sensation, as with their French prototypes. Twachtman worked with Frank Duveneck in Munich during the 1870s. He went to Paris in 1883, and came closer than most of his contemporaries to the art of Monet, especially in late works such as *Hemlock Pool* (1902; Addison Gallery of American Art, Andover, Mass.).

Twombly Cy 1929–

After studying at the Museum of Fine Arts, Boston, the Art Students League, New York, and Black Mountain College, the American painter and graphic artist Cy Twombly moved to Rome in 1957. He developed a distinctive, calligraphic style, his surfaces being covered with seemingly random scribbles and marks, and with occasional scraps of text or diagram. With their emphasis on randomness—Twombly was strongly influenced by John Cage—and process, recording countless graffiti-like marks and erasures, his works reveal a fascination with the deepest sources of creativity. He was inspired by children's art, Surrealist automatism and, more directly, Abstract Expressionism, though his mood is lighter and more ironic.

U

Uccello 1397–1475

Paolo di Dono was a Florentine painter; he was nicknamed "Uccello" (bird) because of his paintings of birds and animals. Younger than Brunelleschi and Donatello, and older than Masaccio, Alberti, and Piero della Francesca, Uccello belonged to a generation of artists concerned with the general movement away from late Gothic forms, towards naturalism. His work is characterized by an obsession with perspective, blended with a passion for clear colors and tapestry-like compositions.

It is recorded that by 1407 Uccello was apprenticed to Lorenzo Ghiberti (1378–1455); he remained in the Ghiberti workshop until 1415, when he joined the guild of painters. Details of Uccello's early activity are not clear, but from 1425 until 1431 he was a master mosaicist at St Mark's in Venice, and was therefore away from Florence during the period when Masaccio was creating the important frescoes in the Brancacci Chapel (1425–8; S. Maria del Carmine, Florence).

Uccello's rapid absorption of new Renaissance ideas on his return to Florence in 1431 is demonstrated by his fresco of Sir John Hawkwood, painted in 1436 on the wall of Florence Cathedral. The foreshortening and modeling give the *trompe-l'oeil* impression that the fresco of this English *condottiere* is a statue—the painting was indeed a substitute for the sculptural effigy originally planned. Uccello's painting of *Four Prophets* of 1443 round the clock face of the cathedral further extends his experiments towards seemingly three-dimensional pictorial space.

In 1445 Uccello painted *The Flood* in the Green Cloister of S. Maria Novella in Florence; here modeling, architectural recession, and light and shadow play important parts. *The Flood* may be seen as a visual interpretation of the theories expounded by Alberti in his *Della Pittura* of 1436. Alberti's two basic art principles—beauty derived from geometry, and decorative form as ornament—are fully realized in this work. Uccello contrasts young, old, clothed, and naked figures, birds, and animals as though to satisfy Alberti's demands in *Della Pittura* for a copious and varied composition. Both the recession to one vanishing point, and the strange doughnut-shaped collar worn by one of the figures in the foreground are characteristic of Uccello's interest in geometrically constructed space.

Uccello's greatest work consists of three panels, painted c1456, representing *The Rout of San Romano* (now in the National Gallery, London; the Uffizi, Florence; and the Louvre, Paris). The work was commissioned by Cosimo de' Medici, and doubtless gave great pleasure to his seven-year-old grandson, Lorenzo, for it is a bloodless but action-packed battle scene depicting the triumph of the Florentine army over that of Siena in 1432. On another level, it serves to mark the power of the Medici banking family in Florentine finance and politics. Uccello's work is a magical combination of scientific perspective and festive love of incident and action. Broken lances serve both to suggest the melée of battle, and to act as perspective lines to lead the eye inward towards the horizon. In the London panel, a foreshortened, fallen knight and curved armor form part of the perspectival checkerboard of events. Uccello has neatly dovetailed the new linear perspective with existing rules relating to the visual impression that warm colors, like red, jump forward, and cold colors, like blue or green, recede.

Uccello: St George and the Dragon; tempera on panel; 52×90cm (20×35in); 1456–60. Musée Jacquemart-André, Paris

Uccello: A Hunt in a Forest; detail; tempera on wood; full size 65×165cm (26×65in); c1468. Ashmolean Museum, Oxford

St George and the Dragon (c1455–60; National Gallery, London) uses similar, but less obvious, perspective tricks; the profiled princess still retains an elongated, Gothic quality. The painting is on canvas, rather than the panel which had been more usual, indicating a change in taste: it is a portable possession of beauty, rather than a fixed devotional object. *A Hunt in a Forest* (c1468; Ashmolean Museum, Oxford), possibly Uccello's last work, is a veritable carnival in paint showing a hunting party. The movement of the animals is stylized, with their front legs raised and their back legs on the ground. This is a repetition of the formula used for the horses in *The Rout of San Romano* and *St George and the Dragon* paintings, and perfectly suggests their springiness.

Uccello's lasting achievement was his ability to overlay basic Quattrocento geometric structure with poetic detail, although the skull beneath the skin is always visible.

Further reading. Pope-Hennessy, J. *Paolo Uccello*, London (1969). White, J. *The Birth and Rebirth of Pictorial Space*, London (1957).

Ugolino da Siena *fl.* 1295–c1339

The Sienese painter Ugolino da Siena was sometimes called Ugolino di Nerio. According to Vasari, he was a pupil of Cimabue. He was active in Siena between 1317 and 1327. His only authenticated work is the high altar painted for S. Croce, Florence (c1320?; panels now scattered, between the National Gallery, London, the Staatliche Museen, Berlin, and the Philadelphia Museum of Art). The style of his painting, and even the details of composition, demonstrate how closely he followed Duccio, whose great *Maestà* (Museo del'Opera del Duomo, Siena) was painted between 1308 and 1311.

Ugolino di Vieri *fl.* 1329–85

Ugolino di Vieri was a Sienese goldsmith. His masterpieces are the Reliquary of the Holy Corporal (1338; Orvieto Cathedral) and the Reliquary of S. Savino (c1338; Orvieto Cathedral), the latter made in cooperation with the otherwise unknown Viva di Lando. The former work, nearly 5 ft (145 cm) in height, is formed like a miniature cathedral: it has pinnacles of amazing delicacy, gargoyles, and even a division of the body of the work into "nave" and "aisles". It is decorated with 32 scenes in enamel, of which the Passion subjects show the influence of similar scenes from Duccio's *Maestà* (1308–11; Museo del'Opera del Duomo, Siena). Ugolino's scenes of *The Miracle of Bolsena* and the early life of Christ in the Orvieto Reliquary of the Holy Corporal are close to the frescoes of Ambrogio Lorenzetti (S. Francesco, Siena).

Ulrich von Ensingen c1350–1419

Ulrich von Ensingen was a German master mason. His most important work, from 1392, was at Ulm Minster. Work on the Minster had been started in 1377 by the Parler family. He altered the design by lengthening the nave to ten bays, and broadening the aisles (since subdivided) to the same width as the nave. At the west end he began the huge tower with its triple bay porch. Its openwork masonry style is a typical German late Gothic feature; it was used by Ulrich in his other great work, at Strasbourg Cathedral, where he built the octagon stage of the north tower after 1399. In 1394 he went to Milan to advise on the building of the cathedral, but stayed there only briefly.

Utamaro Kitagawa 1753–1806

The Japanese artist Kitagawa Utamaro was the greatest master of the *Ukiyoe* print. He may have been the son of his teacher Toriyama Sekien (1712–88). Sekien was a *Kano* artist influenced by contemporary naturalism, which shows in his pupil's detailed and delicate printed picturebook of insects, *Ehon Mushi Erabi* (1788), and in the *Kano* and *Shijo* style landscapes in the printed albums *Kyogesubo* ("The Moon-Mad Monk"), and *Ginsekai* ("The Silver World"). These, and other albums and books, are among the world's most beautiful woodblock productions.

Utamaro's true genius, however, was developed in his sheet prints of the *Ukiyoe* world of women and their admirers. In the 1780s he followed the elegant, somewhat static style of Kiyonaga. During the 1790s his genuine obsession with women led him gradually to elongate his subjects into semi-goddesses; his interest in psychology added a new, electric force to the standard eroticism of this sort of print.

The new style, which soon put Kiyonaga out of fashion, first achieved maturity in the erotic masterpiece, the album *The Poem of the Pillow* (1788). Among his innovations were the half-length portrait, and the use of sumptuous mica backgrounds; both features can be seen in the portrait of the teahouse beauty *Ohisa* (British Museum, London). His figures reach an amazing elongation in the series of prints *The Twelve Hours of the Green Houses* (*c*1795; British Museum, London); the Green Houses were in fact brothels.

Utamaro's later works lack intensity, perhaps because of his dissipated life style, and the death of his mentor, the great publisher Tsutaya. In 1804 he was briefly imprisoned for a politically libelous print of the 16th-century dictator Hideyoshi.

Further reading. Goncourt, E. de *Outamaro: le Peintre des Maisons Vertes*, Paris (1891). Hillier, J. *Utamaro: Colour Prints and Paintings*, Oxford (1979).

Utrillo Maurice 1883–1955

The French painter Maurice Utrillo was born in Paris; he was the illegitimate son of the artist and model, Suzanne Valadon. He began to paint *c*1902, possibly as a therapeutic activity to counteract alcoholism. He is the epitome of the *peintre maudit*, his life being spent in and out of the sanatorium. His views of Montmartre, generally of a few buildings in sharp perspective, have topographical value; at their best, they also show a poetic sensibility to urban solitude. Utrillo's "White Period" (*c*1908–16) contains some of his finest work. In the 1920s his palette grew brighter, and hitherto deserted city squares were often enlivened by small figures.

Kitagawa Utamaro: Reclining Lovers; woodblock print; 25×37cm (10×15in). Victoria and Albert Museum, London

V

Valadon Suzanne 1867–1938

The French painter Suzanne Valadon (born Marie Clémentine Valadon) was a seamstress and circus performer before becoming, at the age of 16, a model for artists such as Renoir, Puvis de Chavannes and Toulouse-Lautrec. Renoir and Degas encouraged her to pursue her own talent for painting, and she developed a highly individual style that—combining the influences of Degas, Gauguin and the Nabis—is characterized by strong colors, emphatic contours and clear compositions. Although she painted some landscapes and still lifes, she was mainly a figure painter; her portraits and nudes give a frank and unsentimental view of women that subverts the male images of women found in both academic and avant-garde paintings of the period, as in her well-known *Blue Bedroom* (1923; Museum of Modern Art, Paris), and her nude self-portrait painted when she was 66 (1938; Museum of Modern Art, Paris). She was the mother of Maurice Utrillo.

Further reading. Warnod, J. *Suzanne Valadon*, New York (1981).

Valdés Leal Juan de 1622–90

The Spanish painter and etcher Juan de Valdés Leal was born in Seville, where he mainly worked, though he was also active at Cordoba. He was an outstanding colorist, whose vigorous handling and decorative Baroque style—full of movement—reflect a restless temperament. This can be seen in many religious compositions, for example *The Temptation of St Jerome* and *The Flagellation of St Jerome* (both 1657; Provincial Museum of Fine Arts, Seville). In other works he shows an interest in unusual iconography.

Valdés Leal's originality is most evident in his *Vanitas* subjects, notably those inscribed *Finis Gloriae Mundi* ("The end of the glory of the world") and *In Ictu Oculi* ("In the blinking of an eye"), the most gruesome and terrifying reminders of the transience of human life ever painted (1672; Charity Hospital, Seville).

Juan de Valdés Leal: St Jerome; oil on canvas; 211×131cm (83×52in). Prado, Madrid

Valentin de Boulogne 1594–1632

The Caravaggesque painter Valentin de Boulogne was active in Rome from *c*1614 until his early death. Despite his French origin, he seems to have received his entire training in Italy, and even his earliest works are marked by the uncompromising naturalism and powerful chiaroscuro effects of Caravaggio. His subject matter, like that of Bartolomeo Manfredi (*c*1580–*c*1620), was also inspired by the example of Caravaggio, in particular by that master's early works, depicting scenes from the low life.

Vallotton Félix 1865–1925

Félix Vallotton was a Swiss artist and engraver whose graphic work placed him among the leaders of the Parisian avant-garde during the 1890s. Born in Lausanne, he trained in Paris at the École des Beaux-Arts and at the Académie Julian. He formed a friendship with Charles Maurin, a Symbolist artist, pioneer woodblock engraver, and social critic. Maurin's influence, together with the 1890 Paris exhibition of Japanese woodblock prints, led Vallotton to reject the sober realism of his early paintings. In 1891 he embarked upon the production of radically simplified woodcuts and lithographs, such as *Burial* (1891), *Assassination* (1893), *The Demonstration* (1893). These depict everyday Parisian life, Swiss landscapes, portraits of leading politicians, writers, and artists, often with social and political satire. He was a friend of the Nabis group, exhibited with them, and collaborated with them on one of the leading avant-garde reviews, *La Revue Blanche* ("The White Review"). By 1901, he had virtually abandoned printed work; instead he began to paint nudes in the style of J.-A.-D. Ingres, such as *Reclining Nude on a Red Carpet* (1910; Petit Palais, Geneva), and landscapes that were indebted to Nicolas Poussin.

Vanbrugh John 1664–1726

The English Baroque architect Sir John Vanbrugh was born in London. He received an army commission in 1686, and was already a successful playwright before he turned his talents—"without thought or lecture"—to architecture. It is not certain when he did this, but by 1799 his reputation was sufficiently well established for him to replace the Comptroller General of the King's Works, William Talman, as the Earl of Carlisle's architect at Castle Howard; his subsequent career was almost exclusively that of a country-house architect working for the Whig aristocracy. It was through this connection that he was appointed Comptroller General in 1702, and received the commission for Blenheim Palace in 1704. He was knighted in 1714.

The speed with which Vanbrugh's mature style emerged belied his lack of formal training. It almost certainly reflected his early association with Nicholas Hawksmoor, Wren's assistant in the Office of Works. Hawksmoor's influence is discernible at Castle Howard, Yorkshire (1699–1726), where the open courtyard arrangement brilliantly paraphrased Christopher Wren's first plan for Greenwich Hospital. Blenheim Palace, Woodstock, Oxfordshire (1705–20), repeated the arrangement, but introduced the principle of compositional movement. This was probably inspired by the example of Elizabethan architecture, and was achieved by the bold massing of wings, pavilions, porticos, and colonnades; each feature varied in height and recession, to produce a theatrical effect that immediately distinguishes Vanbrugh's work from Wren's more cerebral Baroque.

Seaton Delaval, Northumberland (1720–8), Grimthorpe, Lincolnshire (1723–4), and the architect's own house, Vanbrugh Castle, Greenwich (1717), are the most impressive of his late works. The latter—castellated and (after the addition of a south wing in 1720) irregular—provided a remarkable precedent for the asymmetrical Picturesque castles popularized by John Nash early in the 19th century.

Further reading. Bingham, M. *Masks and Facades: Sir John Vanbrugh, the Man and his Setting*, London (1974). Downes, K. *Vanbrugh*, London (1977). Webb, G. *The Complete Works of Sir John Vanbrugh*, London (1928).

Van Loo family 18th century

Although they were of Flemish origin, the Van Loo family dominated French painting in the middle of the 18th century. Jean-Baptiste (1684–1745) was the oldest. He trained in Italy before settling in Paris with his brother Carle in 1719. Jean-Baptiste's two sons, Amédée (1715–95) and Louis-Michel (1707–71), as well as his much younger brother Carle (Charles-André, 1705–65) were all taught by him.

Carle was the most successful member of

Félix Vallotton: Reclining Nude on a Red Carpet; oil on canvas; 73×100cm (29×39in); 1910. Petit Palais, Geneva

the family, though his work was insipid and dull compared with that of his contemporary and traveling companion, François Boucher. The dominating position of the family was not due to great originality or inspiration: it owed more to the wide range of their productions, which included huge altarpieces, royal portraits, and even exotic boudoir scenes.

Vantongerloo Georges 1886–1965

Born in Antwerp, the Belgian artist Georges Vantongerloo was primarily a sculptor, but also a man of many ideas. He joined the *De Stijl* group in 1917, its first year. His Abstract sculptures of this period, with their interlocking masses, often resemble three-dimensional jigsaw puzzles; they are explorations in the interpenetration of planes and solids (for example, *Construction*, 1917; Philadelphia Museum of Art). These enquiries into spatial relationships were of significance for later *De Stijl* architectural projects, such as those by Theo van Doesburg and Cornelis van Eesteren of 1923.

Vantongerloo left *De Stijl* in 1921. In the 1930s he was active in the Parisian Constructivist art circles centered round the magazines *Cercle et Carré* and *Abstraction-Création*.

Vanvitelli Luigi 1700–73

Although of Flemish origin, the architect Luigi Vanvitelli was born in Naples and brought up in Rome. "Vanvitelli" is an Italian rendering of his family name, van Wittel. After he had worked in Rome, Ancona, and Loreto, he was awarded an important commission in 1751 by Charles III: to build a palace in Caserta to house the large court. The facade of the palace is often criticized as monotonous, but it was not built with all the features that Vanvitelli had intended. Within, the palace is notable for the axial play by which the four courtyards are related, and for the monumental staircase. He also designed churches and various public works, including an aqueduct.

Vasarely Victor 1908–1997

The painter Victor Vasarely was born at Pecs, Hungary, and was trained in the design aesthetic of the Budapest "Bauhaus" from 1928 to 1929. In 1930 he left Hungary for Paris, where he worked as a graphic and commercial artist for a number of years. He made his first optical works in the 1930s, but did not evolve his characteristic, geometrical-abstract style until the early 1950s. His so-called "kinetic" works either involve actual movement by the spectator, or give an impression of movement (for example, *Ondho*, 1956–60; Museum of Modern Art, New York). This can be experienced either on a small scale, or in certain large environmental projects that Vasarely has carried out. In the 1960s he progressed from black and white to color and three-dimensional objects. He also moved into the field of mass-produced "multiples" in which a single picture is mass-produced by industrial method.

Further reading. Clay, J. "Vasarely: a Survey of his Work". *The Studio* vol. CLXXIII, London (May, 1967). Joray, M. (ed.) *Vasarely,* Neuchâtel (1965). Rotzler, W. "Victor Vasarely", *Graphis* vol. 27, Geneva (1972).

Victor Vasarely: Sirius II; oil on canvas; 30×20cm (12×8in); 1954. Galerie Denise René, Paris

Vasari Giorgio 1511–73

The Italian painter, architect, and historian Giorgio Vasari was born in Arezzo. He began his training there before moving to Florence in 1524, first to the studio of Andrea del Sarto, then to that of Baccio Bandinelli. After journeys to Bologna and Arezzo, he made two visits to Rome. The first of these was in 1532, together with Francesco Salviati; the second was in 1538. It was during this visit that Vasari abandoned his early style, which had developed from Florentine painting of the 1520s, in favor of the Mannerism of Salviati's 1538 *Visitation* fresco (1538; S. Giovanni Decollato, Rome).

Vasari was an enormously prolific and popular painter, especially in Florence. The Sala dei Cento Giorni in the Cancelleria, Rome, gives an indication of his eclectic style. The scheme derives from that of Peruzzi's for the Sala delle Prospettive (in the Farnesina, Rome); like that work it is enriched with niches for the flanking allegorical figures. The figures seated above the cornice reflect those in Perino's Sala Paolina (Castel S. Angelo, Rome), begun the previous year. The episodes are extended into the spectator's space by steps that reflect those designed by Bramante for the Belvedere. The individual figures abound in artistic quotations, es-

Above: Giorgio Vasari: Self-portrait; oil on canvas; 101×80cm (40×31in); 1568–8. Uffizi, Florence

Vecchietta: The Virgin Receives the Souls of Foundlings (The Ladder of Paradise); fresco; c1446–9. S. Maria della Scala, Siena

pecially from Michelangelo.

Vasari's major achievement was his *Vite* (*Le Vite dei più Eccellenti Architetti, Pittori, e Scultori Italiani . . ., The Lives of the Most Eminent Italian Architects, Painters, and Sculptors*), first published in 1550, revised and expanded version published in 1568. The work established a framework for all subsequent accounts of the Renaissance: its birth (Giotto and the Trecento), its growth (the Quattrocento), and its climax (the High Renaissance and Michelangelo).

Vasari's ability as a painter cannot match his talents either as an historian or as an architect. The end of the 16th century saw an unparalleled growth in the number of official buildings, as houses for new bureaucracies. Few of these new buildings can rival Vasari's Uffizi, designed in 1560. Its long facade is enlivened by motifs borrowed from Michelangelo and Peruzzi. It is further distinguished by the loggia on the ground floor (inspired by that of Sansovino's Library in Venice), which, together with the layout of the twin facades, distantly evokes a Roman forum.

Vecchietta *c*1412–80

Lorenzo di Pietro, known as Vecchietta, was an artist of the Sienese school; he worked as a painter, miniaturist, sculptor, and architect. He probably trained under Sassetta, but was influenced by contemporary Florentine art early in his career. Vecchietta's painting style combined naturalism with a talent for narrative description. Much patronized by Sienese institutions, such as the town government and the hospital of S. Maria della Scala, he left works in various media which were to have considerable influence on artists of the later 15th century. Among the most important of his surviving works are *The Ladder of Paradise* (fresco; *c*1446–9; S. Maria della Scala, Siena), *St Catherine* (fresco; 1461; Palazzo Pubblico, Siena), triptych (1461; Pienza Cathedral), and a bronze *ciborium* (1467–72; Siena Cathedral).

Velázquez Diego 1599–1660

The Spanish painter Diego Rodríguez de Silva y Velázquez was born in Seville. He was of aristocratic Portuguese descent on his father's side, but the surname he chose to use was that of his mother. He was apprenticed to Francisco Pacheco in Seville from 1611 to 1617, and later married his master's daughter.

Some of Velázquez' earliest paintings were religious compositions, but most were of the type known as *bodegón* (the word means eating-house or tavern). They contain naturalistic figures in an interior, preparing or consuming food or drink. *Christ in the House of Martha* (1618; National Gallery, London) combines elements of both religious and *bodegón* types. The main incident takes place in the background, and is seen through an opening in the wall (or reflected in a mirror). The artist's skill in realistic representation of inanimate objects is apparent in the garlic, red pepper, fish, eggs, and simple utensils in the foreground.

In these early *bodegones*, a strong light from low on the left illuminates the scene, as in the *Old Woman Frying Eggs* (1618;

National Gallery of Scotland, Edinburgh) and *The Water-Seller* (*c*1620; Wellington Museum, London). These works are almost tenebrist in character. A similar light effect is seen in some early religious compositions, like the *Immaculate Conception* and *St John the Evangelist* (*c*1618; National Gallery, London). The effect is even more striking in the *Adoration of the Magi* (1619; Prado, Madrid), which is certainly tenebrist. This work is close to being Caravaggesque, whether by direct influence from works of Caravaggio or through parallel tendencies among Spanish contemporaries, is uncertain.

The earliest dated portraits by Velázquez date from 1620. That of the nun *Jerónima de la Fuente* (Prado, Madrid) shows a full-length monumental figure, firmly modeled in a brown habit against a dull green background. The painting is impressive in its characterization and in its simple pattern.

Recognizing his son-in-law's ability, Pacheco encouraged him to seek connections at court and to visit El Escorial. In April 1622, Velázquez went to Madrid for about two months. There he was received by fellow-Andalusians who moved in the circle of Philip IV's favorite, Don Gaspar de Guzmán (later Count-Duke of Olivares). Velázquez executed a portrait of the famous poet *Don Luis de Góngora* (Museum of Fine Arts, Boston), but did not realize his ambition to paint the sovereign. Nevertheless the portrait of Góngora had made a great impression, with its characterization and its subtle modeling in planes (not to be paralleled until Cézanne). Velázquez was soon recalled to Madrid by Olivares.

This time he went accompanied by Pacheco, in July 1623. A month later he painted a full-length portrait of Philip IV and in October was taken into the King's service. However, a bust of *Philip IV* painted shortly afterwards (Meadows Museum and Sculpture Court, Dallas, Texas) is close in its firm outlines and restrained color to the Boston *Góngora*, and is more realistic than the idealized portraits of the King painted in the early 1630s, such as the full-length in brown and silver in the National Gallery, London.

By this period Velázquez had progressed in his career, becoming an Usher of the Chamber in 1627, meeting Rubens in Madrid in 1628, and visiting Italy from 1629 to 1631. He had also executed an important large group of nine figures in *The Triumph of Bacchus*, popularly known as *Los Borrachos* ("The Topers"; 1628–9; Prado, Madrid). In spite of damage and cutting down, the picture is notable for its freedom of handling and its naturalistic conception. It depicts semi-nudes alongside a group of realistic figures, comparable with those in his early *bodegones*. Behind them lies a bleak, broad, windswept landscape of a type that Velázquez was to use in his outdoor portraits of the 1630s. *Los Borrachos* was not a mythological scene but a modern burlesque of one, a realistic piece of playacting on a popular level.

Diego Velázquez: Immaculate Conception; oil on canvas; 135×102cm (53×40in); c1618. National Gallery, London

Half-nude figures appear again in two large compositions that Velázquez executed in Italy in 1630 and took back to Spain: *The Forge of Vulcan* (Prado, Madrid) and *Jacob's Coat* (The Escorial, near Madrid). Both are naturalistic; the placing of the figures in space is more skillful than in his earlier works, and the light effects more subtle. Particularly in *Jacob's Coat*, a Venetian refinement of color reflects the painter's widened experience.

On his first visit to Italy, Velázquez also probably painted two small views of *The Garden of the Villa Medici* (Prado, Madrid). In these he gave free rein to his sensitivity to landscape, the figures being subordinated to it for the first time. The vigorous handling and impasto of these atmospheric sketches recall the work of Titian; we know, from an account by Pacheco, that Velázquez imitated Titian's style in a lost self-portrait.

On returning to Madrid, Velázquez hastened to paint the King, and his son and heir *Baltasar Carlos* (1631; Museum of Fine Arts, Boston). In this first portrait of the Prince, at the age of 16 months, he is accompanied by a dwarf. The infant's superior status is emphasized by the more even light on him and the smoother handling of his face. The warm colors, dominated by deep red tones, seem to revolve round the highlight of his sash. Baltasar Carlos was painted again in a similar attitude, but this time alone and in a cooler color-scheme (1632; Wallace Collection, London). These two entrancing child portraits were to be followed by others, showing the Prince on horseback, in hunting dress, and in the riding school. They demonstrate Velázquez' unique flair for portraying the charms of childhood.

These outdoor portraits, and others of Philip IV, the Cardinal-Infante Fernando, and Olivares, were painted between 1633 and 1636. They were intended either for Philip's new Buen Retiro Palace, or for the reconstructed hunting lodge, the Torre de la Parada. For the Palace, Velázquez also painted the large group picture of *The Surrender of Breda* (1634–5; Prado, Madrid). Here the figures are arranged in balanced masses, parallel to the picture-plane in classical fashion, rather than with Baroque diagonal movement. They are seen against a magnificent atmospheric landscape background of immense depth. *The Boar Hunt* (*c*1636–7; National Gallery, London), from the Torre de la Parada, contains a colorful array of crisply painted figures on a smaller scale. They are in a more enclosed setting, but the landscape and the fresh air are a major feature of the work.

In 1631, Juan Bautista Martínez del Mazo became Velázquez' assistant, and in 1633 his son-in-law. In 1634, the master transferred to him his post of Usher of the Chamber. Velázquez himself continued to receive favors from Philip IV, who frequently visited his studio in the Alcázar to watch him paint. In 1636 he became Gentleman of the Wardrobe, and in 1643 Gentleman of the Bedchamber. Like his later promotions, however, these honors involved him in prolonged struggles with the exchequer officials, in attempts to obtain not only his increased salary, but earlier arrears.

Some outstanding works date from the late 1630s and 1640s, including *The Lady with a Fan* (*c*1638–9; Wallace Collection, London), the epitome of Spanish womanhood, brilliantly toneful and sensitively handled. The dignified *Philip IV in Military Dress* (1644; Frick Collection, New York) is a beautiful harmony of red, silver, gray, and black. The large *The Fable of Arachne* (*c*1644–8; Prado, Madrid) is popularly known as *Las Hilanderas* ("The Tapestry Weavers"). In this painting the varied depth of shadow and diffused light of the foreground are effectively contrasted with the brighter light that is concentrated on the figures representing the main incident in a background recess. The groups of figures are arranged symmetrically on central axes formed by the darkest figure in the foreground and the brightest of the group behind. Both groups recede so little in depth (in spite of some diagonal movement away from the central figures) that this is really a classical rather than a Baroque composition. Especially remarkable are the modeling of forms, by the imperceptible melting of tones into each other, and the skillful placing of the figures in depth, by subtly varied handling and the elimination of unnecessary detail.

Both *Las Hilanderas*, and *The Toilet of Venus* (*c*1644–8; National Gallery, London), Velázquez' only female nude, were probably executed for private patrons. The composition of the latter, based on a system of sweeping curves, is a triumph of discretion, with the model seen from behind and her face reflected imprecisely in the mirror. Her softly modeled body is in the center of the color scheme of unusual harmonies of crimson, gray, and blue.

Late in 1648, Velázquez left Madrid with his assistant, Juan de Pareja, on his second journey to Italy. His purpose was to acquire paintings by Italian masters and casts of antique statues for the Royal Palace in Madrid. In Rome he painted several portraits of members of the Papal Court, culminating in *Pope Innocent X* (1650; Galleria Doria Pamphili, Rome). The realistic characterization of the seated Pope, the tonal rendering of his vestments, and the superbly expressive brushwork make this a masterpiece of formal portraiture. As a preparation for his exacting task, Velázquez had painted an informal half-length portrait of *Juan de Pareja* (1649–50; Metropolitan Museum, New York). Here the handling is vigorous and free, yet so assured that when it was exhibited it achieved immediate fame.

Returning to Madrid in 1651, Velázquez portrayed Philip IV's newly married second wife, *Queen Mariana of Austria* (1652; Prado, Madrid). He also painted a bust of Philip IV (*c*1652; Prado, Madrid) in which the monarch looks weary and disillusioned. Velázquez' appointment as Chief Steward of the Palace in 1652 imposed on him responsibilities so onerous that he had little time for painting. His output in the 1650s was considerably reduced, at the time when his artistic powers were at their greatest. They were, however, displayed to the full in the portrait of Mariana's daughter, the *Infanta Margarita* (1653; Kunsthistorisches Museum, Vienna). This is one of the most alluring pictures of childhood ever created, with entrancing color harmonies of silver, pink, and black in the dress, and red, ocher, and blue in the carpet and tablecloth. A freely brushed glass vase of colorful flowers on the table notably extends these harmonies.

All the brilliant qualities of Velázquez' maturity reached their climax in the large interior group portrait of *The Royal Family*, popularly known as *Las Meninas*, "The Maids of Honor" (1656; Prado, Madrid). The Infanta Margarita is in the foreground with two of her maids of honor

Diego Velázquez: The Toilet of Venus (The Rokeby Venus); oil on canvas; 122×177cm (48×70in); c1648–51. National Gallery, London

and two dwarfs; Philip IV and Queen Mariana are seen reflected in the mirror in the back wall. Velázquez himself, with his brush in hand, stands in front of his large canvas on the left. With astonishing success, the painter has resolved unusual problems of space, perspective, and light. He has unified a complicated composition by his complete command of color and tones, together with skillfully varied brushwork.

Negotiations for the admission of Velázquez as a Knight of the Order of Santiago began in 1658. The prolonged investigation of the painter's antecedents lasted into the following year; his claim was supported by over 100 witnesses, including the painters Zurbarán and Alonso Cano, who had known him in his youth in Seville. But the honor finally accorded to Velázquez at the end of 1659 was not to give him satisfaction for long. His official duties in connection with the Treaty of the Pyrenees, signed by Philip IV and Louis XIV in June 1660, were so exacting that Velázquez eventually returned to Madrid exhausted and died in August of that year.

Though he never approached the inventiveness of Rubens, or the psychological penetration of Rembrandt, and in composition was often more classical than Baroque, Velázquez is one of the great masters of the Baroque age. He is the greatest of all Spanish painters, through his ability to make a satisfying pattern out of every composition, his characterization, and the technical skill with which he realized his intentions. He was, however, a slow worker, in spite of his apparently free brushwork, and he was a perfectionist—as many *pentimenti* in his paintings demonstrate. The number of his works is thus regrettably small.

The steady output of replicas of royal portraits from Velázquez' studio shows that the master employed many assistants, but few of them are identifiable as individual artistic personalities. Even of Martínez del Mazo and Pareja only a few certain works are known. Velázquez' influence was, however, widespread in Spain, affecting first his contemporaries Zurbarán and Cano, then Carreño, Murillo, and Claudio Coello, and later Goya. The works of Terborch, Manet, and J.S. Sargent bear witness to the appeal his paintings have had in other countries.

Further reading. Brown, J. and Garrido, C., *Velázquez: The Technique of Genius*, New Haven (1998). Gudiol, J. *Velázquez*, London (1974). Harris, E., *Velázquez*, Ithaca, N.Y. (1982). Justi, C. *Velázquez und sein Jahrhundert*, Bonn (1888). López-Rey, J. *Velázquez: a Catalogue Raisonné of his Oeuvre*, London (1999). Pantorba, B. de *La Vida y la Obra de Velázquez*, Madrid (1955).

Esaias van de Velde: A Winter Landscape; oil on panel; 26×30cm (10×12in); 1623. National Gallery, London

Velde Esaias van de *c*1591–1630

The Dutch artist Esaias van de Velde was born in Amsterdam. He painted a few semididactic genre pieces of gallant companies feasting, and he also produced pictures of cavalry skirmishes and scenes of plunder. His most typical works, however, are landscapes. These are of his native countryside at different seasons, and are among the first realist landscape paintings of the 17th century. They are characterized by a combination of accuracy of detail and a sense of atmosphere and spaciousness. The color schemes in his mature work tend increasingly towards monochrome. His pictures are often filled with figures, but he abandoned other traditional practices, such as the use of "stage wings" and the bird's eye viewpoint. He had a profound influence on his famous pupil, Jan van Goyen.

Velde Henry van de 1863–1957

Born in Antwerp, the Belgian architect Henry van de Velde studied painting there and in Paris (1884–5). During the early 1890s he was attracted to the work of the English Arts and Crafts movement, and to the ideas of William Morris. In 1892 he turned to graphic design and typography, inventing a style that reflected his interest in Post-Impressionist painting, particularly the work of Gauguin. His first major piece of applied art was the interior of his own house (which he had also built) at Uccle, near Brussels (1895). In 1896 he designed four rooms for Samuel Bing's shop in Paris, "L'Art Nouveau", and in the following year much of this work was exhibited at Dresden.

Unlike that of Victor Horta, van de Velde's brand of Art Nouveau has little direct relationship with nature. Space in his buildings is molded by dynamic but controlled lines of force, further emphasized by the shapes of furniture and furnishings.

Between 1900 and 1914 Van de Velde's career was spent in Germany. In 1901 he was called to Weimar, where he became artistic adviser to the Duke of Saxe-Weimar. His work anticipated the ideals of the Deutscher Werkbund, founded in 1907

Willem van de Velde the Younger: The Battle of Texel; oil on canvas; 150×300cm (59×118in); 1687. National Maritime Museum, Greenwich, London

to improve standards of design in industry. Van de Velde believed in an intuitive approach to design, and could not agree with the Werkbund's new theories of standardization and type. At the Werkbund Exhibition in Cologne in 1914 (to which he contributed the theater), his architecture had already begun to look old-fashioned. In 1914 he resigned his post as Director of the Weimar School of Arts and Crafts, and Walter Gropius took over.

The best-known work of van de Velde's later years is the Kröller-Müller Museum at Otterlo in Holland (1937–54).

Velde family 17th century

Willem van de Velde the Younger (1633–1707), the greatest and most productive of all Dutch marine painters, was the pupil of the marine and landscape artist Simon de Vlieger (*c*1600–53). His early works are primarily straightforward seascapes, but ships and naval battles become increasingly prominent in his paintings, especially after he arrived in London in 1672 with his father, Willem van de Velde the Elder (1611–93). He was subsequently employed there as an official marine artist. His precise knowledge of ship construction was mainly learned from his father, who was a nautical draftsman. The two artists collaborated on many paintings, the son coloring his father's outline drawings. Willem the Younger's marine paintings depict every weather condition, from gale to calm. Their accurately observed effects of light and atmosphere—a great advance on the achievements of earlier painters—were imitated by many English followers, and were particularly admired by J.M.W. Turner and John Constable in the 19th century.

Adriaen van de Velde (1636–72), the brother of Willem the Younger, trained under his father and also with the Dutch landscapist Jan Wijnants (*c*1630/5–84). He painted almost every kind of subject, but is chiefly known for peaceful, sunny landscapes in which figures and grazing animals are prominent. He also produced some winter landscapes, and a few very beautiful beach scenes which have a high-keyed sparkle and lucidity. These paintings, and some etchings of landscapes with cattle, are complemented by a number of idyllic southern landscapes composed of Italianate motifs gleaned from the work of other artists. Adriaen sometimes provided the figures in pictures by other landscape painters.

Verhulst Rombout 1624–98

The Flemish sculptor Rombout Verhulst was active in the northern Netherlands. Born in Malines, Verhulst trained there and in Antwerp. It is uncertain whether he ever visited Italy, but he was living in Amsterdam by 1646. He enlisted as a stonemason in the guild in 1652, and signed several of the most beautiful reliefs, among them *Silence* and *Fidelity*, in the new Amsterdam Town Hall. He obviously enjoyed a higher standing than the other assistants in the workshop of the master sculptor of the project, Artus Quellinus.

Verhulst subsequently turned to carving funeral monuments, including those of Admiral Tromp (*c*1654; The Old Church, Delft), and Admiral de Ruyter (*c*1676; The New Church, Amsterdam). He adapted the local tradition of using variously colored marbles for the architecture and figurative carvings, but infused them with a new monumentality. His effigies are extremely realistic, with a sensuous appreciation of surface textures in the flesh of the faces and hands, and in the freely flowing hair. His sculpture has a robust, Rubensian feeling, conveyed with a brilliant technique of handling marble. He modeled in clay as a preliminary to such schemes, and the sketches that survive have an astounding immediacy (there are examples in the Rijksmuseum, Amsterdam).

The monuments have complex, Baroque cartouches framing the inscriptions, and coats of arms, populated by plump *putti* and other allegorical figures. He naturally applied his talent for portraiture to the carved portrait bust, with results that surpass the paintings of his Dutch contemporaries. Verhulst was also expert in carving narrative scenes in low relief; such scenes traditionally appeared on tombs and on the exteriors of certain public buildings in the Netherlands, for example on the Buttery in Leiden. His style of sculpture prevailed throughout the north Netherlands all during the second half of the 17th century, and forms a crucial component in any estimate of Dutch art in that period.

Vermeer Jan 1632–75

Jan Vermeer van Delft was a Dutch painter who came from Delft. His response to the transient beauty of light and colored surfaces, and his impeccable sense of design, place him among the greatest of all European artists. Very little is known of his life. He was the son of a silk-weaver who also dealt in paintings. His teacher is not known, but certain works suggest that he may have been a pupil of Carel Fabritius, three of whose paintings Vermeer owned at his death. He appears to have inherited his father's art-dealing business, and although he joined the Delft Guild of Painters in 1653, dealing seems to have been his primary source of income. His pictures were used as deposits for unpaid bills, but there are no records of any sales during his lifetime. This has been put forward as a reason why there are so few works by him: fewer than 40 certainly attributable works survive, and these are mostly quite small. There may be some truth in the suggestion that he worked only in his spare time, mainly for his own pleasure, producing perhaps only two or three pictures a year. This may also explain why he was so little known as an artist in his lifetime.

Vermeer's earliest works have religious and mythological themes. They include *Christ in the House of Mary and Martha* (National Gallery, Edinburgh), a painting that relates in its forms and colors to those of Utrecht School artists like Hendrick Terbrugghen, and *Diana and her Companions* (Royal Museum of Art, Mauritshuis, The Hague). The earliest dated painting is *The Procuress* (1656; Gemäldegalerie Alte Meister, Dresden), in which warm yellows and reds echo the colors of Rembrandt school paintings of the 1650s. The later works are generally domestic interiors; in these we see one or two figures, arrested in a moment of time as they occupy themselves with such recreational activities as reading or writing letters, playing musical instruments, drinking, or talking. Occasionally the theme is that of domestic work (as in *The Lacemaker*; Louvre, Paris). In all these later pictures, Vermeer invests essentially mundane activities with a significance out of all proportion to their apparent importance.

His interiors convey an impression of stillness and serenity; an effect that is largely due to his purity of color (in which, after the early period, cool blues and yellows predominate), and his limpid, radiant light. There is an exhilarating, sensuous quality in Vermeer's light, and also in the pearly, translucent highlights that bathe the objects in his paintings—particularly smooth or semitransparent objects, such as jewels. In later pictures Vermeer emphasized the shimmering effect created by the fall of light by using a meticulous *pointillé* technique in which highlights were broken up into very small touches of paint. The soft translucency of Vermeer's light and color has been compared to the glazes on earthenware; this

Jan Vermeer: The Lacemaker; oil on canvas; 24×21cm (9×8in); c1665. Louvre, Paris

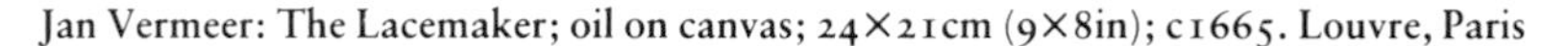

has led some writers to speculate that the artist might once have been engaged in the painting of the tiles and dishes for which Delft was celebrated in the 17th century.

The compositions of Vermeer usually contain very carefully placed horizontals and verticals which are extremely important components of the design. The linear framework formed by rectangular mirrors and maps creates essentially static compositions that enhance the paintings' sense of tranquillity. Spatial organization is generally also complex. There is sometimes little recession, with the image confined to a single figure against a plain background: a figure which, however, has a monumental impact, bearing no relation to the small scale of the painting (for example, *Maidservant Pouring Milk;* Rijksmuseum, Amsterdam). Every object in Vermeer's designs has importance as an abstract volume or shape to the extent that nothing could be altered without destroying the overall harmony. But it is misleading to overemphasize the purely formal aspect of his work: although Vermeer ignores the love of anecdote and incident typical of Dutch genre scenes, his paintings sometimes have a meaning that is not immediately apparent. The musical scenes, for instance, may be representations of profane love; the *Woman Weighing Gold* (National Gallery of Art, Washington, D.C.) represents Vanity.

Symbolism is more obtrusive in a few other paintings, notably in the *Allegory of the New Testament* (Metropolitan Museum, New York) and also in an allegory on the art of painting known as *The Painter in his Studio* (Kunsthistorisches Museum, Vienna). This last work is unusual in Vermeer's oeuvre for its larger scale, as is one of the artist's rare townscapes, the luminous *A View in Delft* (Royal Museum of Art, Mauritshuis, The Hague). In *A View in Delft* (a painting much admired by Van Gogh) and other pictures, the precision of line and detail probably derives from the use of the camera obscura.

Vermeer's work had little influence on other painters. The artist was largely forgotten after his death, and it was not until the 1860s, at the time of the developing interest in naturalism, that he was rescued from relative obscurity. Despite criticisms that his work lacks invention or emotional content, Vermeer's reputation has increased spectacularly in the 20th century. This is due both to his historical importance and to the intrinsic qualities of his work. His fame has led to many attempts at forgeries.

Jan Vermeer: The Painter in his Studio; oil on canvas; 130×110cm (51×43in); 1662–5. Kunsthistorisches Museum, Vienna

Further reading. Liedtke, W. et al., *Vermeer and the Delft School*, New Haven (2001). Wheelock, A. *Johannes Vermeer*, Washington, D.C. (1995).

Vernet Claude-Joseph 1714–89

Claude-Joseph Vernet was a French painter of marine subjects and landscapes. He was trained at Avignon and Aix-en-Provence, and then spent the years 1734 to 1753 working in Italy. There, mainly in Rome, he was the leading painter of marines, evoking the Italian coastline in a manner derived from the early works of Claude Lorrain, or depicting storms and shipwrecks that appealed to pre-Romantic sensibility. He also made landscapes based on Rome and the surrounding Campagna, derived from paintings by Gaspard Dughet, Luigi Vanvitelli, and Andrea Locatelli. He worked for the great Roman families, for French visitors to Rome, and especially for English clients who were making the Grand Tour. His works were admired for their vivid impression of nature, and for their subtle control of tone and light.

In 1753 Vernet began a series of 16 views of the major French seaports (now in the Musée de la Marine, Paris, and the Louvre, Paris); they occupied him until 1765. This was one of the largest official commissions of paintings during the reign of Louis XV. The views are remarkable records of French port life in the 18th century, and important examples of precisely observed realism in a predominantly Rococo age. Vernet continued to paint Italianate landscapes, seascapes, and shipwrecks for an international clientèle, but these eventually became repetitive, and rather dry in style.

Veronese 1528–88

The Venetian painter Paolo Caliari was known as Veronese, because he was born in Verona. By 1541 he was the pupil of the Veronese painter Antonio Badile (1517–60), whose daughter he married in 1566. He is not recorded in Venice until 1555, but he was probably working there a year or two earlier. Even after he settled in Venice he maintained close contacts with Verona. His use of color differs from that of his older contemporaries educated in Venice: Titian and Tintoretto. Veronese achieves a harmony of clear, sharply defined tones that reflects his training in the Veronese school. His work also shows the influence of Brescian artists such as Alessandro Moretto and Girolamo Savoldo.

Veronese was a supreme decorator. Many of his finest pictures, like *The Marriage at Cana* (1562–3; Louvre, Paris), painted for the refectory of S. Giorgio Maggiore in Venice, suffer from their removal from their original setting. But much of his work remains in position, in such buildings as the Doges' Palace and the church of S. Sebastiano in Venice, and the Villa Barbaro at Maser. To describe Veronese as a decorator is not to diminish his status as a painter. He devised a type of painting that was the necessary compliment to the definitive achievement of his contemporaries Il Sansovino and Andrea Palladio in architecture.

In 1551 Veronese worked on the fresco decoration of the Villa Soranzo near Castelfranco, and fragments of these frescoes survive in the cathedral sacristy there. The qualities of clear color, mastery of perspective, and organized design that we find here are carried further in such canvases as the oval *Age and Youth* (*c*1553–4; Sale del Consiglio dei Dieci, Doges' Palace, Venice). In 1555 he received the commission for the ceiling of the sacristy of S. Sebastiano, Venice; this commission was followed by one for the ceiling of the nave, where he painted three masterly canvases of *The Story of Esther and Ahasuerus* (1556; S. Sebastiano, Venice). He continued working for this church until 1565. His painting for the high altar (1558–9) represents St Sebastian and other saints below, and the Virgin with the angels in the clouds above. In 1560 he painted the shutters and gallery of the superb organ, the case of which had been made to his design; this was followed by further paintings. The ensemble at S. Sebastiano forms the finest surviving example of Venetian church decoration from the second half of the 16th century.

In the field of private secular decoration, the same position is held by his frescoes in the Villa Barbaro (now Volpi) at Maser, near Asolo. The villa was built by Palladio *c*1560, and decorated soon afterwards.

Veronese: The Feast in the House of Levi; oil on canvas; 555×1280cm (219×504in); 1573. Gallerie dell'Accademia, Venice

Here we find a number of allegorical and mythological compositions, very much in the manner of those from the Villa Soranzo, and the ceilings of the Sale del Consiglio dei Dieci in the Doges' Palace. In a painted setting of feigned architecture, these compositions are linked with *trompe-l'oeil* effects of people in contemporary dress standing on balconies, or entering through doorways, with a background of delightful landscape prospects. In spite of damage and excessive restoration, these frescoes remain a delight, and represent a major achievement. The canvas of *The Family of Darius at the Feet of Alexander* (date disputed; National Gallery, London) is another splendid example of Veronese's work in the field of private secular painting.

Veronese continued to work in the public sphere. The canvases for the ceilings of the Sale del Consiglio dei Dieci in the Doges' Palace were followed by the decorations in the Sala del Collegio (1575–80). He was commissioned to paint a *Paradise* on the vast end wall of the Sala del Maggiore Consiglio, but death prevented him from carrying it out. He devised a splendid style of decoration for conventual refectories, presenting feast scenes from the gospels in a somewhat secular manner, for instance *The Marriage at Cana* (Louvre, Paris) from S. Giorgio Maggiore, and *The Feast in the House of Levi* (1573; Gallerie dell'Accademia, Venice) from the refectory of the Dominican house of SS. Giovanni e Paolo. In the latter case, the prominence of the secular elements led to his being examined by the Inquisition on a charge of heresy. These paintings combined feigned architecture with figure composition in a manner reminiscent of the decorations at Maser. The backgrounds recall the architecture of the built-in set in the Teatro Olimpico at Vicenza.

In altarpiece design, Veronese favored a type of asymmetrical composition, with a setting of pillars, derived from Titian's altar of Ca' Pesaro in S. Maria dei Frari, Venice. Examples include the *Virgin and Saints* (*c*1551; S. Francesco della Vigna, Venice), and the *Virgin and Saints* from S. Zaccaria (*c*1562; Gallerie dell'Accademia, Venice). He also painted smaller religious pictures such as the *Resurrection* (*c*1570; Gemäldegalerie Alte Meister, Dresden), the *Crucifixion* (*c*1580; Louvre, Paris), and the wonderfully romantic *St Anthony Preaching to the Fishes* (*c*1575–80; Museo e Galleria, Borghese, Rome).

Veronese's portraiture is notable for some very fine full-lengths, both of single sitters and family groups, such as the *Family Portrait* (1558; Palace of the Legion of Honor, San Francisco). He excelled in portraying the relationships of children to their elders. He was assisted in his work by his brother Benedetto, and his sons Carlo and Gabriele who carried on his studio after his death.

Further reading. Osmond, P. *Paolo Veronese: his Career and Work*, London (1927). Pignatti, T. *Veronese* (2 vols.), Venice (1976). Piovene, G. and Marini, R. *L'Opera Completa del Veronese*, Milan (1968).

Verrio Antonio *c*1639–1707

The Italian born artist Antonio Verrio brought the Baroque concept of decorative painting to English art, by collaborating with architects and sculptors at Windsor Castle and Hampton Court. Before coming to England *c*1672, Verrio worked in Naples, where he was influenced by Luca Giordano. The subject of his decorations at Windsor, painted for King Charles II, was the glorification of the English crown. His speciality was the illusionistic ceiling, and in the Royal Chapel, Windsor, he worked with Grinling Gibbons. Verrio succeeded Sir Peter Lely as Court Painter in 1684, and also worked at Chatsworth, Derbyshire, and at Burghley, Northamptonshire.

Verrocchio Andrea del 1435–88

The Italian sculptor and painter Andrea di Michele di Francesco Cioni was born in Florence, the son of a brickmaker. He probably got his first training in the workshop of a goldsmith, Giuliano da Verrocchi, from whom he took his surname. He passed on the artistic heritage of Donatello, especially as a sculptor in bronze. His chief patrons were members of the Medici family. Lorenzo di Credi and Leonardo da Vinci, whose fame for a long time obscured Verrocchio's genius, excelled among the pupils of his large workshop.

One of his earliest works is a bronze candelabrum (1468; Rijksmuseum, Amsterdam), which was originally destined for the Palazzo Vecchio in Florence. Its floral ornaments and architectural motifs are derived from antique prototypes. Between *c*1468 and 1470 he painted the seated *Madonna with Child* (Staatliche Museen, Berlin), the style of which was influenced by the Madonnas of Fra Filippo Lippi. The spatial quality of the two figures, set against a mountainous landscape, shows that he always perceived nature and human figures with a sculptor's eye. Shortly afterwards he painted a small private altar, depicting *Tobias and the Archangel Raphael* (National Gallery, London), which is closely related to an earlier picture of Tobias by Antonio Pollaiuolo.

The monument for Piero and Giovanni de' Medici in the old sacristy of S. Lorenzo, Florence, bears the date of 1472. It excels by its simple construction and abundant decoration. Acanthus leaves grow out of rams' horns, and lions' paws support the sarcophagus, which is set against a diaphanous net of ropes.

Verrocchio's first freestanding statue is

Right: Andrea del Verrocchio: the monument for Piero and Giovanni de' Medici; marble, porphry, and bronze; 1472. Old Sacristy, S. Lorenzo, Florence

Below: Antonio Verrio: The Heaven Room; oil on plaster; c1693. Burghley House, Northamptonshire

the bronze *David* (*c*1473–5; Museo Nazionale, Florence), made for the Medici family. The figure is strongly influenced by its famous forerunner, Donatello's bronze *David* (*c*1433; Museo Nazionale, Florence). However, Donatello's heroic conception here gives place to a calmer and more delicate idealism. The charming bronze *Putto with a Dolphin* (*c*1475–80; Palazzo Vecchio, Florence) originally formed a fountain in a Medici country house. Verrocchio's painting of *The Baptism of Christ* (*c*1474–5; Uffizi, Florence) owes its fame to Leonardo's participation in finishing the picture *c*1480.

At intervals, between 1476 and 1483, Verrocchio worked on the life-sized bronze group of *Christ and St Thomas* (Orsanmichele, Florence), casting Christ *c*1477/8 and St Thomas *c*1482/3. The solemnity of their gestures, and the massive folds of their garments, indicate the master's expressive late style. The famous marble bust of a *Lady with a Bunch of Flowers* (Museo Nazionale, Florence) was carved *c*1478 and was probably influenced by Leonardo's painting of Ginevra dei Benci (*Portrait of a Woman*, *c*1474–6; National Gallery of Art, Washington, D.C.).

Verrocchio's last and undoubtedly greatest work is the bronze equestrian monument of *Bartolommeo Colleoni* (Campo SS. Giovanni e Paolo, Venice), begun *c*1483 and finished, after Verrocchio's death, by Alessandro Leopardi. This gigantic monument combines the lasting influence of Donatello's statuary, as represented by the monument to *Gattamelata* (1446–53; Piazza del Santo, Padua) and the new conception of man as conqueror of his world, which links the late 15th century with the art of the High Renaissance.

Further reading. Passavant, G. (trans. Watson, K.) *Verrrocchio: Sculpture, Paintings, and Drawings*, London (1969). Pope-Hennessy, J. *Italian Renaissance Sculpture*, London (1958). Valentiner, R. *Studies of Italian Renaissance Sculpture*, London (1950).

Vieira da Silva Marie 1908–92

The Portuguese painter Marie-Hélène Vieira da Silva studied sculpture under Antoine Bourdelle and Charles Despiau in 1928. She turned to painting in 1929, and became a pupil of François Dufresne, Othon Friesz, and Fernand Léger. William Hayter, with whom she studied engraving in Paris before the Second World War, had a great influence on her work. This is characterized by abstract linear forms, usually derived from architecture; they are painted in neutral tones, and spiral back to form an interior space (for example, *The City*, oil on canvas; 1950–1; Museum of Modern Art, New York). She should be seen in the general context of the lyrical abstraction movement that flourished in Paris after the Second World War and is sometimes referred to as the School of Paris.

Vien Joseph-Marie 1716–1809

The French painter Joseph-Marie Vien was born in Montpellier. From 1743 to 1750 he worked in Rome, where he must have met A.R. Mengs, the teacher of J.-L. David. Vien's work demonstrates the stylistic possibilities available in the mid 18th century: his *Sleeping Hermit* (Louvre, Paris), a great success at the 1753 Salon, is in the line that leads from the work of Guercino to that of Pier Francesco Mola. His *St Denis Preaching* (1767; St Roch, Paris) has genuine grandeur, its pseudo-Classical manner vaguely derived from Raphael. It met with some praise from Diderot. Vien's best-selling works, in that age of nascent Neoclassicism, were his seminude "Greek" virgins in an antique Pompeian setting, such as his *Greek Girl at the Bath* (1767; Museum of Art, Ponce, Puerto Rico). These works are delicate and whimsical, and Neoclassical only in their trappings.

Vigée-Lebrun Marie 1755–1842

The French portrait painter Marie-Louise-Elisabeth Vigée-Lebrun was the daughter of the pastellist Louis Vigée (1715–67). She married the famous art dealer J.-B.-P. Lebrun. She was much influenced by the works of Rubens (1577–1640) and Anthony van Dyck (1599–1641) and by the softer works of her contemporary, Jean-Baptiste Greuze. Her official career began with a commission to paint a portrait, *Marie Antoinette*, 1779 (now in the Kunsthistorisches Museum, Vienna). She became a member of the Académie in 1783. Her most successful works were portraits of women, painted with a lush, neo-Baroque colorism: they are unashamedly and sentimentally decorative. With the Revolution of 1789 she fled

Maria Viera da Silva: The Golden City. Private collection

France because of her connections with the court; she traveled and worked in many parts of Europe until the Restoration. By then her works had become unfashionable, and she retired to write her *Souvenirs* (published 1835–7).

Vignola Jacopo da 1507–73

The Italian architect Jacopo Barozzi da Vignola came from near Bologna; this northern heritage, and with it the patronage of the Farnese family, were all-important in his architectural life. He started his career as a painter, which influenced much of his early architecture in Rome. He arrived in the city *c*1530, probably through the patronage of the younger Cardinal Alessandro Farnese. He worked for the Farnese family at Caprarola, in the Vatican for Pope Paul III (Farnese), and at the new Farnese ducal palace at Piacenza, begun in 1558. The same patronage made him Michelangelo's successor at St Peters, Rome, in 1564, and on the Roman palaces on the Capitoline Hill.

The influence of Michelangelo was strong in Vignola's work at the Villa Giulio, begun in 1551. Here, with Bartolomeo Ammanati and Giorgio Vasari, he produced a series of interlocking courtyards, opening from the rear of the main casino. The axial and visual arrangement was close to Michelangelo's plan for the Palazzo Farnese. In Vignola's castle-villa at Caprarola (1559), however, the intended fortress plan was made to turn in upon itself, in the form of a circular courtyard. It made an impressive effect through its size and novelty, as did his unfinished Palazzo Farnese at Piacenza.

Vignola is particularly associated with the Gesù in Rome, planned for the Society of Jesus *c*1568. Its broad nave, with side chapels set between the coupled pilasters, and its dome over the crossing, established a type associated with the Jesuit order and Tridentine architecture. Once again, the Farnese family were the driving force both in its construction and in the use of Vignola's design. In contrast with the scale and splendor of the Gesù were his two relatively small exercises in the revised central plan of the Renaissance. At S. Andrea in Via Flaminia (*c*1553), and at S. Anna dei Palafrenieri (1565), he skillfully juggled with two shapes of oval and rectangle. Both these buildings were important during the Roman Baroque period. They strongly influenced the centralized plans of Borromini and Bernini, particularly the latter's S. Andrea al Quirinale, Rome.

In 1562, Vignola published his *Regola delli Cinque Ordini di Architettura* which explained the Classical orders in great detail and established the simple but immensely useful device of the module in correct proportioning. The work was of enormous importance throughout the 16th and 17th centuries and was ultimately published in all the European languages.

Marie Vigée-Lebrun: Madame Grand; oil on canvas; 92×72cm (36×28in); 1783. Metropolitan Museum, New York

Vignon Claude 1593–1670

The French artist Claude Vignon was born at Tours. He trained as a painter in Paris, acquiring there some of the preciosity of Georges Lallemand. During a stay in Rome, probably in 1617, he was influenced in different ways by followers of Caravaggio and of Adam Elsheimer; his work also showed affinities with that of Domenico Feti and Peter Lastman. He was in Paris again in 1622, but later returned to Italy as a picture-dealer. He was made an Academician in 1651. Representative works are in the Louvre, Paris.

Vignon was principally a painter of religious subjects, though his work showed little religious feeling. His early pictures were striking for their richness of color and sweep of execution, producing a rakish, romantic swagger unusual in France at the time. His later work, modified through the influence of Rubens by 1624, is inclined to slovenliness. He had at least 24 children, of whom three were painters: Claude (1633–1703; a follower of his father), Philippe (1638–1701; a portraitist), and Charlotte (b. 1639; a painter of still lifes).

Villard de Honnecourt *fl.* 1225–45

The French architect, artist, and writer Villard de Honnecourt was probably born around the end of the 12th century in Honnecourt, a small town near Cambrai. The sole source of information on Villard is his autograph illustrated Lodge Book in Paris (Bibliothèque Nationale; MS. Fr. 19093). He may have trained at the nearby Cistercian monastery of Vaucelles. His drawings indicate a knowledge of buildings at Vaucelles and Cambrai, Meaux, Laon, Reims, Chartres, and Lausanne. Villard states that he spent a long time in Hungary, which he probably visited between 1235 and 1242. It may be that his book was begun in connection with his visit, and completed after his return. The manuscript was used as an instruction manual in his Lodge; it bears several annotations and additions in two other hands, which were probably made by his successors. Little is known of buildings Villard actually constructed, although he claimed to have designed the choir of an unidentified church, illustrated in his book, with the assistance of a certain Pierre de Corbie. In addition, it has been suggested that Villard designed the collegiate church of St Quentin (built 1225–57).

The Lodge Book consists of 66 folios, most of which are covered with a wide variety of drawings, often accompanied by explanatory captions. Architectural plans and elevations, furnishings, decorative details, applied geometry, examples of masonry, carpentry, and machines are all treated, along with over 200 human and animal figures. These sketches reveal Villard's widespread interest not only in the art of his own day and the recent past, but also in Classical art, which may have been transmitted via Romanesque or Byzantine models. His book provides a rare insight into the working method of a 13th-century architect, indicating that sketchbooks were already an important medium for the exchange of ideas. Its broad scope suggests that Gothic architects were highly versatile, with a profound knowledge of the whole range of the arts and crafts.

Villon Jacques 1875–1963

The French painter known as Jacques Villon was born at Dauville. His real name was Gaston Duchamp, and he was the brother of the painter Marcel Duchamp. From 1894 he lived in Paris, where he published humorous drawings and, influenced by Henri de Toulouse-Lautrec, made posters and engravings. He painted in a Fauvist manner from 1906 until 1911, when Cubism became more important in his work. His intellectual approach led him to form the *Section d'Or* group in 1912. After camouflage work during the First World War his paintings became muted and Abstract (for example, *Race Horse*, 1922; Galerie Louis Carré, Paris). He was forced to live by selling engravings until 1930, when he returned to painting and the use of pure colors.

Jacques Villon: Portrait of Mlle. Y.D.; oil on canvas; 120×89cm (47×35in); 1913. Los Angeles County Museum of Art, Los Angeles

Vischer family
15th and 16th centuries

The Vischer Family were German sculptors and bronze-founders from Nuremberg. For a century, from 1453, theirs was the most important foundry for bronze sculpture in Germany. Also working in Nuremberg, at this time of the city's artistic heyday, were the sculptors Adam Kraft and Veit Stoss, and the painter Albrecht Dürer, who was an important if elusive influence on the later members of the family. The Vischer workshop produced a wide range of bronze sculpture for places all over Germany and eastern Europe. Many works are signed. Whether this indicates responsibility for both casting and design is uncertain, but evidence suggests that such was usually the case.

Hermann the Elder (*ob.* 1488) acquired Nuremberg citizenship in 1453. His many works included the Wittenberg Font (Stadtkirche, Wittenberg) of 1457. It was his son, Peter the Elder (*c*1460–1529) who inherited the business in 1488 and established its great reputation. In that year he supplied a design (Akademie, Vienna) for an architectural framework to surround the shrine of St Sebald (St Sebald, Nuremberg). In the 1490s his work included a powerful bronze figure, the so-called *Branch-breaker* (Bayerisches Nationalmuseum, Munich) and several tomb monuments, for example, the one to Archbishop Ernst von Sachsen (1494–5; Magdeburg Cathedral). He contributed superb life-size figures of King Arthur and Theodoric for Emperor Maximilian's monument (1512–13; Hofkirche, Innsbruck). Construction of the St Sebald shrine was resumed in 1507, was interrupted from 1512 to 1514, and was completed with the assistance of Peter's sons in 1519. Peter the Elder's work is hard and sharp in finish: it displays a monumental dignity and a Gothic style that may have been influenced by his collection of 14th-century wooden sculptures.

It was probably his eldest son, Hermann the Younger (*c*1486–1517), who transformed the original design of the St Sebald Shrine, replacing with truncated canopies the intended elaborate, late Gothic pinnacles. Some of his architectural drawings, made during a visit to Italy in 1515, have survived (Louvre, Paris). That same year he began work on a screen for the burial chapel in St Anna at Augsburg for the great banking family, the Fuggers. The screen was unfinished at Hermann's death in 1517, but was completed by his brother Hans (*c*1489–1550) between 1536 and 1540.

Peter the Younger (1487–1528), a third brother, may also have visited Italy. Much of the sculpture of the St Sebald Shrine is attributed to him. It abounds with mythological and allegorical figures such as sea-gods and *putti*—the influence of the Italian Renaissance in both subject and style. The Paduan sculptor Riccio may have been the inspiration for these, and for the independent bronze statuettes that Peter helped to introduce into Germany, such as his inkwell of 1525 (Ashmolean Museum, Oxford). As well as the usual tomb monuments, such as that to Frederick the Wise (1527; Schlosskirche, Wittenberg), Peter made bronze plaquettes and medals.

Georg Vischer (*c*1520–92), son of Hans, took over the foundry in 1550. Like his uncle he made statuettes, for example an inkwell dated 1547 (Staatliche Museen, Berlin).

Vitale da Bologna 1289/1309–59/69

The Italian painter Vitale d'Aimo de' Cavelli was called Vitale da Bologna, after the city in which he was the most important painter of his period. There are two signed Madonnas by him, one in the Vatican Museums and the other in the Galleria Davia-Bargellini in Bologna, but his work is not easily disentangled from a mass of rather optimistic attributions. Bolognese artists of the 14th century were best known as miniaturists, so that Vitale, a painter of panels and frescoes, is unusual; he seems also to have been a sculptor. To his two signed Madonnas may be added a polyptych in S. Salvatore, Bologna (1353). The style of its narrative panels enables us to attribute to him frescoes in the abbey at Pomposa (1351), frescoes from the church of the Mezzarata (now in the Pinacoteca Nazionale, Bologna) and also the lovely little panels of the *Ador-*

Peter Vischer the Younger: the monument to Peter Frederick the Wise; bronze; height 425cm (167in); 1527. Schlosskirche, Wittenberg

Vitale da Bologna: The Miracles of St Anthony Abbot; panel; 77×37cm (30×15in). Pinacoteca Nazionale, Bologna

ation of the Magi (National Gallery of Scotland, Edinburgh), and *St Anthony Abbot* (Pinacoteca Nazionale, Bologna).

In all these works Vitale displays a feeling for dramatic shapes, blocks of exciting color, and dramatic silhouettes; his works produce an emotional impact almost without regard for subject matter. The *Christ in Majesty* in the apse at S. Maria, Pomposa, is surrounded by a brilliant striped mandorla that dominates the nave; the frescoes at Mezzarata are similarly striking. The Edinburgh *Adoration* is comparatively restful, though highly decorative; the elements of the scene are fitted together with little concern for realistic space, but they tell a complicated story with great economy. This work is probably later than the Davia-Bargellini Madonna and Child (the *Madonna dei Denti*) of 1345, and the Pomposa frescoes of 1351. In his strongly individual art, Vitale was apparently influenced by the International Gothic style.

Vitruvius 1st Century BC

The Roman architect, military engineer, and author Vitruvius worked for both Julius Caesar and for the Emperor Augustus. His books, *De Architectura*, were intended to explain to his presumed patron, the Emperor, the criteria by which excellence in architecture can be judged and attained. He drew freely on the many earlier treatises by Greek artists, and as a result his work is an important source of information and observations about Greek, rather than Roman, architectural practice. It deals with town planning, materials, the use of the orders of architecture, different building types, water supplies, mensuration, and machines for construction and military purposes. His books served the Renaissance as a guide to Greek architecture, although his examples derive more from the Hellenistic than from the Classical period.

Vittone Bernardo 1702–70

Bernardo Vittone was an Italian architect of the late Baroque period. Except for a brief period of study in Rome (1730–2), he practiced exclusively in his native Piedmont, combining the divergent styles of Guarino Guarini and Filippo Juvarra into a highly original synthesis. All his main works are ecclesiastical, and most of them are centrally planned. Vittone was particularly inventive in the various solutions he devised for effecting the transition from the main centralized space into the area of the dome. An example of his skill can be seen in S. Croce at Villanova di Mondovi (1755); despite the complexity of the geometry, the overall effect is one of gaiety, lightness, and serenity.

Vittoria Alessandro 1525–1608

The Italian sculptor Alessandro Vittoria was born in Trento, and received his early training there in the workshop of the Grandi, who were sculptors and bronze-casters. In 1543 he was sent by Bishop Cristoforo Madruzzo of Trento to the studio of Jacopo Sansovino in Venice. Although Sansovino was a major formative influence on Vittoria, the two men had quite different artistic temperaments. In 1547 after a quarrel, Vittoria left, to work as a *stuccatore* in Vicenza.

Alessandro Vittoria: Neptune; bronze; height 50cm (20in); c1580–5. Victoria and Albert Museum, London

The breach was not healed until 1553, when Vittoria returned to Venice. He based himself there for the rest of his career, becoming the most important and influential sculptor working in Venice in the later 16th century, comparable in importance with his exact contemporary, Giambologna, in Florence. The friend of Titian, Tintoretto, Veronese, and Pietro Aretino, Vittoria was a powerful and inventive artist, and exceptionally versatile. He produced brilliant stucco decorations

(Scala d'Oro of the Doges' Palace, Venice) and architectural sculpture (caryatids for the Biblioteca Marciana, Venice); he was an original medallist, and excelled in his age as a portrait sculptor (seen in his bust of *Tommaso Rangone* in the Ateneo Veneto, Venice).

His major work consists of the altarpieces with marble statues that he made for many Venetian churches, for example S. Salvatore, S. Francesco della Vigna, S. Maria dei Frari, and SS. Giovanni e Paolo. It can be argued that he was an even more powerful artist when he worked on a small scale, in bronze (for example, *St John the Baptist, St Francis*, S. Francesco della Vigna, Venice). Like Tintoretto, Vittoria was deeply interested in the work of Michelangelo, and he introduced elements of Michelangelo's style into Venetian sculpture.

Antonio Vivarini (attrib.): The Abduction of Helen; panel; 151×294cm (59×116in); 1445–50. Walters Art Gallery, Baltimore

Vivarini family

15th and 16th centuries

The Vivarini were a family of Italian painters of Venetian origin. No certain dates of birth or death are known. The oldest member of the family was Antonio (*fl.* 1440–76/84), but his brother-in-law Giovanni d'Alemagna (*fl.* 1441–*c*50) was certainly his senior, and is usually included within the group, together with Antonio's brother Bartolommeo (*fl.* 1450–99), and his son Alvise (*c*1445–1503/5).

Giovanni and Antonio, and possibly Bartolommeo, worked on the frescoes of the Ovetari Chapel (church of the Eremitani, Padua) from 1448, alongside Mantegna and Niccolo Pizzolo. At Giovanni's death the family left Padua, having completed only part of the vault. A certain eclecticism is noticeable throughout the works of the Vivarini workshop. Their early works, such as the *Coronation of the Virgin* signed and dated by Giovanni and Antonio in 1444 (S. Pantaleone, Venice), show two influences: a highly decorated late Gothic style, characteristic of Pisanello and Gentile da Fabriano, combined with a style probably derived from Donatello, who was in Padua from 1443 to 1453.

Later, their works came to reflect the influence of Mantegna in the depiction of hard, dry folds, as for instance in Bartolommeo's S. Maria Formosa triptych of 1473. Alvise's S. Ambrogio altar (S. Maria dei Frari, Venice; completed posthumously by Marco Basaiti) shows the saint seated in an open loggia. The architecture of the loggia continues that of the picture's frame, in a manner first used in Venice by Antonello and Giovanni Bellini. The quality of lighting, the musical angels, and the poses of some of the figures in this picture are also reminiscent of Bellini's works.

From 1451 the Vivarini family rarely moved from Venice, but received many commissions for altarpieces from provincial towns on the Italian mainland. Antonio and Bartolommeo signed works both independently and in collaboration throughout their working lives, whereas Alvise worked away from the family

Alvise Vivarini: Virgin and Child with Six Saints; tempera on panel; 146×175cm (57×69in); 1480. Gallerie dell'Accademia, Venice

studio. Their only State commission was achieved as the result of his petition to the Doge in 1488, but at Alvise's death the three paintings contracted for remained unfinished. The Vivarini workshop was second only to Bellini's in the production of religious paintings in Venice in the second half of the 15th and early 16th centuries.

Vlaminck Maurice de 1876–1958

The French painter Maurice de Vlaminck was born in Paris. As an artist he was mostly self-taught, in between activities as a racing cyclist and musician. His meeting with André Derain in 1900 was crucial: the two artists shared a studio at Chatou on the outskirts of Paris. In 1901, the Vincent van Gogh exhibition at the Bernheim-Jeune gallery in Paris convinced him of his métier as an artist: "Van Gogh is my father", he wrote. In portraits, landscapes, and still lifes he painted directly from the tube; his brushwork was turbulent, his color violent. He dismissed all forms of Classical and Renaissance art and wanted to burn the École des Beaux-Arts "with my vermilions".

He and Derain formed the *École de Chatou*, in the group that became known as the Fauves, at the Salon d'Automne of 1905. Vlaminck had probably met Matisse by 1902; his fiercely combative nature led him to repeated denials of Matisse's enormous contribution to Fauvism. His love of Van Gogh meant that the color in his paintings was extremely intense; his impasto was more prominent, and his brush strokes were less organized than those of Derain and Matisse.

In such paintings as *Still Life* (c1907; Musée de l'Annonciade, St Tropez) and *Sailing Boat* (1906; private collection) he made forceful contributions to Fauvism. By 1908, however, like many other artists, he became increasingly interested in the work of Cézanne. The bright, strident color was replaced by darker tones (although metallic blues and sharp reds do appear), the spatial organization became more traditional (he developed a liking for wide and deep perspectives), and the mood grew contemplative. His style changed little in his later years. He worked as a printmaker and book illustrator and also wrote works of poetry and prose.

Bartolomeo Vivarini (attrib.): The Adoration of the Magi; panel; 52×28cm (21×11in); c1475. Frick Collection, New York

Above: Maurice Vlaminck: The Circus; oil on canvas; 60×73cm (24×29in); 1906. Galerie Beyeler, Basel

Further reading. Cabanne, P. *Vlaminck*, Paris (1966). Sauvage, M. *Vlaminck: sa Vie et son Message*, Geneva (1956). Selz, J. *Vlaminck*, New York (1963).

Vos Cornelis de *c*1584/5–1651

The Flemish portrait painter Cornelis de Vos also produced large historical, mythological, and allegorical pictures. His portraits (mainly of Antwerp burghers) are characterized by a prosaic attention to detail, but his portrayals of children are more sympathetic (for example, *Daughters of the Artist*; Staatliche Museen, Berlin). The portraits are sometimes mistaken for those of both Rubens and his friend Anthony van Dyck. In 1637 de Vos, his brother Paul (*c*1596–1678), and his brother-in-law Frans Snyders helped Rubens to provide pictures for Philip IV's hunting lodge near Madrid, the Torre de la Parada. In the subject pictures of de Vos there is a stylistic similarity to the largeness of forms and the rhythmic compositional movements of Rubens.

Vos Marten de 1532–1603

Marten de Vos was an Antwerp painter who studied under Frans Floris. He attained his mastership in 1558, and then spent four years in Rome and Venice. He was especially influenced by the work of Tintoretto, whose brushwork style and figure-types are evident in the St Thomas Altar of 1574 (Royal Museum of Fine Arts, Antwerp). De Vos gained many commissions for altarpieces during the reestablishment of Catholicism in the southern Netherlands, after the iconoclasm of the 1570s. His coloring and brushwork become more inhibited in his later years, but there remains an exuberance of style that anticipates Rubens—for example the angels of the St Luke Altar (1602; Royal Museum of Fine Arts, Antwerp).

Cornelis de Vos: Portrait of the Artist with his Family; oil on canvas; 188×162cm (74×64in); 1621. Musées Royaux des Beaux-Arts de Belgique, Brussels

Vouet Simon 1590–1649

The French painter Simon Vouet was born in Paris. He was in Rome by 1614, after spending some time in Venice. He also visited Naples and Genoa. In 1624 he was elected president of the Academy of St Luke, the respected Roman art academy. On his return to Paris in 1627 he set up a thriving workshop, taking pupils who included the Mignards, Hubert Le Sueur, François Perrier, and Charles Lebrun.

Vouet's early career in Rome indicates the relative popularity there of the Carracci and of Caravaggio. Vouet unhesitatingly followed the latter: his early work, *Birth of the Virgin* (1615/20; S. Francesco a Ripa, Rome) demonstrated the influence of Caravaggio in its dramatic lighting and use of minor figures pointing in towards brightly lit main figures, against a tenebrous stage. Vouet's other works done in Rome show his interest in the works of Giovanni Lanfranco and Guercino, as in *The Virgin Appearing to St Bruno* (1620; Certosa di S. Martino, Naples).

His return to France in 1627 marks the beginning of the modern French school: Vouet became the most influential French artist working in France (Poussin and Claude lived in Rome). Previously the French had relied on foreign artists, or had continued a Mannerist approach derived from the Italian artistic invasion of the previous century. Here, at last, was the modern Italian manner newly arrived from Rome. Vouet introduced a modified Baroque manner, in which a certain emotionalism, color, and atmosphere are linked with a classical balance and restraint. This appealed to French taste far more than the illusionism and wholehearted emotion of the full Baroque, which, for reasons of temperament and religion, would have been spurned.

Vouet's *Presentation in the Temple* (1641; Louvre, Paris), painted for the high altar of the Jesuit Novitiate, takes a monumental view of form, which is simplified by the rather strong lighting. The architecture enlivens the composition, but, in the presentation of steps and main figure groups, both parallel to the picture plane, the work resembles a Veronese more than a Pietro da Cortona. Vouet made important innovations in decorative painting, particularly at the Hotel Séguier, Paris; he worked there in the chapel (1638), library (until 1640) and lower gallery (until 1649; unfinished at his death). His designs survive only as engravings by M. Dorigny. He revived a type of illusionistic decoration that had not been seen in France since the time of Primaticcio (*ob.* 1570), with painted architecture continuing the actual wall architecture. In the chapel at the Hotel Séguier, he disposes the figures in *Adoration of the Magi* behind a painted balustrade.

No single source is sufficient to describe Vouet's decorative manner, which combines elements from Veronese, Guercino, Correggio, and Giulio Romano, as well as the first School of Fontainebleau. Its silvery lightness can be judged from the much damaged fresco of *Parnassus* in the grotto of the Château de Wideville. This is an early work, the illusionism of which (relatively restrained though it is) must have been considered spectacular in French milieu at that date. Vouet's type of illusionism was an alternative to the Caracci system of ceiling decoration then popular in France. It was not copied until Lebrun and Houasse decorated the *Salon de la Guerre*, the *Salon de la Paix*, and the *Salle de l'Abondance* at Versailles in the 1680s. Vouet's accomplishment as a decorative artist also extended to tapestry design, anticipating the talents of his versatile pupil, Lebrun.

When Poussin visited France in 1640, Louis XIII made the famous comment, "Let's see Vouet get out of this one!" The judgment proved premature. Poussin's art was too severe and small-scale for the decorative demands the King made of it: Vouet's was not.

Voysey Charles 1857–1941

The English architect and designer Charles Francis Annesley Voysey was born at Hessle, Yorkshire. He worked with several London architects before establishing his own practice at Westminster in 1881. He was a member of an Arts and Crafts guild and a successful designer of wallpapers, textiles, and simple but slightly mannered furniture. During an architectural career that lasted from 1889 to 1914, he designed numerous country houses (for example, Perrycroft, Colwall, 1893; Broadleys, Windermere, 1898; The Orchard, Chorleywood, 1900). These were puritan restatements of the small country house of late medieval England, with white roughcast walls, sloping buttresses, and emphatic rooflines.

Vrelant William *fl.* 1456–81

William Vrelant was an illuminator from Utrecht whose name is associated with a distinctive style of manuscript painting prevalent in Bruges during the second half of the 15th century. It is characterized by simple, almost crude, miniatures of great energy and verve, painted in bright colors. The text is in notably large characters that complement the straightforward style of the paintings. Vrelant is documented in Bruges from 1456 until his death; an illuminated *Vita Christi* painted by him is recorded, but this manuscript is no longer identifiable. A copy of the *Chroniques de Hainaut* (probably that in the Bibliothèque Royale Albert I, Brussels) is ascribed to one "Guillaume Wyelant", and is the basis for the attribution to Vrelant of many books illustrated in a similar style. This theory has recently been questioned; if it is correct, Vrelant was the head of the most productive workshop in Bruges.

Vries Adriaen de *c*1560–1626

Born in Holland, the sculptor Adrien de Vries worked in Rome, and later in Prague for the Emperor Rudolf II. He also maintained a workshop in Augsburg, where many of his bronze works were cast. The large Hercules Fountain (Maximilienstrasse, Augsburg), finished in 1602, takes its theme and figure-style from the work of Giovanni da Bologna, under whom de Vries trained in Italy. Later, the elegant sinuous forms of his Italian master are rendered by de Vries in a more loosely modeled technique, emphasizing light and shade on the surface of flesh. His work was known as far afield as the court at Copenhagen, for which he designed the Neptune Fountain for Fredericksburg Palace (1617–23).

Vries Hans de 1527–?1604

The Flemish artist Hans Vredeman de Vries was one of the most influential figures in the history of design in the later 16th century. His talents spanned the fields of architecture, painting, furniture, and garden design. His engravings carried throughout Europe an exaggerated form of the style of the School of Fontainebleau. His designs for architectural motifs were used on some of the more ambitious country houses of Elizabethan England, such as Wollaton Hall, Nottingham. Work for State occasions, such as triumphal arches for the entry of Charles V into Antwerp in 1549, prompted his few but important pictures of fantastic architectural settings, for example *Christ in the House of Mary and Martha* (Hampton Court Palace, London).

Vrubel Mikhail 1856–1910

The Russian painter Mikhail Aleksandrovich Vrubel trained at the St Petersburg Academy (1880–4). Afterwards he worked mainly in Kiev until 1889, restoring and painting icons and frescoes in the church of St Kirill and the cathedral of St Vladimir. He visited Venice in 1884, and was influenced by Byzantine mosaics and Renaissance painting. After that he painted in a mystical, flat Byzantine style. From 1889 he lived in Moscow, where he associated with the neo-nationalist circle around Marmontov, experimenting with ceramics, and painting myths (for example the mythical knight *Bogatyr*, 1898; State Russian Museum, St Petersburg). He also became obsessed with the spiritual loneliness of the Demon in Mikhail Lermontov's poem *Demon* (1841), which he illustrated and painted constantly from 1890.

Vuillard Jean-Édouard 1868–1940

The French painter, printmaker, and occasional photographer Jean-Édouard Vuillard was born in Paris. He studied at the École des Beaux-Arts and at the Académie Julian, where he met Pierre Bonnard, Paul Sérusier, Maurice Denis, and others who formed the group of the Nabis. Around 1890, Vuillard had a phase during which he used simplified design, strong color, and energetic brushwork. But this, like the time of the Fauves who were to follow, was short-lived, and he is best remembered for his *intimiste* interiors. In these, a predominantly bourgeois setting (often his mother sewing, or reading, or relaxing) is conveyed in flat color areas, sometimes patterned and textured, and always spatially tense.

Like the rest of the Nabis, Vuillard wanted to go beyond painting: he produced many decorative panels and screens, theatrical designs and lithographs. The Nabis contributed to an avant-garde literary magazine, the *Revue Blanche*. In 1894 its editor, Alexandre Natanson, commissioned Vuillard to paint nine canvas panels in tempera showing Paris park scenes. Each of these was some 7 ft (2.2 m) in height.

In 1899, his series of colored lithographs, *Paysages et Intérieurs*, was published by Ambrose Vollard. He also made etchings and black-and-white lithographs. He became an enthusiastic photographer—photographs sometimes provided the starting-point for his paintings. He was a founder member of the Salon d'Automne in 1903, but unlike his friend Bonnard, he did not continue to develop artistically after 1900. Instead he tended to retreat into a conventional and easily acceptable form of *intimism*.

Jean-Édouard Vuillard: Portrait of Henri Toulouse-Lautrec; oil on card; 25×23cm (10×9in); c1898. Musée Toulouse-Lautrec, Albi

Further reading. Preston, S. *Edouard Vuillard*, New York (1972).

Wagner Otto 1841–1918

Otto Wagner was unquestionably the father and leader of the Viennese school of architecture that produced Adolf Loos, Josef Hoffmann, Josef Olbrich, and others. After training in Vienna and Berlin, he began his career with buildings noted for their classicist approach—an approach he never forsook.

Wagner is chiefly remembered as an architect who reacted against Viennese historicism and for his important contributions to town planning. The Vienna *Stadtbahn* (metropolitan railway) project of the mid 1980s remains a monument to his imagination, technical ingenuity, and concern for the minutiae of detail.

Wagner's most influential book of architectural theory was *Moderne Architektur* (1894). Its crucial point was that architecture must create new forms by taking into account contemporary social needs and advances in technology.

Two of Wagner's post-1900 commissions were of particular importance: the monumental church Am Steinhof (1905), and the Post Office Savings Bank in Vienna (1904–6). The latter work is justly considered a major building in the development of 20th-century architecture.

Walden Herwarth 1878–?1941

The composer, critic, and journalist Herwarth Walden is best known as an energetic propagandist in Germany for Expressionism and the European avant-garde. In 1910 he founded *Der Sturm*, a Berlin-based publishing house and journal. He was the first to promote the work of Oskar Kokoschka and the *Brücke* group; in 1912 he held the first exhibition of the *Blaue Reiter* school; he later published the writing of Kandinsky and others. He exhibited Cubism and Futurism in Berlin in 1913 and followed this with a series of important one-man exhibitions, including those of Robert Delaunay (1913) and Lyonel Feininger (1917).

Wang Hui: Landscape; ink and colors on hanging scroll; 46×30cm (18×21in). Victoria and Albert Museum, London

Wang Chien 1598–1677

The Chinese painter Wang Chien came from T'ai-ts'ang, Kiangsu. He was a contemporary of Wang Shih-min. Like him, he was a member of the Nine Friends group. He rose to be Governor of Lien-Chou Kwangtung, South China. He is known for his large landscapes in the eclectic, orthodox style of his generation.

Wang Hui 1632–1717

Wang Hui came from Ch'ang-shu, Kiangsu. A gifted Chinese artist who followed the orthodox style, he was discovered by Wang Chien, who introduced him to Wang Shih-min. Both of the older men admired Wang Hui's work, and he was taken as a pupil to work in the studio of the elder Wang at T'ai-ts'ang. This gave him access to works of the old masters in Wang Shih-min's collection, and enlarged his experience and his mastery of the styles of his school. Wang Hui was a man of great personal charm, with a wide circle of friends. He was successful at the court of K'ang Hsi, where he held the post of keeper of the Imperial collections of painting and calligraphy (1691–8).

Wang Meng *c*1309–85

The Chinese artist Wang Meng was a nephew of Chao Meng-fu and came from a highly educated family. He was interested in composition and the expression of texture. He painted rich mountain rock formations, occasionally clothing them with colored trees painted in traditional style, but setting up a writhing movement that was quite new. The absence of sky in many of his compositions adds to this rich effect. The scroll *Forest Dwellings at Ch'-u-ch'u* (National Palace Museum, Formosa) is a fine example of the work of this imaginative genius, whose influence on such painters as Wen Chen-ming and Shih T'ao is clear.

Wang Shih-min 1592–1680

The Chinese painter Wang Shih-min came from a prominent scholarly family in T'ai-ts'ang, Kiangsu. He was a contemporary of Tung Ch'i-ch'ang, and was much influenced by him. He was a member of the group called the Nine Friends. He held official posts under the Ming, but retired at the fall of the dynasty. He was a great admirer of the Yuan masters and of Huang Kung-wang in particular. Wang Shih-min, however, used color in the style of Wen Cheng-ming, of whom he must be regarded as a close follower. He worked in a rich, painterly style, but he appears not to have been a great innovator.

Wang Wei 699–759

The Chinese landscape painter Wang Wei was a classically trained scholar poet and official, whose country home was in Wang Ch'uan, Shensi. Wang Wei admired the poetry of Li Po; his own verse was lyrical and evocative.

Wang Wei painted many landscapes, none of which have been preserved. He is credited with the introduction of the art of landscape painting in ink alone, which was regarded, over the centuries, as the greatest school of painting in China. The one work that may bear some echo of his style is the so-called *Wang Ch'uan* scroll, named after his country home. Many copies of the original are recorded; versions in the Seattle Art Museum and the Freer Gallery of Art, Washington, D.C., may be Ming copies of earlier engravings.

Difficult as it is to be certain of the true character of Wang Wei's painting, he stands at the head of the *literati* landscape school. He was revered by all later painters, although his actual paintings quickly became remote in style. He is a striking contrast with his older contemporary, Wu Tao-tzu; although they must have known each other's work, there is no record of their having met.

Wang Yuan-ch'i 1642–1715

Wang Yuan-ch'i was a native of T'ai-ts'ang and a relative of Wang Shih-min. He was thus born into a great family of scholars and achieved considerable distinction, receiving his *chin-shih* degree at

Wang Meng: Fishermen on the Flower Stream; ink on paper hanging scroll; 124×57cm (49×22in). National Palace Museum, Taipei

the age of 29. He was also recognized by the K'ang Hsi Emperor, and was a member of the board for the compilation of the *Pei-wen chai Shu hua p'u*, a comprehensive catalog of painting and calligraphy. Wang Yuan-ch'i's paintings are among the most inventive of the eclectic orthodox school. He was interested in volume and the construction of landscape in a way that was never taken up by artists who followed him, but which seems to point the way to an almost Cubist approach to painting.

Warhol, Andy 1928–87

The American painter, graphic artist, and film-maker Andy Warhol was born Andrew Warhola in Pittsburgh, Pennsylvania, the son of devoutly Catholic immigrants from Czechoslovakia. After a sickly childhood, he studied pictorial design at the Carnegie Institute of Technology in Pittsburgh from 1945 to 1949. Upon graduation, he settled in New York.

During the 1950s Warhol worked as a commercial illustrator, creating whimsical drawings—often related to fashion, especially shoes—for magazines and retail stores. He quickly gained a solid reputation in his field and won several major awards.

About 1960 Warhol switched his focus to the art world. The New York scene at the time was still dominated by the individualistic, emotional work of the Abstract Expressionists, but Warhol created works that used commonplace, impersonal imagery such as Campbell's soup cans, Brillo boxes, and dollar signs. By 1962 he favored photographic silk-screening, a technique that allowed him to remove the artist's "touch." He further minimized his role by often having assistants create these works in his studio, which he labeled "The Factory." Warhol used silk-screening to reproduce photographs from popular culture (a headshot of Marilyn Monroe, a photo of a car wreck) in cold, repetitive series, using the same image again and again and changing only the color of the painted, often monochrome, backgrounds.

It is this body of work, created from about 1961 to 1964, that gained Warhol a place in the pantheon of Western art history. The impersonal, purposefully banal quality of his imagery and technique represented the peak of the Pop art movement, which focused on issues of mass culture rather than the emotions of the artist. Implicit in such work, given the subject matter and cold technique, was a comment on the numbing effects of an increasingly media-saturated society. Such works radically redefined prevailing perceptions of the roles of art and the artist.

During the 1960s Warhol also focused much of his time on film-making. He developed an entourage of downtown New York characters who spent time at his Factory and participated in his experimental films. Some of his films were overtly challenging to the viewer—for instance, *Sleep* (1963) is a six-hour film of a man sleeping. In 1968 Warhol was shot and badly injured by an unstable woman loosely affiliated with the Factory, and this period of his career came to an end shortly thereafter.

In the 1970s Warhol responded to many lucrative commissions for society portraits, creating colorful silk-screens based on Polaroid photographs. These works—as well as subsequent series of portraits of movie and sports stars—were often regarded as purely commercial and devoid of artistic merit. During this period the artist became increasingly fascinated with celebrity and was known as much for frequenting the New York club Studio 54 as for his art. Throughout the decade he developed *Interview* magazine, a publication dedicated to documenting celebrities.

By the end of the 1970s, Warhol was making a series of nearly abstract "Shadow" prints that received some critical acclaim. His career received a boost in 1984, when he collaborated with the up-and-coming artists Jean-Michel Basquiat and Francesco Clemente and became known as the father figure of an important new generation of artists. This came to a halt in 1987, when he died from complications related to routine gall-bladder surgery. The Andy Warhol Museum was opened in Pittsburgh in 1994.

Further reading. Andy Warhol Museum, *Andy Warhol 365 Takes*, New York (2004). Banier, F. and Warhol, A. *Red Books*, Göttingen, Ger. (2004). Feldman, F. et al. *Andy Warhol Prints: a Catalogue Raisonné 1962–1987*, New York (2003). Hackett, P. *The Andy Warhol Diaries*, New York (1989). Warhol, A. *Portrait Drawings*, Cologne (2002).

Andy Warhol: Marilyn Monroe; silk-screen print on paper; 91×91cm (36×36in). Tate Gallery, London

Watteau Antoine 1684–1721

Jean-Antoine Watteau was the outstanding painter of the French Rococo, an artist beside whom the talents of his contemporaries and successors are measured. He was born at Valenciennes; the town had only recently been ceded to France, and during his lifetime he was considered a Flemish artist.

His family was poor and his early years are obscure. He was trained under local artists, and arrived in Paris in 1702 as an assistant to one of them, a painter of scenery for the Paris Opera. This was probably Watteau's first contact with the theater. His master left Watteau in Paris, and he was forced to produce copies of popular old masters on a quasi production-line basis. It may have been at this time that he began to paint in his own right, scenes he would have known during his childhood at Valenciennes, executed in the style of Adriaen Brouwer and David Teniers. Throughout his life his paintings were always based on drawings, and even during these early years in Paris when he was living in poverty, he made many delicate drawings after nature.

Soon after arriving in Paris he came into contact with Claude Gillot. By as early as 1703 Watteau may have been his apprentice. Under Gillot he renewed his association with the theater and with the *Commedia dell'Arte* in particular. This troupe of Italian comedians had taken Paris by storm with their fast, irreverent pantomimes; their scandalous performances had caused them to be expelled from the city in 1697. The memory of the *Commedia dell'Arte* lived on in the productions of French comedians who also based their plays around the traditional characters of Harlequin, Pierrot, and Pantalone. Scenes from the *Commedia* formed most of the subject matter of Gillot's paintings, handled in a matter-of-fact way. Not surprisingly, the paintings

Right: Antoine Watteau: Les Fêtes Venitiennes; oil on canvas; 56×46cm (22×18in); c1718–19 National Gallery of Scotland, Edinburgh

that Watteau made during his apprenticeship with Gillot are *Commedia* scenes that seem, like his master's, to have been painted from actual performances.

It was Gillot who ended Watteau's apprenticeship *c*1707 or 1708, possibly for reasons of professional jealousy. He transferred his apprenticeship to Claude Audran III, a decorator who employed a number of artists to carry out his designs. Under Audran, Watteau absorbed a complete Rococo vocabulary of trellises, birds and monkeys, and chinoiserie.

Watteau was fortunate to have studied under Gillot and Audran, both of whom were modern artists outside the main stream of French academic painting, for by inclination as well as by birth Watteau was an outsider in the Parisian art world.

Audran was the curator of the Luxembourg Palace, and through him Watteau had regular access to *The Life of Marie de Medici* cycle of paintings by Rubens. He was able to study and to copy unhindered a series of paintings by his great compatriot. Rubens' technical ability, his draftsmanship, and his handling of paint were far superior to any painting being produced in Paris at that time, and the *Marie de Medici* cycle became the most important influence in the formation of Watteau's style.

In 1709 Watteau submitted a painting to the competition for the coveted Prix de Rome. He came second, and his fortunes began to improve. Sirois, a dealer with whom he later stayed, commissioned him to paint a contemporary battle scene. Watteau returned to Valenciennes, close to the battle lines of the Duke of Marlborough's campaigns, to make his work as natural as possible. Few of his paintings of military scenes survive, but engravings show that what interested Watteau was not the fight or the glamor of battle but the underlying reality: the camps, the soldiers waiting for orders, and the general inactivity of war. His military paintings are like reports from a modern war correspondent, for he had an acute eye which could select the important in everyday life. This perceptiveness was Watteau's greatest gift, and he used it fully in the type of painting with which his name is most closely linked, the *fête galante*.

It was as a painter of *fêtes galantes* that Watteau was enrolled at the Academy; a new category was specially created for him. The painting he chose to submit for membership was entitled *The Pilgrimage to the Island of Cythera* (1717; Louvre, Paris). The painting has it origins in a scene from a contemporary play, *Les Trois Cousines*. It shows the return of a group of people from Cythera, the island of love, at the moment they realize that the pleasures of love are transitory, and that it is time for them to leave their enchanted island for the boat to the mainland.

Here Rubens was once again an inspiration for Watteau: not so much the Rubens of the *Marie de Medici* cycle, but the Rubens who painted *The Garden of Love* (*c*1634; Prado, Madrid). Seriousness of subject is not generally thought to be an attribute of Rococo painting, and Watteau's exquisitely dressed and perfectly mannered courtiers may seem at first sight as unlikely as his Harlequins and Pierrots to be the vehicles of human passions. But Watteau was above all an artist who understood the theater, with its contrasting layers of artifice and reality.

Restlessness, ill health, and financial motives may have encouraged Watteau's visit to London in 1719. It was probably during his year in England that he created *La Toilette* (1719; Wallace Collection, London). Realistic and freely painted, it shows a Venetian sensuousness quite new to French Painting. At Watteau's death, only a year after his return to Paris from London, his priest persuaded him to destroy a number of "offensive" paintings that were probably similar to *La Toilette*.

It was just before his death that Watteau painted the large *Giles* (*c*1719; Louvre, Paris) as a theater placard for a theatrical troupe. "Giles" was the French adaptation of Pierrot, the scapegoat and outcast derided by his companions. In Watteau's painting he stands isolated and vulnerable, with his stupid face and ill fitting clothes. Watteau may have felt an affinity with Giles for he, too, was an outsider, set apart from his contemporaries by temperament as well as by talent.

Further reading. Adhemar, H. and Huyghe, R. *Watteau*, Paris (1950). Brookner, A. *Antoine Watteau*, London (1967). Goncourt, E. and J. de *French Eighteenth-Century Painters*, Oxford (1981).

Watts G.F. 1817–1904

The English painter George Frederick Watts was born in London, the son of an impecunious pianomaker. At 20, he exhibited *The Wounded Heron* (1837; Watts Gallery, Compton, near Guildford), in which the swirling lines characteristic of his later work already appear. In 1843, some prize money won in the competition for the decoration of the new Houses of Parliament enabled him to travel to Florence, where he spent four years. Italian art, and in particular the rich Venetian coloring, made a powerful impression on him; the results can be seen in the vast *Story from Boccaccio* (1844–7; Keble College, Oxford), and in the works he did throughout his career.

Back in England, his aspirations towards monumental painting were frustrated. His pessimistic mood at this time is reflected in the symbolic *Life's Illusions* (1848–9; Tate Gallery, London), and in the realist *Irish Famine* (1848–9; Watts Gallery, Compton, near Guildford). In 1851 he was adopted as "resident" artist at Little Holland House; members of the artistic set centered there sat for many of his portraits, for example *Countess Somers* (begun 1860; Watts Gallery, Compton, near Guildford). These were of a consistently high standard, and his reputation rested upon them until his old age.

After the breakup of the Little Holland House set in 1875, Watts became a near recluse. But the idealized portraits he had always considered to be his most important achievement won increasing public acclaim through exhibitions, such as the one-man show at the Grosvenor Gallery in 1882. He married in 1886, and spent his last years at Compton, near Guildford, where the Watts Gallery is now located.

Webb Philip 1831–1915

The English architect Philip Webb was born in Oxford. Until 1859 he worked as George Street's assistant, becoming involved in the fledgling Arts and Crafts movement. He later designed furniture for William Morris's firm, but otherwise devoted his career to domestic architecture. For Morris he designed the Red House, Bexleyheath (1859); here he made an unashamed use of red brick, and included simple furniture and fittings to complement the rustic atmosphere. His later houses (for instance No. 1 Palace Green, London, 1868; Smeaton Manor, Yorkshire, 1878) were also generally of brick. He drew on various vernacular building types, to illustrate his belief in architecture as "the art of common building".

Weber Max 1881–1961

The American painter Max Weber, one of the leading figures in the development of American Modernism, was born in Russia, his family emigrating to the United States when he was 10. He studied at the Pratt Institute, New York, and later (1905–9) in Paris, where he absorbed the influences of Cézanne, Matisse and Henri Rousseau. Back in New York, he exhibited at Stieglitz' 291 Gallery, and began to respond to diverse influences such as Cubism and Futurism on the one hand, and Pre-Columbian and Pacific art on the other.

Right: Jan Weenix: A Merry Company amid Ancient Ruins; oil on canvas; 80×107cm (31×42in); 1667. Musée du Petit Palais, Paris

Below: G.F. Watts: Paolo and Francesca; oil on canvas; 152×130cm (60×51in); 1872–5. Watts Gallery, Compton, near Guildford

His *Rush Hour, New York* (1915; National Gallery of Art, Washington, D.C.) shows Futurist inspiration, while *Chinese Restaurant* (1915; Whitney Museum of American Art, New York) illustrates his complete assimilation of Cubism. *Spiral Rhythm* (also 1915; Hirsshorn Museum and Sculpture Garden, Washington, D.C.) was one of the first Abstract sculptures in American art. He later turned to more traditional forms, often painting affectionate evocations of his Jewish childhood.

Further reading. Werner, A. *Max Weber*, New York (1975).

Weenix Jan 1640–1719

The Dutch painter Jan Weenix painted portraits and Italianate landscapes in the manner of his father and teacher, Jan Baptist (1621–60?), but his popularity derived mainly from his slight but charming hunting trophy pictures: still lifes in which dead hares, peacocks, and other game or fowl are surrounded by fruit, flowers, and sometimes also weapons of the chase. These objects were frequently arranged around ornamental urns or other examples of garden sculpture, and placed in the twilight setting of a park.

Wen Cheng-ming 1470–1559

Wen Cheng-ming came from a large family of painters. His home was in Ts'ang Chou. A fine calligrapher and painter, he started life as an official, but retired early in order

Wen Cheng-ming: Cypress and Rock; ink on paper; 26×49cm (10×19in); 1550. William Rockhill Nelson Gallery, Kansas City, Mo.

to devote himself to painting. He was a pupil of Shen Chou, and was the leader of the Wu School of the 16th century. His son, nephews, grandsons, and great-nephews all followed in his path; probably the most notable among these was his great-nephew Wen Po-jen (1502–75).

It was the Wu School of Wen Cheng-ming that flourished when Tung Ch'i-ch'ang was writing his treatises on painting. Although Wen Cheng-ming thought himself close to the Yuan painters, and was a most versatile and spirited artist, his skill and grace worried Tung Ch'i-ch'ang, ever suspicious of the clever painter.

Wen Cheng-ming painted bamboo with great feeling, in the *literati* School of Li K'an and Wu Chen. When he painted landscape he took up the use of color, already introduced by Wang Meng in the 14th century, and employed with great distinction by Shen Chou in the 15th century. Wen was working within a tradition that had its roots in the *literati* traditions of the Yuan dynasty, but he was indeed along the path of change that became so clear in the 17th century.

In a sense, Wen Cheng-ming is the last of the intuitive *literati* painters. His art does not reveal the critical, analytical concerns of the period from Tung Ch'i-ch'ang to Mo Shih-lung.

Wesselmann Tom 1931–

The American artist Tom Wesselmann came to prominence as one of the leading exponents of Pop art. In the early 1960s he rejected the influence of Abstract Expressionists such as de Kooning, and began using both the techniques and the imagery of magazine and billboard advertising. His works focused on the themes of consumerism (his *Still Life* series featured familiar products such as cigarettes, food stuffs, automobiles) and, increasingly, eroticism. In his best-known work, the series *The Great American Nude*, he treads a fine line between undermining the eroticism of advertising, and exploiting it. Painted in flat, artificial colors and with sinuous outlines derived from Matisse, Wesselmann's nudes are large and two dimensional (some are in fact cut-outs standing in three-dimensional settings). Languorously seductive and totally depersonalized, they are featureless except for exaggerated lips, nipples and genitals: *Great American Nude # 57* (1964; Whitney Museum of American Art, New York) for example. This fetishism was made all the more explicit with works such as *Smoker, I (Mouth 12)* (1967; Museum of Modern Art, New York), a huge picture in the shape of lips and a cigarette.

Further reading. Hunter, S. *Tom Wesselmann*, New York (1994).

West Benjamin 1738–1820

The American portrait and history painter Benjamin West was born near Springfield, Pennsylvania. In the mid 1750s he taught himself to paint, and in 1760 he traveled to Rome, where he came under the influence of A.R. Mengs and Gavin Hamilton. He settled in London in 1763 and for the next decade he had no serious rival in his preferred field of history painting. His *Landing of Agrippina at Brundisium with the Ashes of Germanicus* (1766; Yale University Art Gallery, New Haven, Conn.), commissioned by the Archbishop of York, typifies the style of his first London period, with its scrupulous attention to correct antique details. West's conviction that such realism enhanced dramatic content was probably due to his appreciation of Poussin. His most important and influential picture was *Death of General Wolfe* (1770; National Gallery of Canada, Ottawa). Here he succeeded in portraying an incident from contemporary history with all the pathos and heroism of a Classical tragedy, without recourse to allegory or the associative value of antique dress and settings. His rapid climb to success as a narrative painter culminated in his appointment in 1772 as History Painter to George III, who remained his patron for 40 years.

West was eclectic in his choice of styles and subjects, which over his long career ranged from the strict Neoclassical to the extravagantly sublime after 1780. He was capable of great innovation, but in the main his inspiration came from the current ideas of other artists. Nevertheless, he was the most successful history painter of his generation in England. A founder member of the Royal Academy, he succeeded Reynolds as President in 1792.

Weyden Rogier van der 1399/1400–64

The Flemish painter Rogier van der Weyden was the son of a master cutler of Tournai. He is first documented in 1427, when he began his apprenticeship with the Master of Flémalle (Robert Campin). He did not discover his vocation until comparatively late in life. Unfortunately we have no record of his earlier activities—a Tournai document of 1426, mentioning a civic gift of wine to a man of the same name, seems to be a coincidental reference to another person. In 1432 he was admitted to the Tournai guild, but by 1435 he had already moved to Brussels. The following year he was made a civic painter of his adopted city. But he retained his business interests in Tournai and was commemorated by the artist's guild there after his death. Although he received commissions

Benjamin West: Penn's Treaty with the Indians; oil on canvas; 193×274cm (76×108in); 1771. Pennsylvania Academy of the Fine Arts, Philadelphia

from a very wide circle of patrons, both within the Netherlands and abroad, there is no record of his having taveled, with the exception of a visit to Rome *c*1450. None of his paintings is dated, so the chronology of his considerable oeuvre remains uncertain. As he maintained a large workshop, this difficulty is compounded by numerous problems of attribution.

Van der Weyden's earliest surviving works are probably a pair of small diptychs of *The Virgin and Child* and *St Catherine in a Landscape* (Kunsthistorisches Museum, Vienna) and *The Virgin and Child* (Thyssen-Bornemisza Collection, Lugano) and *St George and the Dragon* (National Gallery of Art, Washington). The presence of a number of formal motifs, the handling of light, and the tiny scale of both works betray a knowledge of the work of Jan van Eyck; the facial types of the women and the handling of their drapery indicate a closer association with Robert Campin. A similar combination of influence appears in another early work, the Louvre *Annunciation*. In a number of respects, this picture seems like a critique of the central panel of Campin's Mérode Altarpiece, with the more glaring perspectival errors of its predecessor eliminated. By the time of van der Weyden's *St Luke Drawing a Portrait of the Virgin* (Museum of Fine Arts, Boston) the influence of Campin has become vestigial, while that of Jan van Eyck is paramount. The basic composition is a paraphrase of the latter's *The Madonna of Chancellor Rolin* (*c*1435; Louvre, Paris). Despite this obvious borrowing, *St Luke Drawing the Virgin* exhibits a linear expressiveness absent in its more composed model. It imparts an emotional tension characteristic of van der Weyden's personal style.

This tendency reaches its ultimate expression in the artist's greatest surviving work, the *Descent from the Cross* in the Prado, Madrid. Probably painted in the second half of the 1430s, this altarpiece was commissioned by the Louvain Archers' Guild. Rejecting a naturalistic landscape setting, van der Weyden compressed the ten nearly life-size figures in his composition within a gilded niche simulating the appearance of a sculptured altarpiece of polychromed wood. The tightly interlocked figures seem to seethe in a single convulsion of pain which brutally drives home the anguish of the Passion. Although the *Descent from the Cross* is a work of immense formal and coloristic richness, these characteristics are subordinate to the fundamentally emotional purpose of the design.

Van der Weyden was an extremely prosperous master by *c*1441, but records of this period indicate that he did not disdain to polychrome sculpture and paint banners. During the years 1439 to 1441 he worked on the four panels of *The Justice of the Emperor Trajan and Count Herkinbald* which, until their destruction in 1695,

decorated Brussels Town Hall. A tapestry in Bern records parts of this series, though in a much distorted form. The loss of these pictures is doubly unfortunate, both on account of their evident quality—which is described by several chroniclers—and because they constituted the only major secular narrative cycle that the artist is known to have painted. In 1445 King Juan II gave an altarpiece by master "Rogel" to the charterhouse at Miraflores near Burgos, which indicates that van der Weyden's fame had spread as far as Castile. This work is identical with one of two versions of a triptych dedicated to the Virgin (the smaller in the Staatliche Museen, Berlin, and the larger divided between the Royal Chapel, Granada, and the Metropolitan Museum of Art, New York). During the late 1440s he painted the enormous *Last Judgment* altarpiece, which stands in the hospital founded by the Burgundian Chancellor Nicolas Rolin at Beaune, near Dijon. With its gold background, its sculptural associations (the main composition derives from Gothic tympanum reliefs), and its great emotional intensity, this work is comparable with the earlier *Descent from the Cross*.

Documents reveal that at least one altarpiece by van der Weyden had been exported to Ferrara by 1449. They also show that in 1450 and 1451 he received payments from the Este Court, which were perhaps connected with this lost work. In 1450 he was in Rome, where he is supposed to have admired frescoes by Gentile da Fabriano. It is unlikely that this visit lasted long; he probably visited Florence on the same journey. Two of his surviving works were painted for the Medici: the *Madonna and Child with Four Saints* (Städelsches Kunstinstitut, Frankfurt am Main) and the *Entombment* (Uffizi, Florence). Both were probably painted shortly after his return home, and then shipped to Florence. Although they include certain iconographic motifs derived from Italian art, neither suggests that the artist was particularly interested in Florentine style.

A picture such as the Seven Sacraments Altarpiece (Royal Museum of Fine Arts, Antwerp) probably painted for the Bishop of Tournai in the early 1450s, reveals the continued influence of Jan van Eyck. In the central panel, the placing of the large-scale figures against a vista down a church nave is based upon Jan van Eyck's *Madonna in Church* (c1425–30; Staatliche Museen, Berlin). By extending this basic idea to embrace all three panels, van der Weyden recast the traditional narrative divisions of the triptych format in a way that suggests a section through the nave and aisles of a Gothic church. His Braque Triptych (Louvre, Paris) is probably of similar date. In this small altarpiece, half-length figures of Christ and the saints are set against a distant landscape background in a remarkably original way. It seems probable that later Northern half-length portraits in a landscape setting, which became common at the turn of the 15th and 16th century, derive ultimately from this painting or a related one by the same artist.

Rogier van der Weyden: Madonna and Child with Four Saints; oak panel; 53×38cm (21×15in); c1450–1. Städelsches Kunstinstitut, Frankfurt am Main

With the St John Altarpiece in the Staatliche Museen, Berlin, van der Weyden returned to the format of a simulated triple portal containing three scenes, similar to the one he had employed a decade earlier in the altarpiece of the Virgin for Miraflores. However, the scenes depicted are visually more complex than those in the Miraflores altarpiece. Increased formal and iconographic complexity is also characteristic of the Berlin Bladelin Triptych (Staatliche Museen). By comparison, the diptych of *Christ on the Cross* and *St John and the Virgin* (John G. Johnson Collection, Philadelphia) is a very austere composition, with every nonessential detail eliminated. Rogier's last major work is the St Columba Altarpiece. Probably painted in c1460 for a church in Cologne, it is now in the Alte Pinakothek, Munich. Reminiscences of the whole span of the artist's work, from the Louvre *Annunciation* to the Bladelin Triptych, are combined in this altarpiece. It is a magisterial work, distinguished by exquisite formal and coloristic harmonies.

In addition to a number of other religious works, van der Weyden painted many portraits, both as independent works and combined with bust-length pictures of the Virgin and Child as devotional diptychs. Few of these are documented and it is difficult to establish their chronology. It is clear, however, that the artist developed a new and refined type of aristocratic portrait, by subjectively manipulating the likenesses of his sitters.

Van der Weyden was the third of the great trio of painters who founded the Early Netherlandish school. Although he drew upon Campin and Jan van Eyck, his elegant and emotive style is quite distinct. His many exported works, and his large atelier, which drew artists even from Italy, broadcast his style throughout Europe. It would be no exaggeration to state that he was the most influential Northern painter of the 15th century.

Rogier van der Weyden: Portrait of a Lady; oil on panel; 36×28cm (14×11in); c1450–60. National Gallery, London

Further reading. Davies, M. *Rogier van der Weyden*, London (1972). Friedländer, M.J. *Early Netherlandish Painting* vol. 2, *Rogier van der Weyden and the Master of Flémalle*, Brussels and Leiden (1967). Panofsky, E. *Early Netherlandish Painting* (2 vols.), Cambridge, Mass. (1953). *Rogier van der Weyden*, Brussels (1979).

Whistler J.A.M. 1834–1903

The American painter, graphic artist, and designer James Abbott McNeill Whistler was born in Massachusetts. He spent his boyhood in St Petersburg, where his father supervised the construction of the railway to Moscow. He was sent to West Point military academy but was dismissed for failure in his chemistry studies. After a brief spell with the U.S. Coastal Survey, where he learned to etch maps and plans, he left to study in Paris in 1855. He entered the studio of Charles Gleyre, a painter of the Tugier School, and published his first set of etchings, *The French Set*, in 1858.

These were quickly appreciated by fellow artists such as Henri Fantin-Latour and Alphonse Legros. Whistler adopted the pose of a Bohemian, and remained throughout his career true to the figure of a "dandy" as invented by Baudelaire. The image of a butterfly that he adopted for his signature is an apt expression of his character, and one that fitted in well with the young Parisian art world. In 1858 his first painting, *At the Piano*, was rejected at the Salon (retouched 1859; now in the Taft Museum, Cincinnati). When in the following year it won applause at the Royal Academy, Whistler turned his attention towards London. He was also at this time strongly influenced by Velazquez (1599–1660). He gradually pulled away from the blatant realism of Gustave Courbet towards the restrained light and way of life of England and the English.

In 1859 Whistler bought a house in London. He began depicting the Thames both in a group of etchings and in a long series of oil paintings: *The Thames in Ice* (1862; Freer Gallery of Art, Washington, D.C.), *The Last of Old Westminster* (1863; Museum of Fine Arts, Boston), *Wapping* (1864; John Hay Whitney Collection, New York), and *Old Battersea Bridge* (*c*1872; Tate Gallery, London). During this period he also produced *The White Girl* (1862; National Gallery of Art, Washington, D.C.). The painting was rejected by the Paris Salon, and was exhibited instead at the Salon des Refusés in 1863, where it caused a sensation. In it we can see Whistler at his closest to the English Pre-Raphaelites, particularly Dante Rossetti, but still distinctly individual in style. Whistler's paintings, even when they reflect the current fashion, were never derivative. He had learned from the French artists, particularly from Courbet, to enjoy the medium itself, and was thus insured against the sentimental, small-minded qualities of English genre painting.

J.A.M. Whistler: Finette; drypoint on paper; 29×20cm (11×8in); 1859. British Museum, London

Through his interest in Japanese art, from *c*1863, Whistler was able to expand his aesthetic approach. *Japonisme* eventually offered him a path of development along the lines of self-control and concentration of effort. Some of the early "Japanese" pictures, such as *Purple and Rose, the Lange Lijzen of the Six Marks* (1864; John G. Johnson Collection, Philadelphia), are not much more than costume pieces. He was influenced, like his contemporaries, by Japanese works he saw in London and Paris.

After a brief period of impasse, when Whistler attempted a combination of *Japonisme* and classicism, reminiscent of George Moore, he broke through to a deeper style of self-expression. This began after he traveled to Valparaiso, Chile, and saw the Pacific Ocean for the first time. He worked Japanese balance and harmony into his own simplified decorative schemes in a much more organic way (for example, *Three Figures*, *c*1868; Tate Gallery, London). In his absorption of the ideas of the Orient, he achieved a breakthrough for Western painting. He influenced the art public towards an awareness of Eastern style, not simply bending mannerisms to fit Western ways of seeing, but contributing to a general appreciation of the pure and abstract qualities of Eastern thought and design. It is through his taste for Japanese art and culture that we see Whistler's affinity with Art Nouveau.

J.A.M. Whistler: Nocturne in Black and Gold: the Falling Rocket; panel; 60×47cm (24×19in); c1874. Detroit Institute of Arts

The *Nocturnes* of the 1870s mark the summit of his achievement. His later portraits and his design work, such as the well known *Peacock Room* (1876–7; Freer Gallery of Art, Washington, D.C.), are important steps along the same path. Seen in retrospect, they have won their just place in the development of both American and European painting. But during the artist's lifetime, they seemed as peculiar and outrageous as the public figure that Whistler deliberately cut for himself. It is not surprising that his works and his lifestyle were misunderstood by a critic like John Ruskin: they were a deliberate challenge to the ethics of the previous age.

The notorious Ruskin/Whistler slander trial was caused by the critic's accusation that the painter had slung a pot of paint in the public's face when he produced *Nocturne in Black and Gold: the Falling Rocket* (c1874; Detroit Institute of Arts). One crucial question was, how long had it taken the artist to complete the picture? Whistler's answer was that it contained the experience of a lifetime. In this exchange, two codes, the work ethic and the new aestheticism, met head on. Whistler won the case, was awarded a farthing's damages, and retired abroad, bankrupt.

With the set of etchings he produced in Venice in 1879 and 1880, Whistler brilliantly recouped his losses. On his return he began lecturing on art, publishing his ideas in 1885 in *The Ten o'Clock Lectures.* Here he printed in full the dialogue of the trial, and continued the argument, by declaring his then-radical belief that form and color could exist on their own without material support from subject matter. Whistler made himself known as the chief proponent of the doctrine of "art for art's sake", relating this back to analogies between art and music, and his early use of musical terms in picture titles.

Whistler was elected to the Royal Society of British Artists in 1884. He was married in 1888 and published *The Gentle Art of Making Enemies* in 1890. His final etchings included *The Dutch Series* of the 1890s. He taught at the Académie Carmen from 1898 to 1901, and died in London two years later.

Further reading. Gaunt, W. *The Aesthetic Adventure*, London (1945). Kennedy, E. *The Etched Work of Whistler* (4 vols.), New York (1971). Pennell, R. and J. *The Life of James McNeill Whistler* (2 vols.), London and Philadelphia (1921). Spalding, F. *Whistler*, Oxford (1979). Sutton, D. *James McNeill Whistler: Paintings, Etchings, Pastels, and Watercolours*, London (1966). Weintraub, S. *Whistler: a Biography*, London (1974). Young, A.M., Macdonald, M., and Spencer, R. *The Paintings of James McNeill Whistler* (2 vols.), London and New Haven (1980).

Wiligelmo of Modena *fl. c1100–25*

Wiligelmo of Modena was a Romanesque sculptor of great individuality and powers of expression, who had a profound influence on the history of sculpture. Nothing is known about him except that he was the principal sculptor of Modena Cathedral in Emilia, rebuilt from 1099. A boastful inscription praises him, but gives no clues as to his origin or previous career. It seems likely that he was familiar with a newly emerging school of sculpture in Apulia, and that he admired Ottonian ivories.

The principal source for his art, however, was Roman sculpture, of which many more examples existed at that time in Italy than today. During the building of Modena Cathedral, many Roman reliefs were excavated, and some were incorporated into the facade, alongside Wiligelmo's frieze, carved panels, doorways, and capitals. His frieze, showing scenes from Genesis (from the Creation to the Flood), clearly imitates friezes on Roman monuments, although the iconography is Christian. Some of his other reliefs are unmistakable copies of Roman models.

Wiligelmo's style is expressive and monumental. On the jambs of the west doorway, he employed figures of prophets under arcades, placed one above the other; the method was later taken up in St-Denis Abbey, Paris, and in several Gothic cathedrals of the 13th century. His collaborators, pupils, and followers, although lacking his genius, carried the influence of his style throughout northern Italy and beyond—to Aragon and Catalonia, and to Hungary. The frieze on the facade of Lincoln Cathedral was a faint English imitation of Wiligelmo's Modena frieze.

It has recently been arged that Wiligelmo's frieze was intended for a screen inside Modena Cathedral, and was moved on to the facade in the second half of the 12th century. This theory has, however, been conclusively refuted.

Wilkie David 1785–1841

The Scottish painter Sir David Wilkie was born at Cults, Grampian, where his father was a minister. From 1799 to 1804 he trained at the Trustees Academy, Edinburgh. Before moving to London in 1805, he had already produced rustic scenes influenced by both 17th-century Dutch and recent Scottish genre painting. His reputation was established with *The Village Politicians* (1806; private collection). The painting shows an animated discussion in a shabby alehouse, full of anecdotal incident, and reminiscent of work by Adriaen Ostade and David Teniers. The purchasers of such low-life subjects were largely aristocratic, although they reached a wider middle-class audience through engravings. Official recognition soon capped Wilkie's popularity: he was made Associate of the Royal Academy in 1809, and a full member two years later.

In 1812 he mounted an exhibition of his own work, featuring *Blind Man's Buff* (1812; Collection of H.M. Queen Elizabeth II). The sweetened appearance of the cavorting figures contrasts with that of their boorish predecessors in the first peasant works. *The Letter of Introduction* (1813–14; National Gallery of Scotland, Edinburgh) also represents a branching-out of his art, its subject matter being pitched at a higher social level. In a well-furnished study, a young visitor presents himself to an aged writer, whose suspicious, sidelong look is amusingly echoed in the sniffing of his dog at the stranger's knee. Wilkie's narrative technique was a seminal influence on Victorian genre painting. The tragic tenor of *Distraining for Rent* (1815; private collection) aroused critical displeasure, so the artist, always seeking to attune his style to the taste of his market, did not pursue this vein.

His best-known picture, *Chelsea Pensioners Reading the Waterloo Despatch* (1821–2; Wellington Museum, London), was shown at the Royal Academy. It was accompanied by a lengthy passage describing each of the veterans who are receiving the news of victory outside a tavern on London's King's Road. Its patriotism and sentimental warmth proved enormously appealing; it had to be roped off from the crowds at the exhibition. The subject brought Wilkie's familiar anecdotal genre towards the "higher" category of modern history painting.

The continental tours he undertook for health reasons between 1825 and 1828,

David Wilkie: The First Earring; oil on panel; 74×61cm (29×24in); 1835. Tate Gallery, London

and especially the Spanish Old Masters he saw, led Wilkie to transform his style. This is evident in, for instance, *Empress Josephine and the Fortune-Teller* (1837; National Gallery of Scotland, Edinburgh), with its loose, rapid brushwork and its imposing scale: it is 7 ft (2.5 m) in height. The adoption of this grander manner may result in part from Wilkie taking over from Sir Thomas Lawrence the distinguished post of Painter-in-Ordinary to the King in 1830. He was knighted in 1836. His principal output was now to be portraiture. His *William IV* (1833; Wellington Museum, London), perhaps the finest example, contains passages of bold impasto, notably the plumes of the military helmet.

In 1840 Wilkie visited the Holy Land. His intention, anticipating that of Holman Hunt, was to collect material for historically accurate paintings of biblical subjects. He died on the return voyage.

William of Sens *fl.* 1174–9

William of Sens was a French master mason. He is named in Gervase's account of the burning and repair of Canterbury Cathedral as the man who directed the rebuilding of the choir after the fire of 1174. Presumably from Sens in France, he was at one time also supposed to have been the architect of Sens Cathedral, but this is no longer accepted. He may have known Sens, however, as well as other more recent French buildings, to judge from the evidence of Canterbury choir, which was the first thoroughgoing Gothic design to be executed in England. In 1178, before work was finished, William fell from a scaffold. He retired to France the following year.

William the Englishman *fl.* 1179–84

The master mason known as William the Englishman succeeded William of Sens in 1179, as mason in charge of the new choir of Canterbury Cathedral. He first completed the eastern transepts and then built the Trinity Chapel with Becket's Corona by 1184. The architectural character of these two operations is entirely different: the first is the least French in character, while the other is the most French part of the entire work. For the Trinity Chapel, William of Sens had probably prepared designs which his successor followed faithfully; the transepts, however, called for fresh invention. The transepts were probably the most influential part of the new work at Canterbury.

Richard Wilson: The Valley of Mawddach and Cader Idris; oil on canvas; 102×107cm (40×42in); c1774? Walker Art Gallery, Liverpool

Willumsen Jens 1863–1958

Jens Ferdinand Willumsen was a Danish artist who was a fringe member of the School of Pont-Aven. His artistic activities extended from painting to architecture, ceramics, sculpture, and art criticism. He trained in Copenhagen. In the summer of 1890, during a visit to the popular artists' resort of Pont-Aven in Brittany, he met Gauguin, who initiated him into Pictorial Symbolism. Willumsen quickly adopted the new style of flat, brightly colored, and simplified painting. His bas-relief *A Work from the Quarry* (1891; State Art Museum, Copenhagen) comes close to Gauguin's work in this medium. But his paintings, such as *Breton Women Walking* (1891; J.F. Willumsen Museum, Fredrikssund, Denmark), owe more to Émile Bernard's crude painted surfaces and Sérusier's simplified but lively silhouettes. He retired to Norway in 1892, in search of the pictorial equivalent of the symbolism of Gauguin's "Bible": *Sartor Resartus* (published 1836) by Thomas Carlyle.

Wilson Richard 1714–82

The portrait and landscape painter Richard Wilson was the most important British artist before J.M.W. Turner and John Constable to have devoted most of his career to landscape painting in oils.

He was born at Penegoes in Wales, and from 1729 he studied in London with a minor portrait artist. He painted portraits until 1750; *Admiral Thomas Smith* (c1744; National Maritime Museum, Greenwich) is a good example of his work in this field. In 1750 he went to Italy, staying briefly in Venice before establishing himself in Rome. About 1752 he was persuaded, probably by Claude-Joseph Vernet, to become a landscape painter. In the same year he painted *banditti* and history subjects in the styles of Marco Ricci and Poussin. His earliest dated Italian landscape, *View of Rome from the Villa Madama* (1753; Paul Mellon Center for British Art, New Haven, Conn.) was painted for the Earl of Dartmouth, who later commissioned from

Wilson a superb series of finished landscape drawings in chalk. The landscapes of Wilson's Italian sojourn depict standard views in the environs of Rome and Naples. Their principles of composition were derived largely from Claude and Gaspar Dughet. They were specially admired and collected as souvenirs by English aristocrats making the Grand Tour.

About 1757 Wilson, by then master of a fully developed landscape style, returned to London. There he continued to paint Italian views based on the careful studies from nature he had accumulated during his visit. Seeking recognition as a "serious" painter in the Grand Manner, he again essayed historical landscape with *The Destruction of Niobe's Children* (*c*1760; Paul Mellon Center for British Art, New Haven, Conn.). A version of this painting was shown at the first Society of Artists exhibition in 1760. He was a founder member of the Royal Academy in 1768. In addition to Italian and historical landscapes, Wilson painted country house "portraits" and Welsh views. His five views of Wilton (Collection of the Earl of Pembroke, Wilton, Wiltshire), and his *Snowdon* (1766; Walker Art Gallery, Liverpool), are perhaps his most original contributions to these categories. In his later pictures, the influence of Dutch 17th-century artists, in particular the clear, luminous style of Aelbert Cuyp, becomes increasingly evident. Although he was neglected by patrons toward the end of his life, Wilson had demonstrated the serious purpose of landscape painting. His example inspired English painters well into the next century, and his work foreshadows that of Corot.

Wilton Joseph 1722–1803

The English sculptor Joseph Wilton was born in London, the son of a wealthy plasterer. He had a better training than any English sculptor of his time, being apprenticed to Paul Delvaux at Nivelles, and later joining the workshop of Jean-Baptiste Pigalle in Paris. In 1747 he went to Italy, where he worked successfully for seven years, first in Rome and later in Florence. On his return to London, he established a busy practice in all branches of sculpture. He was a founder member of the Royal Academy in 1769. After inheriting a considerable fortune, he became lazy and extravagant, and too dependent on his large workshop. Although he was the most talented native English sculptor of the 18th century, Wilton was uneven and indecisive in performance; only occasionally did he show in his work the great brilliance of which he was capable.

Witte Emanuel de *c*1617–92

The Dutch painter Emanuel de Witte tackled many subjects but is best known for his church interiors, in which he specialized after moving from Delft to Amsterdam in the early 1650s. His interiors are different from the more objective works of Pieter Saenredam (1597–1665), in that the details and proportions of his buildings are frequently altered, as in *The Choir of the New Church in Amsterdam* (Rijksmuseum, Amsterdam), where the elevation is heightened to stress the church's majestic loftiness. Elsewhere, motifs from different churches are combined in one building, without, however, any loss of architectural homogeneity and authenticity. In some paintings the views are wholly imaginary.

De Witte's massive, silent interiors are generally pierced with dramatic shafts of light, themselves often arbitrary. These,

Emanuel de Witte: The Interior of the Oude Kerk, Amsterdam, during a Sermon; oil on canvas; 79×63cm (31×25in); c1658–9. National Gallery, London

with contrasting pools of shade, heighten the spatial effects and the sense of awesomeness. In this, and in his relatively rich color, de Witte's work is more pictorial than the geometrically organized pictures of Saenredam. De Witte, who achieved little financial success and finally committed suicide, also painted a number of fish-market scenes, some of which contain portraits.

Witz Konrad 1400–45

The Swiss painter Konrad Witz was born at Rottweil in southern Germany. He moved to Basel, becoming a citizen in 1435. The previous year he had been accepted into the artists' guild. About 1435 he was commissioned to paint the so-called "Speculum" Altarpiece. His only signed and dated work, the St Peter Altarpiece, was completed and installed in Geneva Cathedral in 1444.

Witz's altarpieces have long since been dismantled, and many parts are lost. From the Speculum Altarpiece, 12 of the original 16 panels of the wings have survived (Öffentliche Kunstsammlung, Kunstmuseum Basel; Staatliche Museen, Berlin; Musée des Beaux-Arts, Dijon). Their subjects indicate a typological program, wherein scenes from the Old Testament and ancient history prefigure scenes from the New Testament. The latter were probably contained in the missing central section. Only the wings remain of the St Peter Altarpiece (Musée d'Art et d'Histoire, Geneva). They consist of four panels, including the famous *Miraculous Draft of Fishes*—sometimes called *Christ Walking on the Water*. With its view over Lake Geneva, this is one of the first landscape portraits. The painting may be an involved allusion to the deliberations of the Council of Basel (1431–43). Witz's paintings include panels from other dismantled altarpieces, for example, *The Meeting of Joachim and Anna* (Öffentliche Kunstsammlung, Kunstmuseum, Basel).

Witz rejected the Soft style of painting current in southern Germany *c*1430. Through the influence of Robert Campin and Jan van Eyck he forged his own style, whose hallmark is the heavy, firmly molded forms of his figures. With their dignified air, large heads, and narrow shoulders, they dominate the compositions, displaying only restrained emotions. Witz's brand of realism omits the minute detail of Flemish painting, except in the depiction of the surface textures of materials such as wood, stone, flaking plaster, and metal.

Konrad Witz: Miraculous Draft of Fishes (Christ Walking on the Water); tempera on panel; 130×155cm (51×61in); 1444. Musée d'Art et d'Histoire, Geneva

Wolgemut Michael 1434–1519

The German painter Michael Wolgemut was born in Nuremberg where he was the master of Albrecht Dürer from 1486 to 1490. Earlier Wolgemut had taken over the workshop of Hans Pleydenwurff, after the latter's death in 1472; he also married his widow. Wolgemut's personal style as a painter is difficult to reconstruct. His *Mass of St Gregory* at Andechs (1470–1; Schatzkammer und Reliquienkapelle) was painted while he was active in the workshop of Gabriel Mälesskircher in Nuremberg. Although Wolgemut was the leading painter in the city until Dürer returned in 1495, after his first visit to Italy, his many studio assistants collaborated on the large number of altarpieces executed during the years in which he was master of the

Michael Wolgemut: the frontispiece to Hartmann Schedel's "Weltchronik"; woodcut; 1493

workshop, so the exact contribution of Wolgemut himself is often difficult to define. These altarpieces range from the altar of the church of the Virgin at Zwickau (1479), and the Peringsdörff Altar of 1486–8, painted for the church of the Holy Cross, Nuremberg, to late commissions such as the high altar of the town church of Schwabach (1507–8), where the carved elements were executed by a pupil of Veit Stoss.

In the Peringsdörff panels, the influence of Martin Schongauer (*c*1430–91) is added to the precise Netherlandish treatment Wolgemut inherited from Hans Pleydenwurff; the rich, sober coloring creates an immensely decorative effect. Wolgemut collaborated with Wilhelm Pleydenwurff in the design of the woodcuts for the *Schatzbehalter* published in Nuremberg (1491), and for Hartmann Schedel's *Weltchronik* (1493). Albrecht Dürer paid tribute to Wolgemut in his portrait of the aging master, dated 1516 (Germanisches Nationalmuseum, Nuremberg).

Wols 1913–51

The German painter, printmaker, photographer, and writer, Wolfgang Schülze, known as Wols, was born in Berlin in 1913. Although he drew and painted all his life, he had not intended to become an artist. He was a talented musician, but briefly studied ethnography, and then attended the Berlin Bauhaus. In the same year, 1932, he moved to Paris, where he met Amédée Ozenfant, Fernand Léger, Jean Arp, and others.

From 1933 to 1936 Wols lived in Spain with his wife Grety. He then returned to Paris, where he gave his first exhibition of photographs. He continued to paint in his spare time, signing himself "Wols". At the outbreak of the Second World War he was interned for 18 months. It was then that he began his extraordinary improvisations which were first shown in 1946 at the Drouin Gallery, Paris. Done on notepaper, and extremely small in scale, they show a gradual development over a six year period. Their personal imagery derives from variations of figures, creatures, buildings, and boats. Some of them are reminiscent of works by Paul Klee, for instance *Dockland* (1941–2; private collection). Later the open, angular line gives way to the characteristic, spidery network of lines which makes the images impossible to identify. He creates a fantasy world of vegetation, micro-organisms, and tangled nerves, as in *Crane de Poète* (1943; private collection).

On his return to Paris Wols began to paint on a larger scale in a semiautomatic style related to *tachisme* and *art informel.* His use of thick paint was partly influenced by Jean Fautrier. The paintings are Abstract and gestural, like *Taches Rouges* (1949–50; private collection), and only occasionally reveal glimpses of his earlier imagery. Wols remained in Paris to the end of his life. His growing reputation led to commissions for illustrations to works by Sartre, Kafka, and others.

Above: Grant Wood: American Gothic; oil on beaverboard; 76×64cm (30×25in); 1930. Art Institute of Chicago

Below: Wols: Gouache; gouache on canvas; 22×15cm (9×6in); 1949. Collection of John Craven, Paris

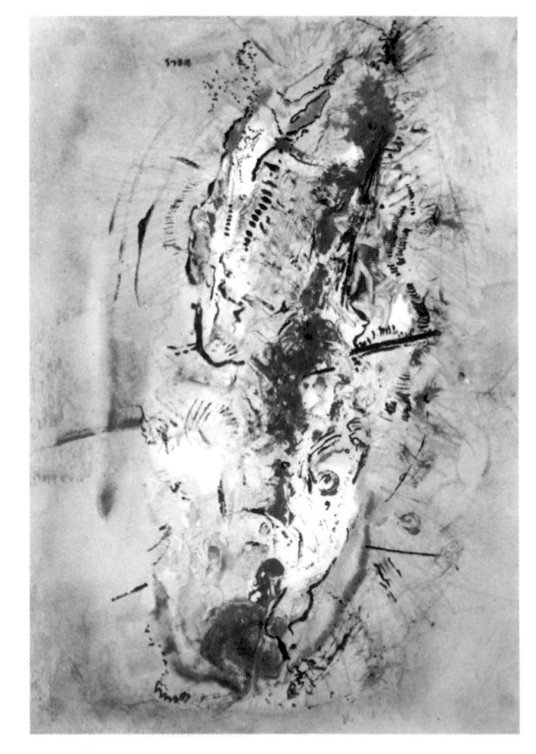

Wood Grant 1891–1942

The American painter Grant Wood was born in Iowa and lived there all his life. For family reasons, he began his artistic training late. In the 1920s he paid several visits to Europe, where he was decisively influenced by the meticulous style of the early Flemish and German masters. His subject matter was the Iowa world that he knew, and he brought both to people and to places an unwaveringly precise vision, evident in his best-known work, *American Gothic* (1930; Art Institute of Chicago).

Further reading. Duggleby, J. *Artist in Overalls: the Life of Grant Wood*, San Francisco (1996).

Wotruba Fritz 1907–75

The Austrian sculptor Fritz Wotruba trained as an engraver, but turned to sculpture, studying under Anton Hanak in 1926. He produced his first stone sculpture in 1928. He took part in the intellectual activity of Vienna during the 1930s; he was particularly associated with Josef Hoffmann. During the Second World War he and his wife lived in Switzerland. In 1945 they returned to Vienna, where he was appointed professor at the Vienna Akademie der Bildenden Kunst. He exhibited widely, and met Henry Moore in 1951. Wotruba worked in stone as well as bronze. His concept of sculpture was architectural and monumental—he portrayed the structure of the human body in a compact mass of geometric forms (for example, *Feminine Rock;* limestone; 1947–8; Middelheim Open-Air Museum of Sculpture, Antwerp).

Wouwermans Philips 1619–68

The Dutch painter Philips Pandsz. Wouwermans was born in Haarlem, the eldest son of a painter; he may have been taught by Frans Hals. He was early influenced by the works of Pieter Verbeecq (*c*1612–*c*54) and by the dune landscapes of Jan Wijnants (1630/5–84). Even more influential were the small genre scenes of outdoor life painted by Pieter van Laer, who in 1638 returned to Haarlem from Rome. Yet Wouwermans was a more productive artist whose subjects were more varied and who, especially in his late years, developed an attractive freedom of handling and light palette. He specialized in landscapes, often with horses; and he also painted encampments, hunts, battles, and dune or seashore views.

Philips Wouwermans: A View on a Seashore with Fishwives Offering Fish to a Horseman; oil on panel; 35×41cm (14×16in). National Gallery, London

Further reading. Rosenberg, J. et al. *Dutch Art and Architecture, 1600–1800*, New York (1966).

Wren Christopher 1632–1723

Sir Christopher Wren was England's greatest Baroque architect. His early years were devoted almost exclusively to scientific pursuits. In 1657, when only 25, he was appointed Professor of Astronomy to Gresham College, London; in 1661 he became Savilian Professor of Astronomy at Oxford University. His career as an architect began in 1663, when he was made a commissioner for the restoration of Old St Paul's, London. His first building, Pembroke College Chapel, Cambridge, dates from this year. When he visited France from 1665 to 1666, it was as an architect rather than as a scientist, and the transition was completed in 1667 when, as a commissioner appointed under the Rebuilding Act, he was made responsible for rebuilding St Paul's Cathedral and the 51 City churches destroyed by the Fire of London. Two years later he was appointed Surveyor General of the King's Works. He held this post until 1714, exercising a virtual monopoly over official architecture.

Wren's earliest buildings are competent and academic, but contain little hint of his future development. The Sheldonian Theatre, Oxford (1664–9), was thus more remarkable for its ingeniously constructed roof (replaced in the late 19th century) than for the originality of its design, which carefully reconstructed Serlio's description of the Theater of Marcellus.

The City churches, begun after his return from France, combined a compositional freedom and a spatial ingenuity that had been entirely lacking in his early buildings. His style developed to sudden maturity with the grandiose interior of St Paul's Cathedral (1675–1710). The exterior is equally impressive. It drew heavily upon the example of 17th-century French ecclesiastical architecture, but the composition of dome and flanking towers was probably suggested by engravings of Borromini's church of S. Agnese, Piazza Navona, Rome (1653–7).

His later work falls into two distinct styles: an austere and monumental classicism, well exemplified by the Royal Hospital, Chelsea (1682–91), and a freer, more

Christopher Wren: St Andrew-by-the-Wardrobe, London; 1685–95

ostensibly Baroque style, anticipated by his second project for St Paul's (1773). This found its fullest expression at the end of his career, in his plans for The Royal Hospital, Greenwich (1696–1707), clearly influenced by Louis Levau's masterpiece, the Collège des Quatre Nations, Paris.

As Surveyor General, Wren worked almost exclusively for the Office of Works. Of his few independent commissions, Trinity College Library, Cambridge (1676–84), reveals the Wren style at its most classical. Tom Tower, Christ Church, Oxford (1681–2), is his most ambitious essay in the Gothic style.

As an architect of European stature, Wren exerted an enormous influence over late-17th- and early-18th-century British architecture. His most talented assistant in the Office of Works was Nicholas Hawksmoor. He was also by far the most important formative influence in the careers of Sir John Vanbrugh, William Talman, Thomas Archer, and James Gibbs.

Further reading. Beard, G. *The Work of Christopher Wren*, Edinburgh (1982). Downes, K. *Christopher Wren*, Harmondsworth (1971). Little, B. *Sir Christopher Wren: a Historical Biography*, London (1975). Sebler, E.F. (trans. Murray, P. and L.) *Wren and his Place in European Architecture*, London and New York (1956). Summerson, J. *Wren*, London (1971). Whinney, M. *Wren*, London (1971).

Wright Frank Lloyd 1869–1959

The American architect Frank Lloyd Wright was not only one of the four or five masters of modern architecture, he was also one of its pioneers, of the generation of Peter Behrens, Auguste Perret, and Adolf Loos. His long career spanned some 70 years, and his influence upon European architecture during the crucial second decade of the 20th century was decisive.

Wright was born in Wisconsin; his parents were of English and Welsh origin. In the 1870s he benefited from the Fröbel Kindergarten system of visual and constructive education, which fostered his strong love of natural forms and his craftsman's respect for natural materials.

In 1888 he began work in the Chicago office of the great American architect Louis Sullivan. This apprenticeship, to a man he never ceased to admire, led to his setting up on his own in 1893. After designing a handful of buildings in the 1890s, Wright evolved his first mature domestic style. This can be seen in his Prairie houses, so called because of their similarity to open-planned American frontier farmhouses: low and spreading, with wide projecting eaves and unbroken horizontal window-strips. The interior spaces flow into one another, and interior and exterior interpenetrate.

This was Wright's "organic" architecture, somewhat Japanese in character, which merged harmoniously with the landscape. Its abstract, spatial features, rather than its 19th-century qualities of craftsmanship, were later admired by the younger generation in Europe. Two fine examples of the Prairie house are the Barton house, Buffalo, New York (1903–4), and the Robie house, Chicago (1908).

At the same time that he was designing these largely traditional constructions, Wright was experimenting with concrete and other new materials in his nondomestic building. From this early, influential period two works stand out for their fusion of the monumental with a new conception of space: the Larkin Office Building, Buffalo, New York (1904), and Unity Temple, Oak Park, Chicago (1906).

Between 1910 and 1930 Wright's output declined. He went through a "baroque", ornamental phase, built a series of houses out of precast concrete blocks, and worked on a number of designs. It was not until the mid 1930s, with two outstanding buildings, that he became as well known in the United States as he was abroad. The first was the Kaufmann house (Falling Water) in Pennsylvannia (1936). This proved that its architect had lost neither his remarkable flair for dramatic siting, nor his sensitivity to both natural materials and the techniques of construction favored by the International style.

In the Johnson Wax Factory, Racine, Wisconsin (1936–9), Wright made use of reinforced concrete mushroom columns and glasstube diffused lighting. He later added a Laboratory Tower (1949). The whole effect was slick and streamlined—a far cry from the aesthetic of rock, wood, earth, and water that influenced Wright's two Taliesin communities. Taliesin West, in the Arizona Desert (1938), was built of what Wright called "desert concrete"—volcanic rocks joined by a minimum of cement.

In the last two decades of his life, Wright became increasingly interested in plans of a nonrectangular format. The Guggenheim Museum, New York (1943–59), is a dazzling triumph of the circle and spiral, and a modern masterpiece of interior space and movement. Despite some wayward projects, Wright was, to the end, an architect of colossal stature.

Further reading. Brooks Pfeiffer, B. and Larkin, D (ed.) *Frank Lloyd Wright: the Masterworks*, New York (1993). Storrer, W. *The Architecture of Frank Lloyd Wright*, Chicago (2002).

Wright of Derby Joseph 1734–97

The English painter Joseph Wright was born at Derby. He was a student of the portrait painter Thomas Hudson, and by 1760 had an established portrait practice in the Midlands. During the next decade he painted his best known pictures, depicting nocturnal industrial scenes and scientific experiments. He emulated in these works the dramatic, artificial lighting effects he had admired in 17th-century Dutch and Flemish pictures, in particular the candlelight scenes of the Utrecht followers of Caravaggio. Wright studied in Italy from 1773 to 1775, and settled permanently at Derby in 1777. At the Royal Academy he exhibited Italian landscapes, portraits, and paintings of literary subjects. In 1784 he

Joseph Wright of Derby: The Earthstopper on the Banks of the Derwent; oil on canvas; 97×121cm (38×48in); 1773. Derby Museums and Art Gallery

declined an offer of full membership in the Royal Academy because of a quarrel concerning the display of his pictures. Versatile in his painting technique, and innovative in his selection and presentation of subject matter, Wright occupies a secure position in the forefront of the English Romantic movement.

Andrew Wyeth: Christina's World; tempera on gesso panel; 81×121cm (32×48in); 1948. Museum of Modern Art, New York

Wu Ch'ang-shih 1844–1927

The Chinese painter Wu Ch'ang-shih came from Huchow in Chekiang. He trained and worked at first as a seal carver, and took up painting later in life. He was a pupil of Jen Po-nien (1839–95) and painted a wide variety of subjects: Buddhist figures, landscape, flowers, bamboo, and trees. His flower painting has survived to epitomize his style, which is bold and yet sensitive. He followed Chu Ta and Li Shan, working in a heavy liquid ink style but adding subtle and beautiful color to produce handsome and often rich painting. His calligraphy is strong and distinctive, and plays an important part in the creation of vitality on the picture surface.

Wu Chen 1280–1354

The Chinese painter Wu Chen was of humble origin, and had a retiring nature. He never undertook official employment, but earned his living as a diviner until his reputation as a painter grew, and he was able to retire from the world to live very quietly in the Chiang Nan area. He was one of the group of painters working in this area, although he was not the most successful of them. His most famous painting is the *Fishermen* handscroll (1342; Freer Gallery of Art, Washington, D.C.), a quiet ink painting on paper depicting the misty landscape of the Hangchow area and the people who live in boats. His ink technique is fluent and gentle, with elements of Kao K'o-kung and Chao Meng-fu, but also of the Hsia-Ma school, from whom he adopted the use of washes and recession expressed in tone. Wu Chen was not highly estimated in his lifetime, but his free and yet controlled use of ink made him an influential artist, admired for his ability to open up the sophisticated Southern Sung style.

Wu Chen: Bamboo; ink on paper; 34×44cm (13×17in). National Palace Museum, Taipei

Wu Tao-tzu c680–c740

The Chinese painter Wu Tao-tzu came of humble parentage, and was left an orphan at Yangti, near Loyang in Honan. However, he was educated, studied calligraphy and poetry, and held minor official positions. He was a man of strong character, recorded as having a quick temper and love of wine, and he was capable of flamboyant energy. His reputation as a painter now rests entirely on contemporary stories, for nothing remains of his work except a few pale copies and engravings. Few painters have excited such admiration and respect in their lifetime. Wu's vitality and speed of work gave rise to wonder. He was able to transmit this energy in his painting, and stories of the life-like quality of his paintings of dragons and horses abound. It was said that in his painting of dragons on one of the palace walls "the scales seemed to be moving and, whenever it was going to rain, they emanated vapors and mist".

Wu Tao-tzu was a Buddhist and painted many murals for both Buddhist and Taoist temples in the two capitals of T'ang. Unfortunately these were all destroyed in the anti-Buddhist rioting of the 9th century. However, the copies and contemporary scraps preserved in such treasuries as the Shosoin, Nara, give an impression of a search for vitality of line and movement, and it is probable that Wu was a master of this modulated line. He was also a master of color and the grand composition. In many ways the antithesis of Wang Wei, he was held by his contemporaries to have been the greatest artist of the dynasty in all aspects of painting. He was perhaps the last of the great exponents of many different styles; he became known as the father of the figure-painters of later periods.

Wyatt James 1746–1813

James Wyatt was the most popular English architect of the late 18th century. He was born in Staffordshire and trained in Italy from 1762 to 1768. His early buildings, such as Heveningham Hall, Suffolk (1780–4), were nearly all in an Adam-inspired classical style. Although this developed into an austere and more personal Neoclassicism, his late reputation rested almost entirely on his talents as a Gothicist. His mature works, beginning with Fonthill Abbey, Wiltshire (1796–1813; destroyed), and including Ashridge, Hertfordshire (1808–13), were frequently vast in scale and displayed a mastery of Gothic detail far in advance of that of any other contemporary architect.

Wyeth Andrew 1917–

The American painter Andrew Newell Wyeth was born in Pennsylvania and was trained by his father, the artist and illustrator Newell Convers Wyeth (1882–1944). His talent showed early and he became well known during his teens. He works in a very exact and realistic style that owes something to Surrealism and a good deal more to photography. His great success, and very wide popularity, can be explained by his style and subject matter, usually the scenery and people of rural America. His best work, for example, *Christina's World* (1948; Museum of Modern Art, New York), is also characterized by a certain melancholy.

Further reading. Meryman, R. *Andrew Wyeth: a Secret Life*, New York (1998). Venn, B. et al. *Unkown Terrain: the Landscapes of Andrew Wyeth*, New York (1998). Wyeth, A. *Andrew Wyeth: Autobiography*, New York (1995). Wyeth, A. and Wyeth, B. *Andrew Wyeth: Close Friends*, Jackson, Miss. (2001).

Y

Yeats Jack 1871–1957

The Irish painter Jack Butler Yeats was born in London, the son of the painter John B. Yeats and brother of the poet William Butler Yeats. He spent most of his formative years in Sligo, Ireland, and memories of his boyhood colored his whole artistic career. He attended South Kensington, Chiswick, and Westminster art schools in London, and went on to be a poster artist in Manchester (1892–3). This, and his experiences as a book illustrator, helped give his early oil paintings their strong linearity and bold flat colors (for example, *The Circus Dwarf*, c1911; private collection). Gradually Yeats made his paint surface more expressive and freed his colors from naturalistic description. By the mid 1920s his canvases resembled those of Oskar Kokoschka and late German Impressionism in the bravura handling of their brushstrokes. His subject matter was imbued with his love of Ireland, whose myths, country fairs, and gypsies continually emerged from and disappeared into the windswept landscapes he painted.

Yevele Henry *fl.* 1356–1400

Henry Yevele was an English master mason; his life is unusually well-documented; its details reveal his enormous versatility, and the achievements that earned him considerable wealth.

Probably born in Derbyshire, Yevele is first recorded in 1356 as a "stonehewer" in London. In 1357 he became mason to the Black Prince and then in 1360 to King Edward III, being granted the office for life in 1369. His most important royal work is the nave of Westminster Abbey, which had been left unfinished in 1269. Building began again in the 1370s. Instead of a Perpendicular design, Yevele completed the remaining six bays in the style of the 13th century. Only the west facade was given the full Perpendicular treatment. At Canterbury Cathedral, it was probably Yevele who rebuilt the Norman nave at the end of the 14th century, but there the design was Perpendicular throughout. It is notable for the illusion of height gained by increasing the size of the arcade at the expense of the clerestory. As at Westminster the aisles, too, are high.

While he was at Canterbury, Yevele was also responsible for the town's fortifications. The massive two-towered west gate is the most prominent of all his surviving military works. These were numerous, and included some building at the Tower of London. It seems likely that Yevele designed the unusual, circular, concentrically planned castle surrounded by a moat at Queenborough, Kent (since demolished).

His domestic buildings probably included the destroyed college at Cobham, Kent, designed as a very early example of the

Jack Yeats: The End of the Season. Private collection

Henry Yevele: the nave of Westminster Abbey; 1370s

quadrangle college plan. More firmly attributed to him are a number of bridges, including work on London Bridge, and the reconstruction of the 11th-century walls of Westminster Hall after 1394.

Finally, Yevele was a designer of monumental works. Tombs, sedilia, and screens all came within his scope, and he may have been responsible for the superbly intricate Neville screen at Durham Cathedral.

Yusho Kaiho 1533–1615

The Japanese painter Kaiho Yusho was (with Eitoku and Tohaku) one of the three great masters of the Momoyama period. He came from an Omi Province Samurai family that had been almost eliminated in the civil wars. The young Yusho entered the Zen Tofukuji Temple at Kyoto for safety, and was taught by Motonobu. His ink brushwork always retained the forthright vigor found in the work of many Samurai artists, especially in his stabbing tree-boughs. His series of landscape screens in the Kenninji (Kyoto) are among the last great monuments of atmospheric and intellectually powerful ink-painting in the Chinese tradition. In his screens for the Myoshinji (Kyoto), he combined gold and other washes with ink in a masterly manner.

Z

Zadkine Ossip 1890–1967

The French sculptor Ossip Zadkine was born in Smolensk, Russia. His mother was of Scottish origin: her family were shipbuilders. He studied and worked in London (1906–8), and settled in 1909 in Paris, to study for a short time at the École des Beaux-Arts under Jean-Antoine Injalbert. From 1914 to 1918 he served in the French Army. He lived in Paris from 1918 to 1941, traveling and exhibiting widely. As an artist in exile, Zadkine lived in New York from 1941 to 1945. On his return to Paris in 1945 he became a Professor of Sculpture at the Académie de la Grande Chaumière. His most famous work is the monument commemorating the 1940 bombing of Rotterdam, *The Destroyed City* (bronze; 1951–3; Quai de Leuvehaven, Rotterdam).

The work done by Zadkine in his late teens and twenties reflects both his involvement with Cubism, and the Parisian circles in which he moved; they included Picasso, Brancusi, Modigliani, and Cocteau. By the time he reached his middle thirties, the geometrical surfaces of his work had opened out, becoming pierced and often elongated.

Further reading. Casson, S. *20th Century Sculptors*, New York (1967). Cogmat, R. *Zadkine*, Paris (1958). Geist, S. "A Memoir of Zadkine", *Artforum*, New York (June 1970). Hammacher, A.M. *Zadkine*, New York (1959). Jianou, I. *Zadkine*, London (1964) and New York (1965).

Zaichu Hara 1750–1837

The individualistic Japanese painter Hara Zaichu was the founder of the *Hara* School. Like many artists of his age, he studied Chinese painters of the Sung and Ming periods, but he formed his true style after adopting some of the naturalistic methods of Okyo, though it is not known whether he met him. The result is sometimes a mixture of *Nanga* and *Shijo* styles, as in *Gathering of Scholars* (British Museum, London). Later in life he added traditional *Yamatoe* techniques and subjects, and the resulting style was favored by royal patrons. His successors, Zaimyo, Zaisho, and Zaisen, all painted for court buildings in Kyoto. The styles used by

Zaichu were very varied, and included Buddhist works.

Zeuxis *fl.* c400 BC

The Greek painter Zeuxis was born in Heraclea in southern Italy but also worked in Greece. To the science of shading developed by Apollodorus he added the use of highlights, which was the next important step in the progress towards the realism of an artist like Apelles. He was said to have painted a boy with grapes in which the fruit looked so natural that birds flew to them. Another famous work was his *Centaur Family*, described in detail by Lucian for its originality of theme and its coloristic technique. Zeuxis became very rich through his art. No original works by him have survived.

Zimmermann brothers
17th and 18th centuries

The German Zimmermann brothers were originally *stuccatori* of the Wessobrunn School. Johann Baptist Zimmermann (1680–1758) became a leading south German fresco painter, and Dominikus Zimmermann (1685–1766) was active as an architect; they worked in partnership on a number of important projects. Their earliest known joint commission, almost at the outset of their careers as independent masters, was the decoration of the church, sacristy, and library of the monastery of Buxheim (1710–12). Dominikus had already begun the decoration of the monastery's Marienkapelle in the previous year. Meanwhile, working independently, Johann Baptist had decorated the abbey church of Edelstetten with stuccos and frescoes (1710), and the sacristy of the abbey church of Waldsee (signed and dated 1710).

In early works such as these, the stucco decorations were both designed and executed by the Zimmermanns. Later, in the stair hall and Festsaal of Schloss Schleissheim (1720–5), Johann Baptist was the executant only, working (with Charles-Claude Dubut) to the designs of Effner. Subsequently Johann Baptist painted superb stuccos to the designs of Cuvilliés in the Munich Residenz (1731–3) and the Amalienburg in the park of Schloss Nymphenburg (1734–9). He used Cuvilliés' designs again, at the end of his career, in the Festsaal of Schloss Nymphenburg itself (1755–7).

At Edelstetten the stuccos belong to the early Wessobrunn foliage type, but in the

Johann Zoffany: Cognoscenti in the Uffizi; oil on canvas; 124×155cm (49×61in); 1772–7/8. Collection of H.M. Queen Elizabeth II

ceiling of the abbey library at Ottobeuren (1715–18), the more loosely composed stuccos tend towards the Rococo. The subsidiary frescoes there include short stretches of balustrade, painted illusionistically; in the ceiling of the abbey library at Benediktbeuern (1725), these are instead included in the actual stuccos. The decorative vocabulary employed there by Johann Baptist reveals the impact of Effner's *Régence* style, and leads on directly to the pilgrimage church of Steinhausen which the brothers began in 1728 (work suspended in 1733).

The relative inexperience of Dominikus as an architect is illustrated by his wild underestimate of the cost of the work at Steinhausen. But its longitudinal oval nave, with aisles rising to the full height of the main vault, is the site of some of the finest Bavarian Rococo decoration in existence. The balustrade motif is used to mask the transition between the real world of the stuccos and the visionary world of Johann Baptist's frescoes; naturalistic forms, including birds and insects, are included in the decorations all over the church.

The parish church at Günzburg (1736–41), by Dominikus alone, together with the elegant Annakapelle at Buxheim (1738–40), designed and decorated by both brothers, are intermediate steps in the development leading to the pilgrimage church of Die Wies. The church was built and decorated by the brothers between 1746 and 1754; its oval nave and galleried choir is developed from Günzburg. The richness and vitality of the decoration mark it out as the climax of his phase of the Bavarian Rococo.

Zoffany Johann 1734/5–1810

The painter Johann Zoffany was born in Germany and received his training there, but his reputation rests upon the portraits and conversation pieces he painted in London and in Rome, where he studied under Mengs for several years. He came to England in 1760, and from 1762 painted a series of theatrical portraits. He became a member of the Royal Academy, and after working in Italy returned to London in 1779. Zoffany was a member of a number of Academies in Italy, and in the 1780s worked in India. He vividly represented the social position and the art-collecting activities of the English nobleman who had taken the Grand Tour (for example, *Charles Towneley among his Marbles*, 1790; Towneley Hall Art Gallery and Museum, Burnley).

Zola Émile 1840–1902

The French novelist and art critic Émile Zola was born in Aix-en-Provence. He was a friend of Cézanne, from adolescence until the publication of his novel *L'Oeuvre* in 1886. He took up art criticism in 1866; he defended Manet and the young Impressionists, and attacked the academic hierarchy. He wrote a brochure on Manet in 1867, and Zola's portrait by Manet (*Portrait of Édouard Manet*) was exhibited at the Salon of 1868 (now in the Musée du Jeu de Paume, Paris). Zola's later criticism was intermittent, and in some ways he felt that Cézanne and the Impressionists had not produced the masterpiece he looked for. Nonetheless, his leadership of Naturalism in the novel went hand-in-hand with the Impressionists' desire to depict modern life.

Zuccarelli Francesco 1702–88

Florentine by birth but Venetian by adoption, the Italian painter Francesco Zuccarelli spent some 15 years in England, on two visits between 1752 and 1771, and was a founder member of the Royal Academy. He sweetened the ideal landscape of Claude to conform with Rococo taste, painting in pastel colors and soft, creamy brush strokes. His landscapes, which also show Dutch influence, may be staffed either by peasants or gods, but usually have the same sweetly pastoral mood. Zuccarelli knew and probably influenced Richard Wilson. It is characteristic of the English taste for "fancy pictures", with figures rather than nature landscapes, that during his lifetime his reputation was far higher than Wilson's.

Zuccaro brothers
16th and 17th centuries

The Italian brothers Taddeo (1529–66) and Federico (*c*1542–1609) Zuccaro were successively the leading exponents of Mannerism in late-16th-century Rome. Both were born near Urbino. It is not known where Taddeo trained, but early in his career he initiated a program designed to reform the art of painting. He deliberately modeled his style on that of the great masters of the earlier 16th-century, such as Raphael and Correggio, and rejected the excessive complexity of Florentine Mannerism of the mid century.

Above: Federico Zuccaro: Portrait of Vincenzo Borghini; black and red chalk on paper; 14×9cm (5½×3½in); c1570–4. British Museum, London

Federico began his career as an assistant to his brother. After Taddeo's early death in 1566, he was responsible for the completion of two of his large-scale fresco cycles in the Sala Regia of the Vatican, and at the Villa Farnese at Caprarola. Federico was to lend his brother's program of reform a wider currency by traveling extensively, both within Italy and abroad. In 1574 he made a journey to France, Antwerp, and England, where he is supposed to have painted a portrait of Queen Elizabeth. Between 1578 and 1579 he completed Vasari's frescoes in the cupola of Florence Cathedral; during the early 1580s he was active in the Doges' Palace in Venice; and in 1585 he was invited to Spain to work in the Escorial.

The eclectic style of Federico also gained authority from his activities as a teacher and theorist. In 1593 he established an academy in his own palace in Rome, and in 1607 he published a treatise propounding his ideals of beauty and design. This was *L'Idea de' Scultori, Pittori e Architetti*, a major document of Mannerist art theory.

Taddeo Zuccaro: Study of a Male Nude; red chalk on paper; 42×29cm (17×11in). Metropolitan Museum, New York

Zurbarán Francisco de 1598–1664

The Spanish painter Francisco de Zurbarán was born in Fuente de Cantos, Badajoz. He was apprenticed in 1614 to Pedro Díaz de Villanueva in Seville. By 1617 he was established in Llerena, Badajoz. There, in 1626, he contracted to paint 21 canvases for the Dominicans of S. Pablo el Real, Seville, and in 1628, 22 canvases for the Merced Calzada in Seville. At the invitation of the municipal authorities he took up residence in Seville in 1629; the move aroused antagonism from the local painters, led by Alonso Cano.

During his apprenticeship in Seville, Zurbarán must have met Velázquez, whose influence is evident in his Llerena period. He early mastered the representation of reality with plastic modeling. His tenebrist style was comparable to that of Caravaggio, as in his *Crucifixion* of 1627 (Art Institute of Chicago). He used the same style in the four works that he contributed in 1629 to the series for the Franciscan College, Seville (surviving panels in the Louvre, Paris, and the Gemäldegalerie Alte Meister, Dresden). These were among many compositions of monastic life that he painted during his career.

In Seville Zurbarán achieved greater luminosity than before in *Birth of the Virgin* (*c*1629; Norton Simon Museum, Pasadena, Calif.), *The Immaculate Conception* (1630; Diocesan Museum, Sigüenza), and the *House of Nazareth* (*c*1630; Art Gallery, Cleveland). In the *Still Life* dated 1633 (Norton Simon Museum, Pasadena, Calif.) he reached a perfection in execution and simplicity in composition, together with a deep mystical content, that make this a masterpiece of European painting.

Francisco de Zurbarán: St Francis Meditating; oil on canvas; 114×78cm (45×31in); 1632. Collection of Dr A.E. Shaw, Buenos Aires

This level of excellence was not maintained in Zurbarán's series of *The Labors of Hercules* and *The Defence of Cadiz* (Prado, Madrid), painted in 1634 in Madrid for the Buen Retiro Palace. But in Seville, from 1638 to 1639, he reached the peak of his achievement in monastic and religious cycles, both in the Hieronymite subjects for the sacristy of the Monastery of Guadalupe (Cáceres), and in the New Testament series for the Charterhouse at Jerez de la Frontera (now in the Musée de Peinture et de Sculpture, Grenoble, and elsewhere).

In the late 1630s Zurbarán had begun to dispatch paintings to the New World, increasingly after 1646, as Murillo's popularity increased, but inevitably their quality declined. In the *Annunciation* (1650; Philadelphia Museum of Art) he lessened the contrast of light and shade, and subsequently he adopted a softer style in parallel with Murillo, as in the *Virgin and Child with St John* (1658; Museum of Art, Diego). After settling in Madrid in 1658, Zurbarán produced a few notable works like the *Immaculate Conception* (1661; Museum of Fine Arts, Budapest) and the *Virgin and Child with St John* (1662; Museum of Fine Arts, Bilbao).

Zurbarán lacked inventiveness. He frequently borrowed compositions from Northern engravings, and his works were sometimes defective in movement, or in cohesion between earthly and celestial figures. Despite this, he has earned increasing fame in modern times through the mystical exaltation or repose reflected in his monastic cycles. He is valued, too, for his skill in naturalistic representation and the subtle use of color and light, both in his monastic pictures and in his rare portraits and still lifes.

During his Seville period, Zurbarán employed many studio assistants, including his son Juan (born 1620), of whom two signed still-life compositions are known (Museum of Art, Kiev, and private collection).

GLOSSARY

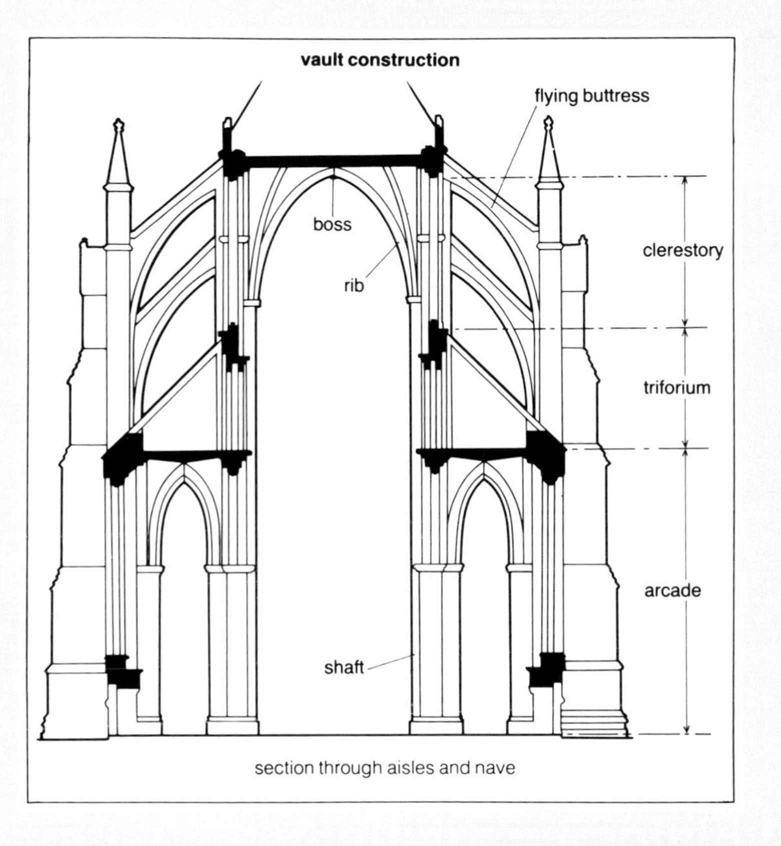

section through aisles and nave

Abbreviations (arch.) architectural term; (Ch.) Chinese; (Fr.) French; (Ger.) German; (It.) Italian; (Sp.) Spanish. Words set in SMALL CAPITALS denote glossary headings of related entries. An * indicates that an entry is illustrated in the glossary.

A

abacus (arch.) flat slab on top of CAPITAL supporting an ARCHITRAVE; *see* CLASSICAL GREEK ARCHITECTURE.

abstract ill-defined and very widely used term which in its most general sense describes any art in which form and color are stressed at the expense, or in the absence of, a representational image.

Abstract Expressionism originally a diverse style of ABSTRACT art developed in the U.S. in the 1940s and 1950s, particularly associated with Arshile Gorky and Jackson Pollock; sometimes known as the NEW YORK SCHOOL. After 1952, sometimes known alternatively as ACTION PAINTING.

abstraction the ABSTRACT work created.

Abstraction-Création (Fr.) **1** group of ABSTRACT artists in Paris in 1931 who promoted nonrepresentational art through their exhibitions. **2** the annual magazine published by the group from 1932 to 1936; its full title was *Abstraction-Création: Art nonfiguratif*.

abutment (arch.) structure supporting the lateral thrust of an ARCH or VAULT; *see* VAULT CONSTRUCTION.

acacia 1 shrub or tree from which gum arabic is produced. **2** obsolete term for object shaped like a roll or bag, shown in the hands of emperors and consuls on CLASSICAL medallions.

academic 1 literally, belonging to an ACADEMY of art. **2** derogatory term meaning conventional, stereotyped, derivative.

academicism the quality of ACADEMIC art.

Academy originally the garden near Athens where Plato taught, and the name given to his school of philosophy. During the RENAISSANCE the term was adopted by philosophical and literary groups, and later by schools established for the training of artists. These academies were characterized by the emphasis on the study of CLASSICAL art and the human form. In the 19th century the academies were associated with conservatism and rejected by many artists who sought alternative creative outlets.

acanthus DECORATIVE MOTIF used in PAINTING and ARCHITECTURE, derived from the scalloped leaf of the acanthus plant.*

acolyte Christian CHURCH officer who assists the priest.

acroterion (arch.) pedestal or figure placed at the three angles of a PEDIMENT.*

acrylic synthetic RESIN polymer. Used in emulsion form as a modern PAINTING MEDIUM and in sheet form in modern SCULPTURE.

Action Painting term coined in 1952 by U.S. critic Harold Rosenberg to describe the type of ABSTRACT EXPRESSIONISM practiced by Jackson Pollock and others, in which the emphasis was on the action of applying paint, sometimes splashing or pouring it over a canvas on the floor.

actor print Japanese print showing an actor in well-known role; popular from the development of the Kabuki theater in the 17th century as part of the UKIYOE movement of GENRE PAINTING.

adobe brick unbaked, sun-dried clay brick used for building.

adsorption close physical interaction between two substances without chemical reaction.

aedicule (arch.) opening, such as door or window, framed by columns, with a PEDIMENT; *see* CLASSICAL GREEK ARCHITECTURE.

Aegean art art from various cultures around the eastern Mediterranean from *c*2800 BC to 1400 BC, including CYCLADIC, Minoan (from Crete), and Mycenaean.

aeolic (arch.) style of Greek ARCHITECTURE found in the 6th century BC; sometimes called Proto-IONIC.

aesthetic concerned with the appreciation of what is beautiful or pleasing.

Aesthetic movement late 19th-century artistic movement in England, promoted by Oscar Wilde and Walter Pater, advocating "art for art's sake".

aesthetics philosophy applied to art, which attempts to formulate criteria for the understanding of the AESTHETIC (rather than utilitarian) qualities of art.

agate semiprecious variety of CHALCEDONY, used in jewelry and as a burnishing tool.

airbrush instrument for spraying paint, propelled by compressed air. Invented in 1893, it has been much used by commercial artists, whether for fine lines, large areas, or subtle gradations of color and tone.

airport art a term, often used pejoratively, for art produced for tourists, based on traditional ethnic forms.

aisle (arch.) division of space at the sides of a CHURCH, parallel to the NAVE and separated from it by PIERS or ARCADES.

aiwan (arch.) recess, niche, or reception hall in ancient Parthian building or MOSQUE.*

Ajanta Indian site of series of caves containing wall PAINTINGS, based on Buddhist legends, dating from *c*200 BC—AD 700.

ajouré (Fr.) pierced or perforated in elaborate patterns, used especially in METALWORK.

Akbar-nama account of the reign of the Mughal Emperor Akbar (1542–1605; reigned from 1556) written in Persian by Abul Fazl (1551–1602). It was frequently illustrated.

akropolis (or **acropolis**) fortifi citadel in Greek cities. "The Acr polis" usually refers to the one Athens.

alabaster 1 in ANTIQUITY, a carbo ate of lime used in Egyptian SCUL TURE, especially for small portab pieces. **2** modern alabaster, a lim sulfate which can be highly po ished but is easily scratched, po ular in 14th-century Europe f tomb EFFIGIES.

alabastron small round-based bott with broad rim, used by ancie Egyptians and Greeks for oin ments. Originally of ALABASTE later, GLASS or CERAMIC.

albumen proteinaceous substan forming the adhesive element egg white, which has been used a PAINTING MEDIUM.

all'antica (It.) style of works of a especially SCULPTURE, that imita ANTIQUE models.

alla prima (It.) technique, common used in PAINTING since the 19 century, whereby an artist com pletes a painting in one sessio without having provided layers UNDERPAINTING.

allegory image that has its meani expressed symbolically.

altar flat-topped block, usually stone, used for sacrifice to a dei or, in a Christian CHURCH, as focal point in services.

altarpiece (arch.) in Christia CHURCH ARCHITECTURE, the pictu or decorated screen behind th ALTAR. It may consist of a sing PAINTING or an elaborate group hinged panels.*

aluminum light, silvery metal used modern SCULPTURE, usually sheet form, sometimes painted.

amber 1 fossilized tree RESIN, used its natural form for jewelry an DECORATIVE objects. Also di solved in oil with other resins produce oil varnish. **2** metal allo consisting of four parts gold one silver.

ambo (arch.) reading desk or pulp in early Christian CHURCH, usual

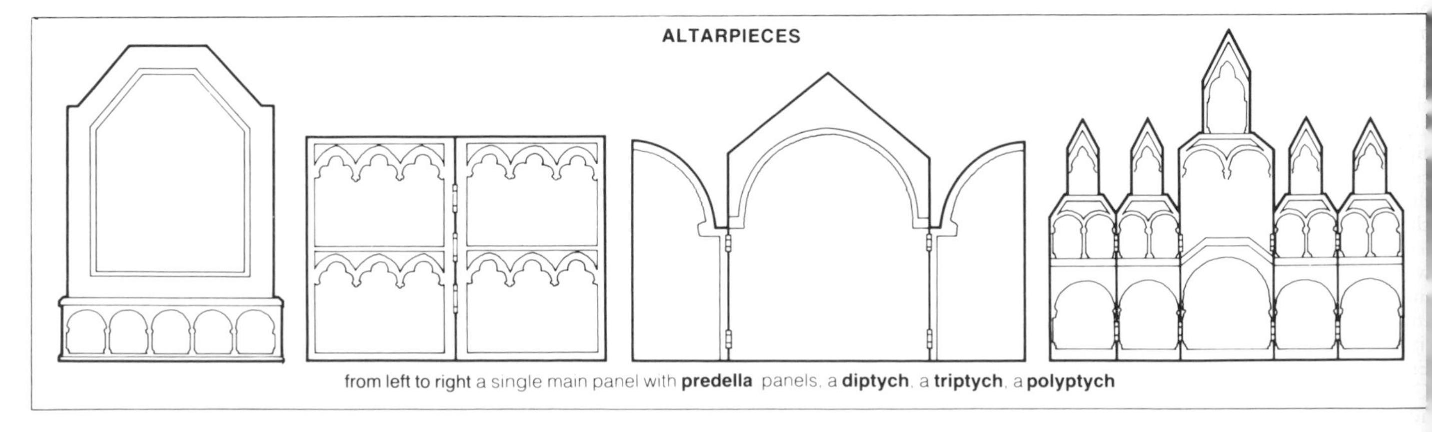
ALTARPIECES

from left to right a single main panel with **predella** panels, a **diptych**, a **triptych**, a **polyptych**

›f stone. Normally there were wo, facing each other on each ›ide of the CHOIR.
bulatory (arch.) continuation of he AISLES of the CHOIR around the APSE, sometimes giving access to smaller chapels; *see* CHURCH.
ethyst purple colored precious stone, used in jewelry.
orino (It., pl. *amorini*) small PUTTO; usually winged.
phitheater arena surrounded by iered seats. Used from the 1st century BC throughout the Roman world for public spectacles.
phora large, two-handled jug used in ANTIQUITY to hold oil, wine, etc.; *see* GREEK VASES.
ulet charm designed to protect he wearer from evil.
alytical Cubism early phase of CUBISM, *c*1907–12, in which natural forms were analyzed and reduced to their essential geometric parts.
atomy structure of the human body. Sometimes refers to the structure of plants or animals.
chorite hermit, recluse.
gular style style of PAINTING and SCULPTURE in Northern Europe from *c*1430–1530 characterized by stiff drapery folds.
imalier (Fr.) 1 member of the 19th-century school of French bronze sculptors who specialized n small animal figures. 2 animal-painter.
imal style 1 ORNAMENT representing animal forms. 2 type of nomad art originating in the 7th century BC in southern Russia and the Caucasus; it was characterized by the predominance of animal MOTIFS, frequently distorted, ornamenting all kinds of portable objects including metalwork, textiles, wood, and bone.
nular vault (arch.) vaulted roof over a ring-shaped (annular) space, between two concentric walls; *see* VAULT CONSTRUCTION.
tefix (arch.) upright architectural ORNAMENT found in CLASSICAL buildings, where it decorated or masked the ends of a roof ridge.
tependium covering for the face of an ALTAR, usually textile or precious metal; sometimes called an altar frontal.
tiphonary (or antiphonal) book containing sections of the Mass that were sung as responses by the choir. From *c*AD 1000 antiphonaries were sometimes ILLUMINATED with scenes from the Bible.
tique, the *see* ANTIQUITY.
tiquity Greek and Roman civilization until the fall of the Roman Empire in the 5th century AD. Greek and Roman SCULPTURE was admired during the RENAISSANCE as an ideal art, and study of the ANTIQUE formed the basis of the curriculum in most art ACADEMIES.
apex (arch.) uppermost point of a triangular or conical form.
apotheosis (Gr., "deification") in CLASSICAL art this represented the entry into Olympus of a famous or heroic figure. In the BAROQUE period it was a popular theme for depicting in an ALLEGORICAL manner the glorification of the artist's patron, usually a prince.
apotropaic having the ability to avert evil influence.
appliqué (Fr.) TEXTILE decoration in which cut fabric shapes are stitched to a fabric ground as a design.
apse (arch.) semicircular or polygonal end of a CHURCH; usually the end of the CHANCEL, at the east end.
aquatint ETCHING process whereby acid is allowed to bite into a copper plate prepared with RESIN which is then inked and printed.
arabesque MOTIF based on interlaced plant forms, found in the FINE and DECORATIVE ARTS, in ARCHITECTURE, and especially typical of Islamic design.*
arca 1 Indian statue of a deity. 2 (Latin) coffin or carved chest, intended to hold the Eucharist or donations in CHURCH.
arcade (arch.) continuous series of ARCHES supported on COLUMNS or PIERS.*
Arcadia rural area of the Peloponnese idealized in the writings of Virgil, which in the RENAISSANCE became a synonym for a life of rustic idyll, hence arcadian.
arch (arch.) curved architectural structure formed by wedges of brick or stone, held together by pressure and supported only at the sides.
archaic 1 art of the ARCHAIC GREEK period. 2 antiquated, out of date.
Archaic Greek art Greek art of the mid 12th century BC to *c*480 BC; one of four convenient divisions of Greek art, the others being GEOMETRIC, CLASSICAL, and HELLENISTIC.
archaistic tending towards the ARCHAIC, in either sense of the word.
architectonic relating to ARCHITECTURE.
architecture 1 science or art of building. 2 the structure or style of what is built.
architrave (arch.) 1 the lowest main section of an ENTABLATURE. 2 molded frame surrounding a door or window.
archivolt (arch.) curved underside of an ARCH, or sometimes the bands of molding that decorate it.
armature framework or skeleton on which a sculptor molds his clay.
Armory Show international exhibition of modern art held in New York in 1913 in the 69th Regiment Armory building. Exhibits included the work of the more AVANT-GARDE U.S. artists and of the SCHOOL OF PARIS. The exhibition was very popular and marked the birth of a real interest in modern art in 20th-century America.
arriccio (It.) coat of lime and sand plaster preparing a wall for PAINTING (especially in FRESCO) on which INTONACO was applied.
Art Deco style of Western ARCHITECTURE, DECORATIVE ARTS, INTERIOR DESIGN, and GRAPHIC DESIGN of the 1920s and 1930s. It was characterized by the combination of DECORATIVE ART NOUVEAU with new geometric forms.
arte povera (It., "poor/impoverished art") term coined by Italian critic Germano Celani in 1967 to describe the work of artists such as Carl André, Richard Long, etc. It stresses the use of ordinary materials such as sand, stones, twigs, etc., and the temporary, noncollectable nature of the work.
articulation the manner in which components of ARCHITECTURE or SCULPTURE are put together or jointed.
artifact (or artefact) 1 any object of human workmanship. 2 (archaeology) an object of prehistoric or aboriginal art, as distinguished from a similar but naturally occurring object.
art informel (Fr.) term coined by French critic Michel Tapié, used from the 1950s to describe the European equivalent to ACTION PAINTING.
Art Nouveau (Fr.) DECORATIVE style popular in Europe in the late 19th and early 20th century; it often employed stylized, curvilinear plant forms. It was known in Germany as JUGENDSTIL.
Arts and Crafts Movement mid 19th-century artistic movement in England, inspired by John Ruskin and William Morris; it attempted to raise the standards of design and craftsmanship in the DECORATIVE ARTS, and to reassert the craftsman's individuality in the face of increasing mechanization.
aryballos 1 tapering oil flask used by ancient Greeks; *see* GREEK VASES. 2 shape of Inca water jar, with conical base.
a secco (It.) technique of MURAL PAINTING on dry plaster.
Ashcan School term used during the 1930s to describe the realist group of artists which evolved from the EIGHT in New York *c*1908 and whose subject was usually the urban environment.
ashlar 1 square-cut stone block. 2 masonry of this stone, evenly laid with very fine joints.

acanthus

acroteria

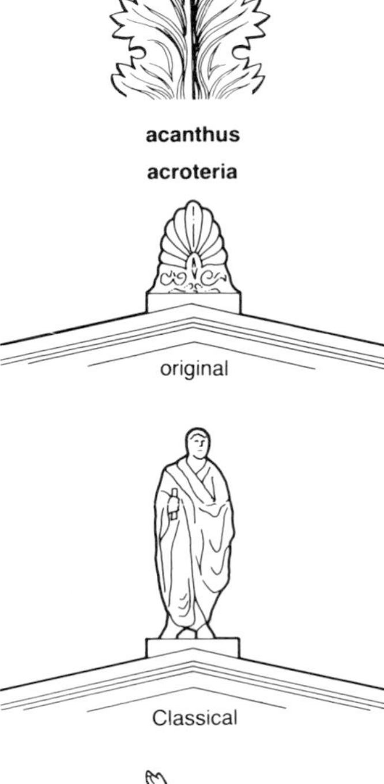

original

Classical

Baroque

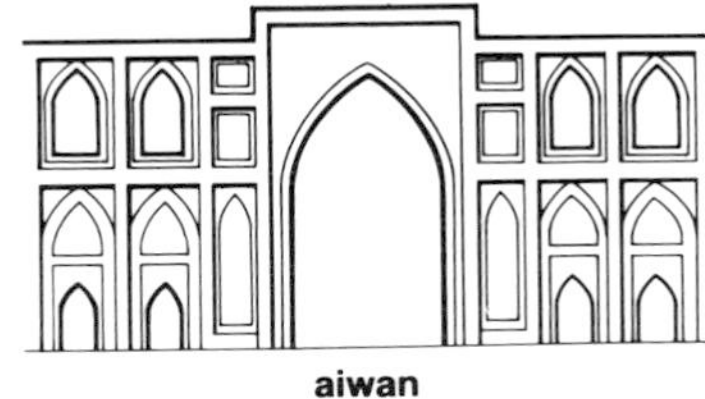

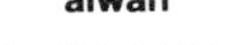

aiwan

the aiwan arch, **above** as used in the early 7th-century palace of Khusrau I at Ctesiphon, **below** as used in a 13th-century *madrasa* in Baghdad

arabesque

assemblage modern art form consisting of objects collected and assembled together; the components are preformed, not made by the artist, and not intended originally as "art material".

atelier (Fr.) studio or workshop.

atlantes (arch.) figures of men used to support an ENTABLATURE. The female equivalent is a CARYATID.

atrium (arch.) 1 forecourt of Roman house leading to various rooms. 2 court in front of Early Christian and ROMANESQUE CHURCHES.

attic 1 in CLASSICAL Greece, of Athens or Attica. 2 (arch.) room with sloping ceiling below roof.

attic order (arch.) square COLUMN of Greek architectural order, or PILASTERS applied to upper story of building.

aureole in PAINTING, light shown encircling the head or body of a holy person.

automata animated figures, probably made in Europe since the 5th century BC. Medieval examples are usually linked with clocks, but also found as table ORNAMENTS; in the 19th century they became fashionable as toys for children.

automatism DRAWING and PAINTING method associated with SURREALISM in which the artist does not consciously create but doodles, allowing the subconscious mind and virtually uncontrolled hand movements to produce an image.

automatist 1 an artist who practices AUTOMATISM; 2 adjective describing the work thus produced.

avant-garde artists whose work is ahead of that of most of their contemporaries; unconventional, experimental, innovative. Also descriptive of the work produced by such artists.

axial related to an AXIS.

axis imaginary line around which the design of a PAINTING, SCULPTURE, or building pivots.

B

bacchanal mythological scene popular in PAINTINGS of the RENAISSANCE and 17th century depicting the revels of Bacchus, Roman god of wine.

backcloth painted scenery in theater design; the term is often used figuratively.

background scene in PAINTING which provides setting for main figures or design; sometimes used synonymously with GROUND.

baluster (arch.) small PILLAR or COLUMN supporting a rail.

balustrade (arch.) series of BALUSTERS, usually edging a terrace or balcony.*

Bamboccianti (It.) group of painters specializing in *bambocciate* (Fr., *bambochades*): LOW-LIFE and peasant scenes popular in the 17th century in the Netherlands and Italy; named after Pieter van Laer, a Dutch painter nicknamed *Il Bamboccio* ("Big Baby").

bamboo tropical giant grasses with woody stems used for furniture in the West in the 19th and 20th centuries. Often incorrectly used to describe 18th- and 19th-century furniture made from other woods, painted and carved to resemble bamboo, in the CHINOISERIE style.

banditti (It.) bandits, or similar "picturesque" characters in PAINTING; especially common in 17th-century European PAINTINGS.

baptistery place where baptism is performed in CHURCH. In early Christian and medieval times, separate buildings were erected and the term applied to them.

Barbizon School group of French landscape painters of the mid 19th century who painted landscape for its own sake, often directly from nature.

Baroque 1 style of ARCHITECTURE, PAINTING, and SCULPTURE originating principally in Italy, of the late 16th to the early 18th century; it exhibited an increased interest in dynamic movement and dramatic effects. 2 "baroque" is sometimes used in a pejorative sense to mean over-elaborate, florid. 3 Baroque period refers to the 17th century, when the style was at its height.

Baroque Classicism CLASSICAL style, exemplified in the PAINTINGS of Nicolas Poussin and the ARCHITECTURE of Carlo Fontana, that flourished during the BAROQUE period.

basilica (arch.) medieval CHURCH in which the NAVE is taller than the AISLES; early churches had an APSE at one end. It was based on the Roman assembly hall, or the design of COLONNADED halls in private houses.*

Basohli Punjab hill state where an individualistic style of PAINTING developed during the later 17th century.

Bauhaus school of ARCHITECTURE and modern art, founded in Weimar, Germany, in 1919 by Walter Gropius, which became the focus of modern design. It moved to Dessau in 1925–6, to Berlin in 1932, and was closed in 1933; *see* NEW BAUHAUS.

bay (arch.) the space formed, usually within a CHURCH, where the limits are indicated by ORDERS, VAULTS, etc., rather than by walls. On an external wall a bay may be indicated by BUTTRESSES.

beading DECORATIVE series of molded beads, found in ARCHITECTURE and furniture.

beam (arch.) horizontal structural member, usually made of wood, bearing a load.

belle peinture (Fr., "beautiful painting") the traditionally esteemed, highly accomplished type of PAINTING that employs the full range of painting skills.

Berlin Secession (Ger., *Berliner Sezession*) association led by the German IMPRESSIONIST painter Max Liebermann which exhibited the work of the BRÜCKE artists in 1908.

bezant 1 gold or silver coin minted at Byzantium. 2 gold ROUNDEL in HERALDRY.

bezel 1 obliquely cut gem face. 2 rim, groove, or mount holding watch-glass or gem in jewelry setting.

Bible moralisée (Fr.) type of Bible originating in the 13th century and designed for the layman, therefore lavishly illustrated.

Biedermeier (Ger.) style of German DECORATIVE ARTS *c*1820–50 emphasizing solid, middle-class comfort; also a style of PAINTING which is banal and sentimental.

biennale (It.) biennial art exhibition.

billet (arch.) ornamentation formed by short cylindrical or rectangular blocks placed at regular intervals in hollow moldings.

billon alloy of gold or silver with a larger proportion of base metal.

biomorphic term derived from "biomorphism", which refers to any DECORATIVE form that represents a living object.

biscuit unglazed white PORCELAIN, popular in Europe from the mid 17th century.

biting ETCHING term meaning the treatment of a PLATE with acid to etch lines in it.

bitumen (also called asphaltum) a brownish-black pigment formed of a mixture of hydrocarbons with oxygen, sulfur, and nitrogen which occurs naturally. It can be partially dissolved in oil to form a semitransparent red-brown color and was much used in the 18th and 19th centuries.

black-figure technique style of decoration of ancient Greek CERAMICS, chiefly of 6th-century BC Corinth. Designs were painted on the object in black metal oxide paint and then incised through to the reddish clay.

Blaue Reiter (Ger., "Blue Rider") group of artists formed in Munich in 1911 by Wassily Kandinsky and Franz Marc. The group was of very varied outlook; other artists who joined it included Paul Klee, Georges Braque, and Picasso.

board various types of stiff pap made from cheap fibers. Boar have been used instead of canv or paper as a PAINTING suppo since the 19th century; types i clude millboard, academy boar and canvas board.

bodegón (Sp., "tavern"; pl., *bod gones*) PAINTING of a kitchen sce with a predominant interest STILL LIFE.

Bodhisattva in Buddhist ICONOGR PHY, one who delays the attai ment of nirvana by compassion f human suffering; it may be tra lated as "Buddha to be".

Body art an art form in which t artist employs and acts on his or h own body, sometimes going as as self-mutilation.

body color 1 WATERCOLOR ma opaque by mixing with white. term used in PAINTING to descri solid, definitive areas of color wh are then completed or modifi with SCUMBLES and GLAZES.

bole 1 Armenian bole is a red cl (ferruginous aluminum silica which can be burnished to a hi polish and is used as a preparati for GILDING. 2 white bole is Chi clay.

Book of Hours book of prayers be said at canonical hours, us privately by laymen. It w common in the 15th century a sometimes richly illustrated.

border DECORATIVE line or desi which delineates edges of a DRA ING, illustration, or manuscri illumination.

boss (arch.) ornamental projectic of wood or stone, placed at t join of vaulting, ribs, etc.; s VAULT CONSTRUCTION.

bottega (It.) shop, workshop, artist's studio.

boxwood very hard, fine-grain wood from an evergreen shrub the genus *Buxus* used for carvi and ENGRAVING.

bracelet ornamental wristband, us ally of precious metal.

bracket (arch.) projection that fur tions as a support; may also DECORATIVE.

brass 1 alloy of copper and zinc. an incised or cast sepulchral pla made of the above material.

bravura describes any style th demonstrates technical or artis flair or brilliance.

brazing process of soldering with alloy of brass and zinc, much us in modern SCULPTURE.

breviary book containing the pra ers, hymns, and lessons to be sa by the clergy at the appropria hours during the day, sometim illustrated.

bridge-spouted vessel traditional p shape found in the CERAMIC wa of Central and South Americ

especially of the central Andes. It has two spouts "bridged" by another piece.
ocade loose term for patterned TEXTILE, especially with woven decoration in gold or silver.
onze 1 alloy of copper and tin, often used for cast SCULPTURE. 2 a sculpture made from this alloy.
onze Age period (mainly 2nd millennium BC) when bronze was the metal chiefly used for weapons and implements.
onzist maker of BRONZE SCULPTURE, plaques, etc.
ücke (Ger., *Die Brücke*, "The Bridge") group of German EXPRESSIONIST painters founded in Dresden in 1905, and including the artists Ernst Ludwig Kirchner and Karl Schmidt-Rottluff.
ush implement for applying paint, usually of hog or sable hair set in a wooden handle.
ush stroke the individual mark made by each application of paint with a BRUSH, usually retaining the mark of the separate brush hairs.
ushwork general term for manner or style in which paint is applied, and often considered by art historians as an identifying characteristic of a particular artist's work.
utalism architectural style of the 1950s associated with Le Corbusier and Alison and Peter Smithson, in which rough REINFORCED CONCRETE is used and no attempt is made to disguise the building materials.
cchero 1 red-colored earth used for making jars, or vase made from this material, in the ancient world. 2 black clayey earth used for certain Etruscan vases.
cranium (Latin; pl. *bucrania*; from Greek *boukranion*, "oxhead") DECORATIVE MOTIF in CLASSICAL and post-RENAISSANCE art based on an oxhead.*
gaku type of ancient Japanese dance, sometimes performed at Buddhist ceremonies.
njinga Japanese scholar-painters working from *c*1700; the term also applies to the work they produced.
on fresco (It.) *see* FRESCO.
rin metal tool used for engraving.
rlap type of coarse canvas, especially jute sacking material.
rnish to polish by rubbing. GOLD LEAF may be burnished by rubbing with a smooth AGATE tool.
st PORTRAIT SCULPTURE showing the sitter's head and shoulders only.
stan "The Orchard", a book of ethics in verse written by the Persian poet Sa'di (*c*1213–92). It was often illustrated.
ttress (arch.) reinforced, projecting wall, usually on the exterior of a building, supporting it at a point of stress. A FLYING BUTTRESS transmits the thrust of a VAULT to an outer support; *see* VAULT CONSTRUCTION.
Byzantine art art of the eastern Roman Empire centered on Constantinople, formerly Byzantium, from the 4th century AD. At various times it embraced both CLASSICAL Greek REALISM and stylized, HIERATIC, Eastern art.

C

cabinet picture small or medium-sized PAINTING executed at an easel and designed for collectors, especially popular from the 17th century; *see* EASEL PICTURE.
cable pattern (arch.) convex ropelike molding found in Norman ARCHITECTURE. Sometimes also refers to similar decoration in goldsmiths' work.
calcite crystalline form of calcium carbonate.
calligraphic style of DRAWING or PAINTING which is particularly free, flowing, and distinctive, like fine handwriting.
calligraphy the art of fine handwriting.
Camden Town Group group of English POST-IMPRESSIONIST painters formed in 1911 around Walter Sickert, including Spencer Gore, Lucien Pissarro, and Augustus John, who applied some of the principles of Paul Gauguin and Vincent van Gogh to contemporary London subject matter.
cameo gemstone or shell of colored layers with the upper layer carved to form a relief design against the contrasting ground.
camera obscura device that uses a lens to project a reduced image of an object onto a flat surface so that the outline may be traced. Popular with artists from the RENAISSANCE to the 18th century.
camera ottica another name for a CAMERA OBSCURA.
campanile (It.) (arch.) freestanding bell tower of CHURCH.
camposanto (It.) cemetery; churchyard.
candelabrum standing candlestick with holders for more than one candle.
canopy (arch.) suspended or projected miniature roof over an ALTAR, seat, STATUE, etc.
cantilever (arch.) a beam supported or fixed at one end carrying a load at the other.
capital (arch.) upper part of COLUMN or PILASTER, directly beneath the ENTABLATURE; *see* CLASSICAL GREEK ARCHITECTURE.
capomaestro (It.) master builder; chief architect.
caposcuola (It.) founder of an artistic or literary movement.
capriccio (It.) literally, a fancy or caprice. In the 18th century it usually referred to a PAINTING in which accurately rendered existing ARCHITECTURE was combined with the imaginary. It also applied to ETCHINGS that represented fantasies rather than actual stories.
Caravaggism tendency to follow the style of Caravaggio, exhibited by the Caravaggisti (17th-century painters working in Rome), who made particularly dramatic use of CHIAROSCURO.
caravansary in the East, an open court surrounded by buildings where caravans rest.
carbon chemical element that occurs in various natural forms including diamond, GRAPHITE, and CHARCOAL, and in all organic compounds. Carbon black, obtained artificially, is one of the oldest black pigments, being derived from the partial burning of wood, bone, and other organic materials.
cardboard board made from pressed paper, used as a support for PAINTING or DRAWING, and in COLLAGE and SCULPTURE.
caricature PAINTING or DRAWING, usually a PORTRAIT, that exaggerates features for humorous or satirical effect.
carnelian (or cornelian) reddish colored form of CHALCEDONY, used in jewelry and for DECORATIVE objects.
Carolingian art European art of the period covered by the reign of Charlemagne (AD 768–814) and his successors until *c*AD 900; usually regarded as the foundation of medieval art.
carpet page in MANUSCRIPT illumination, a page totally filled with DECORATIVE design.
cartography map drawing.
cartoon 1 full-sized DRAWING for transferring design to PAINTING, MURAL, or TAPESTRY. 2 comic drawing; CARICATURE.
cartouche 1 ornamental frame, whether painted, engraved, printed, or sculpted, often in the form of a SCROLL, and containing an inscription, coat of arms, etc. 2 in Egyptian HIEROGLYPHICS, an oval or oblong frame enclosing the names of royalty or divinities.
caryatid (Greek; pl. caryatides) (arch.) figure of draped woman that serves as a COLUMN supporting an ENTABLATURE; *see* ATLANTES. Caryatides are also found as a MOTIF on furniture, for example, as bronze mounts.
casein a phosphoprotein prepared from skimmed milk. When mixed

arcade

after the Ospedale degli Innocenti, Florence, designed by Brunelleschi and begun in 1419

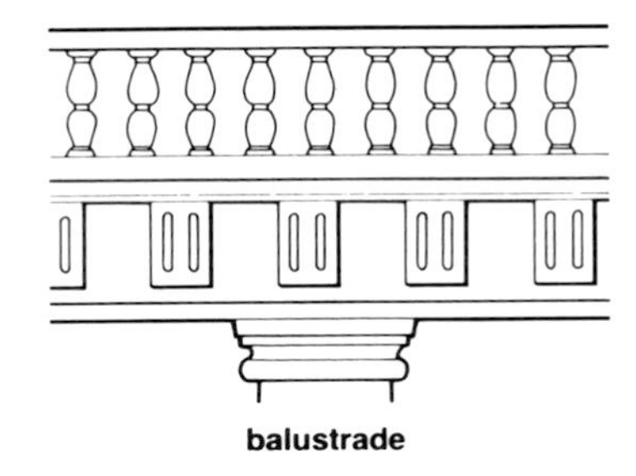
balustrade

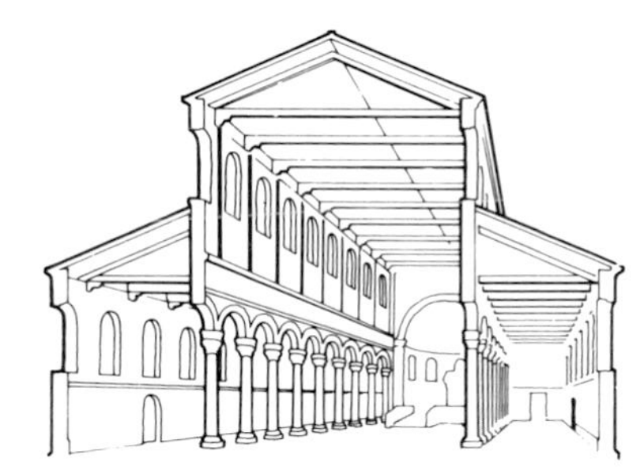
basilica

bucranium

with lime it forms a very strong adhesive that has been extensively used for wood joining, and to a lesser extent as a binding material for paints and GROUNDS.

casino (It.) (arch.) temple or small house, often in a park.

cassone (It.) Italian wooden chest of the 15th and 16th centuries, usually decorated, and often intended to hold a bride's dowry.

castellation (arch.) decoration of a building with battlements and TURRETS, like a castle; the result may be described as castellated.

casting the duplication of a model in METAL or PLASTER by means of a MOLD; the model thus formed is a cast.

catacomb an underground burial chamber for several tombs; the term applies especially to the Early Christian tombs in Rome.

catafalque decorated structure used to display or carry a coffin during a funeral or lying in state.

cedar tree of the genus *Cedrus* with hard, reddish wood that has been used for making furniture.

ceiling (arch.) lining of roof of room, often painted or decorated.

celadon Chinese PORCELAIN or STONEWARE with a distinctive gray-green GLAZE.

cella (also called *naos*) enclosed chamber in Greek or Roman temple housing a cult image.

censer portable incense burner for ecclesiastical use, in which incense is sprinkled on burning charcoal.

centaur mythological creature; a horse with a human torso instead of a horse's head and neck.

ceramics the general term used since the 19th century for POTTERY and PORCELAIN, i.e. fired clay.

ceramic sculpture SCULPTURE in ceramic material.

ceramist one who makes ceramics.

Cercle et Carré Group (Fr., "Circle and Square") group and periodical of International Constructivists formed in Paris in 1929 by Joaquin Torres-Garciá and others to promote ABSTRACT art.

Chac Mool a Mayan god, often represented in SCULPTURE.

chaitya (arch.) term usually reserved for an Indian Buddhist SANCTUARY cut in rock and arranged as a hall with an AISLE on either side separated from it by rows of PILLARS.

chalcedony semiprecious stone; a type of QUARTZ that occurs as different varieties including AGATE and CARNELIAN.

chalice cup, usually of precious metal, used to hold consecrated wine during Mass or Eucharist.

chalk the common name for calcium carbonate, which is found as a natural deposit all over the world, and is composed of the remains of

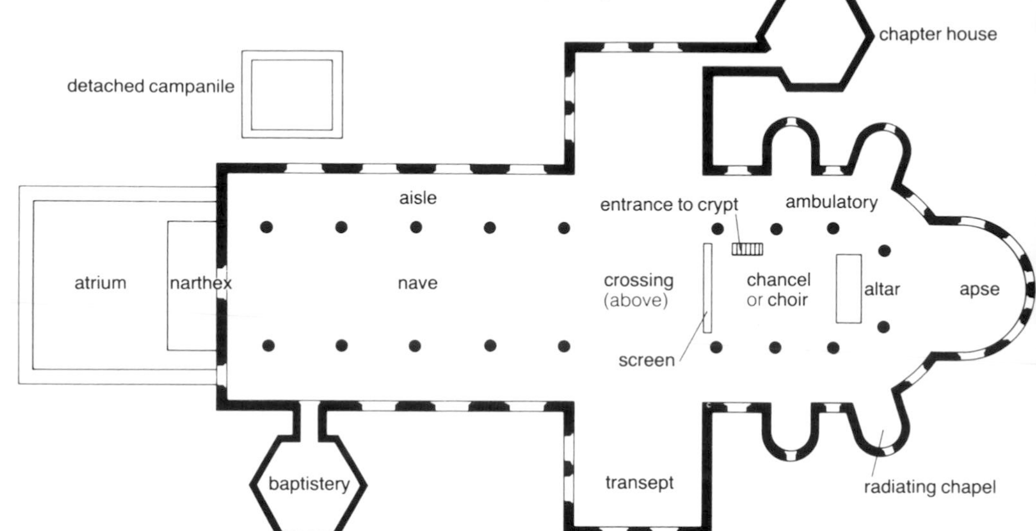

tiny crustaceans. Traditionally used in PAINTING and DRAWING.

chamfered capital (arch.) CAPITAL with square angles cut obliquely.

champlevé enamel (Fr.) decorated METAL, usually COPPER, especially popular in Europe from the 11th century to the 14th; a hollowed-out pattern in the metal was filled with colored GLASS pastes and the whole object fired, thus fusing glass to metal. (Compare CLOISONNÉ ENAMEL.)

Ch'an Chinese Buddhist sect; equivalent of the Japanese ZEN, which produced a rather mystical type of PAINTING.

chancel (arch.) east end of CHURCH containing the ALTAR.

chapter house (arch.) building attached to a monastic or collegiate CHURCH used for the assembly of clergy.

characterization creation of distinct character.

charcoal form of CARBON used for DRAWING.

chase 1 to ornament a metal surface by ENGRAVING with steel tools. 2 to apply the final smoothing to a BRONZE cast. Both processes are known as chasing.

chasuble circular ecclesiastical vestment, with a hole in the center for the head.

château (Fr.) 1 a feudal castle. 2 a large country house.

checker pattern squares of alternate colors.

chert form of QUARTZ.

Che School 15th-century school of Chinese PAINTING, based at Chekiang, that represented the ACADEMIC court tradition.

chevron 1 (arch.) zigzag MOLDING in Norman ARCHITECTURE. 2 pattern of V shapes.*

chiaroscuro pictorial representation of light and shade without regard to color.

Chicago School group of architects working in Chicago between 1871 and 1893 including Louis Sullivan and Daniel Burnham. Their advancements led to the skyscraper.

china term for better quality ceramics such as fine porcelain.

chinoiserie (Fr.) term for a European style of art applied to furniture, CERAMICS, and INTERIOR DESIGN based on imaginary pseudo-Chinese MOTIFS.

chin-shih (Ch., "advanced scholar") the highest grade of the Chinese civil service, from *c*618–1911.

chintz term used in Europe in the 16th and 17th centuries for imported Indian calico, and later for European printed cotton.

chip carving early carved decoration of Northern European oak furniture, executed with a chisel and gouge until about the 16th century.

Chi-Rho a monogram (the Sacred Monogram) formed by the first two letters—X and P (*chi* and *rho*)—of the Greek word for Christ. In religious art it may refer to the Resurrection of Christ.*

choir (arch.) part of CHURCH where service is sung.

choir stalls (arch.) seats arranged in rows on either side of CHOIR, often carved.

chromatic of or relating to color.

chromium metallic element often used to plate other METAL, e.g. in SCULPTURE.

chronogram phrase (often an inscription) written in Roman letters in which those letters that also represent numerals express a date or an epoch.

chrysocolla 1 CLASSICAL name f compounds used in solderi gold, especially green copper mi eral compounds. 2 natural copp silicate, which has been found as pigment.

church 1 building designed f Christian worship. The fi churches were based on t Roman BASILICA, but soon dev oped.* 2 the whole body Christian believers.

ciborium 1 (arch.) vaulted CANO over an ALTAR. 2 vessel for holdi consecrated host.

cimborio (Sp., "drum") (arch.) drum-shaped structure, oft pierced with windows, and su porting a DOME.*

cinnabar red mercuric sulfide used pigment. Artificial cinnabar usually called VERMILION.

cinnabarite mineral ore of CI NABAR.

Cinquecento (It.) the 16th century.

cire perdue (Fr., "lost wax") casti process used in BRONZE SCUL TURE.

cityscape PAINTING or DRAWING city scenery.

cladding coating or covering; e. material covering the FACADE of building.

classic 1 the finest art of its kind in given period. 2 art that adheres high standards of craftsmanshi logic, symmetry, and proportion

Classical 1 Greek art of the 5th ce tury BC. 2 art of the Roman a Greek ANTIQUE world.

Classical Greek architecture apog of Greek architectural desig much imitated in later ARCHITE TURE.*

Classicism the quality of CLASSIC CLASSICAL art. The term is appli in particular to the type of art th

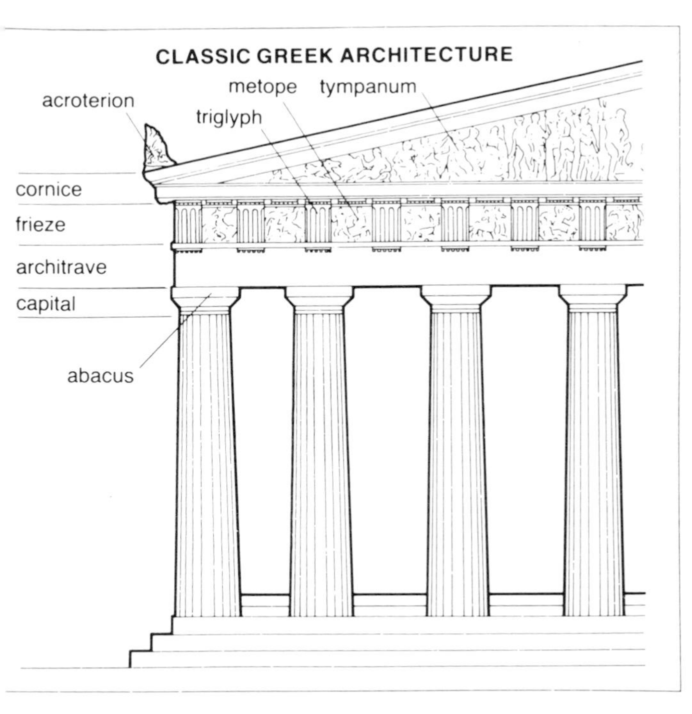

was the antithesis of ROMANTICISM during the 18th and 19th centuries, when it was held to represent the virtues of restraint and harmony, in contrast to dramatic individual expression.
assicizing promoting or tending towards the CLASSICAL.
restory (arch.) upper story of NAVE of CHURCH, pierced with windows; *see* VAULT CONSTRUCTION.
isonné enamel (Fr.) decorated METAL in which a design of metal strips is applied and the compartments *(cloisons)* formed are filled with colored GLASS pastes. Compare CHAMPLEVÉ ENAMEL.)
isonnisme (Fr.) synonym for YNTHETISM.
ister (arch.) covered walk around a space, usually square, with a wall on one side and columns on he other. In Christian monasteries t often links the CHURCH and domestic quarters.
balt metallic element from which various colored pigments were produced in the 19th century.
BrA an association of Dutch, Danish, and Belgian EXPRESSIONIST artists 1948–51. An acronym of he words *Copenhagen*, *Brussels*, and *Amsterdam*.
dex MANUSCRIPT bound as a book.
fer 1 (arch.) ornamental sunken panel recessed into a CEILING or VAULT, which may then be described as coffered. **2** chest for valuable objects.
lage (Fr., "pasting") technique originating with CUBISM in which paper, photographs, and other everyday materials were pasted onto a support, and sometimes also painted.
collé (Fr.) pasted, glued, stuck.
Cologne School PAINTINGS from the Cologne region of Germany, dating from the late 14th century to the 16th.
Colonial style American PAINTING, art, and ARCHITECTURE of the 17th century to the 19th.
colonnade (arch.) row of COLUMNS supporting ENTABLATURE.
colonnette small COLUMN.
Color Field painting PAINTING, usually on a large scale, in which solid areas of color are taken right to the edge of the canvas, suggesting that they extend to infinity.
coloring the way in which color is used in PAINTINGS, or the general impression of color given by a particular PAINTING.
colorism term applied to various periods of PAINTING, e.g. 16th-century Venetian, in which color was emphasized, rather than DRAWING.
colorist artist who specializes in or is famed for his or her use of color.
color modulation composition based on subtle variation of color.
color progression composition based on a clear progression from one color, or group of colors, to another.
colossal order *see* GIANT ORDER.
colossus gigantic STATUE.
column (arch.) cylindrical pillar, either freestanding or supporting another architectural member. In CLASSICAL ARCHITECTURE it consists of a base, a SHAFT, and a CAPITAL; *see* CLASSICAL GREEK ARCHITECTURE.
column-figure human figure, carved in the round, used to decorate columns at church doorways from the 12th century to the 15th.*
column krater Greek vase for mixing wine and water; *see* GREEK VASES.
Commedia dell'Arte (It.) professional, improvised Italian comedy of the 16th and 17th centuries.
commission 1 a work of art ordered by a patron. **2** contract to produce work for a patron.
Composite order *see* ORDERS OF ARCHITECTURE.
composition board BOARD made of cheap pressed or laminated fibers, used as a PAINTING support in COLLAGE and in SCULPTURE.
compound pier *see* PIER.
conceit fanciful device; affectation of style. Used especially in ARCHITECTURE.
Conceptual art art that takes the form of mental images, provoked by various stimuli—visual, tactile, and aural—and in which concepts and ideas are more important than tangible, concrete works of art.
concha (or conch) (arch.) the DOMED roof of a semicircular APSE.*
concrete mixture of sand, stone, and cement used as a building material, especially in the 20th century.
Concrete art term coined in 1929 when Theo van Doesburg became editor of the magazine *Art Concret*; it is sometimes used as a synonym for ABSTRACT art, though the emphasis is not just on geometric or abstract form, but on structure and organization in both design and execution.
condottiere (It.) Italian mercenary; soldier of fortune.
console 1 (arch.) architectural term for scrolled BRACKET. **2** in furniture, a marble-topped side table.
Constructivism international ABSTRACT art movement founded in post-Revolutionary Russia by Antoine Pevsner and Naum Gabo, whose aims were expressed in the REALISTIC MANIFESTO.
conté crayon proprietary manufactured CHALK.
contrapposto (It., "opposite", "antithesis", "placed against") posing of human form in PAINTING or SCULPTURE so that head and shoulders are twisted in a different direction from hips and legs.*
contre jour (Fr., "against the light") technique used in PAINTING and photography of showing the subject placed against a light source, such as a window, rather than illuminated by light at the side.
conversation piece PAINTING of a group PORTRAIT, especially popular in 18th-century England, showing the sitters talking or involved in some other informal activity.

chevron

chi-rho column-figure

cimborio

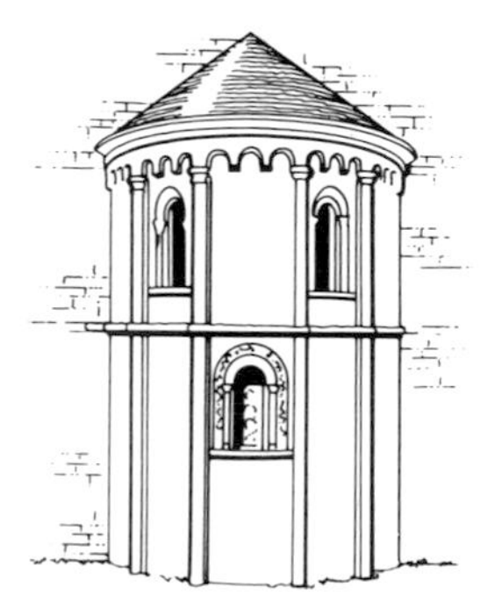
concha

corbel

cool color color tending towards the blue end of the visual SPECTRUM, or which appears to recede in a PAINTING.

cope semicircular ecclesiastical cloak for processions and ceremonies.

copper plate copper plate on which a design is ETCHED or ENGRAVED; often used as term for the image produced by this method.

corbel (arch.) projection on a wall, bearing a weight.*

corbeling (arch.) series of CORBELS built one above the other.

corbel table projecting COURSE resting on a series of CORBELS.

cord-impressed pattern pattern applied to early Japanese and other POTTERY by pressing a piece of cord into the CLAY while still soft.

Corinthian order *see* ORDERS OF ARCHITECTURE.

cornelian alternative spelling of CARNELIAN.

cornice (arch.) **1** upper member of an ENTABLATURE. **2** ornamental molding finishing the part to which it is attached, e.g. at the junction of a wall and CEILING.

cornucopia (Latin) goat's horn overflowing with fruit, flowers, and corn, symbolizing plenty.

coroplast a sculptor in Greek ANTIQUITY whose MEDIUM was chiefly TERRACOTTA, used particularly for making FIGURINES.

cortile (It., "courtyard") courtyard surrounded by ARCADES.

costume piece PAINTING with a chief subject that is a figure or figures in historic or exotic costume.

couching embroidery technique in which thread is sewn on a GROUND using a finer thread, which is visible as a pattern.

coulisse (Fr.) literally, the wings at the side of a stage. In PAINTING, particularly of the BAROQUE period, it refers to a composition in which features at the edge of the picture, e.g. hills and trees, lead the viewer's eye into the painting.

coupled pilaster (arch.) two PILASTERS standing on the same PEDESTAL.

course (arch.) continuous horizontal layer in the stone of a building.

courtyard (arch.) space enclosed by buildings or walls but often open to the sky.

cove (arch.) concave molding, especially between the CEILING and CORNICE of a room.

cowrie small shell, often used as a design MOTIF.

crenellation (arch.) the formation of battlements, in which the openings are known as *crenelles*.

cresting (arch.) line of ORNAMENT finishing a roof or wall.

crewel work textiles made from crewel yarn, a thin, two-threaded strong wool.

crocket (arch.) in Gothic ARCHITECTURE, a carved decoration, usually leaf-shaped, projecting from the sides of pinnacles or gables.

cross-hatching *see* HATCHING.

crossing (arch.) the space in a CHURCH where NAVE, CHANCEL, and TRANSEPTS meet.

cross-in-rectangle (arch.) CHURCH plan, common in Armenia.*

crozier crook-shaped staff carried by bishops.

cruciform cross-shaped; used especially of a CHURCH that has TRANSEPTS.

crypt underground chamber below CHURCH, usually at east end.

crystal (or rock crystal) very hard form of transparent QUARTZ, especially popular in Italy as a carving material.

cube technique MOSAIC technique using cut, cube-shaped stones that can produce more subtle designs than uncut stones.

cubiculum (Latin) (arch.) **1** term used by the Romans for a bedchamber or reclining room, or a small enclosed space, e.g. a box at the theater. **2** term used by the Roman architectural writer Vitruvius (1st century BC) for a recess in a wall designed to receive the end of a BEAM.

Cubism artistic movement *c*1907 to 1915 initiated by Picasso and Braque. It aimed to analyze forms in geometric terms (ANALYTICAL CUBISM) or reorganize them in various contexts (SYNTHETIC CUBISM); color remained secondary to form.

Cubo-Futurism specifically Russian art movement associated with Kasimir Malevich, *c*1913, which combined elements of CUBISM and FUTURISM.

cuerda seca (Sp., "dry cord") DECORATIVE technique used on tiles; an outline is incised in the soft CLAY and the lines are then filled with a greasy MEDIUM that acts as a "resist" so that different glazes will not run together.

cult statue statue of a deity for cult worship.

Cupid synonymous with Amor and Eros; the mythological child of Venus, the Roman god of love, usually depicted as a child holding a bow and arrow. The term is sometimes used to mean simply "cherub" (*see* PUTTO).

cupola (arch.) DOMED VAULT or roof.*

cup painting CLASSICAL Greek decoration of POTTERY vessels that became a sophisticated art form.

cursive form/style flowing, like script.

curtain wall (arch.) outer wall of castle joining towers and gatehouse. Also refers to a wall that divides space without bearing weight.

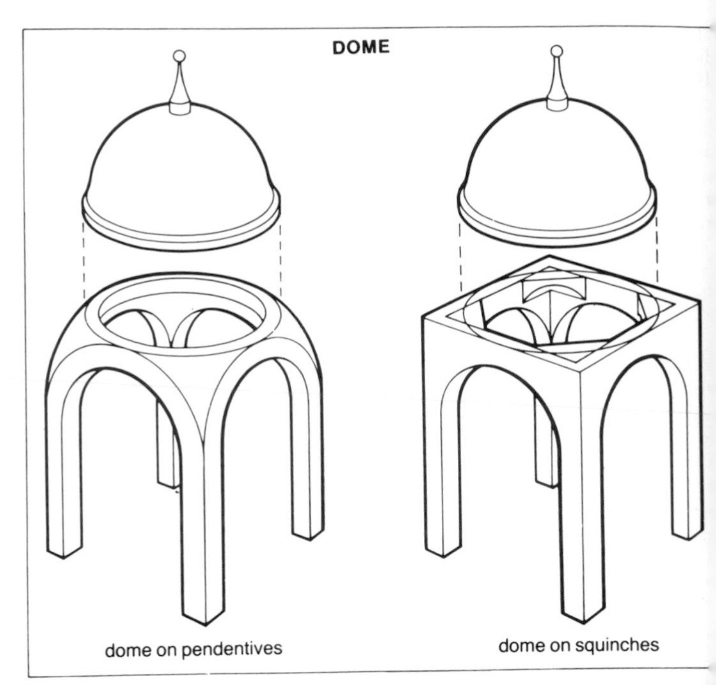

curvilinear based on pattern of curved lines; sinuous.

cushion base base of a CAPITAL associated with early medieval ARCHITECTURE; shaped like a cube but with rounded edges and corners. *See* CUSHION CAPITAL.

cushion capital (arch.) square capital with rounded corners, found chiefly in ROMANESQUE and early medieval buildings; *see* VAULT CONSTRUCTION.

cusp (arch.) point at which two arcs meet in a GOTHIC arch or TRACERY.

Cycladic type of Aegean art from the Cyclades—a group of Greek island—*c*2800 BC to 1100 BC.

cycle series of PAINTINGS linked by a theme, especially used in FRESCO painting.

cypress coniferous tree of the genus *Cupressus*. Often a symbol of mourning. Its rather hard wood may be used for furniture.

D

Dada international "anti-art" movement originating in Zurich *c*1916, involving Marcel Duchamp, Jean Arp, Francis Picabia, among others; a forerunner of SURREALISM; hence Dadaism, Dadaist.

dado (arch.) **1** lower section of a wall, sometimes separated from the upper by a MOLDING. **2** part of a PEDESTAL between the BASE and CORNICE.

Danube School nonexistent as a school, the name loosely refers to several early 16th-century German painters, such as Albrecht Altdorfer and Lucas Cranach, famous for lush landscapes and r coloristic effects.

dappled of variegated color, applied in spots and patches.

Dark Ages period of the Mid Ages from *c*5th century AD to 1 century, formerly considered phase in which philosophy a the arts were ignored or activ hindered. The term has recen come to be seen as pejorative, a EARLY MIDDLE AGES is used inste

Decadent Movement *fin-de-siè* movement associated with Aub Beardsley. It was related to t AESTHETIC MOVEMENT.

Deconstruction a philosophi stance, based on the theories Jacques Derrida, implying that meaning of any work of art is r fixed by the artist's intentions, l is open to constant analysis a comparison with other works art. It has been influential amc art historians and critics and some architectural practice, wh it is linked to POST-MODERNISM.

decorative aesthetically pleasing, namental, nonfunctional.

decorative art the designing and d orating of functional objects materials to give them AESTHE appeal, e.g. CERAMICS, GLASS, f niture, METALWORK, and TEXTII The term is often used to differ tiate this type of work from FINE ARTS (PAINTING, DRAWI SCULPTURE) whose value is prim ily aesthetic.

deësis (Greek) in Byzantine icon raphy, the figure of Christ throned between the Virgin anc John the Baptist.

Degenerate art (Ger., *Entartet Kur* Nazi propaganda term used fr

:1937 for works of modern art
lisapproved of by the party.
lft School 17th-century Dutch
iENRE PAINTING associated with
an Vermeer and Pieter de Hooch.
oth three-dimensionality or reces-
ion, real or suggested.
r Sturm (Ger., "The Storm") mag-
zine and art gallery in Berlin,
ounded by Herwarth Walden;
rom 1910 to 1932 it promoted
UTURISM and EXPRESSIONISM,
articularly the BLAUE REITER
roup.
rvish Muslim religious man,
owed to a life of poverty.
Stijl 1 Dutch art magazine
ounded in 1917 by Theo van
Doesburg and Piet Mondrian. 2
rtists and architects associated
vith the journal who were influ-
ntial in promoting functional
AUHAUS design during the 1920s.
utscher Werkbund (Ger.,
"German Work League") organi-
ation founded in München in
1907 to promote good design in
nachine-made objects.
vice 1 contrivance or invention.
2 design or HERALDIC emblem.
otional associated with, or the
bject of, religious worship.
blerie (Fr.) visual representation
of the powers of Hell or dealings
vith the devil.
dem crown, wreath, or head-
and.
per (arch.) an all-over pattern of
mall square or lozenge-shaped
nits, found in ROMANESQUE and
iOTHIC buildings. The term is also
pplied to a similar pattern in
TAINED GLASS and in the gold
ackground of ILLUMINATED MAN-
USCRIPTS of the 13th, 14th, and
15th centuries.*
phane (Fr.) transparent.
treton (Greek) chased or en-
raved drinking cup; *see* GREEK
VASES.
1 engraved stamp for making a
oin or medal. 2 hollow MOLD for
haping extruded METAL.
uent liquid added to paint to thin
t and make it easier to work with,
.g. turpentine, for OIL PAINTING;
vater, for WATERCOLOR painting.
os GREEK VASE, shaped like a
RATER on a tall base.
rite variety of GREENSTONE or
ADE, used for tools, ORNAMENTS,
nd small SCULPTURE.
tych pair of painted or sculptured
anels hinged or joined together;
specially popular for devotional
ictures in the Middle Ages; *see*
LTARPIECE.
ect carving method of stone
CULPTURE where form is carved
mmediately out of the block and
ot transferred from a model.
ect metal sculpture modern tech-
ique of METAL SCULPTURE, shap-
ing metal by beating or with heat, instead of the traditional CASTING technique.
disegno (It.) literally, "DRAWING" or "design", but during the RENAISSANCE it acquired a broader meaning of overall concept.
di sotto in su (It., "from below upwards") method of illusionistic CEILING PAINTING in which the figures are dramatically FORESHORTENED.
distemper paint based on glue or SIZE MEDIUM, used for PAINTING walls and theatrical scenery.
Divisionism analytical PAINTING technique developed systematically by Georges Seurat; instead of mixing colors on the PALETTE, each color is applied "pure" in individual brush strokes, so that from a certain distance the viewer's eye and brain perform the mixing optically; *see* POINTILLISM, NEO-IMPRESSIONISM.
dogtooth (arch.) 1 small ORNAMENT shaped like a pyramid, with the flat faces cut back. 2 ornament on a MOLDING, in the form of four lobes or leaves radiating from a center, found in 13th-century English ARCHITECTURE.*
dolerite a type of basaltic rock.
dolmen prehistoric monument consisting of a large flat stone on two uprights.
dome (arch.) convex covering set over circular or polygonal base.*
Dong-son prehistoric Indo-Chinese culture; the name derives from the chief site (in Vietnam) in which IMPLEMENTS and ORNAMENTS have been found.
donor giver of a work of art.
Doric *see* ORDERS OF ARCHITECTURE.
draftsman person who draws or sketches plans (particularly of machinery, buildings, etc.).
draftsmanship skill in DRAWING or plan-making.
drapery the arrangement of folds of material, painted or sculpted.
drawing the pictorial representation of objects by a technique that is basically linear, such as pen or pencil. When used for a PAINTING, it refers more specifically to the artist's method of representing form by these means, rather than by the actual use of color and paint.
drum (arch.) 1 circular or polygonal wall supporting a DOME. 2 circular blocks of stone forming a COLUMN.
drypoint COPPER ENGRAVING technique.
dynamism the quality or appearance of power, action, movement. The term may be used figuratively for inanimate objects such as SCULPTURE; hence dynamic.

E

Early Middle Ages *see* DARK AGES.
Earth art *see* LAND ART.
earthenware POTTERY made from red or white CLAY, fired in a KILN at less than 1200°C (2192°F).
easel painting small or medium-sized PAINTING executed at an easel. These were usually intended for collectors and connoisseurs, although the term may also be used generally for any portable painting, as opposed to MURAL painting; also called CABINET PICTURE.
eave (arch.) lower edge of a roof, overhanging a wall.
ebony heavy, hard-grained black wood of the species of tree *Diospyros ebenum*, used for furniture and DECORATIVE objects.
Ecce homo (Latin, "Behold the man") the pictorial representation of Christ's presentation to the people by Pontius Pilate before the Crucifixion.
École de Paris *see* SCHOOL OF PARIS.
écorché (Fr., "flayed") describes a figure drawn or modeled without skin to show the musculature; used by the artist as an aid to DRAWING, PAINTING, or SCULPTURE.
Edo 1 former name for Tokyo. 2 name of the period of Japanese history from 1615 to 1868.
effigy PORTRAIT or model of a figure, especially when part of a stone tomb.
Eight, the group of New York artists formed in 1907 and later known by this name. They opposed the restrictive practices of the National Academy of Design, and for their own works turned instead to depicting the contemporary American scene.
electrum natural alloy of silver and gold used in the ancient world for METALWORK.
Elementarism modified form of NEO-PLASTICISM propounded by Theo van Doesburg in the 1920s, which caused a rift with Piet Mondrian by introducing diagonals instead of a rigid horizontal and vertical format.
elevation (arch.) 1 the face or side of a structure. 2 DRAWING or plan of the side of a building.
ellipse an oval shape traced by a point moving in one plane, so that the sum of its distance from two fixed points remains constant.
emblema elaborate MOSAIC panel set into a plain floor or MOSAIC. The term may also be used for any distinct DECORATIVE panel set in a larger area, e.g. a carpet.
emboss to MOLD, stamp, or carve a surface to produce a design in RELIEF.

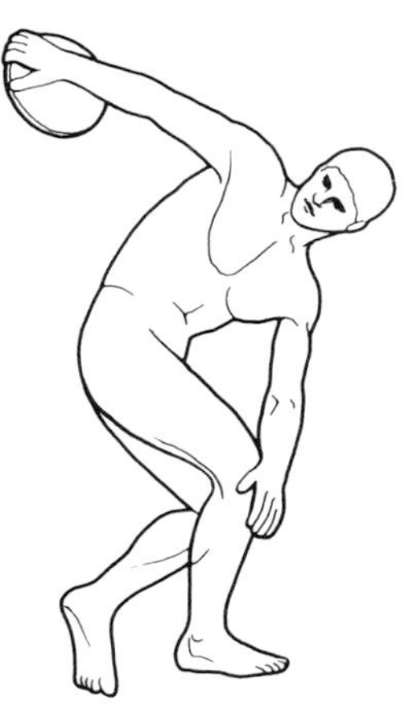
contrapposto
after the Discobolus (Discus-thrower) by Myron; 5th century BC

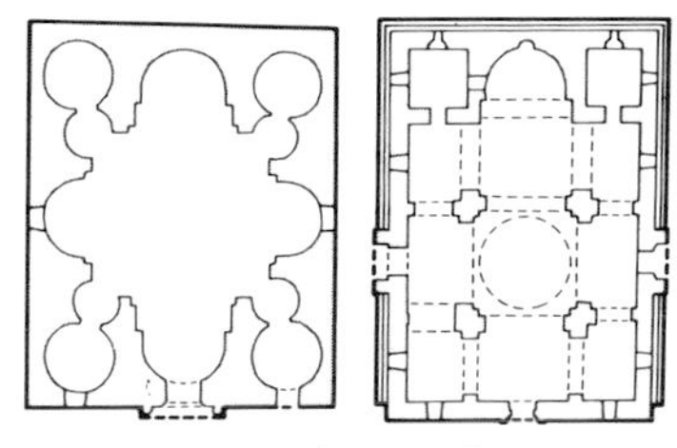
cross-in-rectangle
two examples of Armenian cross-in-rectangle church plan

cupola

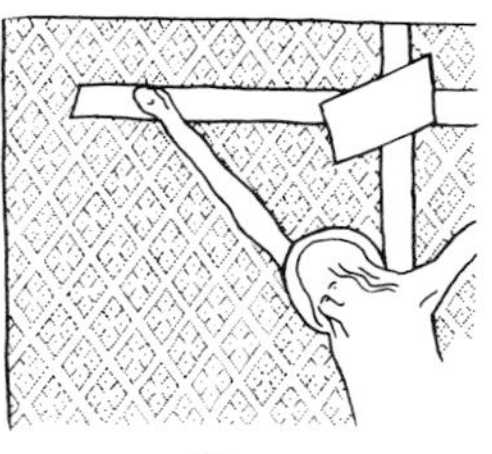
diaper

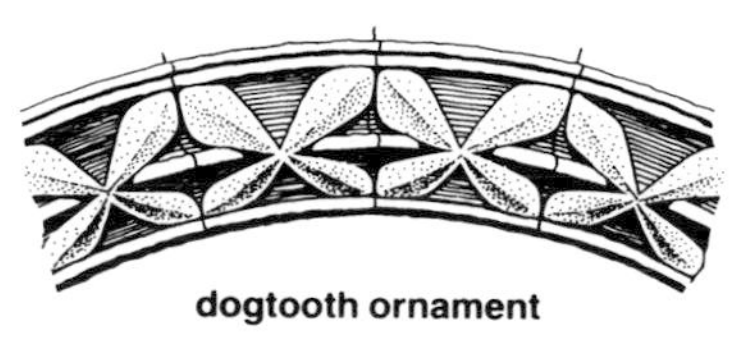
dogtooth ornament

emulsion a combination of two non-miscible liquids in which drops of one are suspended in the other. It is not established how far emulsions have been used as PAINTING media, but the technique used by the 15th-century Flemish painters may have employed an egg/oil emulsion.

enamel 1 vitreous substance (usually lead/potash GLASS) fused to METAL at high temperature (about 800°C; 1472°F) and often used for DECORATIVE objects; *see* CLOISONNÉ ENAMEL And CHAMPLEVÉ ENAMEL. **2** the object so produced.

enamel paint paint based on thickened linseed oil and RESIN, which dries to a very hard and glossy surface.

enamel painting PAINTING with colored ENAMELS, often used for small objects of METAL or GLASS.

encaustic technique ancient technique of PAINTING with wax and PIGMENTS fused by heat.

engraving 1 the technique of incising lines on wood, METAL, etc. **2** the impression made from the engraved block.

Enlightenment 18th-century philosophical movement that stressed the importance of reason.

enlumineur (Fr.) illuminator (of MANUSCRIPTS).

entablature (arch.) upper section of a CLASSICAL ORDER consisting of ARCHITRAVE, FRIEZE, and CORNICE.

entasis (Greek) (arch.) a slight swelling of the contour of a COLUMN, designed to counteract the optical illusion of concavity and generally found in CLASSICAL ARCHITECTURE.*

environmental sculpture a development in contemporary SCULPTURE which is conceived as part of the environment shared, rather than just observed, by the viewer.

epistolary (from Latin *epistolarium*) "Book of Epistles" used for the Mass or Eucharist.

equilateral triangle triangle with three equal sides and angles.

erechtheum temple of the Acropolis in Athens, built *c*421–406 BC.

erotic art art devoted to the expression or arousal of sexual feeling.

Erster Deutscher Herbstsalon (Ger., "First German Autumn Salon") art exhibition held in Berlin in 1913, organized by August Macke and Wassily Kandinsky.

etch 1 term used in LITHOGRAPHY for the solution of gum arabic and nitric acid used to render the non-drawn area of a litho stone insensitive to grease. **2** (verb) to eat into, e.g. with acid.

etching 1 process in which the design is drawn on a METAL plate through a wax ground; the design is cut into the plate with acid and printed. **2** PRINT produced by this method.

ethnographic art art inspired by a particular racial culture.

ewer pitcher, jug.

exedra (arch.) semicircular or angular recess in a wall, common in Greek and Roman ARCHITECTURE.

Expressionism artistic movement of the 20th century in which the expression of emotion and feeling is emphasized rather than the representation of nature; hence Expressionist, Expressionistic. *See also* BLAUE REITER and BRÜCKE.

extender inert pigment used to bulk a paint or to lower the tinctorial strength of another pigment.

eye cup BLACK-FIGURE Greek vase with a stylized eye MOTIF.

F

facade (arch.) face of a building, usually the main face.

facet one side of a many sided object, e.g. a cut gem.

facture quality or style of execution or handling, especially of a PAINTING.

faience 1 type of tin-glazed EARTHENWARE, often used for architectural purposes. **2** archaeological term for ancient Egyptian wares of glazed powdered QUARTZ.

fantasy (or the Fantastic) dreamlike, visionary, or grotesque image which is the product of the artist's imagination.

Fauves (Fr.) originally a derogatory term (*Les Fauves*) meaning "wild beasts", used for a group of painters who exhibited at the Salon d'Automne in Paris in 1905, including Matisse; hence Fauvism, Fauvist.

felt 1 (arch.) watertight fibrous building material used as underlining for roofs. **2** in papermaking, the blanket that carries the PAPER and squeezes moisture from it.

feminist art works of art exploring or promoting the feminist program; the movement was strongest in the 1970s but continues as a strand in artistic practice.

fête (Fr.) festival; saint's day; bazaar.

fête champêtre (Fr.) PAINTING of somewhat idealized rural festivities, popular in the 17th and 18th centuries.

fête galante (Fr.) an elegant FÊTE CHAMPÊTRE of the type popularized in the 18th century by Antoine Watteau.

fetish object found in various cultures (especially African) used as the focus of a magic or religious ceremony.

fiberglass 1 woven glass fiber fabric. **2** molded plastic containing glass fiber, used for SCULPTURE, furniture, etc.

fictive imaginary, creating an illusion. Most frequently used in descriptions of TROMPE L'OEIL painted ARCHITECTURE.

figural figurative, relating to figures or shapes.

figuration 1 form, shape. **2** ornamentation with design. **3** depiction of figures, especially human.

figurative art synonym for REPRESENTATIONAL ART.

figure drawing (and figure PAINTING) DRAWING or painting in which the human figure predominates, usually full length.

figurine small model or SCULPTURE of the human figure.

filigree fine woven mesh of gold and silver threads, used for mounting precious objects, e.g. GEMS, or in bookbinding.*

Fin de Siècle late 19th-century style of ART NOUVEAU, also associated with the SYMBOLIST and DECADENT movements.

fine art art whose value is considered to be aesthetic rather than functional, i.e. ARCHITECTURE, SCULPTURE, PAINTING and DRAWING, and the GRAPHIC ARTS. Compare DECORATIVE ART.

finial (arch.) the ornamental termination of part of a building such as a SPIRE or PEDIMENT.

fire to bake in a KILN, especially POTTERY and PORCELAIN. The process converts "raw" CLAY to a hard, usable material.

Flamboyant (arch.) the last phase of French Gothic ARCHITECTURE, from *c*1460, characterized by elaborate, flowing window TRACERY.

flint hard stone, mainly silica, used for making primitive tools and in building.

floral motif design based on flower forms, often used for textiles.

flourish curved ORNAMENT used in CALLIGRAPHY or MANUSCRIPT illumination.

flower painting still-life PAINTING of flowers, associated chiefly with Eastern art and the Dutch painters of the 17th century.

fluorescent having the property of absorbing radiation in the invisible, ultraviolet range, and emitting it as visible light. Fluorescent paint has been used in modern PAINTING for its vivid color and dramatic optical effect.

flute decoration of shallow vertical grooves in COLUMNS or on furniture; hence fluted, fluting.

Fluxus an informal grouping of international AVANT-GARDE artists centered around specific events and manifestos during the 1960s and 1970s. Inspired by some of the same ideas as DADA, they sought to challenge rigid defi[...] tions of art by engaging in dive[...] media such as PERFORMANCE A[...] VIDEO ART, and concerts.

flying buttress *see* BUTTRESS.

fold feature of drapery represen[...] in PAINTING or SCULPTURE, of[...] used to characterize a style; [...] MULDENSTIL.

foliated (arch.) covered with leaf [...]namentation.

folio 1 sheet of paper folded to fo[...] two leaves. **2** book of the larg[...] common size.

folk art NAIVE art of peasant or n[...] literate societies, including th[...] FINE ART and DECORATIVE ART.

font vessel, usually stone, in[...] CHURCH, used to hold the wa[...] for baptism.

foreground in PAINTING, the pl[...] nearest to the viewer.

foreshortening the use of the laws[...] PERSPECTIVE in art to make [...] individual form appear three[...]mensional.

forge 1 to shape metals by heat a[...] hammering. **2** the place where t[...] is done.

form the shape or appearance [...] artist gives to his or her subject[...]

formalism the tendency to adhere [...] conventional forms at the expe[...] of the subject matter.

format shape, style, or arrangeme[...] which may be repetitive or ster[...]typed.

formica laminated plastic used [...] modern furniture and SCULPTU[...]

forum Roman public meeting pla[...] "The Forum" refers to the ci[...] center of ancient Rome.

found object an object that is fou[...] not made, by the artist, and [...] then defined and displayed a[...] work of art; also known as [...] *objet trouvé* and associated w[...] SURREALISM and DADA.

free painting PAINTING done for [...] own sake, and not as decorat[...] of an object.

French chalk finely ground mag[...]sium silicate used with RESIN [...] LITHOGRAPHY to protect the im[...] from the acid when ETCHING [...] stone.

fresco (It.) MURAL PAINTING on fr[...] plaster; sometimes called *bu[...] fresco* ("true fresco") to distin[...]ish it from painting A SECCO, [...] dried plaster.

fresco secco (It.) misleading te[...] synonymous with PAINTING [...] SECCO.

frieze 1 part of an ENTABLATURE [...]tween the ARCHITRAVE and C[...]NICE, sometimes decorated [...] relief. **2** horizontal band of de[...]ration along the upper part o[...] wall or on furniture. **3** woo[...] cloth.

frit 1 mixture of calcified sand u[...] in making GLASS. **2** glasslike c[...]

position used in making PORCELAIN. 3 ground glass used in making POTTERY.

ontal 1 facade of, or covering for, the front of an ALTAR. 2 as an adjective, *frontal* describes images of the human figure or of deities in which the face is emphasized; hence frontality.

ontispiece 1 book illustration opposite title page. 2 (arch.) main FACADE, PEDIMENT, or BAY of a building.

ottage (Fr., "rubbing") the technique of placing paper over textured objects or surfaces and rubbing with a wax crayon or graphite to produce an image.

Chinese Bronze Age food vessel of c700 BC.

nctionalism the artistic theory that form should be determined by function, especially in ARCHITECTURE and the DECORATIVE ARTS, and that this will automatically produce objects that are aesthetically pleasing.

turism Italian artistic movement founded in 1909 by Filippo Marinetti, which exalted the modern world of machinery, speed, and violence.

G

ble (arch.) triangular part of a wall at the end of the roof ridge.

ble end (arch.) gable-shaped CANOPY over a door or window, or a gable-topped wall.

llery (arch.) 1 an upper story in a CHURCH above the AISLE. 2 in Elizabethan or Jacobean ARCHITECTURE, a long room, usually extending the full length of the house. 3 place where works of art are displayed.

lvanized iron iron coated with zinc to prevent rust.

rgoyle (arch.) waterspout projecting from the gutters of a building (especially in GOTHIC ARCHITECTURE), often in the form of an open-mouthed grotesque human or animal head.

rnet deep red GEM stone.

n precious or semiprecious stone used in jewelry and DECORATIVE objects.

nji eponymous hero of a Japanese novel, *The Tales of Genji*, written by Lady Murasaki c AD 1000.

nre 1 style, type. 2 PAINTING of scenes of daily life, popularized by 17th-century Dutch painters.

ometric abstraction loose and somewhat inaccurate term for ABSTRACT art in which the image is composed of nonrepresentational geometric shapes. It has been used of various artists and movements, including the SUPREMATISTS, Piet Mondrian, and Ben Nicholson.

Geometric style Greek style of decoration, flourishing from c900 to c725 BC, based on linear and angular shapes.

gesso (It.) name used for any mixture of an inert white PIGMENT with glue, used as a GROUND for PAINTING; strictly, a mixture in which the inert pigment is calcium sulfate. *Gesso grosso* is coarse gesso made from sifted Plaster of Paris, used for the first ground layer in medieval Italian panel paintings. *Gesso sottile* is fine crystalline gypsum, made by slaking Plaster of Paris in excess water.

gestural art the type of GEOMETRIC ABSTRACTION that emphasizes brushwork and the artist's movements.

giant order (arch.) COLUMN or PILASTER that extends over more than one story of a building; also known as colossal order.

gilding the coating of a surface with GOLD LEAF; hence gilded.

gilt silver or other METAL, decorated with GOLD LEAF.

giornata (It.) the area of work in MURAL or MOSAIC that could be finished in one day. In FRESCO PAINTING, it refers to the area of INTONACO applied each day. In true fresco, the joins of the *giornate* are usually visible.

glass material produced by fusing silica with an alkaline flux, e.g. potash or soda, by heat.

glass fiber *see* FIBERGLASS.

glass painting technique of decorating GLASS, not very clearly distinguished from glass enameling, although it may be more transparent and smoother. Early glass PAINTING was not FIRED, and therefore not permanent.

glaze 1 transparent layer of paint applied over another; light passes through and is reflected back, modifying or intensifying the underlayer. 2 vitreous layer made from silica, applied to POTTERY as decoration or to make it watertight.

glazing 1 process of applying glaze. 2 window design or construction.

gloria aureole or NIMBUS around the head of a deity, or a head ORNAMENT representing this.

glyptic art term usually used for SCULPTURE in which the design is incised, sometimes to produce an image for CASTING A SEAL.

golden section geometrical proportion, usually expressed as a finite line divided so that the shorter length bears the same relation to the longer as the longer does to the whole. Originally thought to be a naturally harmonious and pleasing relationship.

gold leaf gold, very thinly beaten so that it can be used for GILDING.

gorget piece of armor to protect the throat.

gorgoneion (Greek) representation of the Gorgon's head.

Gospel lectionary volume containing the four Gospels.

Gothic the last period of medieval art and ARCHITECTURE. Early Gothic usually refers to the period 1140–1200; High Gothic c1200–50; late Gothic from 1250. *Gothic* was used in the RENAISSANCE as a pejorative adjective for medieval ARCHITECTURE.

gouache 1 opaque WATERCOLOR paint. 2 a work executed in the gouache MEDIUM.

gradual 1 verses sung or recited immediately after the epistle at Mass. 2 a book of the choral parts of the Mass.

graffiti (It.) DRAWINGS or words scribbled in random fashion on a wall.

grande machine (Fr.) phrase meaning literally "great work" or composition, used for PAINTINGS of monumental construction.

granite very hard crystalline rock, much used in building.

granulation the decoration of metalwork, particularly gold and jewelry, with a pattern of tiny balls.*

graphic related to DRAWING or engraving; vividly descriptive.

graphic art broad term for techniques of illustration on paper, particularly in black and white or monochrome, such as DRAWING, ENGRAVING, LITHOGRAPHY.

graphic design the art of combining images and text to convey a message and a visual impression, e.g. book design, magazine design, and POSTER design.

graphics design or decoration, including PHOTOGRAPHY, associated with typographic work and illustration.

graphite crystalline form of CARBON, used in PENCILS.

grattage (Fr., "scraping") technique used by 20th-century artists in which an upper layer of paint is partially scraped away to reveal the contrasting under layer.

Greek cross cross with arms of equal length, often used as an architectural ground plan.

Greek orders of architecture *see* DORIC, IONIC, CORINTHIAN, and ORDERS.

Greek vases range of pots of different sizes, used for different purposes, most of which were often decorated if not painted.*

greenstone nephrite (a variety of JADE) or similar types of stone containing feldspar.

grid-plan term used in town planning to denote a right-angled

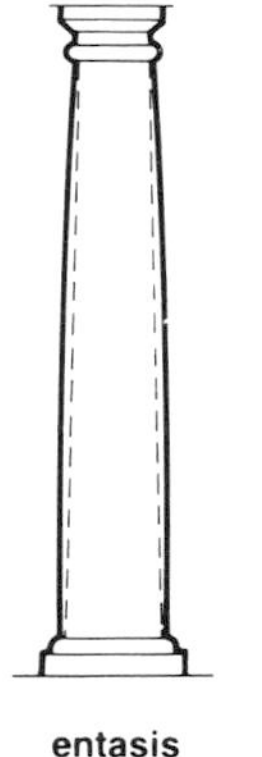

entasis

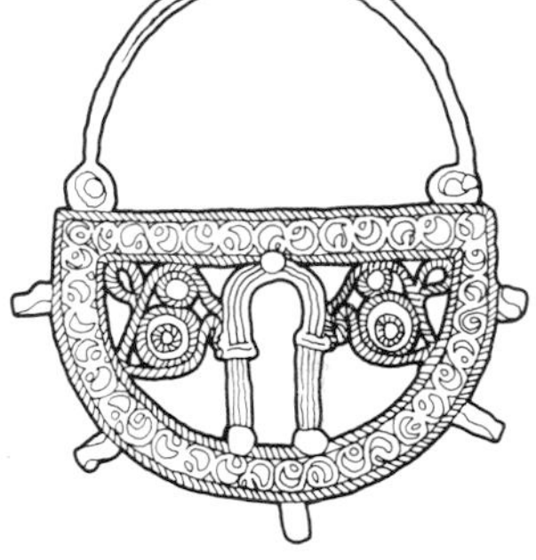

filigree

granulation

grotesque

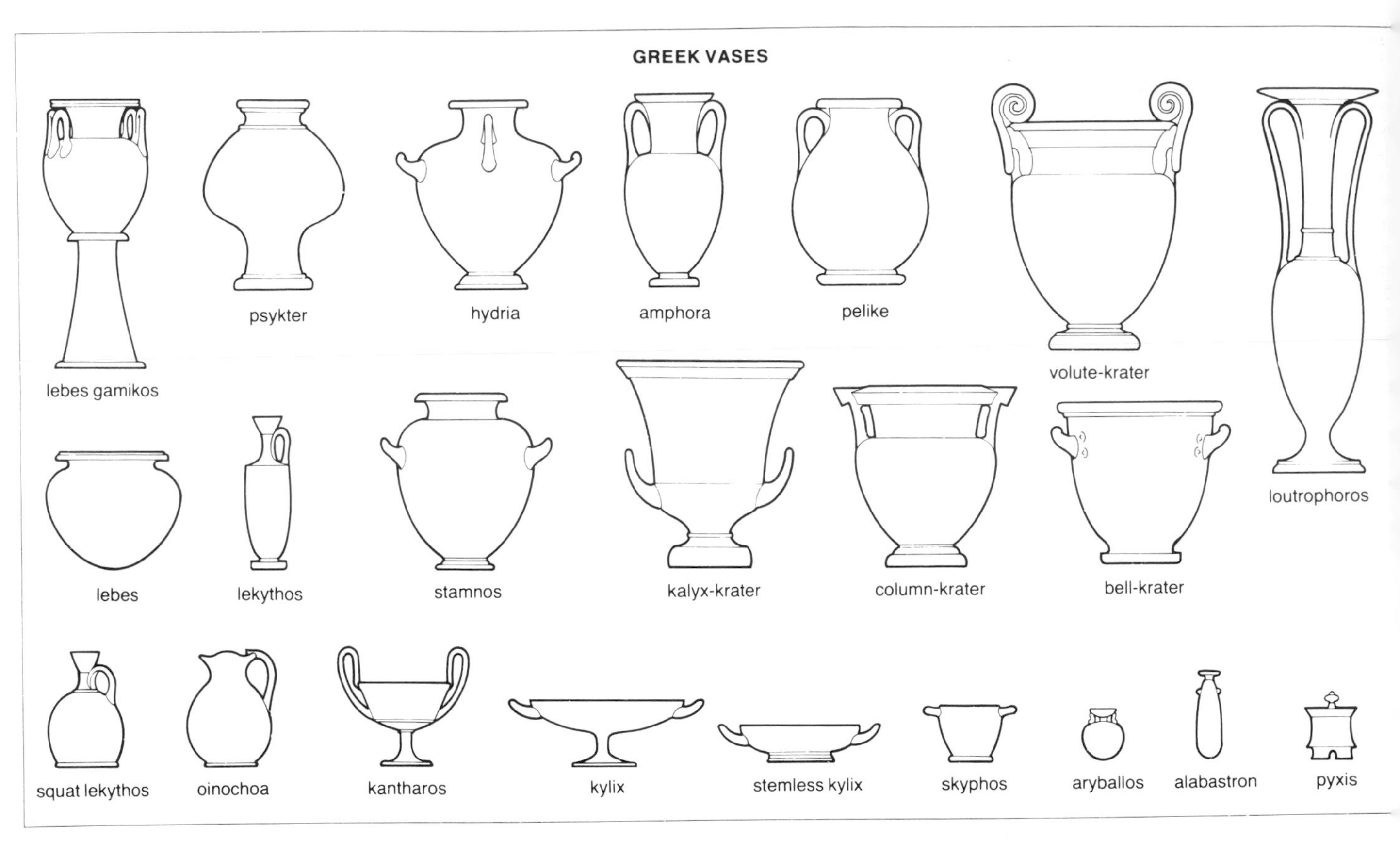

latticelike layout, imposed regardless of the terrain. It is thought to have originated in Greece in the 5th century BC.

griffin mythological creature with an eagle's head and wings and a lion's body.

grisaille technique of monochrome PAINTING in shades of gray, used as UNDERPAINTING or to imitate the effect of RELIEF.

groin (arch.) ARCH supporting VAULT *(see* VAULT CONSTRUCTION), or the intersection of two barrel vaults.

grotesque fanciful ORNAMENT, based on animals, fruit, flowers, and human forms; found in Roman buildings and reused during the RENAISSANCE; also known as *grotesquerie* and *grotteschi.**

grotto artificially constructed cave, often a feature of landscaped parks and gardens.

ground 1 synonym for BACKGROUND. **2** layer of preparation on a support to receive paint. **3** in ETCHING, the acid-resistant material spread over the metal plate before the design is etched. **4** in POTTERY, the CLAY forming the body of a vessel on which a design is executed.

groundline base on which a geometrical design or pattern is constructed, e.g. in Greek vase PAINTING.

ground plan (arch.) plan of building as seen from above.

guild medieval form of professional association that regulated standards of craftsmanship and commercial activity.

Gulistan (Persian) literally, "the Place of Flowers", the title of one of the two works by the 13th-century poet Sa'di.

gypsum chemically, calcium sulfate dihydrate, an inert white material used to make PLASTER of Paris and CEMENT. Varieties of gypsum include ALABASTER; *see* GESSO.

H

haematite red iron oxide, naturally occurring as an ore; the source of red-brown earth PIGMENTS.

Hafiz one of the great Persian lyric poets; he lived from *c*1325 to 1389/90 and worked mainly in Hiraz. His compositions were often illustrated.

haiga Japanese PAINTING illustrating a HAIKU poem.

haiku Japanese poem of three lines and 17 syllables, developed from the 17th century.

half-tone tone in DRAWING, PAINTING, or in a screen pattern for reproduction; between the darkest and the lightest.

half-tone process printing process using dots to indicate different tones and densities.

hall church (arch.) CHURCH with a NAVE and AISLES that are about the same height.*

hallmark official mark for gold, silver, and platinum, to indicate the standard of purity.

halo circle of light surrounding head of saint or divinity; associated with Christian art although it dates back to ancient Greece and Egypt; *see* NIMBUS.

hamam (or *hammam)* in Islamic ARCHITECTURE, the public baths or bath house, usually DOMED.

Happening spontaneous event or display; a feature of American and Western European art since the 1960s.

hard edged 1 in PAINTING, term coined in 1959 to describe ABSTRACT (but not geometric) painting, using large, flat areas of color with precise edges. **2** linear style; the opposite of SFUMATO.

hatching DRAWING technique that uses closely spaced parallel lines to indicate toned areas. When crossed by other lines in the opposite direction, it is known as cross-hatching.

Heian period of Japanese art, from AD 784 to 1185.

Hellenic Greek culture of the 11th century BC to 323 BC.

Hellenistic Greek culture after Alexander the Great (from 323 BC) to the late 1st century BC.

hemicircle semicircular figure.

hemp herbaceous plant produci[ng] tough fiber, used in making ro[pe] and canvas.

heraldry art or study of armor[ial] devices; hence heraldic.

herm pillar-sculpture that appear[ed] in Greece in the 6th century [BC,] usually in the form of a beard[ed] male figure.

hexagon plane figure with six si[des] and angles; hence hexagonal.

hieratic style in which certain fix[ed] types, often sacred, are repeate[d,] e.g. in Egyptian or Byzantine a[rt.] It may also be applied to any [art] that uses severe, rigid figu[res] rather than naturalistic ones.

hieroglyphs 1 picture writing, used by the Egyptians. **2** duri[ng] the RENAISSANCE the term was a[p]plied to emblems whose messa[ge] could be deciphered.

Hieronymite belonging to the or[der] of St Jerome.

high art art that strives to attain t[he] highest AESTHETIC and moral qu[al]ities in content and expression.

High Baroque the peak of the Itali[an] BAROQUE style, *c*1625–75.

highlight in PAINTING, a highlight [is] the brightest area, indicating li[ght] falling on a prominent plane [or] point; hence highlighting.

hiragana one of the Japanese s[ys]tems of syllabic writing, used [in] newspapers, etc.

historiated ARCHITECTURE or SCU[LP]TURE decorated with narrat[ive] subjects. A historiated initial is an initial in an ILLUMINATED MANUSCRIPT containing a narrative scene.*

story painting PAINTING with a subject that is a significant historical event—CLASSICAL, actual, or literary. From the 16th to the 19th century, it was more highly esteemed than other forms of painting, especially by the ACADEMIES.

orizon the line at which sky and earth appear to meet.

ours in the Christian Church, prayers to be said at set times of day.

u a Chinese Bronze Age storage vessel.

ydria a Greek pottery water vessel; *see* GREEK VASES.

ydrodynamic concerning the forces acting on or produced by liquid.

ygroscopic having the ability to readily take up and retain water from the atmosphere.

I

on (Greek, "image", "portrait") in Byzantine, Greek, and Russian Orthodox church art, the representation of Christ or the Virgin, or saints, in MOSAIC or PAINTING; tending to be stereotyped or HIERATIC; hence iconic.

onoclasm (Greek, "image breaking") widespread destruction of religious images, especially in the Byzantine Empire during the 8th and 9th centuries; hence iconoclast, iconoclastic.

onography the identification of subject matter in works of art; hence iconographic.

onology the interpretation of subject matter in works of art.

onostasis in Russian or Byzantine churches, the screen on which ICONS are placed.

eal art art of various periods that is based on the artist's conception rather than visual perception, e.g. the art of the High RENAISSANCE, or of 17th-century CLASSICISM.

eated imagined, conceived.

eogram symbol, e.g. Chinese writing, which expresses an idea without actually expressing the sound of its name.

iom characteristic, local language or style of art.

nudi (It.) nude figures.

uminated manuscript handwritten book on VELLUM or PARCHMENT, usually medieval, decorated with miniature PAINTING, borders, and DECORATIVE capital letters.

usionism the use of optical and perspectival principles to create the illusion of painted objects being three dimensional; hence illusionist, illusionistic.

imagery collection of images or forms giving expression to the artist's idea of objects or people.

impasto thick mass of paint or pastel; hence impasted.

Impressionism 19th-century French art movement, from 1874. Various artists such as Pissarro, Monet, Renoir, and Sisley were linked by their common interest in capturing immediate visual impressions and an emphasis on light and color; hence IMPRESSIONIST; Impressionistic.

incised line line cut into the surface of an object; used in CERAMICS as a decoration, or in PAINTING, when it is made in the GROUND layer, as a guide for painting.

indulgence the remission of a sin by the Roman Catholic Church.

industrial design the art of designing manufactured products, taking into account both function and appearance.

inert pigment white PIGMENTS of low refractive index, therefore poor hiding power, e.g. GYPSUM, CHALK, aluminum hydroxide. They may be used in preparing GROUNDS, as EXTENDERS in paint, or as the substrate on which a LAKE PIGMENT is precipitated.

infilling (arch.) area of stone filling a window or ARCH, from which TRACERY is usually cut.

ink fluid for writing or DRAWING; used also in printing processes.

ink box box containing solid block of ink; used for Eastern drawing and CALLIGRAPHY when mixed with water.

ink painting Japanese and Chinese PAINTING technique, using ink in the same way as WATERCOLOR.

inlay the decoration of furniture, POTTERY, METALWORK, etc., by inserting patterns of wood, stone, etc., into the body of the object so that the surface is level.

Installation art an art form that emerged in the 1960s; the artist creates and installs an entire environment where viewers can experience and interact with the work.

intaglio decoration produced by cutting into a surface, used in ENGRAVING, ETCHING, GEM carving.

intarsia (It.) the decoration of wood with INLAY work, especially in 15th-century Italy.

interior design the art of planning the configuration and furnishings of an architectural interior.

International Gothic since the 19th century described the style of art prevalent from *c*1375–1425, balanced between naturalistic and idealistic values and characterized by delicate, rich coloring.

International style an influential style of ARCHITECTURE beginning in the 1920s, characterized by strict geometry and a lack of ornamentation. Major architects working in this style included Le Corbusier and Mies van der Rohe.

intimisme (Fr.) French GENRE PAINTING of domestic, intimate interiors, such as the work of Pierre Bonnard and Édouard Vuillard; hence *intimiste*.

intonaco (It.) the smooth layer of LIME plaster that receives the paint in FRESCO PAINTING.

Ionic the second CLASSICAL order of Greek ARCHITECTURE; *see* ORDERS OF ARCHITECTURE.

isocephaly characteristic of Greek CLASSICAL art whereby figures in a group are all shown at the same height, regardless of distance or recession.

Italianate style 1 in an Italian manner. **2** (arch.) the adaptation of Italian RENAISSANCE palace styles, especially so in the U.S. *c*1840–65.

J

jade very hard stone, which may be blue, green, white, or brown; highly prized in Chinese art for carvings and jewelry. It is composed of calcium and magnesium, with sodium or aluminum.

Jagged style (or *Zackenstil*) sharp, hard-edged style of drapery folds, characteristic of German ROMANESQUE art.

jamb vertical side of a doorway or fireplace.

Japonisme the influence of *Japonaiserie*—Japanese imports, e.g. prints and furniture, brought to Europe in the mid 19th century—on European PAINTING.

Jasper ware type of stoneware POTTERY introduced by Josiah Wedgwood in 1774. Originally pure white but sometimes stained with cobalt oxide to produce "Wedgwood blue".

joiner furniture maker.

journeyman under the medieval GUILD system, a craftsman who had completed his apprenticeship but had not become a MASTER, and therefore worked for a daily wage as a master's assistant.

Jugendstil (Ger.) German term for ART NOUVEAU.

Junk sculpture ASSEMBLAGE SCULPTURE produced since the 1950s, using scrap materials and cast-off everyday objects.

K

kabuki popular Japanese theater of the 17th century, often depicted in prints.

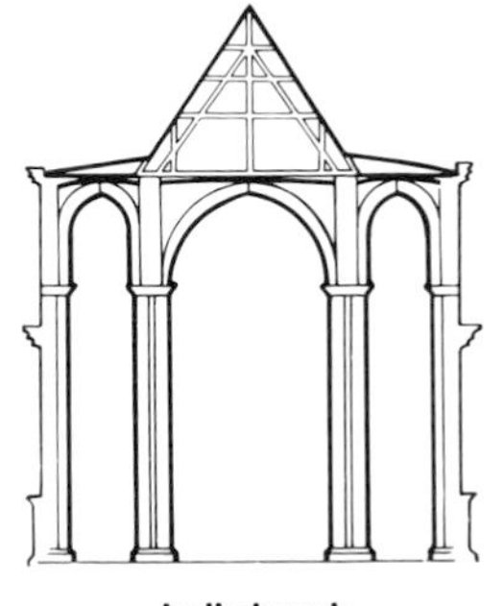

hall church
section through aisles and nave

historiated initial

key design
an example

Kalighat Indian temple in Calcutta, built in 1809 and dedicated to the Buddhist deity Kali.

kalyx-krater Greek bowl for mixing wine and water; *see* GREEK VASES.

Kano school of Japanese PAINTING; began with the 15th-century work of Kano Masanobu and flourished in Kyoto until the 19th century.

kaolin (Ch., "clay") substance used in the manufacture of hard-paste PORCELAIN and sometimes in the GROUNDS of PAINTINGS. Chemically it is hydrated silicate of ALUMINUM.

karst an underground region where cavities and drainage result from the dissolution of rock.

keros flaring-topped tumbler shape found in PRE-COLUMBIAN pottery and goldwork.

key design geometrical pattern of repeated horizontal and vertical straight lines, found in ancient Greek art.*

keystone (arch.) central wedge-shaped block of an ARCH.

Khamsa "The Quintuplet", the title of the major collection of poems by the great Romantic epic Persian poet Nizami (*b.* *c*1141–1209).

kiln oven in which POTTERY is fired.

kinetic SCULPTURE designed to move and thus produce optical effects; first made in the 1920s, but most popular from 1960 onward.

kitsch (Ger.) mass-produced vulgar articles of the kind manufactured for souvenirs; it has become a pejorative term for anything thought to be in flamboyant bad taste. An ironic embrace of kitsch has characterized the work of many POP and POST-MODERN artists.

knop DECORATIVE swelling in the stem of a glass or cup.

kouroi *see* KOUROS.

kouros Archaic Greek statue of standing youth (pl. KOUROI).

krater ancient Greek storage vessel; different shapes were used for water and wine: *see* COLUMN KRATER and KALYX-KRATER.

Kuan yin *see* BODHISATTVA.

Kufic script angular, square type of Arabic script; sometimes found in DECORATIVE ROMANESQUE and GOTHIC art. *See* NASHKI

Kunstschau (Ger., "Art show") 1908 exhibition by artists who had resigned from the Vienna SECESSION, including Oskar Kokoschka and Gustav Klimt.

kylix shallow, two-handled Greek drinking cup; *see* GREEK VASES.

lacquer a waterproof resinous VARNISH that can be highly polished. True lacquer is obtained from the tree *Rhus verniciflua* found in China and Japan. Another type is obtained from the lac insect, *Coccus lacca*, used in shellac, a commercial polish preparation. Modern commercial "lacquers" are coating materials that dry by the evaporation of solvent.

lake pigment PIGMENT produced by precipitating an organic dye onto an INERT PIGMENT (known as the substrate). Dyes must be treated in this way; otherwise they would dissolve in the MEDIUM.

lancet (arch.) tall, narrow, acutely pointed window, a feature of Early English ARCHITECTURE (13th century).

Land art the creation of works of art in the landscape or emerging from the forms of the landscape itself. These works are also called EARTH ART or earthworks.

landscape 1 PAINTING, DRAWING, or ENGRAVING in which the scenery is the principal subject. **2** scenic areas of a painting or DRAWING.

landscape architecture design or planning of landscape elements; synonymous with landscape gardening.

lantern 1 (arch.) small structure or TURRET on top of a DOME, with windows to allow light to enter.* **2** lamp.

lapis lazuli deep-blue semiprecious stone, used for jewelry, and from which the PIGMENT ultramarine is extracted.

La Tène style style of DECORATIVE ART that appeared *c*5th century BC in Europe and was fully developed in Celtic art of the pre-Roman period; the name is derived from a site in Switzerland where metal objects and weapons in this style have been found.

lay-in initial stage of traditional oil PAINTING technique, where a DRAWING is "laid in" with a MONOCHROME to produce a full tonal design.

layout design or plan; particularly used in ARCHITECTURE, garden design, and GRAPHIC DESIGN.

lead heavy, bluish-gray malleable METAL, used as a DRAWING material, in building, pottery GLAZES, printing, and SCULPTURE.

leather animal skin that is made flexible by dressing and tanning; used for clothing, bags, bottles, footwear, etc.

leitmotif (Ger.) MOTIF that recurs throughout a design and is associated with a particular person or meaning.

lekythos (Greek) ancient Greek oil jug; *see* GREEK VASES.

Leonardesque in the style of Leonardo da Vinci.

letter-cutter someone who makes the punches for type founding.

li Chinese Bronze Age food vessel, formed of three cone-shaped containers merged together at the top.

lierne rib (arch.) short RIB connecting the intersections of weight-bearing ribs in GOTHIC vaulting; *see* VAULT CONSTRUCTION.

life drawing DRAWING from the live human model.

light 1 brightness or illumination, especially in PAINTING. **2** (arch.) division of a window indicated by vertical MULLIONS.

lignin the material of which the cell walls of wood are composed.

lime calcium oxide used for making PLASTER.

limestone lime carbonate rock of various types, much used for building.

limner 1 obsolete term for an illuminator of medieval MANUSCRIPTS. **2** 16th-century term for a miniaturist or portraitist. **3** 18th- and 19th-century term for an untutored, NAIVE portraitist.

linear artistic style that emphasizes lines and contours; hence linearity and linearism.

linear perspective method of indicating spatial recession in a picture by placing objects in a series of receding planes; parallel lines receding from the onlooker's viewpoint will appear to meet at a VANISHING POINT.

line engraving 1 the art or process of hand-engraving in INTAGLIO and copper plate, using a BURIN. **2** a PRINT taken from such a plate.

linen cloth woven from flax.

lino cut PRINT produced by carving a design into a block of linoleum.

lintel (arch.) horizontal beam above a door or window.

literati 1 Chinese scholarly or literary PAINTING style, developed from the 10th century. **2** literary or scholarly people.

lithography printing method in which a design is drawn on stone with a greasy crayon and then inked.

local color in PAINTING, the color of an object seen against a white background in daylight, not influenced by cast shadows. Alternatively it may be defined as the color natural to each part, independent of the general color scheme or light and shade.

loggetta (It.) (arch.) small ARCADE or open GALLERY.

loggia (It.) (arch.) covered COLONNADE or ARCADE, open on at least one side.

London Group group of English artists who were influenced by POST-IMPRESSIONISM, and who exhibited together from 1913.

lost wax *see* CIRE PERDUE.

low life tavern scenes, etc., depicted in GENRE PAINTING.

low relief *see* RELIEF.

lozenge (arch.) diamond shape wi four equal sides.

luminosity appearance of reflectir light, or ability to do so.

lunette semicircular window, or PAINTING or MOTIF of that shape.

lunula crescent-shaped ORNAMEN particularly from Bronze A Europe.

lux unit of illuminance expressed lumen per square meter. (The ill minance of a surface is the lum nous flux [quantity of light p second] falling on a unit area.)

Lyrical abstraction term coined the French painter Georg Mathieu in 1947 to describe t more DECORATIVE style of *L'A Informel* and ABSTRACT EXPRE SIONISM.

lyricism an intensely poetic, DECOR TIVE quality.

M

macerate to break up and soften material in water.

madrasa Muslim school or college

Maenad mythological female fo lower of Bacchus.

Maestá (It.) representation of t Madonna and Child enthron and surrounded by a host of a gels and saints.

malachite green copper mineral us for jewelry and in the DECORATI ARTS. Chemically, it is natur basic copper carbonate. It is al the source of a green PIGMENT.

mandala circular figure, symbolic the universe in several religion particularly Buddhism.

mandorla (It., "almond") in ear Christian art, an almond-shap outline around a divine persona (especially Christ) showing hi endowed with divine light.* was abandoned in the RENA SANCE.

manganese metallic element or met oxide; since the 19th century has been the source of blue and v olet PIGMENTS and used in CERA ICS to produce a purple color.

maniera (It.) according to the wr ings of Georgio Vasari, the "st ishness" associated with the art 16th-century Italy. *Bella manie* was considered the highest artis expression of the age, epitomiz in the work of Raphael a Michelangelo.

manikin simple jointed model of t human figure, used by the artist a model for drapery, etc., in t absence of a sitter.

maniple ecclesiastical vestment the form of a strip, hanging fro the left arm.

annered using the exaggerated characteristics of any style. Before the 1930s the term was often synonymous with Italian MANNERISM.
annerism artistic style originating in Italy *c*1520–90 that tends to employ distortion of figures and emphasize an emotional content; hence Mannerist.
an of sorrows the image of Christ, wounded and wearing the crown of thorns. It was a popular theme in the Italian RENAISSANCE and in late medieval German art.
anuscript handwritten or typed (but not printed) book.
aquette small-scale model made by a sculptor or a stage designer as a preliminary three-dimensional "sketch" for the final work.
arble type of LIMESTONE used since ANTIQUITY for SCULPTURE and building. It occurs in various colors, from pure white to black, often veined.
arbling DECORATIVE effect produced by staining or PAINTING in streaks to resemble MARBLE.
archigian literally, "of the marches" or border country; often used to refer to the East Italian Marches.
arine PAINTING or DRAWING of a sea subject.
arl CLAY and LIME soil, applied to the ground as fertilizer.
arouflage (Fr.) the gluing of a canvas to a flat, rigid support; a method employed by artists and in conservation.
ask a replica of the face, whether for theatrical purposes or as a PORTRAIT made after someone's death.
asonry stonework.
asque theatrical or musical amateur entertainment, with or without dialogue, popular during the 16th and 17th centuries.
ass term generally used figuratively of PAINTING and SCULPTURE that has the appearance of weight, volume, and solidity.
aster in the medieval GUILD system, one who was entitled and able to practice his art on his own.
aster mason skilled, senior mason.
aster mountain landscape style of Chinese landscape PAINTING of the late 10th century, in which small figures and rocks in the foreground are dominated by a massive mountain in the background.
aster painter eminent or highly skilled painter who employs assistants and is qualified to teach students.
asterpiece originally a test piece of work done by the medieval apprentice in order to qualify as a MASTER of his GUILD. The term is now used more freely to mean a work of outstanding importance or quality.
mat 1 small carpet. **2** non-reflective.
matière (Fr.) material, in the sense of the substance of which something is made.
mat-painted ware pottery decorated mainly with linear patterns in a MAT, manganese paint; chiefly found in mainland Greece *c*1900–1550 BC.
matrix MOLD, usually of COPPER, for CASTING printing type and other METAL objects.
mausoleum (arch.) **1** the tomb of Mausolus of Caria at Halicarnassus, *c*350 BC. **2** large, imposing structure erected as a tomb.
meander motif repetitive ornamental pattern of lines, in a SCROLL or KEY DESIGN.
medal small metal commemorative plaque, usually an award.
medallion 1 large MEDAL, usually bearing a PORTRAIT. **2** prominent oval or circular MOTIF. **3** the central motif of a Persian carpet.
medium generally, the means or material with which an artist expresses himself. In PAINTING, the medium is the liquid in which PIGMENT is mixed and thinned, e.g. linseed oil.
megalith large monumental stone.
megaron 1 ceremonial hall in Mycenean palace. **2** Mycenaean or Minoan dwelling.
mensuration mathematical rules for determining measurements.
mercedarian from the Spanish *merced*, "market".
Mesolithic period Middle Stone Age, in European history dated *c*10,000 to 3000 BC, between the Paleolithic and Neolithic periods.
metal 1 solid crystalline substance, usually opaque, ductile, dense, e.g. gold, silver, COPPER, iron. **2** molten GLASS, in glassmaking processes.
metalwork objects shaped from METAL.
metamorphic having, or suggesting, the ability to change shape.
Metaphysical painting (It., *Pittura Metafisica)* movement of *c*1915–18 associated with the painter Giorgio de Chirico. Paintings in this style juxtapose enigmatic imagery, often in empty streets or landscapes.
métier (Fr.) subject in which an artist specializes.
metope (arch.) space between TRIGLYPHS in a Doric frieze *(see* ORDERS OF ARCHITECTURE).
mezzanine (arch.) intermediate level between two floors.
mezzotint 1 method of copper ENGRAVING. **2** a PRINT produced by this method.
mica mineral, chiefly composed of aluminum silicate.
Middle Ages in European history, the period between the end of CLASSICAL ANTIQUITY and the end of the RENAISSANCE (5th–15th century AD).
mihrab niche in the QIBLA wall of a MOSQUE, indicating the direction of Mecca.
millefiori (It.) pattern formed in glassmaking by fusing rods of colored GLASS in a bundle and then slicing across the bundle to show a cross section.
mimbar (arch.) PULPIT in a MOSQUE.
minaret (arch.) slender tower of a MOSQUE from which worshipers are called to prayer.
Ming Chinese dynastic period, 1368–1644; the name is mainly associated with the fine CERAMICS produced at that time.
miniature very small piece of work, such as the illustration in a medieval MANUSCRIPT. During the RENAISSANCE and the 18th and 19th centuries, the term was more specifically applied to small PORTRAITS painted on ivory.
Minimal art modern art that rejects texture, subject, atmosphere, etc., and reduces forms and colors to the simplest; hence Minimalism, Minimalist.
minster a monastic or collegiate CHURCH.
mis-en-page typographical term meaning "making up"; generally, the LAYOUT or composition.
missal book containing all the texts of the Mass, sometimes illustrated.
miter bishop's headdress.
mixed media the combination of different materials in the same work, sometimes including PERFORMANCE.
mobile KINETIC SCULPTURE probably originated by Alexander Calder in 1932; the sculpture is hung from wires so that it is moved by air currents.
Möbius strip a mathematical figure: the surface formed by joining the ends of a rectangle after twisting it through 180°, i.e. producing a single continuous surface and continuous curved edge.
model 1 figure to be copied, e.g. in life DRAWING: PATTERN. **2** to shape in three dimensions, for example in CLAY. By extension the word also means to paint or draw something that is given the appearance of three-dimensionality, e.g. the human figure.
model book PATTERN BOOK used for reference by artists in the MIDDLE AGES; usually containing copies from existing works.
modeling 1 three-dimensional representation of objects. **2** the artist's depiction or grasp of solid form.

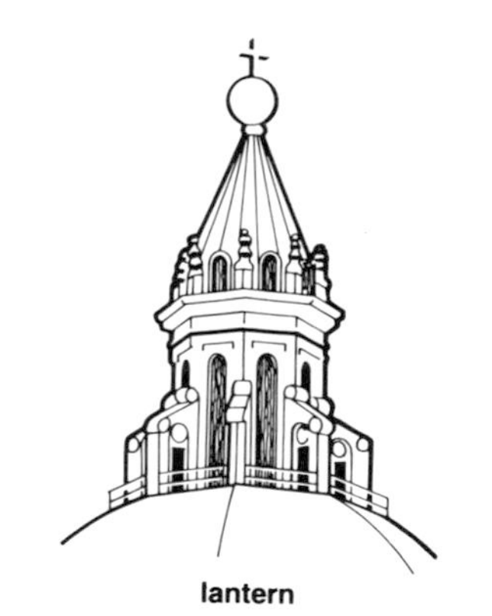
lantern
after the lantern of the duomo, Florence

mandorla

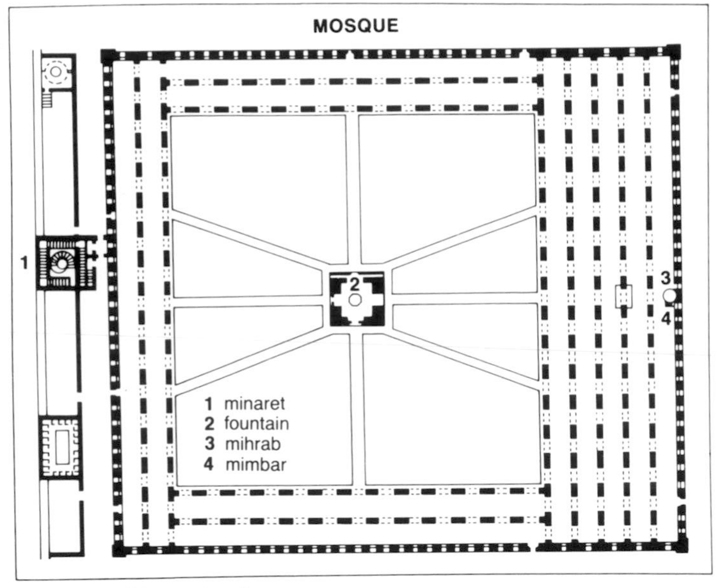

an example of the courtyard mosque,
the groundplan of the mosque of Ibn Tulun, Cairo, built 876–9

modello (It.) preliminary sketch, drawn or painted. Sometimes quite elaborate and occasionally done in competition for patronage or a COMMISSION.

modernism the theory of modern art that rejects past styles and promotes contemporary art as the true reflection of the age; hence modernist.

Modern Movement name derived from Nikolaus Pevsner's book *Pioneers of the Modern Movement* for the FUNCTIONALIST ARCHITECTURE and design of the 1920s and 1930s.

modular unit (arch.) prefabricated building component.

module standardized part used in the construction of ARCHITECTURE, furniture, etc., which can therefore be prefabricated.

moiré TEXTILE or METAL textured to produce a rippled effect.

mold shape or pattern in which a cast image is reproduced; hence molded, to mold.

molding a strip of stone or wood, plain or decorated, used to ornament a wall or piece of furniture.

Momoyama period of Japanese art from 1573 to 1615.

monel an alloy of 25–30 percent COPPER and 60–70 percent nickel, used as an acid-resist material.

monochrome picture done in various tones of one color only, especially black and white; hence monochromatic.

monogram two or more letters of an artist's name, as a signature.*

monotype printing process that takes an impression from a METAL or GLASS plate, producing only one PRINT of each design, which must then be redrawn.

monstrance in CHURCH, a vessel in which the Host is displayed, on the ALTAR or in procession.

monumental 1 connected with, or serving as, a monument. **2** used figuratively of PAINTINGS and other art forms to mean imposing or massive.

Moorish belonging to the culture of the northwest African Muslim peoples of mixed Berber and Arab origin.

morphography the scientific description of form.

morphology study of the form of animals, plants, or language.

mortar building material made from LIME, sand, PLASTER of Paris, and fibrous materials mixed with water, which sets by hydration or carbonation. The term may refer to this mixture in the wet state, or to any similar mixture used as a cement for stone or brick.

mosaic design formed from small pieces of stone, glass, marble, etc.

Mosan art art of the 12th and 13th centuries in the valley of the River Meuse, which flows from northeast France to the Low Countries; it produced the first great school of ENAMEL painters using the CHAMPLEVÉ technique.

mosque Muslim place of worship.*

mother-of-pearl hard, pearly substance forming inner layer of mollusk shells and used in DECORATIVE METALWORK, jewelry, and inlaid furniture.

motif a repeated distinctive feature in a design.*

mouvementé (Fr.) animated, dynamic.

mucilages complex organic compounds of vegetable origin, with gluelike properties, used as an adhesive; hence mucilaginous, pertaining to mucilages.

mud brick (arch.) brick made from unbaked CLAY.

Mughal art of the courts of the Muslim rulers in India, 1526–1707; also spelled Mogul and Moghal.

Muldenstil (Ger., "troughed style") style of GOTHIC drapery in which the folds form a trough pattern.

mullion (arch.) the vertical member that divides a window into two or more LIGHTS; *see* TRACERY.

multiple a kind of art produced since the 1960s, theoretically made in unlimited numbers as consumer articles; the opposite of the traditional "limited edition".

Munich Secession withdrawal in 1892 of German artists in Munich from the traditional institutions; it remained relatively conservative, and was followed by the VIENNA SECESSION (1897) and the BERLIN SECESSION (1908).

mural 1 concerning walls. **2** picture painted on a wall.

muse in Greek and Roman mythology, nine goddesses who inspired poetry, music, etc., and are identified in PAINTING by their various attributes.

mythological painting PAINTING of subjects chosen from Greek and Roman CLASSICAL mythology, popular from the 15th century to the 19th.

N

Nabis (Fr., *Les Nabis*) group of French artists working from *c*1892 to 1899, influenced by Gauguin in their use of color and lightly exotic DECORATIVE effects. They included Pierre Bonnard, Jean-Édouard Vuillard, Félix Vallotton, and Paul Sérusier.

Nagasaki School 18th-century school of Japanese REALISM in PAINTING. It was very influential on modern painting.

naive the work, style, or art of untaught artists, usually crudely naturalistic.

Nanga School Japanese school of BUNJINGA or LITERATI PAINTING, active from the late 17th century to the late 19th.

naos synonym for CELLA.

narrative painting PAINTING that relates a story or incident, most popular during the Victorian period.

narthex (arch.) porch across the west end of a CHURCH, used by those not yet taking full communion, e.g. penitents.

nashki the flowing form of Arabic script (compare KUFIC).

natron the natural form of sodiu[m] carbonate; also known as sod[a] ash and used chiefly for POTTER[Y] GLAZES.

naturalism accurate, detailed repr[e]sentation of objects or scenes [a]s they appear, whether attractive [or] otherwise. The term was first use[d] of the 17th-century CARAVAGGIS[TI] (compare REALISM).

nave (arch.) main body or AISLE [of] CHURCH.

Nazarenes group of Germa[n] painters working in Rome in th[e] early 19th century; inspired b[y] Northern art of the 15th and ear[ly] 16th centuries.

neck-amphora Greek POTTERY sto[r]age jar; broader-lipped than th[e] ordinary AMPHORA.

necropolis cemetery, especially in th[e] ancient world.

Neoclassicism the late 18th-centu[ry] European and American sty[le] lasting from *c*1770 to 183[0,] which reacted against the wor[st] excesses of the BAROQUE and R[O]COCO, reviving the ANTIQUE. It im[]plies a return to CLASSICAL sourc[es] which imposed restraint and sim[]plicity on PAINTING and ARCHITE[C]TURE.

Neo-Expressionism term given to a[n] international art movement th[at] began in the 1960s and 1970s as [a] reaction against the perceive[d] stark, sterile nature of MINIMA[L]ISM and other purely ABSTRAC[T] movements. It was characterize[d] by large-scale, crudely drawn, ga[r]ishly colored canvases depicti[ng] violent or erotic subject matt[er.] Begun largely in Germany, in th[e] early 1980s it dominat[ed] American art.

Neo-Gothic revival of the GOTH[IC] style in 18th-century Englan[d,] especially in ARCHITECTURE.

Neo-Impressionism the developme[nt] of IMPRESSIONISM through Georg[es] Seurat's scientific analysis a[nd] treatment of color; *see* DIVISIO[N]ISM; POINTILLISM.

Neolithic period later Stone Ag[e,] *c*8000–1800 BC.

neon inert gas that emits light wh[en] an electric current passes throu[gh] it; neon lights have been used [in] modern SCULPTURE since t[he] 1950s.

Neo-Palladian *see* PALLADIAN.

Neo-Plasticism synonymous with [DE] STIJL. The term was coined by Pi[et] Mondrian for his type of GEOME[T]RIC ABSTRACTION, restrict[ed] to nonrepresentational horizon[tal] and vertical forms, primary co[l]ors, and black and white.

Neoplatonism philosophical and [re]ligious system, mixing Platon[ic] ideas and Eastern mysticis[m,] which developed from Alexand[ria] in the 3rd century AD.

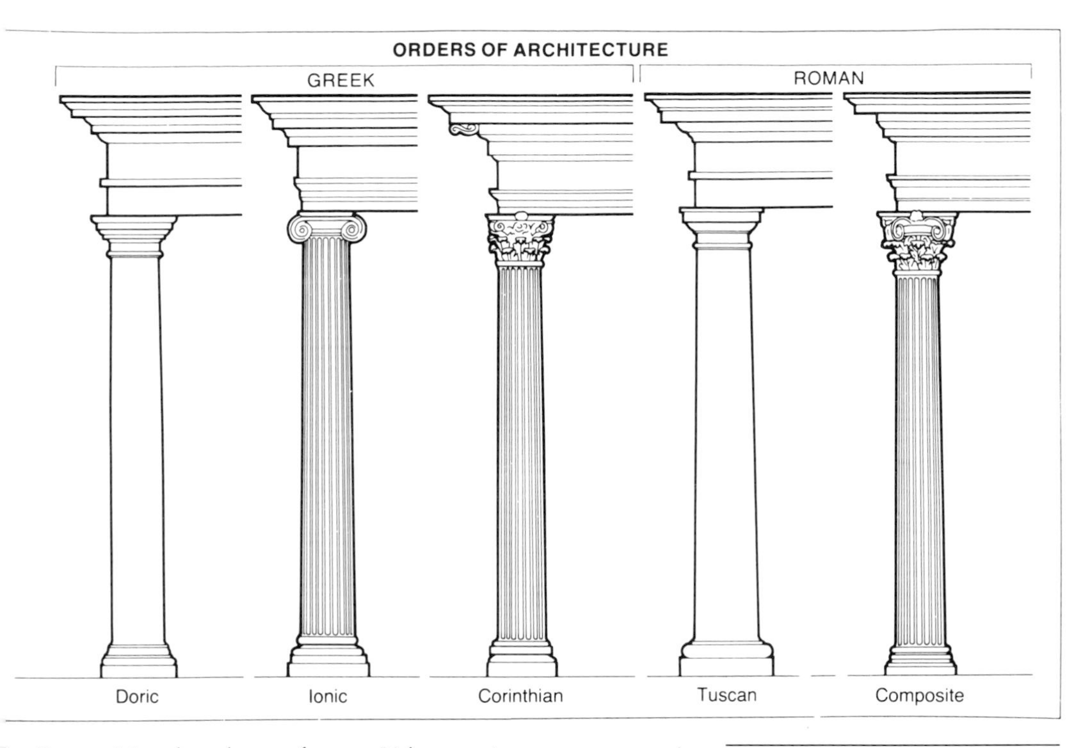

monograms

artists' monograms: top left Albrecht Dürer (1471–1528), top right Pieter Pourbus (*fl.* (1520–84), below left Max Klinger (1857–1920), below right John Tenniel (1820–1914)

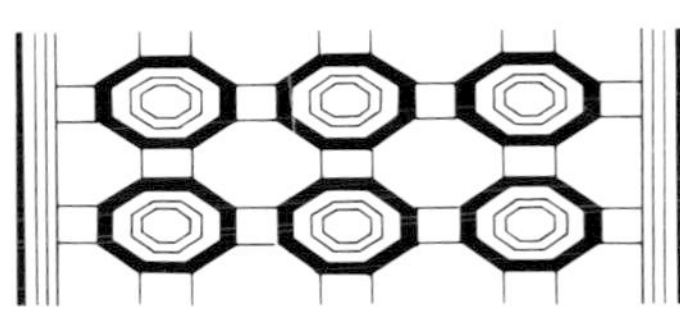

motif

four examples

eo-Romanticism broad term for several 20th-century European art movements that draw on mystical, dreamlike subjects; expressive, emotional forms; and SURREALISM.

ephrite variety of JADE; *see* GREENSTONE.

ereid in Greek mythology, a sea nymph.

et vault (arch.) GOTHIC vault in which the LIERNE RIBS form a net-like pattern; *see* VAULT CONSTRUCTION.

eue Künstlervereinigung (Ger., "New Artists' Association") founded in Munich in 1909 with Wassily Kandinsky as president, and influenced by the Munich JUGENDSTIL and FAUVISM. Kandinsky and Franz Marc later formed the BLAUE REITER group.

ew Bauhaus the BAUHAUS founded in Chicago by Laszlo Moholy-Nagy, which later became the Institute of Design.

ew English Art Club antiacademic, pro-IMPRESSIONIST art club founded in 1886. Its founder members included Walter Sickert and Wilson Steer.

ew Realism (or *Nouveau Réalisme*) term coined in 1960 by the French critic Pierre Restany for art derived partly from DADA and SURREALISM, which reacted against more ABSTRACT work, especially by using industrial and everyday objects to make JUNK art or SCULPTURE.

ew Secession a group of artists who broke away from Max Liebermann's BERLIN SECESSION in 1910 under the leadership of Max Pechstein to promote AVANT-GARDE art.

New York School the core of ABSTRACT EXPRESSIONISM in New York in the 1940s and early 1950s, including Jackson Pollock, Willem de Kooning, and Mark Rothko.

niche (arch.) recess in a wall, often containing a statue.

niello 1 black alloy of powdered silver, LEAD, COPPER, and sulfur, fused to METALWORK; especially popular during the RENAISSANCE in Italy. **2** silver plaque decorated with niello.

nimbus halo or light around a sacred image.*

niobid antique statuary of Niobe and her daughters. In Greek mythology, Niobe, the daughter of Tantalus, died weeping for her 12 children who were killed and was turned to stone.

Nizami Persian poet (1135–1203/17) whose works were frequently illuminated, especially his KHAMSA ("Quintet").

No or **Noh** traditional Japanese dance-drama with heroic theme.

nocturne night scene.

Nomad art name given to DECORATIVE ART of the 7th century BC, also known as ANIMAL STYLE.

Northern Renaissance non-Italian Western art of the period *c*1420–*c*1600.

nymphaeum (arch.) Roman "temple of the nymphs" or house of pleasure, often with statues.

O

obelisk (arch.) tall, four-sided free-standing PILLAR. It originated in Egypt as a solar symbol.*

objet trouvé (Fr.) *see* FOUND OBJECT.

oblate person dedicated to a monastery or religious work.

obsidian type of volcanic rock.

obverse the face of a coin or MEDAL showing the head or main design.

Oceanic art art of the South Pacific region.

ocher (or ochre) natural earth of silica and CLAY, colored by iron oxide. It may be yellow, red, or brown and is used as a PIGMENT.

octagon plane figure with eight sides and angles; hence octagonal.

oculus (arch.) the circular window at the west end of a CHURCH; it may also mean an illusionistic PAINTING of a window or circular opening.

œil de boeuf (Fr., "bull's eye") a small octagonal vestibule in the Palace of Versailles, lit by a small circular window; the name has been adopted for similar rooms elsewhere.

oeuvre (Fr.) the total output of an artist.

offset litho LITHOGRAPHIC technique in which ink is transferred from a plate to a rubber roller and then onto the paper.

oil viscous liquid of vegetable or mineral origin, used in PAINTING and printing. "An oil" or "oils" is often used as shorthand for OIL PAINTING.

nimbus

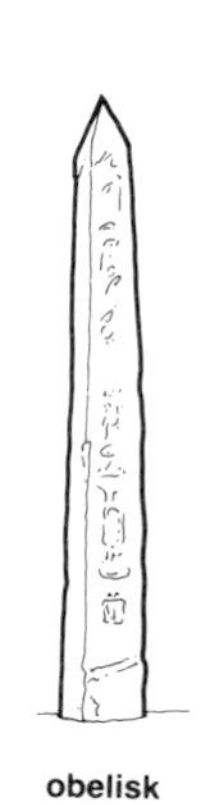

obelisk

oil painting PAINTING in an OIL MEDIUM, using linseed, walnut, or poppy oil.
oil sketch *see* SKETCH.
oinochoa ancient Greek vessel for dipping wine from the bowl and filling drinking cups. *See* GREEK VASES.
onyx variety of CHALCEDONY.
opaque impermeable to light; not TRANSPARENT or TRANSLUCENT.
Op art abbreviation of Optical art; 1960s movement in PAINTING in which the illusion of movement was created by the juxtaposition of contrasting geometrical shapes, tones, lines, and colors.
openwork lacy-patterned METALWORK of gold and silver threads (*see* FILIGREE). The term is also used for similarly patterned TEXTILES, lace, etc.
order arrangement, sequence.
orders of architecture the five CLASSICAL orders, each composed of a COLUMN, having a base, SHAFT, CAPITAL, and ENTABLATURE with ARCHITRAVE, FRIEZE, and CORNICE. There are three Greek orders: Doric, IONIC, and Corinthian. These were adapted by the Romans, who added Tuscan and Composite.*
ore naturally occurring mineral, in aggregate form from which metal is extracted.
organic 1 resembling or related to a living organism **2** (chemically) containing CARBON.
oriel (arch.) bay window on an upper story.
Orientalizing Greek style of art originating in the late 8th century BC in Corinth.
ornament 1 decoration or DECORATIVE object. **2** ecclesiastical accessories of worship, e.g. ALTAR, service book.
ornamented decorated, term used especially of three-dimensional objects.
Orphic Cubism term coined *c*1912 by Guillaume Apollinaire for the branch of CUBISM associated with Robert Delaunay, emphasizing color and the analysis of light and its connexion with nature; also known as Orphism.
orthogonal in LINEAR PERSPECTIVE, an orthogonal is a line apparently at right angles to the PICTURE PLANE, which will appear to meet a parallel line at the VANISHING POINT.
Ottoman Turkish dynasty founded in the early 14th century by Othman I. The name is also applied to the later Turkish Empire.
Ottonian art German art of the period 919–early 11th century, under the Ottonian emperors; notable for MANUSCRIPT illumination, BRONZE CASTING, MURAL PAINTING.
outline edge of shape; contour.
outsider art art made by people considered to be from outside conventional society, including the mentally ill.
oxide chemically, a binary compound with oxygen, i.e. oxygen and one other element, e.g. rust, which is iron oxide. Metal oxides have been used as PIGMENTS and in POTTERY GLAZES.

P

pagoda (arch.) Chinese or Indian sacred building or tower.
paint PIGMENT dispersed in MEDIUM.
painterly a term coined by the art historian Heinrich Wölfflin to describe one of two contrasting styles in PAINTING: LINEAR, which emphasizes contours; and painterly, which emphasizes color and tone; hence painterliness.
painting 1 process of applying paint. **2** object produced by applying paint to a flat support, e.g. a wall or canvas.
palanquin Eastern covered carrying litter.
Paleolithic period the oldest Stone Age culture in Europe, *c*30,000–10,000 BC.
palette 1 slab of wood, METAL, or glass used by the artist for mixing paint. **2** figuratively: the range of colors used by the artist. **3** in ancient Egypt, a carved or plain slab used by scribes or for grinding cosmetics.
palette knife flexible, spatula-shaped knife for mixing or applying thick, bodied paint.
palette knifing use of the palette knife for applying paint.
Palladian style English architectural style, from *c*1715, in imitation of the style of Andrea Palladio; a reaction against the BAROQUE in favor of the CLASSICAL; also called Neo-Palladian.
pallium 1 man's cloak worn by the ancient Greeks. **2** archbishop's vestment. **3** ALTAR cloth.
palmette ornamental palm-leaf MOTIF.
Panathenaic term describing Greek vases made for or acquired at the *Panathenaia*, the national festival of Athens celebrating the union of Attica under Theseus.
pandit Hindu learned in Sanskrit, philosophy, and religion; also spelled pundit.
panel 1 flat piece of wood or metal used as a PAINTING support. **2** distinct area or compartment as part of a design.
panel amphora AMPHORA on which the design is set in a PANEL, separated from the body of the vase by a border.
panel painting PAINTING on a wood or METAL PANEL.
panorama PAINTING of a view or landscape; especially large-scale painting around a room or rolled on a cylinder.
pantheon literally, a temple "of all the gods"; usually the one at Rome, built *c*27–25 BC. Sometimes also used as a collective noun for all the gods.
paper tissue made of vegetable fiber.
papier collé (Fr., "pasted paper") collage of paper and card, first used by Georges Braque, *c*1912.
papier mâché (Fr., "chewed paper") paper pulped with glue and then molded, baked, and polished.
papyrus reed plant with a stem that was used by the Egyptians as writing "paper".
parapet (arch.) low wall around a balcony or similar structure.
parcel gilt silver or furniture gilded in parts.
parchment animal skin from calf, sheep, lamb, goat, or kid, used for writing, PAINTING, bookbinding.
parterre level space in a garden or ornamental flowerbed.
Parthenon the chief temple of Athena in Athens, on the Acropolis, built *c*447–433 BC.
pastel stick of PIGMENT mixed with gum or work executed in this MEDIUM. Because pastel tends to be light and chalky in tone, the word is also used to describe pale, light colors.
pastellist artist working in PASTEL.
pastiche 1 work in the style of another artist. **2** (derogatory) work made from fragments of another work or works.
pastoral idealized landscape PAINTING or country scene.
pastose impasted; thickly painted.
paten shallow dish used for bread of the Mass or Eucharist.
patron someone who patronizes or supports the arts and artists; hence patronage.
pattern model, design, or repeated DECORATIVE design.
pattern book book of MOTIFS and designs used as a reference book by artists and INDUSTRIAL DESIGNERS.
pavilion 1 pleasure house in garden or park. **2** building attached by wings to the main block or projecting from it.
pearl lustrous GEM produced by mollusks.
pectoral ORNAMENTED metal breastplate.
pedestal 1 support for statue, etc. **2** part of an ORDER consisting of PLINTH (or base), die (or DADO), and cap (or CORNICE).
pediform foot-shaped.
pediment (arch.) in CLASSICAL GREEK ARCHITECTURE, a triangular GABLE under the roof of a building or similar triangular field.
pelerinage (Fr.) account of a pilgrimage, sometimes illustrated.
pelike (pl. *pelikai*) large Greek storage jar; *see* GREEK VASES.
pen DRAWING instrument used with ink, sometimes made of quill.
pencil DRAWING instrument of lead or similar; in the MIDDLE AGES the term also meant a brush.
pendant 1 projecting or suspended BOSS in GOTHIC ARCHITECTURE. decoration at the end of a GABLE roof. **3** one of a pair of works.
pendant vault VAULT decorated with hanging stone BOSSES or TERMINALS; found in late GOTHIC ARCHITECTURE; *see* VAULT CONSTRUCTION.
pendentive (arch.) curved triangular section of vaulting in a DOME.
pensieri (It.) small models made as preliminaries to larger models when making SCULPTURE.
pentimento (It.) area of a PAINTING where the artist has changed his mind. Such changes may become visible in an OIL PAINTING as it ages, because of the increased transparency of the paint, or may be detected by X radiographs or infrared examination.
Performance art works in which the artist performs an act or acts, as HAPPENINGS or BODY ART.
peristyle (arch.) COLONNADE around a CLASSICAL temple or court, or an inner court in a large house surrounded by a colonnade.
Perpendicular (arch.) the English GOTHIC style of *c*1335 to *c*153[illegible] (between Decorated and Tudor); its most characteristic feature is vertical window TRACERY.
personification the image of something embodying ideas or as an example, such as the figure of a deity in human form.
perspective method of representing objects on a two-dimensional surface so that they appear three-dimensional; *see* LINEAR PERSPECTIVE.
Perspex *see* PLEXIGLAS.
pewter alloy of tin and lead, used mainly for tableware.
pH the standard measure of acidity given as a figure on a scale of 1[illegible] units. A pH value of less than 7 indicates acidity; a value greater than 7 indicates alkalinity.
phalerae (Latin) metal BOSS or disc worn as an ORNAMENT or decorating a horse's harness.
phiale broad, flat Greek vase.
photography method of producing an image by the chemical action of radiation, such as light, on a sensitive film.
photolithography LITHOGRAPHIC process in which the plates are made photographically.

otomontage picture combining juxtaposed photographic images.
oto-Realism a style of PAINTING in which the painter reproduces the effects created by photography; it is also used in illusionistically realistic SCULPTURE.
ysiognomy the study of a person's character from his physical attributes; hence physiognomic.
ano nobile (It.) (arch.) the first and main floor of an Italian RENAISSANCE palace.
azza (It.) square, open space surrounded by buildings.
ctogram (or pictograph) pictorial symbol, especially in so-called PRIMITIVE ART.
ctorial illustrative, or expressed in pictures; hence pictorialism.
cture field the surface area of a PAINTING, also called the picture plane.
cture plane *see* PICTURE FIELD.
cturesque quaint, charming. From the 18th century onward "the Picturesque" acquired a more specific meaning, particularly in connection with LANDSCAPE PAINTING, landscape gardening, and ARCHITECTURE; it suggested a deliberate roughness or rusticity of design, and was to some extent transitional between CLASSICISM and ROMANTICISM.
er (arch.) solid support between door or window openings, or supporting a bridge; usually square, but can be cylindrical, hence cylindrical pier. A compound pier in GOTHIC ARCHITECTURE is a group of SHAFTS. *See* VAULT CONSTRUCTION.
età (It.) representation of the Virgin Mary holding the dead body of Christ.
etra dura (It.) hard or semiprecious stone, e.g. AGATE, CHALCEDONY, used as inlaid or MOSAIC type work on furniture and other articles; in the plural, *pietre dure*, it implies the use of several different types of stone.
etra serena (It.) grayish sandstone quarried near Fiesole, Italy, and much used for building.
gment a colored solid, usually dispersed in a MEDIUM to form paint.
laster (arch.) rectangular attached COLUMN that projects from a wall by less than one third of its width.
llar (arch.) vertical supporting member; unlike a COLUMN, it may be square.
lotis (Fr., "stilts") in modern ARCHITECTURE, the rows of reinforced concrete COLUMNS often used to support a building, while leaving the ground free.*
nnacle (arch.) conical-or pyramid-shaped ORNAMENT on top of a SPIRE, especially in GOTHIC ARCHITECTURE.
plan design or DRAWING; *see* GROUND PLAN.
plane 1 mathematically a plane is defined as a surface "such that a straight line joining two points lies wholly in it." 2 the term *plane* may also be used to describe a predominantly flat surface.
plaque DECORATIVE or commemorative RELIEF in PLASTER, PORCELAIN, or METAL.
plaquette small metal PLAQUE, usually cast by the CIRE PERDUE method and popular from the 14th century to the 16th.
plaster material for surfacing walls, usually interior. Made by mixing dry materials, including CLAY, LIME, and GYPSUM, with water, applying it to the wall, and allowing it to set by evaporation, carbonation, or hydration. Plaster of Paris is calcium sulfate hemihydrate. It is often used for making MOLDS.
plastic 1 synthetic polymer that can be molded by heat and pressure. 2 describes anything molded or modeled; the opposite of GLYPTIC. 3 often also used of the three-dimensional values of a PAINTING.
plastic form three-dimensional forms of art such as SCULPTURE, POTTERY, and ARCHITECTURE.
plate 1 shallow dish. 2 piece of METAL or GLASS used in printing, ENGRAVING, and photographic processes. 3 collection of (silver) plated objects. 4 metal tableware, for domestic use.
Plateresque Spanish architectural style from *c*1520, with elaborate RELIEF decoration.
plate tracery (arch.) of windows, early form of GOTHIC TRACERY with simple wide MULLIONS.
plating layer of thin METAL applied to an object, or the application of this layer.
plaza (Sp.) marketplace, square.
plein air (Fr., "open air") term for a PAINTING executed outdoors, or giving the impression of naturalism by skillful handling of atmosphere.
Plexiglas (U.S. trademark) acrylic sheeting used in modern SCULPTURE (also known as Perspex). Transparent Plexiglas is often used for glazing pictures.
plinth (arch.) 1 the rectangular stone slab or block that forms the lowest member on which a COLUMN or statue stands. 2 projecting base of a wall.
plywood thin board composed of several layers of wood glued together with the grain crossed to give strength.
pochade (Fr.) sketch, especially one made outdoors.
podium (arch.) 1 continuous base of a building or room. 2 raised platform.
poesie (It., "short poems") PAINTINGS based on a poetic or literary source, especially from the RENAISSANCE.
pointillism (Fr.) the NEO-IMPRESSIONIST technique pioneered by Georges Seurat, using dots of pure color instead of mixing paint on the palette; hence *pointillé, pointillist; see* DIVISIONISM.
polychrome painted in several colors; usually used of SCULPTURE; hence polychromy.
polyester synthetic RESIN polymer, used to make synthetic fibers and PLASTIC.
polygon many-sided figure; hence polygonal, polygony.
polymorphic painting multiform PAINTING produced by some modern KINETIC artists. The appearance of the work changes according to the position of the observer.
polyptych painted work (usually an ALTARPIECE) of more than three panels; *see also* DIPTYCH, TRIPTYCH.
polyurethane synthetic RESIN based on ethyl carbonate, used to make VARNISHES and LACQUERS.
pompe-funèbre (Fr.) funeral ceremony.
Pop art art derived from the popular culture of the 1960s, including commercial illustration, comic strips, and advertising images. American and British equivalent of NEW REALISM.
porcelain hard, refined CERAMIC material invented by the Chinese in the 7th century.
porch (arch.) covered entrance, usually at the main door of a building.
porphyry hard volcanic stone used since ANTIQUITY for SCULPTURE.
portal (arch.) imposing entrance of a building.
portico (It.) (arch.) covered COLONNADE at the entrance to a building.
porticus (Latin) (arch.) small PORCH built on the north or south side of English pre-Conquest CHURCHES. Sometimes a *porticus* was built on both sides, thus forming rudimentary TRANSEPTS.
portrait drawn or painted image of a person, usually naturalistic and identifiable; hence portraiture, portraitist. *See also* BUST.
pose the stance or attitude of the human figure, or group of figures, in PAINTING or SCULPTURE.
poster public placard developed as an art form from the 19th century onward.
Post-Impressionism term coined by the art theorist Roger Fry for the style of art of Cézanne, van Gogh, and Gauguin.
post-modernism a term initially applied to ARCHITECTURE and

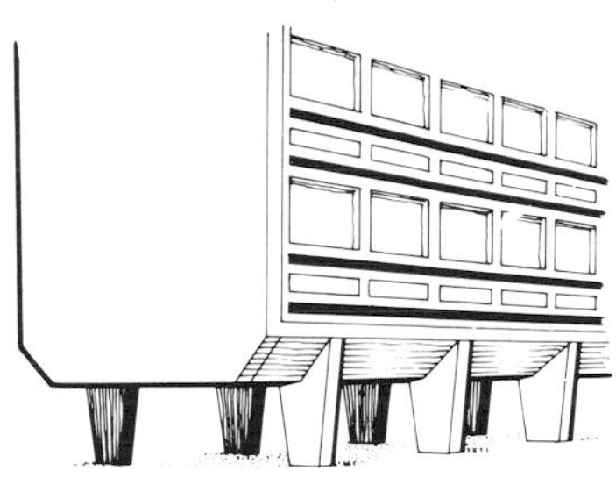

pilotis
after the Unité d'Habitation, Marseilles, designed by Le Corbusier; built 1947–52

rustication

implying a reaction to the strictures of MODERNIST theory and an eclectic use of past MOTIFS, particularly NEOCLASSICAL ones; it was later applied, more vaguely, to other visual arts. Generally speaking, it implied the rejection of FORMALISM and art for art's sake, embracing instead an art based on ideas and often engaging social issues and audience interaction.

Post-Painterly abstraction term coined by the American critic Clement Greenberg for a group of ABSTRACT artists working in the 1960s. It includes a number of specific styles and movements, such as COLOR-FIELD PAINTING and MINIMAL ART.

Post-Structuralism a form of critical analysis modifying the ideas of STRUCTURALISM and generating entirely new and often enlightening structures within which to examine works of art.

Poussinist adherent of the French late 17th-century theory, inspired by the work of Nicolas Poussin, of *poussinism*: the supremacy of line (draftsmanship) over color.

Prairie School a term that was applied to a group of architects working in the American Midwest in the early 20th century; the leading figure was Frank Lloyd Wright.

Pre-Columbian American art and culture before 1492.

predella 1 a platform on which an ALTAR stands. 2 lower part of painted ALTARPIECE.

Prehistoric art art of the Stone Age, which may be divided into PALEOLITHIC, MESOLITHIC, and NEOLITHIC periods.

Pre-Raphaelite Brotherhood English association of artists, *c*1848–54, including Rossetti, Holman Hunt, and Millais. The group had no clear, unifying doctrine but shared an interest in art of the 15th century prior to 1495, the start of the High RENAISSANCE.

presbytery (arch.) east end of a CHURCH, between the CHOIR and High ALTAR; sometimes synonymous with SANCTUARY.

primary colors red, blue, and yellow; the colors that can be mixed to produce other colors, but cannot themselves be produced from mixtures.

priming the preparation of a GROUND on which to paint.

primitive art 1 art of a prehistoric culture. 2 early European, non-naturalistic art. 3 untrained, NAIVE art. However, the notion of the "primitive", when seen as a supposed contrast to the developed West, has fallen out of favor.

print 1 any image, pattern, or lettering produced on fabric or PAPER by a variety of GRAPHIC processes. 2 to make an impression or image by such a process. Usually means letter-printing; printmaking involves producing an image that is aesthetically pleasing or illustrative.

prismatic prism shaped; related to prisms. Prismatic color is produced by light passing through a TRANSPARENT prism and synonymous with spectral color.

process works modern works of art in which the process of creation itself becomes the subject of the work.

profile 1 DRAWING, outline, or silhouette of a figure, especially the human figure viewed from the side. 2 (arch.) section of a MOLDING. 3 cross section of any structure.

proof 1 first impression of a PRINT made for the artist or as a limited edition. 2 the first example taken from any printing MEDIUM.

proportion ratio or relationship of dimensions.

Protogeometric style Greek vase-PAINTING style of the 11th century BC that began to replace the former freehand, LINEAR decoration with more severe, precise shapes; the forerunner of the true GEOMETRIC STYLE.

psalter a book containing the text of the psalms, sometimes illustrated.

pueblo (Sp.) communal village built by certain Native American peoples, e.g. the Hopi.

pulpit raised platform, from which the sermon is delivered in church.

pumice light volcanic stone consisting of silicates of aluminum, sodium, and potassium; used as an abrasive and for polishing.

Purism movement founded in 1918 by Le Corbusier and Amédée Ozenfant that aimed to purify CUBISM of any DECORATIVE elements, emphasizing pure outline and impersonality. It had little influence on PAINTING, more on ARCHITECTURE and design.

putto (It.; pl. *putti*) figure of a child in PAINTING or SCULPTURE; *see also* AMORINO.

pyramid Egyptian stone or brick tomb; rising from a square base to a triangular apex.

pyrolusite natural manganese dioxide; the ore from which manganese is extracted.

pyroxilin (or pyroxylin) cellulose nitrate used as LACQUER or synthetic MEDIUM.

pyxis (Greek) (pl. *pyxides*) a small box or casket, usually made of boxwood, used by the ancient Greeks and Romans to hold medicines. It was normally cylindrical; *see* GREEK VASES.

qibla west wall of a MOSQUE, indicating the direction of Mecca.

quadrangle rectangular or square figure, or four-sided courtyard.

quadratura (It.) Italian BAROQUE illusionistic PAINTING of an interior, using PERSPECTIVE to create the impression of an open, limitless space.

quadriga chariot drawn by four horses abreast.

quartz natural, crystalline form of silica; also known as rock crystal.

quatrefoil 1 (arch.) four-arc opening in GOTHIC TRACERY. 2 four-lobed DECORATIVE MOTIF.

Quattrocento (It.) 15th century.

quincunx an arrangement of five objects with four at the corners of a square and one in the center.

radiating chapel (arch.) chapel radiating from the APSE or AMBULATORY of a CHURCH.

raku Japanese POTTERY used for the tea ceremony; molded, not thrown on a wheel.

ramie East Asian plant with a strong fiber used for weaving.

Rayonnant (arch.) style of GOTHIC ARCHITECTURE of the late 13th and 14th centuries, usually referring to the TRACERY of windows, e.g. ROSE WINDOWS. It preceded the FLAMBOYANT style.

Rayonnism development of ABSTRACT art by the Russian artists Michail Larionoff and Natalia Gontcharova, *c*1913, which was an offshoot of CUBISM and in some respects the forerunner of FUTURISM.

ready-made name given by Marcel Duchamp—exponent of DADA principles—to prefabricated objects exhibited as works of art.

realism 1 style of PAINTING dating from the 19th century, typified by Courbet, that makes a deliberate choice of everyday subject matter (Realism). 2 the opposite of ABSTRACT or distorted (similar to NATURALISM). 3 in Greek CLASSICAL SCULPTURE, work that is not stylized or idealized.

Realistic Manifesto manifesto produced in 1920 by the brothers Naum Gabo and Antoine Pevsner, which questioned the figurative role of SCULPTURE.

recession in PAINTING, the illusion of depth or distance achieved through the use of color or PERSPECTIVE.

rectilinear based on straight lines; hence rectilinearism.

Rectilinear style (arch.) the la phase of GOTHIC ARCHITECTU *c*1335–*c*1530, characterized l vertical TRACERY; also called PE PENDICULAR.

recto the opposite of VERSO, i.e. t front or "right" side of a coi MEDAL, or PAINTING, or the righ hand page of an open book.

red-figure technique the technique the finest ancient Greek vas PAINTING, in which figures we drawn in black and the bac ground blocked in in black so th the figure stood out in the r GROUND-color. Compare BLAC FIGURE TECHNIQUE.

reductivist Minimalist (*see* MINIM ART).

refectory (arch.) dining hall, esp cially of a monastery or college.

refractive index a measure of t amount that light is bent on pas ing from one optical MEDIUM another, e.g. from air to water from a paint medium into a PI MENT particle.

régence style French ROCOCO style *c*1705–30.

Regency style the style of English a *c*1811–30, i.e. during the regen and reign of King George IV.

Regionalists American painters the 1930s and 1940s who d picted midwestern life.

register in GRAPHIC ART, the alig ment of corresponding parts produce separate colors in t same image.

reinforced concrete concrete rei forced with METAL wire to gi increased strength.

relative humidity a measure of a mospheric humidity expressed a percentage of the maximu amount of moisture that could contained by a given volume of a at a given temperature (abbre ation, RH).

relief sculpture, carving, etc., which forms project and depth hollowed out; the type of relief determined by the degree to whi the design stands out; thus *al rilievo* (high relief) and bas reli (low relief), in which the proje tion is slight.*

relief line in Greek RED-FIGURE va PAINTING a "relief line" was us for details of DRAWING, so-call because it stood out from the su face on which it was drawn.

relief process any GRAPHIC process which the areas not to be seen a cut away, so that the design stan out in RELIEF on the block; t term is applied to WOODCUTS, LIN CUTS, etc.

reliquary vessel for sacred relic often in precious METAL.

Renaissance (Fr., "rebirth") the p riod of Italian art from *c*1400 1520 characterized by increas emphasis on REALISM and the rediscovery of CLASSICAL art. The "Early Renaissance" is sometimes deemed also to include the art of the 14th century. High Renaissance refers to the period of the finest achievements of Leonardo, Raphael, and Michelangelo, c1495–1520. *See also* NORTHERN RENAISSANCE.

oussé (Fr., "pushed back") METAL decorated by hammering from the side not seen, so that the design stands out in RELIEF.

poussoir (Fr.) device in PAINTING: objects are placed in the FOREGROUND to direct the eye to the center of the painting.

presentational art art that attempts to show objects as they really appear, or at least in some easily recognizable form.

redos ornamental screen behind an ALTAR.

served describes the areas of decoration on CERAMICS, gilded objects, etc., that are left in the color of the base or body of the object.

sin 1 natural organic compound secreted by some plants and insects, used in VARNISHES, LACQUERS, and PAINTS. 2 synthetic substance formulated to resemble the natural resin.

table 1 raised shelf, ledge, or frame containing ornamental panels, at the back of an ALTAR. 2 painted or carved ALTARPIECE of one or more fixed panels.

tardataire (Fr.) archaic.

veal (arch.) the inside surface of a door or window, cut at right angles to the face of the wall.

vetment (arch.) wall built to hold back a mass of earth, water, etc.; also called a retaining wall.

H *see* RELATIVE HUMIDITY.

yton drinking vessel, usually ceremonial, in the form of an animal head or human figure; found in Greek, Assyrian, and Minoan art; *see* GREEK VASES.

(arch.) projecting band or MOLDING on a VAULT or ceiling; *see* VAULT CONSTRUCTION.

vault (arch.) a cross VAULT with arched ribs across the sides and diagonals of the BAY that support, or seem to support, the INFILLING; *see* VAULT CONSTRUCTION.

dgepole (arch.) the horizontal timber at the ridge of a roof where the rafters are fastened.

dge rib (arch.) a supporting or DECORATIVE RIB running along the central axis of a VAULT; *see* VAULT CONSTRUCTION.

mpa School school of Japanese PAINTING founded by Tawaraya Sotatsu, *fl.* c1600–30.

caille (Fr.) 1 scallop-shell ORNAMENT popular from c1730.* 2 shell or stone decoration of ROCOCO gardens and grottoes. 3 among French art historians, sometimes synonymous with Rococo.

Rococo elegant, DECORATIVE style of c1730–80. During the 19th century the term acquired pejorative connotations, meaning trivial or over-ornate.

Romanesque (arch.) style of ARCHITECTURE that lasted from 1000 to 1150 in France and to the 13th century in the rest of Europe; characterized by massive VAULTS and rounded ARCHES. The term is also applied to the FINE and DECORATIVE ARTS of the period.

Romanist collective name applied particularly to those Northern artists who visited Rome and were influenced by Italian art during the 16th century, e.g. Maerten van Heemskerck.

Romanticism the late 18th- and early 19th-century antithesis to CLASSICISM; the imagination of the artist and the choice of literary themes predominated. Leading Romantic painters included Eugène Delacroix and J.M.W. Turner.

rood screen screen separating the NAVE and CHOIR in a CHURCH.

rosette circular ORNAMENT, especially in ARCHITECTURE, shaped like a formalized rose.

rose window (arch.) circular window with radiating TRACERY, found in GOTHIC ARCHITECTURE.

rotunda (arch.) round building or internal room surmounted by a DOME.

roughcast rough preparation of sand and lime applied to a wall prior to the smooth PLASTER.

roundel circular panel, PAINTING, MEDALLION, or ornamental STAINED-GLASS window.

rubbing synonymous with FROTTAGE.

rubenisme *see* RUBENISTE.

Rubeniste adherent of the French late 17th-century theory, inspired by the work of Peter Paul Rubens, of *rubenisme*: the supremacy of color over line, in PAINTING. Compare POUSSINIST.

rustication (arch.) masonry in which blocks of stone are emphasized by the deep joints and roughened surfaces; most commonly found in Italian palaces from the 16th century.*

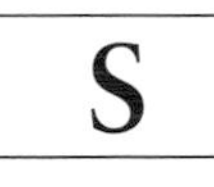

sacra conversazione (It.) in Christian ICONOGRAPHY, the image of the Virgin and Child with saints, as a group PORTRAIT.

sacristy (arch.) room attached to a CHURCH in which the vestments and sacred vessels are kept and where priests are attired.

Safavid Persian dynastic period, c1502–1736.

salon large room.

Salon French annual exhibition (held from 17th century onwards) of PAINTING and SCULPTURE by members of the ACADEMY; traditionally hostile to innovation.

Salon des Indépendents (Fr.) exhibition of the Société des Artistes Indépendents of 1884, including Seurat and Signac. The society had no selection jury.

Salon des Réfusés (Fr., "Salon of the Refused") exhibition of 1863 promoted by Napoleon III to show works rejected by the Paris SALON.

salon painting the style acceptable to the Paris SALON; by implication dull and stereotyped.

sanctuary (arch.) holiest part of temple or CHURCH, containing the ALTAR.

sand painting applying colored sand to glue on a canvas.

sandstone rock formed of sand or QUARTZ particles bonded together with CLAY, calcium carbonate, and iron oxide; it has a warm color and is easily worked, and has therefore been popular for building and carving.

sarcophagus a stone coffin, often decorated, especially common in ANTIQUITY.

sardonyx onyx in which the white layers alternate with sard (a yellow or orange-red CARNELIAN).

sarsen boulder carried and deposited by ice during the glacial period.

satin silky fabric with a glossy surface.

satyr mythological attendant of the Greek god Dionysos; usually depicted in PAINTING as a goat-footed creature with horns and tail, or with the feet, ears, and tail of a horse.

scallop shell-shaped ORNAMENT.

scalloped capital (arch.) block CAPITAL whose four sides have a series of curves or SCALLOPS.

scapigliatura (It.) Bohemianism.

scarab ancient Egyptian representation of a sacred beetle, associated with the idea of resurrection. Usually made of stone or FAIENCE and inscribed.

scaraboid roughly resembling a SCARAB.

scène galante *see* FÊTE GALANTE.

scenographic using PERSPECTIVE in PAINTING to create the illusion of depth.

schema (pl. *schemata*) simplified synopsis or representation of a general type.

schematic representing objects by symbols or diagrams.

high relief

low relief

relief

rocaille

an example of the scallop-shell ornament

schematized in SCHEMATIC form.

schist rock composed of bands of different minerals that can be split into thin layers.

scholar-painter the Japanese equivalent of *wen-jen hua* (or "literary men's PAINTING") in Chinese art; a literary-minded amateur who painted for pleasure.

School of Fontainebleau there were two schools; the first, under Francis I (*c*1528–58), was fundamentally MANNERIST, directly influenced by expatriate Italian masters. The second, under Henry IV (1589–1610), was more mediocre.

School of Paris (*École de Paris*) 1 a broad name for various modern art movements originating in Paris including Nabism (see NABIS), Fauvism (see FAUVES), CUBISM, and SURREALISM. 2 school of medieval MANUSCRIPT illuminators in Paris from the mid 13th century to the early 15th century.

School of Pont-Aven not a true "school" but the group of painters, generally SYMBOLISTS, who worked at Pont-Aven, France, during the late 19th century, including the NABIS and Gauguin.

screen partition, often carved or painted.

scroll 1 architectural ORNAMENT, similar in form to a scroll of parchment. 2 scroll of paper or silk, popular in Eastern art. A hand scroll is about 30cm (12 in) wide and up to 30m (100 ft) long, and unrolls from right to left to give a continuous picture, viewed section by section. A hanging scroll, as the name implies, is hung like a PAINTING. Both are usually painted in ink or WATERCOLOR.

scroll work ornamentation of spiral lines.

sculpture object carved or modeled in wood, stone, etc., or cast in metal for an aesthetic, nonfunctional purpose; alternatively, the process of producing it; hence sculptor. The term "sculptural" is used to describe art (including PAINTING and DRAWING) that has pronounced three-dimensional qualities.

scumble an OPAQUE or semiopaque layer of paint applied over another so that the first is partially obliterated, producing a slightly broken effect.

scuola (It.) school of art; a group of artists working under the same influence or master.

seal engraved GEM or METAL stamp used to make an impression in a wax seal on a document; usually identifiable, it therefore serves as a signature.

seascape PAINTING or DRAWING of the sea and shipping.

secco painting (It., "dry") method of wall PAINTING onto dry PLASTER, using PIGMENTS in lime water or an egg MEDIUM. Often used for retouching FRESCO.

Secession (Ger., *Sezession*) term used for withdrawal of German and Austrian artists from ACADEMIES in the late 19th century.

section 1 figure or view produced by cutting through an object. 2 in book production, a sheet of PAPER, folded and ready for sewing.

Section d'Or (Fr., "Golden Section") offshoot of CUBISM; members of the group included Fernand Léger, Marcel Duchamp, Frank Kupka, and Jacques Villon. The members were linked by an interest in a mathematical system of proportion and the harmonious use of color. There was a *Section d'Or* exhibition in 1912 and a magazine of the same name.

sedilia series of stone seats in a CHURCH on the south side of the CHANCEL, used by the clergy.

segmental arch (arch.) ARCH with a contour that is a section of a circle but less than a semicircle.

Seicento (It.) 17th century.

self-portrait PORTRAIT of and by the artist.

Semiabstraction the name used by Picasso and his circle for ABSTRACTION.

semidome (arch.) DOMED ceiling of an APSE, less than the full DOME height.

semiotics a form of linguistic and general critical analysis concentrating on whatever is signified by the words or by other elements of an artistic work.

sennit plaited straw or palm leaf fibers.

sepia blackish brown secretion of ink from cuttlefish and squid, used as a DRAWING MEDIUM and in WATERCOLOR.

serial painting art form of the 1960s involving the repetition of an image with slight variations.

serpentine sinuous, winding.

Seven and Five Society English art association formed in 1920 by seven painters and five sculptors, including Ben Nicholson and Barbara Hepworth; originally FIGURATIVE, but became ABSTRACT.

sfumato (It., "evaporated") using subtle gradations of tone and softened lines.

shade absence of direct light; tone of a particular color.

shading use of darker tones to indicate shadowed areas.

shaft (arch.) 1 part of a COLUMN between the base and CAPITAL. 2 in medieval ARCHITECTURE, a slender column; *see* VAULT CONSTRUCTION.

Shah-nama "Book of Kings", a verse history of Persian kings written by the Persian poet Firdawsi (*c*935–1020/6). Its text was a popular subject for illustration in the Arab world.

shallow relief low relief or bas relief; *see* RELIEF.

shaped canvas canvas stretched on a frame before PAINTING to form a three-dimensional support.

sheet print single sheet Japanese PRINT.

shell outer case, especially of marine mollusks.

Shijo school of Japanese PAINTING that emphasized NATURALISM and REALISM, founded by Matsumura Goshun in the 18th century. It lasted into the 20th century.

shogun Japanese hereditary commander and ruler, under the Emperor. The institution lasted from 1192 to 1867; the title means "General".

Sibyl CLASSICAL prophetess associated with the oracles, e.g. at Delphi.

signet ring ring containing a personal seal.

silhouette 1 MONOCHROME PAINTING, dark on light or light on dark, with a well-defined outline. 2 PROFILE PORTRAIT cut from black paper and mounted on white; popular in the 18th and 19th centuries.

silk thread or cloth made from the fiber produced by the silkworm.

silk screen method of color reproduction in which colored inks are squeezed through a stencil prepared on a silk screen.

silver gilt silver gilded with gold.

silver leaf thinly beaten silver, applied like GOLD LEAF.

silverpoint DRAWING with a silver wire or stylus.

sinopia 1 red-brown earth PIGMENT used in DRAWING for FRESCO. The name is derived from the place of origin; the town of Sinope on the Black Sea. 2 the name is also generally applied to the drawing on the ARRICCIO, prior to PAINTING the fresco, whether or not it is in this pigment.

Siren 1 mythological creature, half bird, half woman, who lured sailors to their death by sweet singing. 2 mythological serpent.

Situationist associated with the International Situationist Movement formed in Italy by Asger Jorn and the Lettrist International Movement formed in France by Guy Debord, it cut across national and political divisions. The group's work was characterized by an anarchic, DADA spirit.

situla art DECORATIVE bronzework that appeared *c*600 BC in the Mediterranean area and later in Celtic art.

size gelatine or animal glue, or oth materials such as starch and gun used to stiffen fabrics, to redu the porosity of a surface, or as PAINTING MEDIUM.

sketch 1 rough DRAWING as the pr liminary to a more finished co position. 2 since the 18th centu a complete but slight or quick executed drawing, PAINTING, WATERCOLOR.

skyphos ancient Greek drinking cu *see* GREEK VASES.

slate grayish rock of natural al minum silicate formed when CL is hardened by pressure. It is eas split into plates or sheets a often used in building.

slip CLAY, thinned with water, f decorating or coating pottery.

smalti small pieces of MOSAIC co posed of colored vitreous mate als or glass fused in a KIL sometimes onto a TERRACOTTA PORCELAIN base.

soapstone steatite or hydrated si cate of magnesia; a soft stone, ea ily carved and polished and oft used for small objects; also used an ingredient in the manufactu of PORCELAIN.

Socialist Realism the official, cons vative, post-Revolutionary style art in Russia.

social realism since the 19th centu the term refers to the convinci portrayal of subjects in a social political context; in the last ce tury, applied more specifically art that deliberately recorded commented on political or soc conditions and events.

soffit (arch.) underside of an ARCH some other feature.*

soft ground etching ETCHING tec nique developed in the late 18 century that renders textures.

Soft style the German equivale (Ger., *Weicher Stil*) of the INTE NATIONAL GOTHIC, *c*1375–142 distinguished by soft, curviline forms. It was replaced by t sharp, ANGULAR STYLE of DRAPER

Sonderbund (full name, *Sonderbu Westdeutscher Kunstfreunde u Künstler*) league of art lovers a artists, founded in Dusseldo *c*1909. The first president w Karl Ernst Osthaus, a notab patron of modern art.

Sondergotik (Ger.) late Goth German architectural style equi alent to the French FLAMBOYA and the English PERPENDICULAR.

Sound art a form of SCULPTURE INSTALLATION ART in which t sonic element is foremost and t visual element is normally the e position of the generation sound.

spandrel (arch.) 1 triangular ar contained by one side of ARCH. 2 the surface between tw

adjacent arches and the MOLDING above. 3 surface of VAULT between two adjacent RIBS or any similar triangular surface.
azialismo (It.) also known as *Movimento Spaziale*; the movement, founded by Lucio Fontana in 1947, that rejects the idea of EASEL PAINTING in favor of the development of form and color in space.
ectrum the range of colors produced when white light passes through a TRANSPARENT PRISM.
hinx the Greek name for a creature with a human head and lion's body; in Egypt, usually male; in Greece, female.
ral line or form that winds continually along or up a central AXIS; hence spiral COLUMN, spiral staircase, etc.
re (arch.) tapering, slender cone on top of a tower.
lit stitch embroidery stitch used for very fine work; the needle is pushed through an untwisted silk thread as it is sewn, to produce something that looks like a chain stitch.
uare up method of transferring or enlarging a preliminary DRAWING by superimposing a network of squares and transferring each to the intended support.
uinch (arch.) ARCH built diagonally from the corner of a square building supporting a spire or DOME.
ffage figure figure in ARCHITECTURE or LANDSCAPE PAINTING intended to indicate the scale or provide a point of interest.
ined glass GLASS colored with metal oxides; joined with LEAD strips to form designs, mostly for windows in CHURCHES.
inless steel chrome steel, nonrusting; used in modern SCULPTURE and ARCHITECTURE.
r vault (or stellar vault) medieval VAULT in which the intermediate and LIERNE RIBS form a star pattern; *see* VAULT.
sis stoppage, stagnation.
tuary collection of STATUES, or the making of statues.
tue carved or molded figure in STONE, CLAY, BRONZE, etc.
tuette small statue.
atite *see* SOAPSTONE.
el alloy of iron and carbon used in SCULPTURE, building, furniture.
eple (arch.) tower of a CHURCH, including the SPIRE, LANTERN, etc.
la (pl. *stele* or *stellae*) Greek stone slab, marking a grave or with an inscription.
llar vault *see* STAR VAULT.
llate star shaped.
mma (It.) escutcheon, coat of arms.
ncil design cut in a card or plate used for brushing color through to the paper beneath.

still life PAINTING of inanimate objects such as fruit, flowers, dead game.
stipple patterning tone built up with small dots and dabs of color.
stirrup jar ancient Greek jar with an arched handle at the top.
stirrup spout pot CERAMIC pot shape, chiefly found in PRE-COLUMBIAN culture and in Mexico and Peru; it has a semicircular hollow handle, leading to a spout shaped rather like a stirrup.
stoa (arch.) roofed PORTICO, usually facing onto a public place, with a wall at the back and a COLONNADE at the front.*
stole ecclesiastical vestment in the shape of a narrow strip of fabric worn over the shoulders, reaching the knees, or a similar piece in front of the ALTAR.
stone 1 rock used for building and SCULPTURE. **2** gemstone.
stoneware hard POTTERY made from CLAY plus a fusible stone (usually feldspar) and fired at 1200–1400°C (2200–2500°F) so that the stone is vitrified.
stopping out in ETCHING, the prowtection of areas of a PLATE with VARNISH to prevent acid from attacking those areas during BITING.
strapwork ornamentation of interlaced bands, like straps of leather, common in the 16th century.*
stretcher frame, usually of wood, on which fabric is stretched prior to PAINTING.
striation 1 pattern of narrow stripes. **2** the representation of drapery by parallel lines, found in BYZANTINE and ROMANESQUE ART.*
strigil ancient Greek or Roman skin scraper, used by athletes.
stringcourse (arch.) MOLDING running horizontally along a wall.
Structuralism a form of critical analysis, based on the concept of underlying structures, linked to SEMIOTICS and to elements of cultural anthropology. In art, it seeks to uncover the cultural phenomenon and signs that work together to generate meaning in a work.
stuccatore (It.) plasterer, someone who works in STUCCO.
stucco slow-setting lime and marble PLASTER that can be modeled and carved for decorating interiors.
stuccoist *see* STUCCATORE.
studiolo (It.) small office or work room.
study detailed preparatory DRAWING for a larger work; more detailed and complete than a SKETCH.
stupa ancient Indian burial mound, often housing relics of the Buddha.
style 1 ancient writing implement. **2** manner of artistic expression, particular to an individual, school, or period.

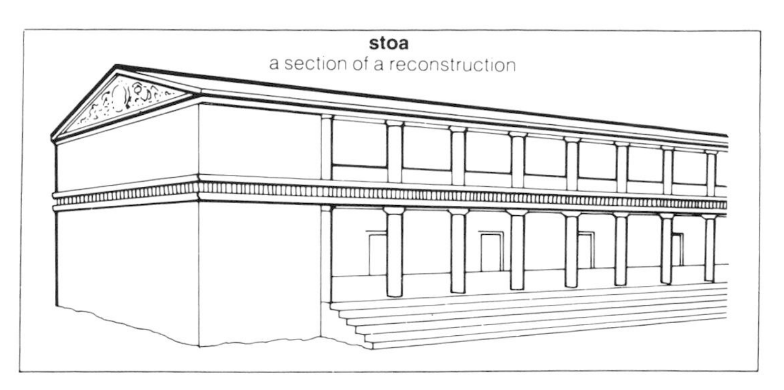

stoa
a section of a reconstruction

stylized 1 conforming to a recognized style. **2** based on natural forms that are then simplified according to a conventional SCHEMA or stereotype, hence stylization.
stylobate (arch.) continuous base of a COLONNADE.
suite a sequence of rooms or a set of matching furniture. It can also mean a series of DRAWINGS, PAINTINGS, or PRINTS linked by a common theme, often literary.
Sung Chinese dynasty dating from AD 960 to 1278.
support canvas, PAPER, PANEL, wall, etc., on which a PAINTING or DRAWING is executed.
Suprematism Russian ABSTRACT art movement of 1913–15, led by Kasimir Malevich, that used geometric elements.
surimono Japanese color PRINTS commemorating festive occasions, e.g. births, weddings, New Year.
Surrealism movement in art and literature between the two World Wars that tried to fuse actuality with dream and unconscious experience, using AUTOMATISM among other techniques; hence Surreal, Surrealist.
swag carved or painted festoon of garland or drapery.*
swastika ancient symbol, often used in decoration, of a cross with four arms, all bent at right angles to the same direction.
Sweet style sentimental style of marble SCULPTURE associated with the workshop of the della Robbia family in Florence in the mid 15th century.
syllabary a set of SYMBOLS or characters representing syllables, used as an alphabet.
symbol image of something representing something else; hence symbolic, symbolism, symbolize.
Symbolist *see* SYMBOLIST MOVEMENT.
Symbolist movement (sometimes generally known as Symbolism) art movement that appeared *c*1885 in France, originating in poetry; a reaction against both REALISM and IMPRESSIONISM, it aimed at the fusion of the real and

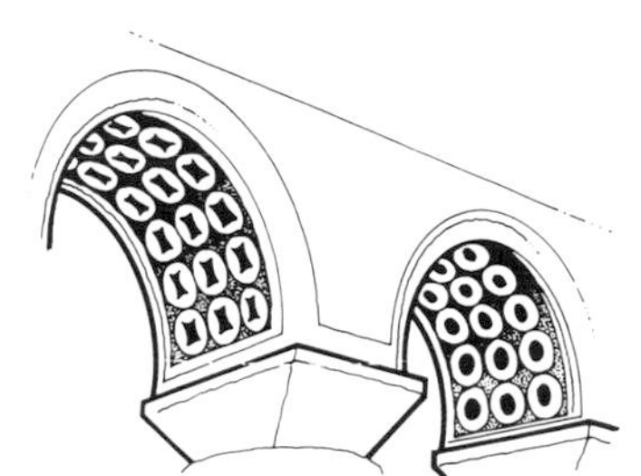

decorated soffits

strapwork

striation

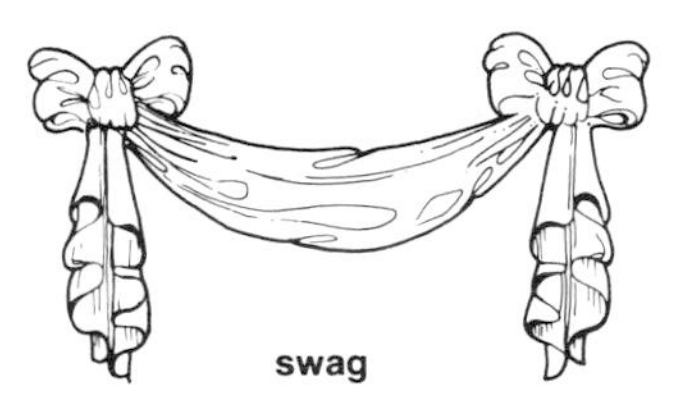

swag

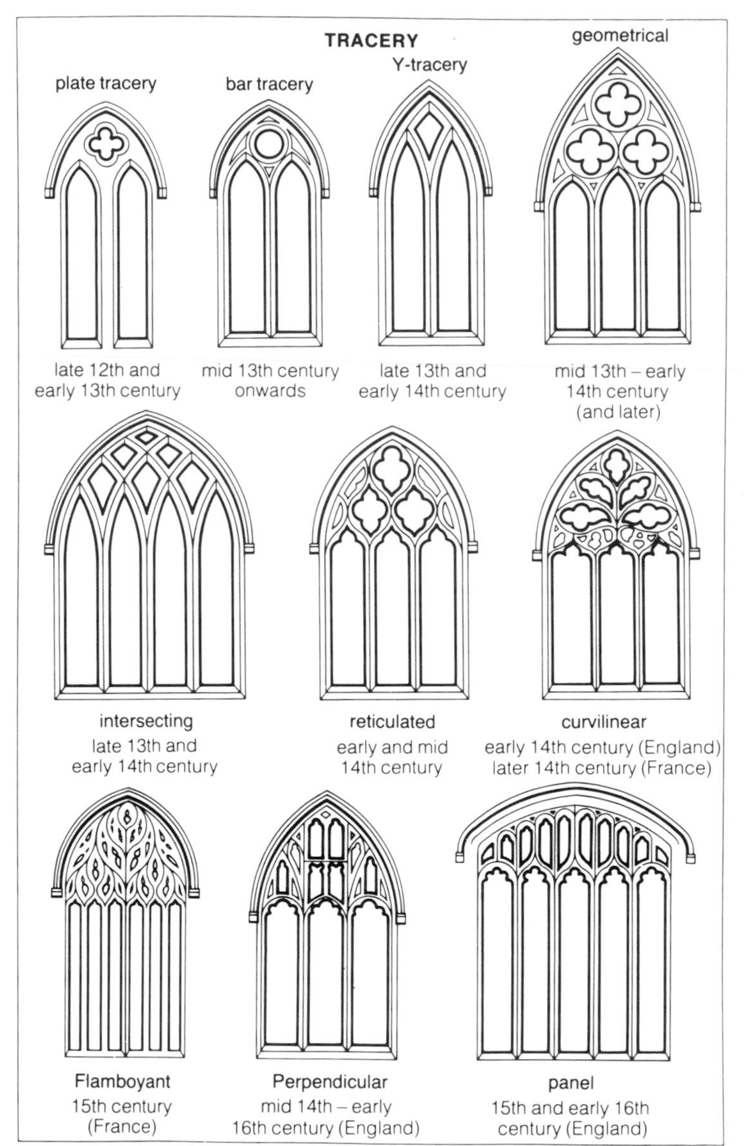

spiritual worlds, the visual expression of the mystical.

Synchromism an American movement of 1913 promoted by Morgan Russell and Stanton Macdonald-Wright; influenced by Orphism (*see* ORPHIC CUBISM), using ABSTRACT form and color.

Synthetic Cubism the second phase of CUBISM, after 1912, using COLLAGE.

Synthetism a branch of POST-IMPRESSIONIST PAINTING associated with Gauguin, *c*1888, chiefly employing flat areas of color, strong contour lines, and simple forms; also called CLOISONNISM.

tabernacle (arch.) niche or receptacle containing the Holy Sacrament, usually above the ALTAR.

tableau vivant (Fr.) motionless group of people arranged to represent a scene.

Tachisme term coined in 1952 by the French critic Michel Tapié, referring to the technique of PAINTING in irregular dabs (from the French word *taches,* or spots) and in an apparently haphazard manner.

tactile perceived by touch. The term "tactile values" was introduced to art criticism in 1896 by Bernard Berenson to describe the textural qualities of PAINTINGS.

tapestry wall hanging of silk or wool with a nonrepeating pattern or narrative design woven in by hand during manufacture.

tarashikomi Japanese method of PAINTING "wet on wet".

teak the hard wood of a tropical tree, *Tectona grandis*, used for furniture and veneers.

technique method of execution.

tectonic related to building and construction.

tempera 1 general term for any MEDIUM used for PAINTING. **2** (egg) tempera, when a whole egg or yolk is used as a medium.

templon COLONNADE in a Middle BYZANTINE CHURCH that closes off the CHANCEL.

Ten, the group of American painters, *c*1895, influenced by IMPRESSIONISM.

tendril ornamental curving line resembling plant stem or curl of hair.*

Tenebrism style of 17th-century PAINTING associated with Caravaggio making much use of strong CHIAROSCURO.

terminal (arch.) PEDESTAL or similar structure supporting a sculpted head or figure, placed in gardens to define the boundaries; also known as a term or HERM.

terracotta (It., "baked earth") hard, fired but unglazed, brownish-red clay used for POTTERY, SCULPTURE, and building.

terribilità (It.) awesomeness.

tessellation pattern of MOSAIC or pavement floor, composed of blocks of stone, marble, etc.

tesserae (pl. of *tessera*; Latin from Greek, meaning "four-sided") fragments of inorganic material such as stone, GLASS, and MARBLE, cut into cubes and used in MOSAIC.

tetraconch building composed of four CONCHAS.

tetramorph composite figure containing the SYMBOLS of the four Evangelists.

textile woven fabric.

texture the surface of a material, especially as perceived by touch.

thiasos company celebrating the festival of the gods, especially Bacchus.

tholos ancient Greek DOME-shaped building or underground tomb.

thyrsos spear topped with a pinecone ORNAMENT, carried by Dionysos as a symbol of revelry.

tile flat piece of CERAMIC, decorated or used for roofing.

tile hanging wall covering of overlapping rows of slates or tiles.

tint hue, or shade of a color.

tonality quality of color, light, and shade in PAINTING.

tondo (It.) circular picture or RELIEF.

tone 1 atmosphere, character. **2** intensity of color or hue. **3** degree of lightness or darkness.

topography the art of mapping in detail the features of a geographical region.

toreutics objects, especially metal, that are chased, carved, EMBOSSED, or the study of these.

torsion twisting.

torso human body (or statue) apart from the head and limbs, i.e. t trunk.

Tosa School Japanese school PAINTING founded in the 15th ce tury that stressed native traditio in art.

totem pole carved wood pillar dec rated with mythological figur made by certain Native Americ peoples, especially those of t northwest Pacific coast.

tou Chinese bronze vessel; globul with a cover and a flared base.

tow flax fibers.

town planning science or art of pla ning the layout of cities.

townscape picture of a town.

trace to draw or copy, especia from a DRAWING on a superi posed TRANSPARENT sheet.

tracery (arch.) ornamental sto work in window openings, esp cially in GOTHIC ARCHITECTURE Bar tracery dates from *c*1245 a has narrow shafts of sto branching out to form a DECOR TIVE pattern; it is more delica and elaborate than plate trace which has more solid stone.

transept (arch.) transverse arm o cross-shaped CHURCH.

transformable synonymous w POLYMORPHIC PAINTING.

transition change of style or, in PAINTING, of color.

Transitional style (arch.) the sty that developed between ROMA ESQUE and GOTHIC.

translucency the property of tran mitting light without being co pletely TRANSPARENT.

transparent allowing light to pa through.

trascoro (Sp.) space behind t CHOIR in CHURCH.

travertine very pure LIMESTO found at the sources of certa Italian rivers; used for buildin especially in Rome.

Trecento (It.) 14th century.

trefoil three-lobed ORNAMENT, fou in GOTHIC TRACERY.

trellis lattice of wood, etc.

tribune (arch.) **1** upper story in CHURCH, above the AISLE. **2** bishop's throne. **3** raised floor a Roman BASILICA.

triclinium ancient Roman dini room or table.

Tridentine derived from the Rom Catholic Council of Trent, Ita (1545–63); orthodox Rom Catholic doctrine.

triforium (arch.) passage in the w of the NAVE, between the ma ARCADE and CLERESTORY; *see* VAU CONSTRUCTION.

triglyph (arch.) projecting blo with three vertical grooves, fou alternately with METOPES in Doric FRIEZE.

Trinità (It.) representation of t Holy Trinity.

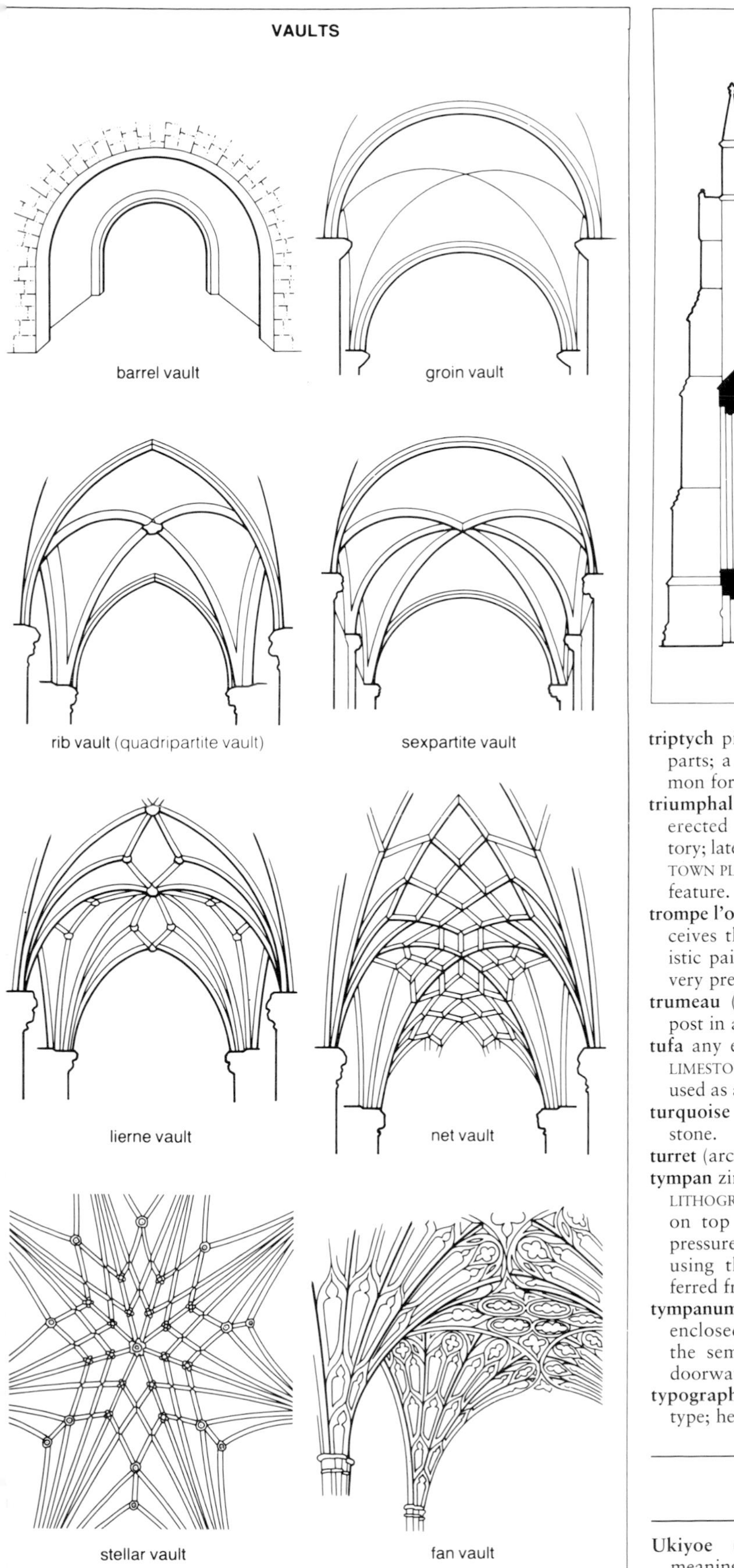

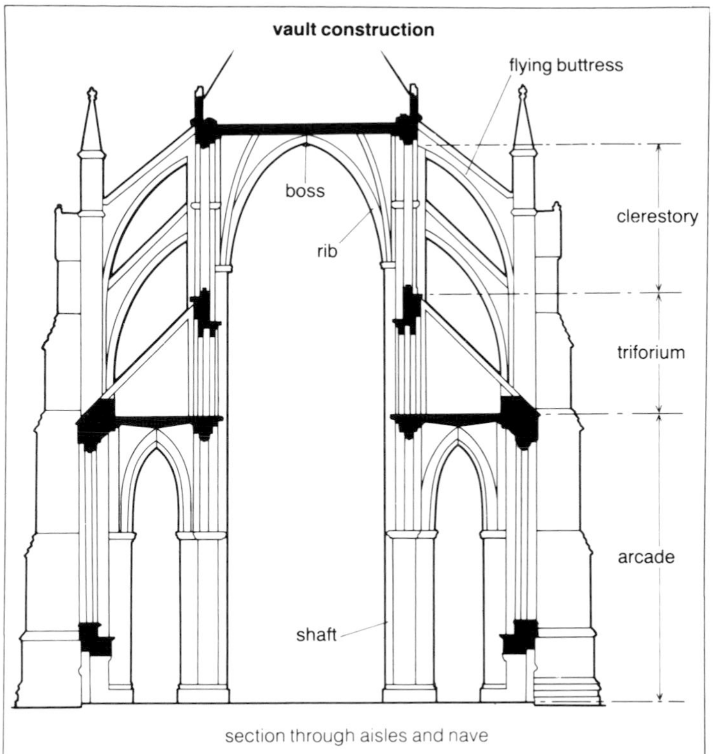

section through aisles and nave

triptych picture or carving in three parts; a form of POLYPTYCH common for ALTARPIECES.

triumphal arch Roman monument erected to commemorate a victory; later adopted by 19th-century TOWN PLANNING as an architectural feature.

trompe l'oeil (Fr.) PAINTING that "deceives the eye"; type of illusionistic painting characterized by its very precise NATURALISM.

trumeau (Fr.) (arch.) stone center post in a doorway.

tufa any easily hewn rock such as LIMESTONE used for building. Also used as a synonym for SANDSTONE.

turquoise blue-green semiprecious stone.

turret (arch.) small tower.

tympan zinc or brass sheet used in a LITHOGRAPHIC transfer press. It lies on top of the PAPER and when pressure is applied to the top of it using the scraper, ink is transferred from the stone to the paper.

tympanum (arch.) triangular surface enclosed by a PEDIMENT, or the semicircle above an arched doorway.*

typography the art of composing type; hence typographer.

tendril

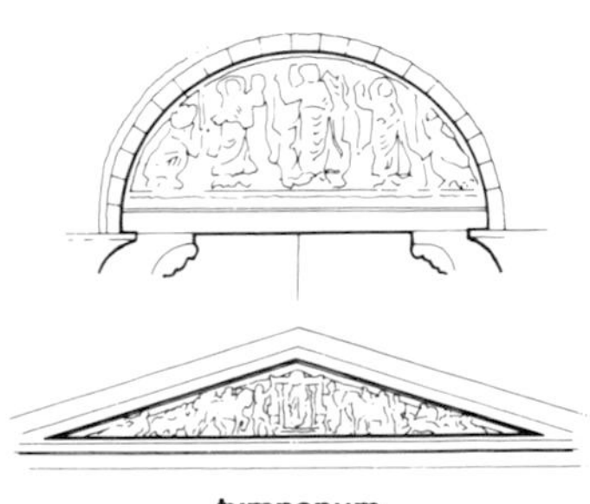
tympanum
above Romanesque, **below** Classic Greek

U

Ukiyoe (or Ukiyo-e) Japanese, meaning "pictures of the floating world". GENRE PAINTING, and later

WOODBLOCK prints, with subjects such as actors, domestic scenes, and courtesans.

undercutting term used for CASTING, indicating the area of a MODEL that prevents the removal of the MOLD parts without destroying the impeding parts of the model. Also used to describe the cutting away of the solid matter between an outlying part of a carving and the main part of the block or to describe the area that has been thus cut away.

underpainting the first layer of a PAINTING that establishes forms and tone and is then modified by GLAZES and SCUMBLES.

urn Roman covered vase used for the ashes of the dead.

ustad the Persian title, "Master".

Utrecht School group of painters in Utrecht including Terbrugghen and Honthorst, 1610–20, who had visited Rome and were influenced by the REALISM and lighting of Caravaggio.

ziggurat

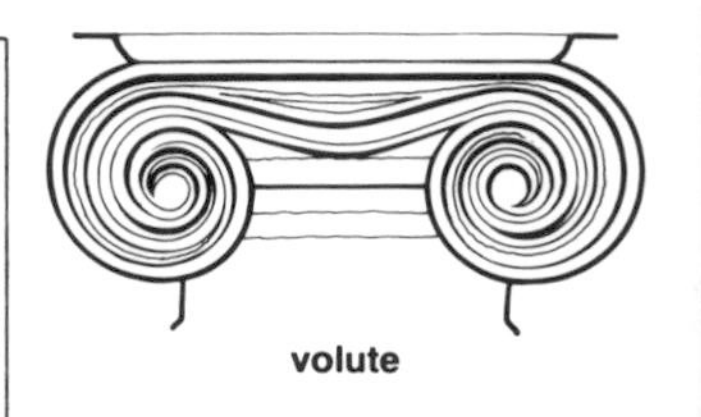

volute

V

Valori Plastici (It.) artists' association and their magazine, produced in Rome in 1918 by the supporters of *Pittura Metafisica*, aiming at a revival of CLASSICAL and ACADEMIC art.

value lightness or darkness on a scale of black-white, or from the lightest to the darkest tone of a color.

valve (arch.) leaf of a folding door.

vanishing point point at which the receding parallel lines in a PAINTING appear to meet; *see* LINEAR PERSPECTIVE.

vanitas STILL-LIFE PAINTING, popular from the 17th century, which contains objects as reminders of the impermanence of temporal life and of mortality.

varnish natural or synthetic resinous solution applied to furniture and PAINTINGS to saturate color and give a glossy surface, and as a protective layer.

vault (arch.) arched roof or ceiling in stone.*

vault construction in GOTHIC ARCHITECTURE, the architectural structure for directing pressures to maintain VAULTS.*

vaulting series of VAULTS, or style of vault.

vegetal motif plant MOTIF.

vellum fine calf skin used for writing, PAINTING, and bookbinding.

velvet silk textile with a soft pile of looped threads. Modern velvets are made from other fibers.

ventail armor protecting the neck or the lower part of a helmet.

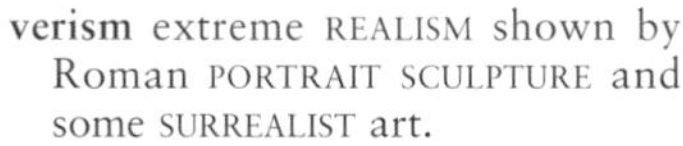

verism extreme REALISM shown by Roman PORTRAIT SCULPTURE and some SURREALIST art.

vermilion brilliant red PIGMENT; natural or synthetic mercuric sulfide.

vernacular architectural style using native, local materials and styles.

verso reverse of coin, MEDAL, or PAINTING or left-hand page of an open book; *see* RECTO.

Video art a form of INSTALLATION ART using television, usually with video tape, and normally displaying looped material. Its popularity began in the 1970s.

Vienna Secession radical movement led by Gustav Klimt in an attempt to improve Austrian art, *c*1897. It had strong links with JUGENDSTIL and ART NOUVEAU.

vignette small ORNAMENT in a book or on GLASS; or a PAINTING with no obvious edges or softened edges.

Villanovan belonging to the Iron Age culture of Etruria before 700 BC; after this date it is known as Etruscan.

vine rinceau (Fr.) SCROLL WORK; a tendril pattern.

Vingt, Les (Fr., "The Twenty") group of AVANT-GARDE Belgian artists who held annual exhibitions 1883–93.

virtual volume appearance of three dimensionality possessed by an image that is virtual, not real; i.e., from which light rays appear to diverge.

virtues personification of the seven virtues (Faith, Hope, Charity, Prudence, Justice, Temperance, Fortitude) often depicted as CLASSICAL gods and goddesses.

virtuosity special skill of execution.

vista long view, e.g. along an avenue of trees.

vitreous glaze in POTTERY, a glaze that is vitrified (or becomes glass-like) on FIRING.

Vitruvian derived from the writings of Vitruvius (1st century BC), author of *De Re Architectura*.

volute (arch.) spiral SCROLL ORNAMENT, usually on Greek IONIC CAPITALS; also on furniture.*

Vorticism short-lived English AVANT-GARDE movement, the most prominent member of which was Wyndham Lewis. Its name derives from a magazine published by the group in 1914: *Blast! A Review of the Great English Vortex*.

votive offered or consecrated in fulfillment of a vow.

voussoir (Fr.) (arch.) one of a series of wedge-shaped stones forming an ARCH.

W

wall arcade (arch.) series of ARCHES attached to a wall.

wallpaper strong PAPER used to decorate interior walls; it probably came into use by 1480.

warp thread stretched on a loom for weaving, through which the WEFT threads are passed.

wash the application of diluted WATERCOLOR over a large area to establish a general TONE.

watercolor PAINTING executed in a water-soluble MEDIUM.

wax plastic substance produced by bees, or of vegetable origin, used for modeling.

weft thread that is woven in and out of the WARP threads on a loom.

welding fusing together pieces of metal or plastic with heat.

Westwerk (arch.) wet part of CHURCH in CAROLINGIAN and OTTONIAN ARCHITECTURE, having an APSE, towers, sometimes a TRANSEPT, in addition to the usual arrangement at the east end.

whorl spiral or circular pattern.

Wiener Werkstätte an organization of designers formed in Vienna in 1903 to promote JUGENDSTIL arts and crafts.

wing **1** side piece of a composite PAINTING such as an ALTARPIECE. **2** block projecting from main building. **3** sides of stage in the theater.

wood the material obtained from trees; hardwood is dense, close grained, and obtained from deciduous trees; softwood obtained from coniferous trees.

woodblock PRINT produced from design on a wooden block.

woodcut PRINT made from a WOO BLOCK, cut so that the desi stands out in RELIEF.

workshop place in which art obje or PAINTINGS are execute "Workshop work" is usually n by the MASTER but by his assistan

wrought iron iron that is forged rolled (but not cast) into elabora shapes, e.g. for gates, balconies.

Wu School school of Chinese PAIN ING founded by Shen Chou in t 15th century.

Y

Yamato-e the school of Japane PAINTING from the 10th to t 15th century that preserved nati traditions.

yew evergreen coniferous tree, t wood of which is used in cabin making.

Yuan Chinese Mongol dynas 1279–1368 (between SUNG a MING).

Z

Zen Japanese form of Buddhism.

Ziggurat (arch.) ancient Babyloni and Assyrian pyramid-shap construction.*

zigzag pattern formed of lines th make abrupt right and left tur in Norman ARCHITECTURE, zigz is synonymous with CHEVRON.

zoomorphic based on animal forn or the worshiping of gods w have assumed an animal form.

INDEX

Page numbers in *italics* refer to illustrations or their captions.